The Nexus of Corporate Sustainability Management, Accounting, and Auditing

Albertina Monteiro
ISCAP, CEOS, Polytechnic of Porto, Portugal

Ana Pinto Borges
ISAG - European Business School, Porto, Portugal & Research Centre in Business Sciences and Tourism (CICET - FCVC), Porto, Portugal & Research Centre in Organizations, Markets and Industrial Management (COMEGI), Porto, Portugal

Elvira Vieira
ISAG - European Business School and Research Center in Business Sciences and Tourism (CICET-FCVC), Porto, Portugal & Applied Management Research Unit (UNIAG), Instituto Politécnico de Bragança, Bragança,Portugal & IPVC—Polytechnic Institute of Viana do Castelo, Viana do Castelo, Portugal

A volume in the Advances in Finance, Accounting, and Economics (AFAE) Book Series

IGI Global
Publishing Tomorrow's Research Today

Published in the United States of America by
IGI Global
Business Science Reference (an imprint of IGI Global)
701 E. Chocolate Avenue
Hershey PA, USA 17033
Tel: 717-533-8845
Fax: 717-533-8661
E-mail: cust@igi-global.com
Web site: http://www.igi-global.com

Library of Congress Cataloging-in-Publication Data

CIP Data Pending
ISBN: 979-8-3693-5663-0
eISBN: 979-8-3693-5665-4

British Cataloguing in Publication Data
A Cataloguing in Publication record for this book is available from the British Library.

Table of Contents

Detailed Table of Contents

Capital structure is a classic issue that has been widely studied in the last decades. Its relevance in corporate social responsibility (CSR) shows to be pertinent, but not sufficiently explored, namely in what concerns the role of capital structure on CSR. Based on a bibliometric analysis from the Scopus database for the period from 2010 and February 2023, the authors look to the past to follow the evolution of scientific production and trends on capital structure and CSR over the last decades and then try to understand in which direction the research in these subjects is moving. The results show the dominance of documents on capital structure and CSR in the period 2020-2022. The main conclusions about the studies analyzed is that companies with high levels of indebtedness face lower capacity to invest in CSR activities and firms with more CSR activities are more likely to use less debt. However, the last conclusion in not consensual. This study offers an overview of the state of the art, contributing to understanding the relationship between CSR and capital structure and identifying several avenues for future research.

Helena Costa Oliveira, CEOS.PP, ISCAP, Polytechnic of Porto, Portugal
Inês Sousa, ISCAP, Polytechnic of Porto, Portugal
Susana Bastos, CEOS.PP, ISCAP, Polytechnic of Porto, Portugal

Considering the significant impact of sustainability on companies' performance, implementing strategies and measuring them is essential. The sustainability balanced scorecard integrating sustainability into traditional perspectives (finance, customers, internal processes, and learning and growth) can be an efficient strategic management and performance assessment tool. This study aims to analyze the sustainable development goals a company prioritizes and propose their integration into the balance scorecard to monitor them. This study develops a case study through a qualitative analysis based on documentary analysis and interviews. The balanced scorecard developed for the energy company is aligned with its mission and values, considering the sustainable development goals that the company aims to achieve (SDGs 8, 9, 12, and 17). This study contributes to the literature on the sustainability-balanced scorecard. The model presented can be useful for other companies that intend to use management tools to measure sustainability.

Federico Galán-Valdivieso, University of Almería, Spain
Isabel Cristina Mañas-Álvarez, University of Almería, Spain
María José Rodríguez-Martínez, University of Almería, Spain
María del Mar Gálvez-Rodríguez, University of Almería, Spain

Sustainable reporting implies that a company not only takes action to help meet the Sustainable Development Goals (SDGs), but also that it is transparent with its stakeholders to show its efforts and commitment. Previous literature is scarce in studies that focus on certain SDGs, particularly planet-related, and perhaps even more scarce in delving into specific actions taken to meet the targets. From a sample of the 51 biggest Spanish companies in terms of revenue, the authors analyse their 2022 sustainability reports. The results show that the most committed companies are also the most transparent when disclosing information about SDGs, and that, in line with previous research, SDGs 12 and 13 are the most addressed by companies. The analysis also allows us to conclude that firms lack real commitment and transparency, since the vast majority of them do not mention which specific actions are being taken to meet the sustainable goals.

This study aims to analyze the level of environmental disclosure (ED) and its determinants. Employing a mixed-methods approach, this investigation employs content analysis in corporate reports spanning from 2016 to 2020. Furthermore, multiple regression analysis on panel data is utilized to identify the drivers of ED extent. Findings from this study indicate an upward trend in the ED index, which is slightly higher in Brazil, with the sustainability report, the most widely used means of disclosure, showing the highest levels of ED. Global Reporting Initiative (GRI) indicators related to environmental compliance, emissions, and energy exhibit the highest levels of disclosure. Moreover, GRI standards adoption, CEO duality, and workers diversity are identified as significant influencers of ED extent in both countries. This research contributes valuable insights to both academic literature and practical application by scrutinizing the extent of ED in private and listed Portuguese companies and identifying influential factors.

This study focuses on the companies of the Águas de Portugal Group, which operate in the water and sanitation sector, and aims to perform a content analysis of the auditor's reports and, specifically, of the key audit matters (KAM) disclosed from 2017 to 2021. Although it is not mandatory to disclose KAM, 57% of companies disclosed KAM in the period under review. Content analysis shows a high similarity in the number and content of KAM disclosed by companies in the period in which the same firm audits them. The categories of KAM disclosed are investment - recognition and measurement; impairment of investments; impairment of debts; revenue - recognition of downward activity; revenue - expense recovery deviations; and process of split. Audit responses to disclosed KAM mainly included inspections, followed by analytical procedures and inquiries, with reperformance being the least common procedure.

With signaling lens, this study aims to analyze whether the environmental, social, and governance (ESG) performance disclosure is influenced by sustainability strategies and global reporting initiative (GRI) standards adoption. The data obtained from the Refinitiv Eikon database, for Chinese listed companies, are subject to correlation and regression analysis for panel data. The findings reveal that the presence of business ethics and human rights policies have a positive impact on ESG performance disclosure. Additionally, stakeholder engagement level and GRI standards adoption are predictive variables for ESG performance disclosure. Exclusive analysis in the China's industrial sector restricts the results generalization. This study explores the effect of sustainability strategies on ESG performance disclosure.

The primary research objective is to analyze the influence of cultural and gender diversity (board cultural diversity and board gender diversity and executive's member gender diversity) on the companies Environmental, Social, and Governance (ESG) performance reporting and the mediating effect of workforce and human rights policies. This study utilizes data sourced from healthcare listed companies within the European Union (EU). Structural Equation Modelling (SEM) is employed to examine the interplay among various constructs. Results show that board cultural and gender diversity has a positive impact on ESG performance reporting. However, the workforce only improves the relationship between board gender diversity and ESG performance reporting. This study contributes to the literature by incorporating multidimensional perspectives of diversity into one general framework that stresses the mediating role of workforce in the interactive effect of cultural and gender diversity initiatives with ESG reporting practices. Moreover, by promoting ESG measures that apply global gender diversity and equality, the findings have practical implications for human resource policies and development at the organizational level.

This study analyses the social responsibility (SR) information disclosed by the Portuguese mercies that are part of the Union of Portuguese Mercies and that had a website. These non-profit organizations prefer to disclose SR information on their homepage, adopting mainly a text format balanced with images. Around half of them disclose between four and ten pages of SR information, with larger mercies disclosing more SR information pages than the smaller ones. The SR information disclosed mainly refers to their activities, rather than environment and/or human resources, and few disclose codes of conduct and/or ethics. This study contributes to the literature of SR disclosure in three ways. First, it adds empirical evidence related to a different type of non-profit organization that has not been studied. Second, it provides evidence that the Portuguese mercies use their websites mainly to disclose SR information about their work area and activities. Third, it shows that the disclosure of SR information depends a lot on the characteristics of each type of non-profit organization.

Preface

Organizations face major challenges in incorporating the sustainable development goals (SDGs) into their business strategies. Continuous reflection on the relationship between SDGs and organizational performance is essential for developing business models that integrate economic, ecological, and social considerations. New reporting regulations and stakeholder pressures have made sustainability accounting and auditing more crucial than ever. By adopting sustainable practices and understanding their social environmental impacts, organizations can drive sustainability forward.

The Nexus of Corporate Sustainability Management, Accounting, and Auditing contributes to the dissemination of knowledge within the areas of management, accounting, and auditing. It is dedicated to these themes and the way they are integrated into organizations within the scope of sustainability. Covering topics such as corporate governance, ethical practices, and sustainable corporate reporting, this book is an excellent resource for managers, executives, accountants, auditors, graduate students, postgraduate students, academicians, researchers, policy makers, regulators, consultants, advisors, and more.

This book consists of 12 chapters, which cover a variety of research topics.

The first chapter carries out a bibliometric analysis. Specifically, the authors analyse scientific production existing on capital structure and Corporate Social Responsibility (CSR), identifying trends and several avenues for future research.

The second chapter is centred on the energy sector. This study analyses the SDGs prioritised by an energy company and proposes their integration into the Balanced Scorecard for monitoring. Research develops a case study through a qualitative analysis based on documentary analysis and interviews. The Balanced Scorecard developed, aligned with the company's mission and values, prioritises SDGs 8, 9, 12 and 17.

The third chapter is also centred on the SDGs, in this case those related to the planet. Based on the 2022 sustainability reports of 51 of Spain's largest companies (in terms of revenue), the study results reveal that the companies most committed to the SDGs are also the most transparent in disclosing information about them. In addition, the study identifies the SDGs that are most addressed by companies (SDG 12 and SDG 13) and finds that most of the companies analysed are not completely transparent as they do not mention in their reports the actions they are taking to achieve the sustainable goals.

The following six chapters focus also on sustainability reporting. The fourth chapter assesses the level and determinants of environmental sustainability disclosure in Portuguese and Brazilian Companies. This study, based on content analysis on corporate reports covering 2016 to 2020, identify the Global Reporting Initiative (GRI) indicators show the highest levels of environmental disclosure, and factors that significantly influence the extent of environmental disclosure in both countries. Results reveal that the GRI indicators related to "environmental compliance", "emissions" and "energy" show the highest levels of disclosure. In addition, the adoption of GRI standards, CEO duality and employee diversity are identified as factors that significantly influence the extent of ED in both countries. The fifth chapter, based on a content analysis of the auditors' reports on key audit matters (KAM) disclosed between 2017 and 2021 by companies in the Águas de Portugal Group, evaluates the effectiveness of KAM disclosures, common audit challenges in the sector and relevance of KAM to stakeholders. The results show that fifty-seven per cent of the companies disclose KAM from 2017 to 2021 and a similarity in the number and content of the MCS. In addition, the study reveals that the categories of KAM disclosed are investment; impairment of investments; impairment of debt; revenue (recognition of downward activity); revenue (expense recovery variances); and demerger process. Finally, the content analysis also allowed to verify that the audit responses to the disclosed KAM were mainly related to inspections, analytical procedures and enquiries. The next chapter, based on sample of Chinese listed companies, analyses the effect of business ethics and human rights policies, stakeholder engagement and Global Reporting Initiative (GRI) standards adoption on Environmental, Social, and Governance (ESG) performance reporting. Study Results show that the model variables explain 58% of the dependent variable variance. Still on the subject ESG performance reporting, the seventh chapter asses the influence board cultural and gender diversity on ESG performance reporting in EU Healthcare companies. This research results show that board diversity has a positive impact on ESG performance reporting. Results also show that the workforce variable improves the relationship between board gender diversity and dependent variable. The eighth chapter includes a study applied to Portuguese mercies and analyses the disclosure of information on social responsibility on their website. The results of the study show that these organisations disclose information on social responsibility on their homepage, mainly opting for a text format balanced with images and disclosing information on work and activities, and that larger mercies disclose more pages of social responsibility information than smaller ones. The nineth chapter focuses on determinants of sustainability reporting quality. Empirical evidence reveals that quality index is low and influenced by activity sector. The requirement for non-financial reporting (European directive) only has a significant effect on the quality of Portuguese companies' sustainability reporting in the environmental dimension.

The last three chapters are related to sustainability strategies. The tenth article aims to gain a better understanding of ESG dynamics and whether this can be shaped through a dialogical process between stakeholders. This case study shows that the level of materiality related to ESG issues is dependent on a two-way conversation in which stakeholders. This research reveals that stakeholders are not seen as primary users, but as real 'co-producers' of information. The penultimate chapter identifies and analyses the CSR practices adopted by construction companies listed on the Brazilian Stock Exchange between 2010 and 2020. The research findings indicate a positive evolution in the social stance of organizations within the construction sector despite these practices being not mandatory. The last chapter, whit focus on the connections between organisational and individual accountabilities for sustainability control, stresses the importance of incorporating the individual level of accountability and socialising accountability form to incorporate into sustainability monitoring studies, and highlight potential research avenues for scholars conducting research into sustainability management, accounting and/or control.

Albertina Monteiro
ISCAP, CEOS, Polytechnic of Porto, Portugal

Ana Pinto Borges
ISAG – European Business School, Porto, Portugal & Research Centre in Business Sciences and Tourism (CICET – FCVC), Porto, Portugal & Research Centre in Organizations, Markets and Industrial Management (COMEGI), Porto, Portugal

Elvira Vieira
ISAG – European Business School and Research Center in Business Sciences and Tourism (CICET-FCVC), Porto, Portugal & Applied Management Research Unit (UNIAG), Instituto Politécnico de Bragança, Bragança,Portugal & IPVC—Polytechnic Institute of Viana do Castelo, Viana do Castelo, Portugal

ACKNOWLEDGMENT

All the chapters were double-blind review. The editors would like to acknowledge the help of all the people involved in this project and, more specifically, to the authors and reviewers that took part in the review process. Without their support, this book would not have become a reality.

First, the editors would like to thank each one of the authors for their contributions. Our sincere gratitude goes to the chapter's authors who contributed their time and expertise to this book.

Second, the editors wish to acknowledge the valuable contributions of the reviewers regarding the improvement of quality, coherence, and content presentation of chapters. Most of the authors also served as referees; we highly appreciate their double task.

Finally, the authors are deeply grateful to ISAG – European Business School and Research Centre in Business Sciences and Tourism (CICET – FCVC), for all support.

This work was supported by national funds through FCT/MCTES (PIDDAC): UNIAG, UIDB/04752/2020 (DOI 10.54499/UIDB/04752/2020) and UIDP/04752/2020 (DOI 10.54499/ UIDP/04752/2020).

Chapter 1
Capital Structure and Corporate Social Responsibility:
From the Past to the Future

Elisabete S. Vieira
https://orcid.org/0000-0003-3593-368X
GOVCOPP Unit Research, University of Aveiro, Portugal

Mara Madaleno
https://orcid.org/0000-0002-4905-2771
GOVCOPP Unit Research, University of Aveiro, Portugal

ABSTRACT

Capital structure is a classic issue that has been widely studied in the last decades. Its relevance in corporate social responsibility (CSR) shows to be pertinent, but not sufficiently explored, namely in what concerns the role of capital structure on CSR. Based on a bibliometric analysis from the Scopus database for the period from 2010 and February 2023, the authors look to the past to follow the evolution of scientific production and trends on capital structure and CSR over the last decades and then try to understand in which direction the research in these subjects is moving. The results show the dominance of documents on capital structure and CSR in the period 2020-2022. The main conclusions about the studies analyzed is that companies with high levels of indebtedness face lower capacity to invest in CSR activities and firms with more CSR activities are more likely to use less debt. However, the last conclusion in not consensual. This study offers an overview of the state of the art, contributing to understanding the relationship between CSR and capital structure and identifying several avenues for future research.

DOI: 10.4018/979-8-3693-5663-0.ch001

INTRODUCTION

One of the research fields that has gained significant attention in the last decade is CSR, a business model based on ethical behavior, which practices tend to improve society, the environment, and their stakeholders. According to the Commission of the European Communities (CEC, 2001), CSR has been defined at that time as "a concept whereby companies integrate social and environmental concerns in their business operations and in their interaction with their stakeholders on a voluntary basis" (p.8). The fact that CSR is voluntary and not legally enforced, is a challenge associated with CSR implementation.

Although the vast and growing interest in CSR issues by society and researchers, the costs and benefits associated with activities of CSR are still not fully understood because of its complexity (Harjoto, 2017; Villarón-Peramato et al., 2018), namely in what concerns implementation costs, the lack of standardization, and its voluntary nature.

A significant part of past studies on CSR focused on the association between CSR and a firm's financial performance (e.g., Margolis et al., 2009; Nelling & Webb, 2009; Barnea & Rubin, 2010; Jo & Harjoto, 2011; Barauskaite & Streimikiene, 2021; Pradhan & Nibedita, 2021), finding, overall, a positive relationship between CSR and performance. Analyzing specifically the banking sector, Wu et al. (2016) find also evidence of a significant and positive relationship between CSR and financial performance. Indeed, there is evidence that by adopting sustainable practices, firms experience an improvement in their competitiveness and profitability.

Other empirical studies explore the impact of CSR on firm value, finding that CSR brings several advantages to companies' value (Lin et al., 2017; Liu & Tian, 2019; Chen et al., 2020). Consumers are more aware of sustainability issues, being more likely to buy from responsible entities, which improves their brand images and gains the loyalty of their employees (e.g., Nelling & Webb, 2009). Another advantage of adopting CSR practices is that it improves the stakeholders' confidence and assurance in the firm's operations, contributing to the reduction of firms' risk (Jo & Na, 2012; Benlemlih et al., 2018; Albuquerque et al., 2019).

Firms with high CSR enjoy several benefits, namely the reduction of agency problems, the decrease in the cost of capital, the improvement of transparency in financial information, as well as the social and environmental contract between companies and society (Lu et al., 2017; Mahmood et al., 2023).

Although the literature has studied the effect of CSR on companies' value, financial performance, and idiosyncratic risk (Harjoto, 2017), there is a gap in what concerns the study of the relationship between CSR and capital structure, both in what concerns the impact of CSR practices on capital structure, and the influence of capital structure on CSR initiatives. In addition, the existing evidence is not consensual. Moreover, the effect of CSR on debt maturity is a subject that has not gathered much attention from researchers (Benlemlih, 2017).

Intending to cover this gap, and reconcile the research on the relationship between capital structure and CSR, this chapter intends to examine research trends on this topic, considering the CSR as a business approach where firms are conscient of their responsibility for the impact they have on society and the environment. Consequently, companies go beyond considering only the profits, but also their effects on employees, customers, community, and the planet. It can include ethical business practices, charitable donations, environmental sustainability efforts, and initiatives to improve social well-being. To accomplish this objective, this study analyses the characteristics of documents published on this topic for the period from 2010 to February 2023, summarizing the past, present, and future research trends on this subject, using bibliometric analysis based on the Scopus database and Vosviewer visualizations.

This chapter contributes to the literature as it is, to the best of our knowledge, the first to carry out a bibliometric analysis on this subject. It identifies the most influential works, performing an integrated analysis. In addition, the article identifies, among other aspects, the most prominent authors, the countries where the studies were carried out, the most cited documents, and the dominant keywords. Based on the trends of the empirical studies, we suggest some avenues for future research.

The remaining chapter is structured as follows. The next section presents a brief coverage on the literature, followed by the methodology, and the bibliometric analysis results. After that, the chapter shows the most cited documents and the next section briefly covers the trends in the research during the analyzed period. Finally, a conclusion and avenues for future research are presented.

LITERATURE REVIEW

Capital structure tends to influence CSR activities since higher levels of debt motivate creditors to have a monitoring role more vigorous, and to mitigate the conflicts of interest (Jensen, 1986; Diamond, 1991), which suggests that, because of interest payments and monitoring reasons, leverage tends to prevent overinvestment in CSR (Barnea & Rubin, 2010). Pradhan and Nibedita (2021) find evidence that firms with high levels of indebtedness face low capacity to invest in CSR activities.

Complementary, Mahmood et al. (2023) conclude that firms with low levels of leverage spend more cash on CSR activities.

Concerning the impact of CSR on capital structure, the conclusions are not consensual. Although some studies find evidence that CSR initiatives influence negatively the capital structure, others find no evidence of a significant relationship between the two variables.

Several authors, such as Harjoto (2017), Ezzi et al. (2020), Pucheta-Martínez et al. (2020, 2022), Oware and Mallikarjunappa (2021) and Hsu et al. (2023) find evidence of a negative association between CSR and capital structure. According to Pucheta-Martínez et al. (2022), companies that reveal CSR information as a corporate governance tool, present lower levels of capital. Mahmood et al. (2023) find evidence of a negative association between CSR and leverage, but only for firms with high CSR, since this relation is not statistically significant in the case of firms with low CSR practices. Hsu et al. (2023) find that companies with better CSR performance are more likely to reduce the use of debt. Considering a sample of high-technology firms, Grabinska et al. (2021) conclude that only the employee component of CSR has a significant influence on capital structure, finding no evidence of a significant role of the other components of CSR practices on capital structure.

Since CSR act as a mechanism to reduce the risk of companies (Pastor et al. 2008; Jo & Na, 2012; Benlemlih et al., 2018; Albuquerque et al., 2019), the firms that use CSR practices should enjoy a lower cost of capital. Indeed, CSR signals the market about management reliability, ethical values, and governance practices, reducing information asymmetry, enhancing investor trust in the firm's future cash flows, and reducing the cost of capital.

Several studies find evidence that CSR practices reduce the cost of equity (Hail & Leuz, 2006; Chen et al., 2009; Ghoul et al., 2011; Reverte, 2012; Xu et al., 2015). Xu et al. (2015) conclude that firms with high CSR performance benefit from the lower cost of equity. Ellili (2020) find similar results for the relationship between the environmental, social, and governance (ESG) and the cost of capital. Hail and Leuz (2006), Chen et al. (2009), and Reverte (2012) argues that companies' cost of equity can decrease due to the reduction of agency costs, as well as the information asymmetry problems. Ghoul et al. (2011) find evidence that a firm's equity cost is lower for the ones that present superior CSR performance, concluding also that information asymmetry is more serious for firms with low CSR. Cheng et al. (2014) conclude that firms with higher CSR performance enjoy better access to finance, decrease agency costs and improve reporting transparency, which diminishes the information asymmetry.

In what concerns the cost of debt, previous studies present two distinct arguments: the overinvestment sight and the risk mitigation viewpoint (Goss & Roberts, 2011), which influences distinctly the relationship between CSR and the cost of debt. According to the overinvestment perspective, managers overinvest in CSR practices to enjoy their own benefits, to the detriment of shareholders' interests. Consequently, higher CSR performance is expected to influence positively the cost of debt (Sharfman & Fernando, 2008; Menz, 2010). Based on the risk mitigation viewpoint, banks are more likely to give better loan conditions to socially responsible companies, so CSR investments might reduce the financial risk (Boutin-Dufresne & Savaria, 2004; Lee & Faff, 2009) and, consequently, lower the cost of debt (Ye & Zhang, 2011; Cooper & Uzun, 2015; Zhou et al., 2016; Xu et al., 2021). Kim et al. (2021) argue that firms incurring CSR practices improve their reputation, which results in a lower cost of debt.

Overall, the empirical evidence on the relationship between CSR and capital structure suggests that firms with high levels of indebtedness face low capacity to invest in CSR activities and companies with more CSR activities tend to use less debt.

METHODOLOGY

This study adopts the bibliometric analysis as a research methodology, since it offers an objective criterion to assess the development in a specific field of research, acting as a comprehensive tool for measuring the production and quality of research (Cobo et al., 2015; Salinas-Ríos & García López, 2022), and making it easier to identify new directions for future research (Xu et al., 2018; Donthu et al., 2020). According to Arslan et al. (2022), this methodology is considered suitable for conducting quantitative analyses on extensive data sets and monitoring their changes over time.

The search took place on 6th February 2023, and applied to the Scopus database (https://www.scopus.com/search/). Although the usage of the Web of Science (WoS) or the Scopus databases influence the outcome of bibliometric analyses (Stahlschmidt & Stephen, 2022), the authors opt to use the Scopus database to detriment of WoS for several reasons. Comparing WoS and Scopus databases, Vieira and Gomes (2009) conclude that Scopus provides 20% more coverage than WoS; Chadegani et al. (2013) document that Scopus covers a superior number of journals but is limited to more recent articles (and our research is based on a topic that is explored in a near past); Harzing (2019) notes that Scopus produced higher measures than WoS; and Martín-Martín et al. (2020) conclude that Scopus offered twice as much exclusive content as WoS. Additionally, several authors conclude that Scopus is one of the favorite databases for academic researchers (Boyle & Sherman, 2006; Marlowe & Clarke 2022). According to Elsevier (2020), Scopus has extensive access to academic literature, offering continuous admission to research output worldwide. However, the Scopus database in not free of limitations, such as the Elsevier's decision to consider document citations only from 1996 can be a disadvantage for users that want to understand the development of a specific field of research whose ancestries encompass farther back in time and can result in a skewed h-index for researchers with extended careers. The analysis was also supported by the VOSviewer.

The following filters were selected in the Scopus database to obtain the documents to implement the bibliometric analysis:

1. Criterion of research: The authors done the following combination of keywords, concentrated on the main topics they want to explore: (TITLE-ABS-KEY ("capital structure") AND TITLE-ABS-KEY ("corporate social responsibility" OR "CSR") OR TITLE-ABS-KEY ("environmental social and governance" OR "ESG")). The ESG was considered, since this score it is usually used to proxy for CSR practices. With this criterion, it was obtained 60 results;
2. Limit the study field to "articles", to exclude other type of publications, such as conference papers, trying to select relevant documents. While articles are intended to have a lasting influence and be cited by scholars for a long period of time, a conference paper, on the other hand, provides a forum for presenting preliminary results or ongoing research. Using this filter, the publications decline to 50;
3. Set the language to "English", for reasons of language knowledge. The number of records continues to be 50.

Using the filters 1 to 3, (TITLE-ABS-KEY ("capital structure") AND TITLE-ABS-KEY ("corporate social responsibility" OR "CSR") OR TITLE-ABS-KEY ("environmental social and governance" OR "ESG")) AND (LIMIT-TO (DOCTYPE, "ar")) AND (LIMIT-TO (LANGUAGE, "English")), the output consists of 50 documents, which are the basis of this study.

Figure 1 shows the methodological approach adopted and the steps followed to obtain the number of publications used in the study, adapted from the flowchart for systematic reviews (e.g., Page et al., 2021).

Figure 1. Sample selection process.

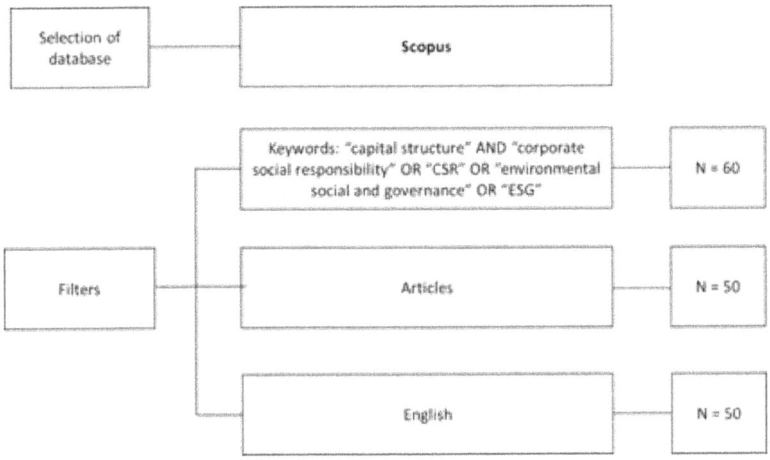

The final database includes 50 articles, whose documents were published between 2010 and 6th February 2023.

BIBLIOMETRIC ANALYSIS RESULTS

Based on the methodological selection process, Figure 2 shows the number of articles published each year.

Figure 2. The number of articles published by year: 2010- 6th February, 2013.

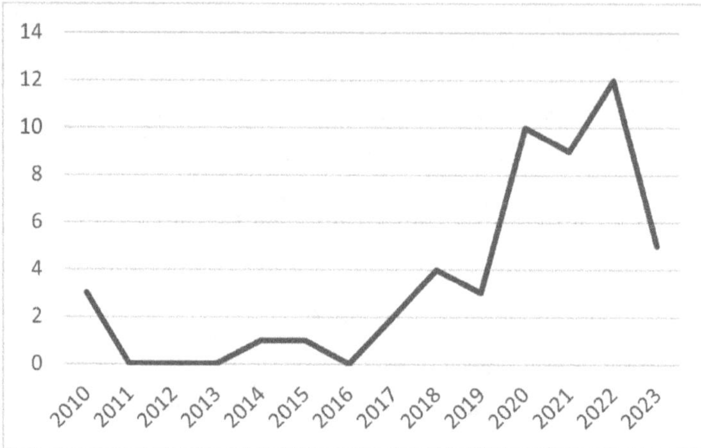

The first three papers on capital structure and CSR were published in 2010. From this year to 2017, the increase in published articles presents a steady growth. However, the evolution from 2018 onwards is more significant, showing an increasing interest in researchers about the relationship between capital structure and CSR in recent years. The highest number of publications is registered in 2022 (12 documents). It is possible that researchers identify gaps in the literature, and try to cover them with new studies. The year of 2023 lists 5 articles, but it is considered only January and the first six days of February. These results show that the research on capital structure and CSR has room to grow.

Figure 3 reports the documents published by the authors' affiliation country, to analyze the origin of the research contributions by region.

Figure 3. Articles published by the authors' affiliation country during the period 2010- 6th February, 2013.

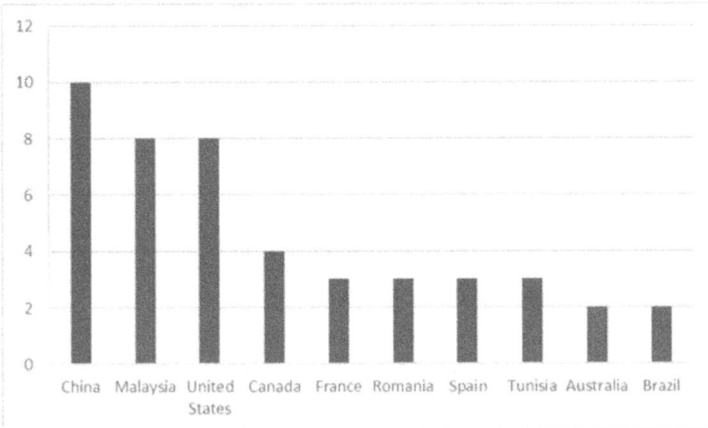

Analyzing the scientific production of the top 10 countries, it is evident that the major part of the articles is concentrated on Asian countries (China, with 10 articles, and Malaysia, with eight), followed by North America (United States and Canada, with eight and four documents, respectively). Western Europe (France and Spain), as well as East Europe (Romania and Tunisia), represent each 13% of publications. Finally, Australia and Brazil register two publications both. This evidence shows that research departing from some countries or regions is still in need of research, such as from European countries, South America and Africa.

The documents published by source title (Journal) over the period covered by this analysis can be observed in Figure 4.

Figure 4. Articles published by Journal during the period 2010- 6th February, 2013.

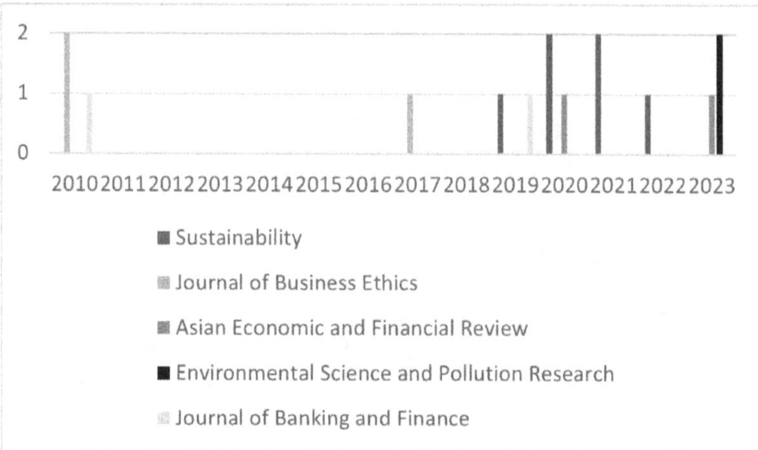

The top five scientific journals with the most relevant publications related to capital structure and CSR are the *Asian Economic and Financial Review*, the *Environmental Science and Pollution Research*, the *Journal of Banking and Finance*, the *Journal of Business Ethics*, and the *Sustainability*. It is interesting to note that there are oscillations in the publishing journals over time. In the first years, the documents were mainly published in the *Journal of Business Ethics* and the *Journal of Banking and Finance*, whereas in the last period (2020-2023), the articles have been published in the *Asian Economic and Financial Review*, the *Environmental Science and Pollution Research* and in the *Sustainability*, showing an increase of publications in journals dedicated to environmental and sustainability issues. It reflects the increased concern about social issues, not only by society in general but also by researchers, in particular.

The key authors on this field during the period considered, are García-Sánchez, I.M., and Martínez-Ferrero, J., both from the University of Salamanca, Kammoun, I., from the University of Sfax, Tunisia, and Khatib, S.F.A., from the University Teknologi, Malaysia, with two published articles each one.

Another strength of the bibliometric analysis is to identify the most cited articles. The Scopus database (option "view citation overview") provides the h-index (Hirsch, 2005), which shows the interaction between the number of citations and the number of publications, which is shown in Figure 5.

Figure 5. h-index during the period 2010- 6th February, 2013.

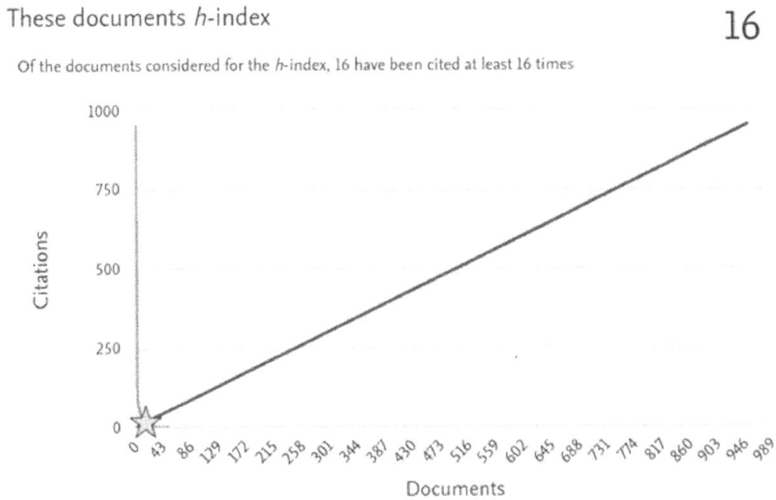

The h-index is 16, indicating that, from the 50 documents selected, 16 have been cited at least 16 times over the period from 2010 to 6th February 2023.

MOST CITED DOCUMENTS

Based on the h-index, the authors analyze the most cited articles during the study period. Table 1 shows the top 16 publications, in descending order of the number of citations.

Table 1. Top 16 cited documents during the period 2010-2013.

N.	Document Title	Authors	Year	Journal	Citations
1	Corporate Social Responsibility as a Conflict Between Shareholders	Barnea, A., Rubin, A.	2010	Journal of Business Ethics, 97(1), 71-86	951
2	Employee well-being, firm leverage, and bankruptcy risk	Verwijmeren, P., Derwall, J.	2010	Journal of Banking and Finance, 34(5), 956-964	129
3	Nudging toward diversity in the boardroom: A systematic literature review of board diversity of financial institutions	Khatib, S.F.A., Abdullah, D.F., Elamer, A.A., Abueid, R.	2021	Business Strategy and the Environment, 30(2), 985-1002	70

continued on following page

Table 1. Continued

N.	Document Title	Authors	Year	Journal	Citations
4	Corporate social responsibility, environmental leadership and financial performance	DiSegni, D.M., Huly, M., Akron, S.	2015	Social Responsibility Journal, 11(1), 131-148	65
5	Does corporate social responsibility reduce the costs of high leverage? Evidence from capital structure and product market Interactions	Bae, K.-H., El Ghoul, S., Guedhami, O., Kwok, C.C.Y., Zheng, Y.	2019	Journal of Banking and Finance, 100, 135-150	62
6	Corporate Social Responsibility and Firm Debt Maturity	Benlemlih, M.	2017	Journal of Business Ethics, 144(3), 491-517	47
7	Corporate governance, law, culture, environmental performance and CSR disclosure: A global perspective	Lu, J., Wang, J.	2021	Journal of International Financial Markets, Institutions and Money, 70, 101264	45
8	Exploring the Impact of Legal Systems and Financial Structure on Corporate Responsibility	Gainet, C.	2010	Journal of Business Ethics, 95(SUPPL. 2), 195-222	41
9	Corporate social responsibility and degrees of operating and financial leverage	Harjoto, M.A.	2017	Review of Quantitative Finance and Accounting, 49(2), 487-513	31
10	How does corporate social responsibility change capital structure?	Yang, S., He, F., Zhu, Q., Li, S.	2018	Asia-Pacific Journal of Accounting and Economics, 25(3-4), 352-387	28
11	Corporate social responsibility, corporate governance and business performance: Limits and challenges imposed by the implementation of directive 2013/34/EU in Romania	Gh Popescu, C.R.	2019	Sustainability (Switzerland), 11(19), 5146	28
12	CSR as entrenchment strategy and capital structure: corporate governance and investor protection as complementary and substitutive factors	Villarón-Peramato, Ó., Martínez-Ferrero, J., García-Sánchez, I.-M.	2018	Review of Managerial Science, 12(1), 27-64	27
13	The influence of corporate governance on corporate sustainability: new evidence using panel data in the Iberian macroeconomic environment	Cancela, B.L., Neves, M.E.D., Rodrigues, L.L., Gomes Dias, A.C.	2020	International Journal of Accounting and Information Management, 28(4), 785-806	25
14	Does corporate social responsibility affect cost of capital in China?	Yeh, C.-C., Lin, F., Wang, T.-S., Wu, C.-M.	2020	Asia Pacific Management Review, 25(1), 1-12	21

continued on following page

Table 1. Continued

N.	Document Title	Authors	Year	Journal	Citations
15	Sustainability assessment: Does the oecd/g20 inclusive framework for beps (base erosion and profit shifting project) put an end to disputes over the recognition and measurement of intellectual capital?	Popescu, C.R.G.	2020	Sustainability (Switzerland), 12(23), 10004, 1-22	18
16	Rethinking capital structure decision and corporate social responsibility in response to COVID-19	Huang, H., Ye, Y.	2021	Accounting and Finance, 61(3), 4757-4788	18

The 16 most cited documents were cited 1606 times. Although there are two articles with more than 100 citations, the study of Barnea and Rubin (2010) is by far the one with the highest number of citations (951), followed by the article of Verwijmeren and Derwall (2010), which was cited 129 times. The other citations are between 18 and 70. In what concerns the year's production, the period that received fewer citations was the period 2011-2014. The most cited documents are from 2010 (1121) and 2021 (133), which shows that, after rising to a peak in 2010, the interest in research on this theme has again raised, which agrees with the evidence of Figures 2 and 4. Regarding the source, the *Journal of Business Ethics* has three records on the most cited documents.

Several studies focus on the influence of capital structure on CSR (Barnea & Rubin, 2010; Gainet, 2010; Verwijmeren & Derwall, 2010). Considering a sample of US firms, Barnea and Rubin (2010) find evidence that leverage is negatively related to CSR expenditures, concluding that, although managers tend to overinvest in CSR for their own benefit, they are only disposed to overinvest in CSR practices when they do not suffer with the costs of such practices, which are in line with the agency theory arguments. These results are in line with the ones of Verwijmeren and Derwall (2010), for the same market. Gainet (2010) examines also the impact of financial structure on CSR and environmental responsibility, but considering a sample of 16 European countries. The results show that firms with a low percentage of the debt and with a high number of publicly held shares, are more likely than their counterparts to motivate themselves to social and environmental practices, concluding that capital structure influences CSR, in accordance with the evidence of previous studies carry on the US market (Barnea & Rubin, 2010; Verwijmeren & Derwall, 2010).

Others studies focus on the inverse relationship, i.e., the influence of CSR on capital structure (DiSegni et al., 2015; Benlemlih, 2017; Harjoto, 2017; Villarón-Peramato et al., 2018; Yang et al., 2018). Considering a sample of US firms during the period between 1991 and 2011, Harjoto (2017) analyses the effect of CSR on companies' level of operating and financial leverage. The results show that, overall, CSR reduces the firms' financial leverage, which suggests that companies diminish their debt financing and maintain higher liquidity to honor their implicit contracts with stakeholders (Bae et al., 2011). Separating the financing types, the results show that CSR is positively related to operating leverage, but negatively associated with financial leverage, which supports the trade-off theory between operating and financing debt, agreeing with other authors' studies, such as Li and Henderson (1991) and Trezevant (1992). The author concludes that CSR behaves as a substitute for corporate debt tax shield in situations where companies' financial leverage is low.

Yang et al. (2018) explore the impact of CSR on information asymmetry between companies and creditors, considering a sample of Chinese-listed firms both on the Shanghai and Shenzhen Stock Exchanges. The authors find evidence that companies that engage in CSR strategies have more indebtedness than their counterparts, which contrasts with the results of Harjoto (2017). However, the authors suggest that a possible reason for this result is that CSR statements enhance transparency and diminish information asymmetry between creditors and managers, so that companies can take advantage of financial benefits, maintaining higher levels of leverage. In addition, the results show that the existence of CSR reports lowers the speed of capital structure adjustment. Finally, there is evidence that CSR statements enable firms to maintain higher levels of long-term leverage, compared to companies that do not use CSR practices.

The difference in results between the studies based on the US and the Chinese markets may be also related to the fact that, in the US, firms raise their funds mainly on the equity market, whereas in China, companies tend to raise funds from the external debt market (Pessarossia & Weill, 2013).

Villarón-Peramato et al. (2018) also study the effects of CSR on company debt, considering the agency and signaling perspective of CSR, examining also the external and internal control, to understand their role in reducing or complementing the capital structure as a mechanism of a CSR entrenchment plan, considering an international sample with 21 countries from several continents, covering the period 2003-2010. Overall, the results show that CSR impacts positively the level of debt, functioning as a moderating procedure of agency conflicts between shareholders and managers. This result confirms the ones of Yang et al. (2018). In addition, the authors find evidence that firms with more independent and diverse boards present higher levels of debt, concluding that there is a moderating effect of board independence and diversity in resorting to CSR activities as entrenchment tools.

More specifically, DiSegni et al. (2015) and Benlemlih (2017) analyze the association between CSR and capital structure, exploring debt maturity, and finding different results. DiSegni et al. (2015) analyze the US firms that constitute the Dow Jones Sustainability Indexes for the period from 2008 to 2010, finding evidence that firms associated with practices of social responsibility and environmental sustainability have significantly higher long-term leverage than their counterparts in the industry and related sector. However, Benlemlih (2017), studying the relationship between CSR and a company's debt maturity for a big sample of US companies for the period between 1991 and 2009, finds evidence that the higher the social responsibility of firms, the lower the debt maturity, which contrasts with the results of DiSegni et al. (2015). In addition, its results show that high CSR firms have a low cost of equity, suggesting that CSR is associated with a decrease in investments financed with long-term debt and an increase in investments financed with short-term debt or equity. While DiSegni et al. (2015) argue that their results might happen because firms try to signal the market about their concern on social issues, namely to reduce the cost of capital, or that they can be related to the assumption that firms that depend on long-term debt are more aligned with the interests of society, as well as with sustainability, Benlemlih (2017) concludes that high CSR companies resort to the debt maturity to control CSR overinvestment problems and to signal the market about their performance and their facility to access to the debt market.

Other studies explore the impact of CSR on the cost of capital, such as the ones of Bae et al. (2019) and Yeh et al. (2020). Bae et al. (2019) explore the effect of CSR on the costs of high leverage, considering a large sample of US firms, finding that CSR mitigates this type of cost, supporting the stakeholder value maximization perspective of CSR. This conclusion meets the results of Ghoul et al. (2011) and Benlemlih (2017), and is in alignment with the reason pointed out by DiSegni et al. (2015) to justify their results. Yeh et al. (2020) explore the impact of CSR on companies' cost of equity and debt capital, considering a sample of Chinese firms for the period 2008-2011, concluding that the companies with higher CSR performance can decrease the cost of debt. However, the results show that the capital structure does not act as a significant moderating function between CSR performance and both the cost of equity capital and the cost of debt, which does not support the predictions of the agency theory and the information asymmetry hypothesis. Based on the empirical results, the authors conclude that in the Chinese market, CSR investment is still at legal and compliant extents, experiencing further information asymmetry and reduced market efficiency in the country's financial sector.

Huang and Ye (2021) explore the joint impact of capital structure and CSR on companies' risk during the COVID-19 pandemic in the US context. The results show that companies with excessive leverage confront higher risk during the pandemic period, which is in line with other studies which find that firms with high leverage react more negatively to market performance (e.g. Ding et al., 2021). In addition, the authors split the sample into two subsamples (overleveraged firms versus their counterparts). Although the results remain unchanged for overleveraged firms, in what concerns the underleveraged subsample, when indebtedness increases, there is a significant risk reduction. According to the authors, this effect may be justified by the trade-off theory, since underleveraged companies do not deplete their debt capacity to maximize the interest tax benefits, having space for debt increase until it gets the optimal point. The authors concluded that, during the COVID-19 pandemic, companies with excessive levels of debt face a high corporate risk, being this effect more prevailing among companies with inferior CSR Performance. Moreover, companies with a low debt level are protected, nevertheless their CSR practices.

In the top cited articles, Lu and Wang (2021) explore the influence of corporate governance characteristics on CSR disclosure and a company's environmental performance, considering a sample based on ESG information from the Sustainalytics database, and financial data obtained in the Thomson Reuters Eikon database, considering the period from 2010 to 2017. The results show that environmental performance impacts positively CSR disclosure, which supports the voluntary disclosure theory. The authors find evidence that the separation of board chair and CEO positions, the ESG committees, and gender diversity on boards are effective mechanisms of corporate governance to obtain higher environmental performance and increase the level of CSR disclosure. However, the authors find no association between executive compensation to ESG goals and environmental performance, concluding that executive compensation to achieve ESG targets may not be an efficient practice because it may encourage managers to disclose more information, but the environmental performance cannot be improved. Concerning the capital structure issue, the results show that a firm's debt is positively related to the environmental performance and with the CSR disclosure, which evidence is consistent with the assumptions of the agency theory and the free cash flow hypothesis (Jensen & Meckling, 1976; Fama & Jensen, 1983; Jensen, 1986). Thus, it suggests that debt can be used as a monitoring and control mechanism to reduce agency costs as well as the managers' self-serving behavior.

Some studies focus on corporate governance characteristics (Gh Popescu, 2019; Cancela et al., 2020; Khatib et al., 2021). Focusing on Romania, a country that is making efforts to process European integration, Gh Popescu (2019) finds evidence that it is crucial to intensify corporate governance practices as well as CSR responsibility in firms so that it can be possible to create equilibrium among sustainability, competitiveness, productivity, and businesses' performance.

Cancela et al. (2020) analyze the relationship between corporate governance and corporate sustainability performance, considering an Iberian sample of non-financial firms, covering the period from 2013 to 2017. The evidence suggests that corporate sustainability performance has distinct determinants, according to the different dimensions of performance. The authors find that the economic dimension of performance is influenced by public debt, board size, board diversity, and the existence of an audit committee. The determinants of environmental performance are the board size and the presence of both the audit and the CSR committees. The social component of performance is explained by the board size, the audit committee, and the capital structure. Consequently, the authors conclude that the level of indebtedness plays a significant role in social performance and that the presence of a CSR committee contributes to obvious environmental concerns, but not the economic and social components of performance.

According to Khatib et al. (2021), that carry on a systematic review to analyze the research on board diversity, focusing on financial institutions, the authors conclude that there is still a scarcity of research concerning the relationship between board diversity, in all their attributes and several topics such as capital structure and CSR.

Finally, Popescu (2020) tries to assess sustainability, focusing on demonstrating associations between intellectual capital, sustainability assessment mechanisms, and the consequences of CSR, considering an international sample of 44 countries, from different continents. According to the methodology adopted, the authors conclude that the number of general recommendations of the Base Erosion and Profit Shifting Project, as well as those associated with the alignment of the economic elements on Intellectual Capital was decreasing. The different economies tend to focus more on the functions and relevance of some vital factors, such as the capital structure of companies and the potential of intellectual assets, namely capital and intellectual property.

In summary, based on the results of the most cited document, the authors conclude that leverage impacts negatively CSR expenditures and that CSR contributes to decreasing the cost of debt. However, in what concerns the effects of CSR activities on the capital structure, the results are mixed, justifying additional research on this phenomenon. These conclusions are in accordance with the literature review done before.

Moreover, the findings suggest that the results can be different, depending on the type of countries analyzed, such as the US (e.g., Harjoto, 2017) and the Chinese market (e.g., Yang et al., 2018). The studies focused on the effects on the debt maturity are scarce and the results are no consensual, which is a gap that can be explored in the future. Some of the more recent studies on the top 16 articles, such as the ones of Cancela et al. (2020), Khatib et al. (2021) and Lu and Wang (2021) focus on the topic of corporate governance, and its influence on CSR and capital structure, which suggest a new trend of research. As Khatib et al. (2021) said, there is still a scarcity of research concerning the relationship between corporate governance characteristics and other finance topics, such as capital structure and CSR. These gaps and contradicting results in the literature need further exploration.

The dominance of the more cited articles in the analyzed period reflects the academic and practical interests in the intersection of capital structure and CSR.

TRENDS IN THE RESEARCH

Based on the keyword analysis, the connection of the main research themes is presented in Figure 6.

Figure 6. Network analysis with keywords (VOSviewer)

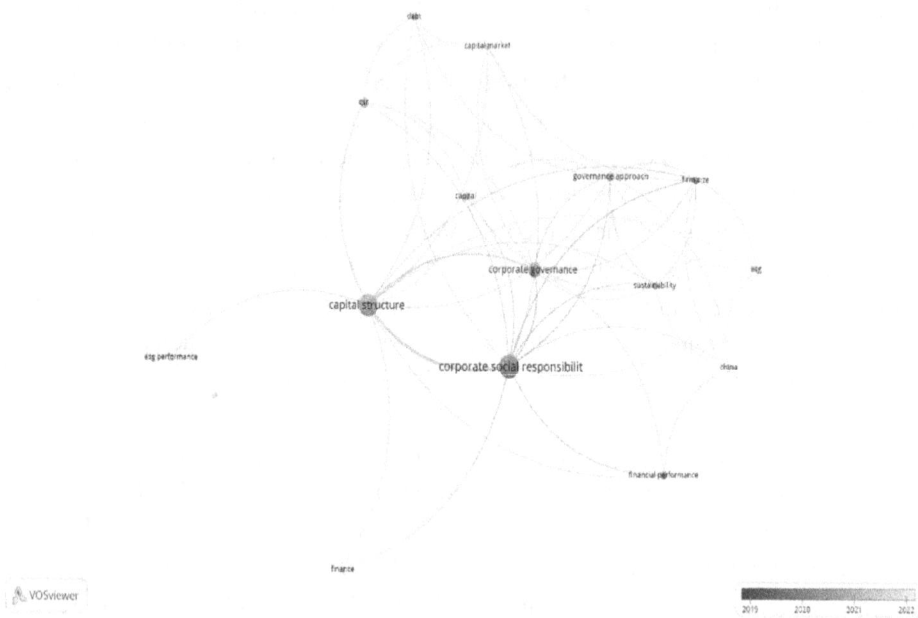

As it can be seen, the research on capital structure and CSR is transversal for the period under review. First, the studies focus on capital structure and financial performance. More recently (2021-2022), there are key turning points and emerging topics beyond capital structure and CSR, such as corporate governance characteristics, finance, and ESG performance, which can be seen as emerging topics, being clusters with potential growth in future research.

The density map indicates that the core and most important keyword that has been widely used in the existing literature is "corporate social responsibility". The next keywords with more relevance are "capital structure" and "corporate governance".

The connection of the countries with publications is shown in Figure 7.

Figure 7. Network analysis with countries (VOSviewer)

There are three clusters. China, related to Pakistan; Indonesia, related to Malaysia, Nigeria, and Tunisia; and the United States of America, related to Canada. The countries associated with more recent studies are developing countries. The density map indicates that the three countries that have been widely analyzed in existing literature are the United States, China, and Malaysia.

Some countries and regions are in lack research, which may open doors for future studies.

CONCLUSION

This study analyses the trends in capital structure and CSR for the period between 2010 to February 6th 2023, using bibliometric analysis from the Scopus database. Considering the sample selection process, 50 publications were analyzed. To the best of the authors knowledge, this is the first to carry out a bibliometric analysis on this subject. It identifies the most influential works, performing an integrated analysis.

This work identifies the most influential works, countries of publications, the sources with more records published, the authors, keywords, and citations, focusing on the 16 studies with more citations.

The increase in publications in the last five years may reflect the recognition from society about the benefits of the firm's adoption of sustainable practices to improve the welfare of society, the environment, and stakeholders.

Results show that García-Sánchez, I.M., Martínez-Ferrero, J., Kammoun, I. and Khatib, S.F. are the authors with the highest publications in the analyzed period. China is the country with the higher number of publications, broadly followed by Malaysia and the US. The most cited article is from Barnea and Rubin (2010), with 951 citations.

Based on the results of the 16 publications with more citations, it was concluded that leverage impacts negatively CSR expenditures (Barnea & Rubin, 2010; Verwijmeren & Derwall, 2010) and that CSR contributes to decreasing the cost of debt (Bae et al., 2019; Yeh et al., 2020).

Concerning the relationship between CSR and capital structure, the results are mixed, with some studies finding a negative relationship (e.g., Harjoto, 2017) and others finding a positive association (Yang et al., 2018; Villarón-Peramato et al., 2018). There is also no consensual evidence of the influence of CSR on debt maturity. While DiSegni et al. (2015) find evidence that CSR has a positive impact on long-term leverage, Benlemlih (2017) concludes that the higher the social responsibility of firms, the lower the debt maturity. The mixed results motivate additional research.

Concerning the relationship between capital structure and CSR, the findings suggest that leverage is negatively related to CSR expenditures. However, there is a gap in the empirical evidence on the moderating effect of corporate governance characteristics on the impact of CSR practices on the capital structure, which brings future research opportunities. Khatib et al. (2021) suggest that there is still a scarcity of research concerning the relationship between board diversity, in all their attributes and several topics such as capital structure and CSR. Moreover, the evidence shows that CSR contributes to decreasing the cost of debt. However, the results concerning the relationship between CSR practices and leverage are not consensual, which still leaves room for further studies.

Additionally, to remain the drive in the capital structure and CSR research though it is a recognized scope, more publications may emerge from some unexplored regions, such as European countries, South America and Africa, in which CSR practices can be in different stages of evolution since it is voluntary, and not legally enforced.

Based on the bibliometric analysis, the main theories that are associated with the results are the trade-off theory, the agency theory, the signaling hypothesis and the information asymmetry hypothesis and the free cash flow hypothesis. Harjoto (2017) and Huang and Ye (2021) find evidence that supports the trade-off theory concerning the capital structure. Villarón-Peramato et al. (2018) conclude that CSR moderates the agency conflicts between shareholders and managers. However, whereas the results of Yeh et al. (2020) do not support the predictions of the agency theory and the information asymmetry hypothesis, Lu and Wang (2021) support the assumptions of the agency theory and the free cash flow hypothesis. The signaling hypothesis was supported by DiSegni et al. (2015) and Benlemlih (2017).

This study has some limitations, such as the fact that it had been conducted a bibliometric analysis which considers only the Scopus database, causing potential biases in database coverage. Thus, in the future, it would be valuable to use another bibliometric source, such as the WoS database. In addition, the keywords selection can influence the final sample, so, it is recommended a more careful and detailed selection of the keywords in a future study. Nevertheless, this study shows some findings that can conduct researchers to some new avenues for further research on this subject.

This study is important for researchers and managers, because it aids them to understand the consequences of CSR practices on financing decisions, helping managers to make more efficient financial decisions. This study contributes to knowledge in several ways. Firstly, by showing some consistent results, such as the fact that firms that are more indebted, tend to have less practices of CSR, and the findings that are not consensual, and needs more research, such as the impact of CSR on the capital structure, as well as on the type of debt used. Secondly, showing the main theories associated with this subject. Finally, suggesting some avenues for further research, based on the bibliometric analysis, and on keywords trends.

Beyond the previous suggestions for future research, it is possible to identify specific focus of studies that could deepen the understanding of the relationship between capital structure and CSR, covering some gaps on literature, such as exploring sector-specific differences, geographical variations, cultural differences, institutional particularities, and the impact of regulatory frameworks and legal systems. It will be also interesting to explore the difference between CSR quality (assurance) and CSR quantity (disclosure), which is not yet explored.

Finally, other research opportunities can focus on the specific case of the family business, since it is not yet explored, and family firms are internationally frequent, or explore the differences between the impact of CSR and capital structure, for firms with high levels of leverage versus firms with low levels of leverage.

REFERENCES

Albuquerque, R., Koskinen, Y., & Zhang, C. (2019). Corporate social responsibility and firm risk: Theory and empirical evidence. *Management Science*, 65(10), 4451–4949. DOI:10.1287/mnsc.2018.3043

Arslan, H. M., Chengang, Y., Bilal, , Siddique, M., & Yahya, Y. (2022). Influence of senior executives' characteristics on corporate environmental disclosures: A bibliometric analysis. *Journal of Risk and Financial Management*, 15(3), 136. DOI:10.3390/jrfm15030136

Bae, K., Kang, J., & Wang, J. (2011). Employee treatment and firm leverage: A test of the stakeholder theory of capital structure. *Journal of Financial Economics*, 100(1), 130–153. DOI:10.1016/j.jfineco.2010.10.019

Bae, K.-H., El Ghoul, S., Guedhami, O., Kwok, C. C. Y., & Zheng, Y. (2019). Does corporate social responsibility reduce the costs of high leverage? Evidence from capital structure and product market Interactions. *Journal of Banking & Finance*, 100, 135–150. DOI:10.1016/j.jbankfin.2018.11.007

Barauskaite, G., & Streimikiene, D. (2021). Corporate social responsibility and financial performance of companies: The puzzle of concepts, definitions and assessment methods. *Corporate Social Responsibility and Environmental Management*, 28(1), 278–287. DOI:10.1002/csr.2048

Barnea, A., & Rubin, A. (2010). Corporate Social Responsibility as a Conflict Between Shareholders. *Journal of Business Ethics*, 97(1), 71–86. DOI:10.1007/s10551-010-0496-z

Benlemlih, M. (2017). Corporate Social Responsibility and Firm Debt Maturity. *Journal of Business Ethics*, 144(3), 491–517. DOI:10.1007/s10551-015-2856-1

Benlemlih, M., Shaukat, A., Qiu, Y., & Trojanowski, G. (2018). Environmental and social disclosures and firm risk. *Journal of Business Ethics*, 152(3), 613–626. DOI:10.1007/s10551-016-3285-5

Boutin-Dufresne, F., & Savaria, P. (2004). Corporate social responsibility and financial risk. *Journal of Investing Spring, 13*(1), 57-66.

Boyle, F., & Sherman, D. (2006). Scopus: The product and its development. *The Serials Librarian*, 49(3), 147–153. DOI:10.1300/J123v49n03_12

Cancela, B. L., Neves, M. E. D., Rodrigues, L. L., & Dias, A. C. (2020). The influence of corporate governance on corporate sustainability: New evidence using panel data in the Iberian macroeconomic environment. *International Journal of Accounting and Information Management*, 28(4), 785–806. DOI:10.1108/IJAIM-05-2020-0068

Chadegani, A., Salehi, H., Yunus, M., Farhadi, H., Fooladi, M., Farhadi, M., & Ebrahim, N. (2013). A comparison between two Main academic literature collections: Web of science and Scopus databases. *Asian Social Science*, 9(5), 18–26. DOI:10.5539/ass.v9n5p18

Chen, G., Wang, B., & Wang, X. (2020). Corporate social responsibility and information flow. *Accounting and Finance*, 61(2), 2759–2807. DOI:10.1111/acfi.12683

Chen, K., Chen, Z., & Wei, K. (2009). Legal protection of investors, corporate governance, and the cost of equity capital. *Journal of Corporate Finance*, 15(3), 273–289. DOI:10.1016/j.jcorpfin.2009.01.001

Cheng, B., Ioannou, I., & Serafeim, G. (2014). Corporate social responsibility and access to finance. *Strategic Management Journal*, 35(1), 1–23. DOI:10.1002/smj.2131

Cobo, M., Matínez, M., Gutiérrez-Salcedo, M., Fujita, H., & Herrera-Viedma, E. (2015). 25 years at knowledge-based systems: A bibliometric analysis. *Knowledge-Based Systems*, 80, 3–13. DOI:10.1016/j.knosys.2014.12.035

Commission of the European Communities. (2001). Green Paper: Promoting a European framework for Corporate Social Responsibility. Retrieved from https://ec.europa.eu/commission/presscorner/detail/en/DOC_01_9

Cooper, E. W., & Uzun, H. (2015). Corporate social responsibility and the cost of debt. *Journal of Accounting & Finance*, 15(8), 11–29.

Diamond, D. (1991). Monitoring and reputation: The choice between bank loans and directly placed debt. *Journal of Political Economy*, 99(4), 689–721. DOI:10.1086/261775

Ding, W., Levine, R., Lin, C., & Xie, W. (2021). Corporate immunity to the COVID-19 pandemic. *Journal of Financial Economics*, 141(2), 802–830. DOI:10.1016/j.jfineco.2021.03.005 PMID:34580557

DiSegni, D. M., Huly, M., & Akron, S. (2015). Corporate social responsibility, environmental leadership and financial performance. *Social Responsibility Journal*, 11(1), 131–148. DOI:10.1108/SRJ-02-2013-0024

Donthu, N., Kumar, S., & Pattnaik, D. (2020). Forty-five years of Journal of Business Research: A bibliometric analysis. *Journal of Business Research*, 109, 1–14. DOI:10.1016/j.jbusres.2019.10.039

El Ghoul, S., Guedhami, O., Kwok, C. C., & Mishra, D. R. (2011). Does corporate social responsibility affect the cost of capital? *Journal of Banking & Finance*, 35(9), 2388–2406. DOI:10.1016/j.jbankfin.2011.02.007

Ellili, N. O. (2020). Environmental, social, and governance disclosure, ownership structure and cost of capital: Evidence from the UAE. *Sustainability (Basel)*, 12(18), 7706. DOI:10.3390/su12187706

Elsevier (2020). Scopus: Content Coverage Guide. Retrieved from https://www.elsevier.com/__data/assets/pdf_file/0007/69451/Scopus_ContentCoverage_Guide_WEB.pdf

Ezzi, F., Jarboui, A., & Zouari-Hadiji, R. (2020). CSR categories and R&D investment: The moderating role of managerial emotional intelligence. *Management & Marketing*, 15(1), 17–37. DOI:10.2478/mmcks-2020-0002

Fama, E. F., & Jensen, M. C. (1983). Separation of ownership and control. *The Journal of Law & Economics*, 26(2), 301–325. DOI:10.1086/467037

Gainet, C. (2010). Exploring the Impact of Legal Systems and Financial Structure on Corporate Responsibility. *Journal of Business Ethics*, 95(S2, SUPPL. 2), 195–222. DOI:10.1007/s10551-011-0854-5

Gh Popescu, C. R. (2019). Corporate social responsibility, corporate governance and business performance: Limits and challenges imposed by the implementation of directive 2013/34/EU in Romania. *Sustainability (Basel)*, 11(19), 5146. DOI:10.3390/su11195146

Ghoul, S. E., Guedhami, O., Kwok-Chuck, C. Y., & Mishra, D. R. (2011). Does corporate social responsibility affect the cost of capital? *Journal of Banking & Finance*, 35(9), 2388–2406. DOI:10.1016/j.jbankfin.2011.02.007

Goss, A., & Roberts, G. S. (2011). The impact of corporate social responsibility on the cost of bank loans. *Journal of Banking & Finance*, 35(7), 1794–1810. DOI:10.1016/j.jbankfin.2010.12.002

Grabinska, B., Kedzior, D., Kedzior, M., & Grabinski, K. (2021). The Impact of CSR on the Capital Structure of High-Tech Companies in Poland. *Sustainability (Basel)*, 13(10), 5467. DOI:10.3390/su13105467

Hail, L., & Leuz, C. (2006). International differences in cost of equity capital: Do legal institutions and securities regulations matter? *Journal of Accounting Research*, 44(3), 485–531. DOI:10.1111/j.1475-679X.2006.00209.x

Harjoto, M. A. (2017). Corporate social responsibility and degrees of operating and financial leverage. *Review of Quantitative Finance and Accounting*, 49(2), 487–513. DOI:10.1007/s11156-016-0598-5

Harzing, A. W. (2019). Two new kids on the block: How do Crossref and Dimensions compare with Google Scholar, Microsoft Academic, Scopus and the Web of Science? *Scientometrics*, 120(1), 341–349. DOI:10.1007/s11192-019-03114-y

Hirsch, J. (2005). An index to quantify an individual's scientific research output. *Proceedings of the National Academy of Sciences of the United States of America*, 102(46), 16569–16572. DOI:10.1073/pnas.0507655102 PMID:16275915

Hsu, S. C., Wu, K. T., Wang, Q., & Chang, Y. (2023). Is capital structure associated with corporate social responsibility? *International Journal of Corporate Social Responsibility*, 8(1), 6. DOI:10.1186/s40991-023-00081-9

Huang, H., & Ye, Y. (2021). Rethinking capital structure decision and corporate social responsibility in response to COVID-19. *Accounting and Finance*, 61(3), 4757–4788. DOI:10.1111/acfi.12740

Ikram, M., Sroufe, R., Mohsin, M., Solangi, Y. A., Shah, S. Z., & Shahzad, F. (2019). Does CSR influence firm performance? A longitudinal study of SME sectors of Pakistan. *Journal of Global Responsibility*, 11(1), 27–53. DOI:10.1108/JGR-12-2018-0088

Jensen, M. C. (1986). Agency costs of free cash flow, corporate finance, and takeovers. *The American Economic Review*, 76, 323–329.

Jensen, M. C., & Meckling, W. H. (1976). Theory of the firm: Managerial behavior, agency costs and ownership structure. *Journal of Financial Economics*, 3(4), 305–360. DOI:10.1016/0304-405X(76)90026-X

Jo, H., & Harjoto, M. (2011). Corporate governance and firm value: The impact of corporate social responsibility. *Journal of Business Ethics*, 103(3), 351–383. DOI:10.1007/s10551-011-0869-y

Jo, H., & Na, H. (2012). Does CSR reduce firm risk? Evidence from controversial industry sectors? *Journal of Business Ethics*, 110(4), 441–456. DOI:10.1007/s10551-012-1492-2

Khatib, S. F. A., Abdullah, D. F., Elamer, A. A., & Abueid, R. (2021). Nudging toward diversity in the boardroom: A systematic literature review of board diversity of financial institutions. *Business Strategy and the Environment*, 30(2), 985–1002. DOI:10.1002/bse.2665

Kim, S., Lee, G., & Kang, H. G. (2021). Risk management and corporate social responsibility. *Strategic Management Journal*, 42(1), 202–230. DOI:10.1002/smj.3224

Lee, D., & Faff, R. (2009). Corporate sustainability performance and idiosyncratic risk: A global perspective. *Financial Review*, 44(2), 213–237. DOI:10.1111/j.1540-6288.2009.00216.x

Li, R., & Henderson, G. V.Jr. (1991). Combined leverage and stock risk. *Quarterly Journal of Business Economics*, 30(1), 18–39. https://www.jstor.org/stable/40473011

Lins, K. V., Servaes, H., & Tamayo, A. (2017). Social capital, trust, and firm performance: The value of corporate social responsibility during the financial crisis. *The Journal of Finance*, 72(4), 1785–1824. DOI:10.1111/jofi.12505

Liu, L., & Tian, G. G. (2019). Mandatory CSR disclosure, monitoring and investment efficiency: Evidence from China. *Accounting and Finance*, 61(1), 595–644. DOI:10.1111/acfi.12588

Lu, F., Kozak, R., Toppinen, A., D'Amato, D., & Wen, Z. (2017). Factors influencing levels of CSR disclosure by forestry companies in China. *Sustainability (Basel)*, 9(10), 1800. DOI:10.3390/su9101800

Lu, J., & Wang, J. (2021). Corporate governance, law, culture, environmental performance and CSR disclosure: A global perspective. *Journal of International Financial Markets, Institutions and Money*, 70, 101264. DOI:10.1016/j.intfin.2020.101264

Mahmood, A. N., Arslan, H. M., Younas, Z. I., Komal, B., Ali, K., & Mubeen, M. (2023). Understanding the dynamics of capital structure, corporate governance, and corporate social responsibility in high and low-leveraged US and Chinese firms. *Environmental Science and Pollution Research International*, 30(16), 1–18. DOI:10.1007/s11356-022-24843-3 PMID:36710308

Margolis, J., Elfenbein, H., & Walsh, J. (2009). Does it pay to be good? A meta-analysis and redirection of research on the relationship between corporate social and financial performance (March 1, 2009). Retrieved from https://ssrn.com/abstract=1866371

Marlowe, J., & Clarke, A. (2022). Carbon accounting: A systematic literature review and directions for future research. *Green Finance*, 4(1), 71–87. DOI:10.3934/GF.2022004

Martín-Martín, A., Thelwall, M., Orduna-Malea, E., & Delgado López-Cózar, E. (2020). Google Scholar, Microsoft Academic, Scopus, Dimensions, Web of Science, and OpenCitations' COCI: A multidisciplinary comparison of coverage via citations. *Scientometrics*, 126(1), 871–906. DOI:10.1007/s11192-020-03690-4 PMID:32981987

Menz, K. M. (2010). Corporate social responsibility: Is it rewarded by the corporate bond market? A critical note. *Journal of Business Ethics*, 96(1), 117–134. DOI:10.1007/s10551-010-0452-y

Nelling, E., & Webb, E. (2009). Corporate social responsibility and financial performance: The "virtuous circle" revisited. *Review of Quantitative Finance and Accounting*, 32(2), 197–209. DOI:10.1007/s11156-008-0090-y

Oware, K. M., & Mallikarjunappa, T. (2021). Corporate social responsibility and debt financing of listed firms: A quantile regression approach. *Journal of Financial Reporting and Accounting*, 19(4), 615–639. DOI:10.1108/JFRA-07-2020-0202

Page, M. J., McKenzie, J. E., Bossuyt, P. M., Boutron, I., Hoffmann, T. C., Mulrow, C. D., & Moher, D. (2021). Updating guidance for reporting systematic reviews: Development of the PRISMA 2020 statement. *Journal of Clinical Epidemiology*, 134, 103–112. DOI:10.1016/j.jclinepi.2021.02.003 PMID:33577987

Pastor, L., Sinha, M., & Swaminathan, B. (2008). Estimating the intertemporal risk-return trade off using the implied cost of capital. *The Journal of Finance*, 63(6), 2859–2897. DOI:10.1111/j.1540-6261.2008.01415.x

Pessarossia, P., & Weill, L. (2013). Choice of corporate debt in China: The role of state ownership. *China Economic Review*, 26, 1–16. DOI:10.1016/j.chieco.2013.03.005

Popescu, C.R.G. (2020). Sustainability assessment: Does the oecd/g20 inclusive framework for beps (base erosion and profit shifting project) put an end to disputes over the recognition and measurement of intellectual capital? *Sustainability, 12*(23), 1-22.

Pradhan, A. K., & Nibedita, B. (2021). The determinants of corporate social responsibility: Evidence from Indian firms. *Global Business Review*, 22(3), 753–766. DOI:10.1177/0972150918814318

Pucheta-Martínez, M. C., Bel-Oms, I., & Gallego-Alvarez, I. (2022). Corporate social responsibility reporting and capital structure: Does board gender diversity mind in such association? *Corporate Social Responsibility and Environmental Management*, 1–13. DOI:10.1002/csr.2437

Pucheta-Martínez, M. C., Olcina-Sempere, G., & Lopez-Zamora, B. (2020). Female directorship on boards and corporate sustainability policies: Their effect on sustainable development. *Sustainable Development (Bradford)*, 28(1), 56–72. DOI:10.1002/sd.1965

Reverte, C. (2012). The impact of better corporate social responsibility disclosure on the cost of equity capital. *Corporate Social Responsibility and Environmental Management*, 19(5), 253–272. DOI:10.1002/csr.273

Salinas-Ríos, K., & García López, A. J. (2022). Bibliometrics, a useful tool within the field of research. *Journal of Basic and Applied Psychology Research*, 3(6), 9–16. DOI:10.29057/jbapr.v3i6.6829

Sharfman, M., & Fernando, C. (2008). Environmental risk management and the cost of capital. *Strategic Management Journal*, 29(6), 569–592. DOI:10.1002/smj.678

Stahlschmidt, S., & Stephen, D. (2022). From indexation policies through citation networks to normalized citation impacts: Web of Science, Scopus, and Dimensions as varying resonance chambers. *Scientometrics*, 127(5), 2413–2431. DOI:10.1007/s11192-022-04309-6

Trezevant, R. (1992). Debt financing and tax status: Tests of the substitution effect and the tax exhaustion hypothesis using firms' responses to the economic recovery tax act of 1981. *The Journal of Finance*, 47(4), 1557–1568. DOI:10.1111/j.1540-6261.1992.tb04670.x

Verwijmeren, P., & Derwall, J. (2010). Employee well-being, firm leverage, and bankruptcy risk. *Journal of Banking & Finance*, 34(5), 956–964. DOI:10.1016/j.jbankfin.2009.10.006

Vieira, E. S., & Gomes, J. A. N. F. (2009). A comparison of Scopus and Web of Science for a typical university. *Scientometrics*, 81(2), 587–600. DOI:10.1007/s11192-009-2178-0

Villarón-Peramato, Ó., Martínez-Ferrero, J., & García-Sánchez, I.-M. (2018). CSR as entrenchment strategy and capital structure: Corporate governance and investor protection as complementary and substitutive factors. *Review of Managerial Science*, 12(1), 27–64. DOI:10.1007/s11846-016-0212-1

Wu, M., Shen, C., & Chen, T. (2016). Application of multi-level matching between financial performance and corporate social responsibility in the banking industry. *Review of Quantitative Finance and Accounting*, 49(1), 29–63. DOI:10.1007/s11156-016-0582-0

Xu, H., Xu, X., & Yu, J. (2021). The impact of mandatory CSR disclosure on the cost of debt financing: Evidence from China. *Emerging Markets Finance & Trade*, 57(8), 2191–2205. DOI:10.1080/1540496X.2019.1657401

Xu, L. D., Xu, E. L., & Li, L. (2018). Industry 4.0: State of the art and future trends. *International Journal of Production Research*, 56(8), 2941–2962. DOI:10.1080/00207543.2018.1444806

Xu, S., Liu, D., & Huang, J. (2015). Corporate social responsibility, the cost of equity capital and ownership structure: An analysis of Chinese listed firms. *Australian Journal of Management*, 40(2), 245–276. DOI:10.1177/0312896213517894

Yang, S., He, F., Zhu, Q., & Li, S. (2018). How does corporate social responsibility change capital structure? *Asia-Pacific Journal of Accounting & Economics*, 25(3-4), 352–387. DOI:10.1080/16081625.2017.1354710

Ye, K., & Zhang, R. (2011). Do lenders value corporate social responsibility? Evidence from China. *Journal of Business Ethics*, 104(2), 197–206. DOI:10.1007/s10551-011-0898-6

Yeh, C.-C., Lin, F., Wang, T.-S., & Wu, C.-M. (2020). Does corporate social responsibility affect cost of capital in China? *Asia Pacific Management Review*, 25(1), 1–12. DOI:10.1016/j.apmrv.2019.04.001

Zhou, H., Li, G., & Lin, W. (2016). Corporate social responsibility and credit spreads: An empirical study in Chinese context. *Annals of Economics and Finance*, 17(1), 79–103.

KEY TERMS AND DEFINITIONS

Bibliometric Analysis: It is a quantitative method employed to assess scholarly publications, such as journal articles, conference proceedings, and books. It entails scrutinizing publication patterns, citations, and co-citations to comprehend different facets of academic communication within a specific field or subject. With this technique, academics can recognize patterns, monitor the evolution of scientific research across time, and realize future trends of research.

Capital Structure: It refers to the specific combination of debt and equity used by the companies to finance their assets, which allowas them to implement their operations and to growth.

Corporate Governance: Corporate governance involves a set of regulations, procedures, and methods through which the management and oversight of a company is conducted, in ordet to protect the investors and the other stachholders.

Corporate Social Responsibility (CSR): CSR is a business strategy that involves incorporating social and environmental considerations into its activities and relationships with stakeholders, entailing companies choosing to take accountability for their effects on society and the environment that go beyond what is required by law.

H-Index: It is a metric used to quantity the productivity and impact of the work done by researchers. It is calculated having as reference the number of publications as well as the number of citations of these specific publications. It reflects the highest number of scientific papers that a researcher has published that have received at least the same number of citations.

Information Asymmetry: It referes to the fact that one side of the deal (managers) has more information that the other side, that has limited access to the information (investors), which can impact choices concerning investments, loans, and other financial dealings.

Scopus Database: It is a large database, with multidisciplinary peer-reviewed literature, such as scientific journals, books, and conference proceedings.

Chapter 2
Sustainability-Balanced Scorecard for an Energy Company: Case Study

Helena Costa Oliveira
CEOS.PP, ISCAP, Polytechnic of Porto, Portugal

Inês Sousa
ISCAP, Polytechnic of Porto, Portugal

Susana Bastos
CEOS.PP, ISCAP, Polytechnic of Porto, Portugal

ABSTRACT

Considering the significant impact of sustainability on companies' performance, implementing strategies and measuring them is essential. The sustainability balanced scorecard integrating sustainability into traditional perspectives (finance, customers, internal processes, and learning and growth) can be an efficient strategic management and performance assessment tool. This study aims to analyze the sustainable development goals a company prioritizes and propose their integration into the balance scorecard to monitor them. This study develops a case study through a qualitative analysis based on documentary analysis and interviews. The balanced scorecard developed for the energy company is aligned with its mission and values, considering the sustainable development goals that the company aims to achieve (SDGs 8, 9, 12, and 17). This study contributes to the literature on the sustainability-balanced scorecard. The model presented can be useful for other companies that intend to use management tools to measure sustainability.

DOI: 10.4018/979-8-3693-5663-0.ch002

1. INTRODUCTION

Sustainability plays a dominant role in the surrounding environment, influencing society and the economy, and affecting people and companies. Adherence to sustainable practices is essential to ensure a healthy environment for society and future generations. Several companies are concerned with managing a more sustainable economy by becoming more socially responsible. In addition to worrying about success and profit, organizations are also concerned about the impact of their actions and decisions on society and the planet. More and more consumers are becoming aware of sustainability, thus influencing their purchasing decisions. People prefer products that do not put the environment at risk, even if they are more expensive, therefore supporting companies that adopt ethical and sustainable practices.

In addition to sustainable practices, organizations are concerned with sustainability management and looking for effective measurement tools. The Balanced Scorecard (BSC), a strategic management tool that helps measure the performance of several areas, can be adapted to measure social and environmental impacts. By integrating sustainability into the BSC, companies can measure their sustainable practices and the impact of their decisions, not being guided only by the financial aspect. Therefore, this integration allows companies to evaluate and improve their social and environmental responsibility performance.

This paper aims to develop a BSC that integrates the sustainability issues of Makeen Energy Portugal, S. A., a company in the energy sector. The purpose is to analyze the company´s prioritized Sustainable Development Goals (SDGs) and integrate them into the BSC. Documentary analysis and interviews were used to carry out this case study.

This study contributes to the literature on BSC and sustainability. The proposed model will be useful for companies that intend to use management tools to measure sustainability and integrate it into their strategy, aligning their practices with long-term sustainability objectives. The proposed indicators could serve as a reference for other companies prioritizing the SDGs studied.

The paper is divided into five sections. Section two presents the literature review, section three the methodology, and section four the case study. The paper ends with final considerations about the case study.

2. LITERATURE REVIEW

Sustainability is the set of processes and actions to maintain the vitality and integrity of nature and meet the needs of present and future generations. Sustainability has an increasing impact on companies' performance and therefore, it is necessary to implement strategies, to ensure competitive advantages over competitors (Ali et al., 2022). Although this concept is not new, many companies still do not know how to measure outputs (Kalender et al., 2016).

Sustainability management is interpreted as formulating, implementing, and evaluating decisions and actions related to environmental and socioeconomic sustainability (Bell et al., 2008), including decisions and actions at individual, organizational, and social levels. However, these are often carried out only at the operational level, and not at the company's strategic planning level (Kalender et al., 2016).

In 2015, the United Nations proposed 17 Sustainable Development Goals (SDG) with 169 targets to be achieved by 2030. These define the priorities and aspirations of global sustainable development for 2030 and seek to mobilize international efforts around a set of objectives and common goals. The SDGs require global action by governments, businesses, and civil society to eradicate poverty and create a life of dignity and opportunity for all, within the planet´s limits (United Nations, 2015). One way to create more value in the future and generate a competitive advantage in the market is to combine these SDGs with management tools such as the Balanced Scorecard (BSC) (Rösner et al., 2022 and Figge et al., 2002). There are several approaches, including the combination of corporate social responsibility, the SDGs, and the BSC, to support strategic alignment, aiming for sustainability and creating value for the company (Sarkar et al, 2019).

The BSC is a strategic management tool that aims to identify problems related to business strategy and, consequently, find their causes and resolution (Kaplan et al., 1996). The BSC presents a long-term vision and focuses on tangible and intangible measures, presenting four organizational analysis perspectives (Financial, Customer, Internal Processes, and Learning and Growth). A company will only obtain attractive financial results if it knows how to satisfy its customers, optimize existing internal processes, and remain innovative (Butler et al., 2011).

The BSC evolved to integrate financial, and economic issues but also social and environmental. Some authors now call it the Sustainability Balanced Scorecard (SBSC) (Figge et al., 2002 and Butler et al., 2011). The use of SBSC as a formal control tool implies informal controls (such as cultural or administrative) (Mio et al., 2022). Sustainable development cannot occur without complementarity of controls (formal and informal) (Lueg et al., 2016, Florêncio et al., 2023). Most of the research presents the SBSC as a tool for the sustainable development of companies. However, little literature focuses on the role of SBSC as a corporate tool to achieve global sustainable development.

The development of the BSC depends on the organization´s needs. It is important for outlining a strategic plan and converting the original model into an operational system, adjusted to the organization´s context (Cobbold et al., 2001).

Companies are concerned about understanding the importance and correctly implementing sustainability strategies. Still, the most important thing is implementing a system with a strong connection between environmental/social management and financial benefits (Kalender et al. 2016). The BSC can stabilize and ensure proactiveness in the environmental strategy (Hsu et al, 2010).

Integrating environmental and social concerns into traditional management systems allows alignment to financial issues. The resources and skills will create value not only for a competitive strategy, but also for an environmental strategy, and can have positive downstream effects (Christman et al., 2000).

Practical decision-support tools can be used to achieve sustainability objectives, facilitate processes, and assist in organizational change and learning (Gladwin et al., 1995). SBSC contributes to translating the vision, values, and sustainability strategies into actions, showing how intangible assets can contribute to companies´ sustainability (Bieker et al. 2001).

The integration of the three pillars of sustainability (environmental, social and economic) in global business management, through the BSC, allows to consider sustainability management, both in times of crisis and in moments of success; promotes environmental management and ensures that the three pillars are fully integrated (Figge et al., 2002). In addition, it provides relevant information, allowing an accurate evaluation performance; and generates synergies with the strategic management of other business units (Hsu et al., 2010).

According to Hansen et al. (2016), the SBSC develops and manages sustainability strategies, allowing the integration of strategic objectives in the three dimensions of sustainability, reducing costs and improving efficiency, replacing three independent variables through an integrated management strategy.

There are several cases of integrating sustainability into organizational management through tools such as the BSC.

Pereira and Oliveira (2020), propose an SBSC for a city council, that isolated the pillars of sustainability, creating a new perspective called sustainability. According to the authors, this approach is stronger for organizations that want to make sustainability a key factor in their strategy. It can become decisive when a company has a relevant social impact and wants to highlight its relevance.

Araújo et al. (2020), propose an SBSC for the Brazilian company with the most significant agricultural land in Brazil. Through analysis, it evaluated the company's vision, strategy, and possible strategic objectives, allowing us to filter issues from an environmental point of view and understand the main concern for building the strategic map.

For Mendes et al. (2012) the BSC can contribute significantly to improving the quality of services provided in the case of waste management. Furthermore, it gives results in real-time, contributing to better strategic planning, with communication and learning as its main pillars.

Based on the study by Elbanna et al. (2015) the SBSC contributed to filling a gap in testing organizational development using the BSC in the hotel industry.

The SBSC can also be designed to develop a strategic map for implementing and monitoring environmental education programs in universities (Andrade Guerra et al., 2018). By developing and implementing environmental concerns into the principles and infrastructures, universities have become increasingly proactive in promoting social change with a view to sustainable development. These concerns can be translated into environmental education programs, raising awareness among students and the entire surrounding community. With the implementation of the BSC, the authors identify positive aspects such as respect for existing resources in the university environment. Another issue mentioned was the possibility of structuring strategic objectives within a university context, in an integrated and interconnected way.

There are still cases of success in the banking sector. Gazi et al. (2022), evaluate the SBSC internal indicators in the banking system in Northern Cyprus. Sustainable development management increases companies´ effectiveness and efficiency and ensures sustainable measurement based on BSC practices. The study investigates the relationship between organizational culture, innovation performance, intrapreneurship, and the effectiveness of the company's accounting information systems and the BSC.

Due to its flexibility and ease of adaptation to each company´s peculiar characteristics, the BSC can be applied in several sectors, from the agricultural to the banking sector.

3. METHODOLOGY

3.1. Purpose of the Study

This paper presents a case study and aims to develop a BSC for Makeen Energy Portugal S.A., which belongs to the energy sector and focuses on sustainability. The choice of the energy sector was because it is a complex and comprehensive sector regarding the various aspects of sustainability. Furthermore, studying this sector is essential to promote balanced economic development, ensure environmental protection, and improve quality of life. The research questions are (1) What perspectives will be used in the BSC? (2) How can sustainability be integrated into the BSC? (3) How do we reflect this integration in the strategic map?

Makeen Energy Portugal S.A was chosen because it is a global market leader in the energy industry, concerned with the development of responsible energy solutions. It is determined to play an active role in the sustainable transformation of the market in which it operates. It has a broad portfolio of services and businesses such as equipment, services and spare parts; facilities management, engineering and project management; Liquefied Petroleum Gas (LPG) filling facilities and Liquefied Natural Gas (LNG) supply solutions; power plants and facilities that convert plastic waste into oil (Makeen Energy, 2022). The company employs around 300 employees and operates in Portugal, Spain, and Portuguese-speaking African Countries (PALOP - *Países Africanos de Língua Oficial Portuguesa*).

The company's purpose is aligned with its values, highlighting proactivity and particular concern not only for employees and business partners but also for the entire surrounding society. The following values govern the company (1) be proactive and take control, (2) get involved passionately, (3) share knowledge – make others good, (4) understand and help customers, (5) leave no one behind, (6) address any problem freely and constructively (Makeen Energy, 2023a).

The SDGs that Makeen Energy prioritizes are decent work and economic growth (SDG 8), industry, innovation and infrastructure (SDG 9), responsible consumption and production (SDG 12), and partnerships for the goals (SDG 17) (Makeen Energy, 2023b).

3.2. Data Collection and Analysis

This case study will be carried out based on qualitative analysis and data will be collected through documentary analysis and interviews. Four employees were interviewed - the head of the financial department; the coordinator of the continuous improvement department; the head of the quality, environment, and safety department; and the head of the continuous improvement department. They were selected based on their roles and potential contribution to the purpose of the study. The interviews took place between May and June 2023 and had an average duration of 20 minutes. The content of the interviews was analyzed using NVivo software. Several documents available on the company website and provided by them were analyzed, such as reports and accounts, risk and opportunity assessment matrices, continuous improvement reports, Kaizen reports, and audit reports.

All the data obtained from interviews and documental analysis underwent an active and continuous recursive process of reading, examination, speculation, searching, selecting, viewing, and interpretation (Davie, 2008).

Based on documents and interview analysis, a BSC was proposed for the organization. It started by identifying the perspectives to be integrated, and the respective objectives and indicators, aligned on a strategic map. The final BSC translates the organization's mission, values, and principles to align all employees with the company's strategy.

4. RESULTS AND DISCUSSION

To construct the BSC there were considered the four traditional perspectives (economic, customer, internal processes, and learning and growth). Each perspective must follow the principle "responsible energy solutions for people and planet" since this is the company's motto. Makeen Energy is a global market leader in the energy sector and is therefore determined to play an active role in the sustainable transformation of the energy market.

4.1. Economic Perspective

Economic growth guarantees the prosperity of the company and its products. The implementation of the SDGs will have a positive impact on sustainability and reduce the company's ecological footprint. In the long term, the company will ensure that its products and services are in demand and profitable. Considering the SDGs that the company prioritizes SDG 8 (promoting inclusive and sustainable economic growth, full and productive employment, and decent work for all) fits in this perspective.

The objectives of the economic perspective are directed towards economic growth and competitive advantage. Three goals were defined - growth in turnover, increase in working capital, and increase in profit. The growth in turnover and the increase in profit impact economic growth, and therefore, meet the features of SDG 8. This SDG also seeks to dissociate economic growth from pollution and environmental degradation. Although the increase in the working capital will not directly impact SDG 8, it will increase the company's short-term resources. Therefore, the company can consider some investments to make capital profitable and generate profit. Table I presents the objectives, initiatives, and indicators proposed from the economic perspective.

Table 1. Objectives, indicators, and initiatives from the Economic Perspective

Objectives	Indicators	Initiatives
Growth in turnover (SDG 8)	(Sales N - Sales N-1)/Sales N-1	Create a portfolio of expertise for sales
Increase in working capital	% Trade working Capital = Inventories + customers - suppliers	Negotiation of better payment and receipt terms; Stock Reduction
Increase in profit (SDG 8)	EBITDA/Sales volume	Cost control measures and increased turnover; Active approaches to the market; Analysis of the Win rate of the proposals sent

Source: Own Elaboration

4.2. Customer Perspective

The customer perspective drives service innovation. Based on the customers' needs, solutions are designed with less environmental impact and guaranteed sustainability. Customer satisfaction must consider that the product/service meets the statements of sustainable production, which is concerned with reducing waste and the proper treatment of waste. The delivery of this product/service may result in a higher cost for the company in the short term, even though attracting new customers will eventually return these costs.

From the customer's perspective, three objectives were defined - improvement of products and services provided; integrity and ethics; and expansion of the network of business partners and market. The SGD associated with this perspective is SDG 7 (strengthening the means of implementation and revitalization of the global partnership for sustainable development) and is related to the expansion of the network of partners and market expansion, thus reinforcing the global partnership for sustainable development, sharing market knowledge, technology, and diversifying resources.

Although it does not directly impact SDG 17, improving the products and services provided is essential for the organization's success and competitiveness. The ability to adapt is very important to maintaining satisfactory products/services for the customer. Integrity and ethics aim to have a transparent and honest relationship with the client to contribute to long-term success and lasting business relationships with partners.

Table II presents the objectives, initiatives, and indicators proposed from the customer perspective.

Table 2. Objectives, indicators, and initiatives from the Customer Perspective

Objectives	Indicators	Initiatives
Improvement of products and services provided	Customer satisfaction surveys	Analysis of customer responses
Integrity and ethics	Number of customer complaints	Preparation of the code of conduct
Expansion of the network of business partners and market (SDG 17)	Number of new customers, Number of new/renewed contracts	Create a portfolio of expertise for sale; Open Book; Early renegotiations

Source: Own Elaboration

4.3. Internal Process Perspective

The internal process perspective focuses on the efficiency and quality of the company's internal processes to achieve strategic objectives and implement improvement initiatives. Five goals were defined for this perspective – production efficiency, reduction of accidents with environmental impact and reduction in the use of fossil energy, compliance with legislation, increased demand for services/products, and process standardization. The SDG related to this perspective is SDG 12 (ensuring sustainable consumption and production patterns).

The objectives that directly affect SDG 12 are all related to sustainable management and the efficient use of natural resources. Considering this SDG, it is important to significantly reduce the release of waste and chemicals into the air, soil, and water, to minimize negative impacts on human health and the environment. Production efficiency is equally important, as it involves optimizing resources to maximize production and reduce waste, costs, and time.

The remaining objectives indirectly impact SDG 12. Regarding compliance with legislation, organizations must ensure that their processes are completely aligned and in compliance with legal requirements to protect the organization against legal risks and minimize the negative impact of its operations on the environment. Another objective considered is increasing customer demand for an organization's products/services. Companies must balance between increasing demand and adopting sustainable practices throughout the production process, always considering sustainable production. Finally, the standardization of processes was also considered an objective to be achieved. This allows for greater efficiency and quality, never forgetting the promotion of responsible practices that reduce environmental and social impact.

Table III presents the objectives, initiatives, and indicators proposed from the internal process perspective.

Table 3. Objectives, indicators, and initiatives from the Internal Process Perspective

Objectives	Indicators	Initiatives
Production efficiency (SDG 12)	Production per capita = Production per machine hour worked	Application of Kaizen methodology; Development of investment plans
Reduction of accidents with environmental impact and reduction in the use of fossil energy (SDG 12)	Number of accidents/incidents resulting from normal activity, with environmental impact; Amount spent on fines; Fossil fuel consumption/sales volume; % emission of contaminated waste compared to clean/treated waste	Environmental training and awareness; Environmental Management System based on ISO 18001:2015; Risk assessment and definition of prevention measures
Compliance with legislation	Number of non-conformities/Audit	Carrying out regular internal audits; Validation of the closure of non-conformities; External audits
Increased demand for services/products	Order Intake (in euros)	Assessment of Current Opportunities
Process standardization	Number of continuous improvement/Lean/ Kaizen certifications; Number of documented processes/total processes	Exhaustive survey of processes

Source: Own Elaboration

4.4. Learning and Growth Perspective

The learning and growth perspective focuses on continuous learning and growth, recognizing that sustainable development and continuous improvement require constant investment in these topics.

The objectives selected for this perspective are valuing human capital and increasing employee efficiency, creating protocols with various entities, reducing electricity consumption, investing in hybrid/electric cars, reducing accidents, and digital archiving practicing. Considering the SDGs the company aims to achieve, the SDGs that fit into this perspective are SDG 8 (also referred to in the economic perspective) and SDG 9 (building resilient infrastructure, promoting inclusive and sustainable industrialization, and fostering innovation).

The valorization of human capital, the increase in the efficiency of employees, and the reduction in the accident rate are two important objectives that directly impact SDG 8. In this organization, human capital is fundamental, so it is necessary to invest in training, working conditions, and the well-being of employees. Employees' efficiency will increase if they feel valued and involved in the organization. Makeen has objectives that will directly impact the company's sustained economic growth but also raise awareness among employees with some actions the company encouraged (such as the initiative to collect rubbish on beaches).

If these objectives are met, we automatically face the protection of human rights and decent work, thus promoting motivating and safe work environments.

Creating protocols with various entities contributes to achieving SDG 9, contributing positively to sustainable development.

The reduction in electricity consumed and the implementation of digital archiving practices reduce the company's costs and thus contribute to the company's economic growth and sustainability. Another critical sustainable practice is the increase in hybrid/electric cars. This goal promotes environmental sustainability by reducing dependence on fossil fuels and mitigating climate change.

Table IV presents the objectives, initiatives, and indicators proposed from the internal process perspective.

Table 4. Objectives, indicators, and initiatives from the Learning and Growth Perspective

Objectives	Indicators	Initiatives
Valuing human capital and increasing employee efficiency (SDG 8)	Employee satisfaction survey Training hours per employee Invoicing/Employee	Development of an action plan; Creation of efficient work processes; Definition of training plans
Creating protocols with various entities (SDG 9)	Number of protocols created	Participation in job fairs; Protocols with educational establishments
Reducing electricity consumption	Electricity consumption/hours worked	To raise awareness among employees
Investing in hybrid/electric cars	Number of electric and hybrid vehicles/Total number of vehicles	Acquisition of Hybrid/electric vehicles
Reducing the level of accidents (SDG 8)	Number of accidents/total hours worked Short hours/Total hours worked	Reinforcement of training and control of jobs; Control of security measures
Digital archiving practicing	Number of prints per month	Check the viability of the process; Raise awareness of employees regarding digital archives

Source: Own Elaboration

4.5. Strategic Map

After obtaining the necessary inputs for developing the BSC, a strategic map was designed to establish the relationships between the objectives of the four perspectives.

Several dynamic connections were identified between the objectives, whether upward, downward, or at the same level from each perspective. In general, the macroeconomic objectives, which are influenced by all the others, are increased profit and growth in turnover. The entire organization impacts these two objectives.

According to all interviewees, the objectives developed to create this map are aligned with the company's vision, mission, and values. Customers and employees are highly present on the map, which reflects their importance in the organization (See Figure 1: Strategic Map).

Figure 1. Strategic Map

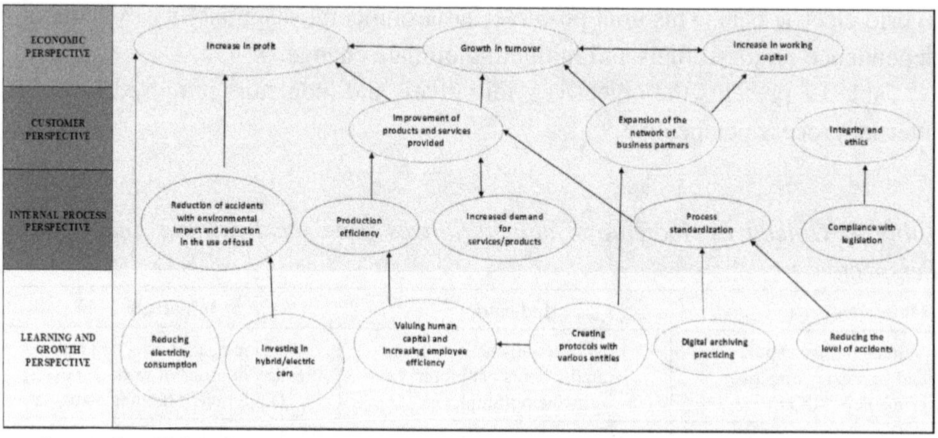

Source: Own Elaboration

5. CONCLUSION

Organizations have an essential role in building a fairer and more sustainable society. This paper studies the integration of sustainability into the business strategies at Makeen Energy Portugal. This world-leading company works in the energy sector and plays an active role in the sustainable transformation of the energy industry, developing responsible energy solutions that impact the planet. This integration was carried out using the BSC, where four perspectives were identified - economic, customer, internal processes, and learning and growth. In addition to identifying objectives, indicators, and initiatives, interconnection with the SDGs prioritized by the company was sought. This contributed to the measurement and compliance with SDGs 8, 9, 12, and 17.

Following the company´s vision, mission, and values, sustainability was effectively integrated into the BSC. It was also aligned with financial, operational, and strategic goals, including long-term environmental and social responsibility. All the objectives were visually represented in the strategic map, crucial tools for having a holistic view of key components and relationships of the drive strategic objectives.

The BSC model presented meets the organization's vision, mission, and values, which are key concepts of cooperation with customers and the well-being of employees. For good worker performance (considered the base of the strategic map), initiatives were identified, such as defining action plans and evaluating processes such as downtime, waiting times, and rework, thus contributing to greater efficiency and per capita production.

This work contributed to the literature about the BSC. The results achieved can be used by other companies that intend to implement the BSC integrating sustainability. They can also serve as motivation for measuring sustainability.

As limitations of the study, we highlight that the conclusions are restricted to the case study and cannot be generalized. In addition, the analysis needs more quantitative data which restricts the ability to provide numerical evidence and statistical validation of the findings. Furthermore, the study does not encompass the measurement of all SDGs, meaning it does not offer a comprehensive assessment of progress across these goals.

Future investigations may focus on the integration of sustainability in the BSC considering SDG 4 (Equality Education), SDG 5 (Gender Equality), and SDG 10 (Reduce Inequalities), despite not being addressed in the present study are equally important as they have equity and justice as their principles. We also suggest developing national and international quantitative studies to sustain policymakers and provide guidance for the general implementation of sustainability.

ACKNOWLEDGMENT

This work is financed by Portuguese national funds through FCT – Fundação para a Ciência e Tecnologia, under the project UIDB/05422/2020.

REFERENCES

Ali, I., Sami, S., Senan, N. A. M., Baig, A., & Khan, I. A. (2022). A study on corporate sustainability performance evaluation and management: The sustainability balanced scorecard. *Corporate Governance and Organizational Behavior Review*, 6(2), 150–162. DOI:10.22495/cgobrv6i2p15

Araújo, L., Oliveira, H. C., & Gomes, L. (2020). Sustainability Balanced Scorecard for a Brazilian agricultural and livestock company. E3S Web of Conferences, 159, 04005. DOI:10.1051/e3sconf/202015904005

Bell, S., & Morse, S. (2008). *Sustainability indicators: Measuring the immeasurable*. Earthscan.

Bieker, . (2001). *Sustainability management with the Balanced Scorecard*. The Institute for Economy and the Environment at the University of St. Gallen.

Butler, J. B., Henderson, S. C., & Raiborn, C. (2011). Sustainability and the balanced scorecard: Integrating green measures into business reporting. *Management Accounting Quarterly*, 12(2), 1.

Christmann, P. (2000). Effects of 'Best Practices' of Environmental Management on Cost Advantage. *Academy of Management Journal*, 43(4), 663–680. DOI:10.2307/1556360

Cobbold, I., & Lawrie, G. (2001). Strategic Alignment: Cascading the Balanced Scorecard in a Multi-national Company, Balanced Scorecard Case Study - Crosshouse.2GC Working Paper, Active Management, December

Davie, S. (2008). An autoethnography of accounting knowledge production: Serendipitous and fortuitous choices for understanding our social world. *Critical Perspectives on Accounting*, 19(7), 1054–1079. DOI:10.1016/j.cpa.2007.03.011

De Andrade Guerra, J. B. S. O., Garcia, J., De Andrade Lima, M., Barbosa, S. B., Heerdt, M. L., & Berchin, I. I. (2018). A proposal of a Balanced Scorecard for an environmental education program at universities. *Journal of Cleaner Production*, 172, 1674–1690. DOI:10.1016/j.jclepro.2016.11.179

Dunphy, D., Benveniste, J., Griffiths, A., & Sutton, P. (Eds.). (2000). *Sustainability: The corporate challenge of the 21st century*. Allen & Unwin.

Elbanna, S., Eid, R., & Kamel, H. (2015). Measuring hotel performance using the balanced scorecard: A theoretical construct development and its empirical validation. *International Journal of Hospitality Management*, 51, 105–114. DOI:10.1016/j.ijhm.2015.09.004

Figge, F., Hahn, T., Schaltegger, S., & Wagner, M. (2002). The Sustainability Balanced Scorecard-Linking sustainability management to business strategy. *Business Strategy and the Environment*, 11(5), 269–284. DOI:10.1002/bse.339

Florêncio, M., Oliveira, L., & Oliveira, H. C. (2023). Management Control Systems and the Integration of the Sustainable Development Goals into Business Models. *Sustainability (Basel)*, 15(3), 2246. DOI:10.3390/su15032246

Gazi, F., Atan, T., & Kiliç, M. (2022). The Assessment of Internal Indicators on The Balanced Scorecard Measures of Sustainability. *Sustainability (Basel)*, 14(14), 8595. DOI:10.3390/su14148595

Gladwin, T. N., Kennelly, J. J., & Krause, T. (1995). Shifting paradigms for sustainable development: Implications for management theory and research. *Academy of Management Review*, 20(4), 874–907. DOI:10.2307/258959

Hansen, E. G., & Schaltegger, S. (2016). The Sustainability Balanced Scorecard: A Systematic Review of Architectures. *Journal of Business Ethics*, 133(2), 193–221. DOI:10.1007/s10551-014-2340-3

Hsu, Y.-L., & Liu, C.-C. (2010). Environmental performance evaluation and strategy management using balanced scorecard. *Environmental Monitoring and Assessment*, 170(1-4), 599–607. DOI:10.1007/s10661-009-1260-7 PMID:20020324

Kalender, Z. T., & Vayvay, Ö. (2016). The Fifth Pillar of the Balanced Scorecard: Sustainability. *Procedia: Social and Behavioral Sciences*, 235, 76–83. DOI:10.1016/j.sbspro.2016.11.027

Kaplan, R. S., & Norton, D. P. (1996). *The balanced scorecard: Translating strategy into action*. Harvard Business School Press.

Lueg, R., & Radlach, R. (2016). Managing Sustainable development with management control systems: A literature review. *European Management Journal*, 34(2), 158–171. DOI:10.1016/j.emj.2015.11.005

Makeen Energy (2022) Responsible energy solutions on a sustainability journey Available online: global-compact-2022_responsible-energy-solutions-on-a-sustainability-journey.pdf

Makeen Energy. (2023a) About us Available online: https://www.makeenenergy.com/about-us/who-we-are

Makeen Energy. (2023b) Our work with the UN SDGs Available online: https://www.makeenenergy.com/commitments/sustainable-development-goals

Mendes, P., Santos, A. C., Perna, F., & Ribau Teixeira, M. (2012). The balanced scorecard as an integrated model applied to the Portuguese public service: A case study in the waste sector. *Journal of Cleaner Production*, 24, 20–29. DOI:10.1016/j.jclepro.2011.11.007

Mio, C., Costantini, A., & Panfilo, S. (2022). Performance measurement tools for sustainable business: A systematic literature review on the sustainability balanced scorecard use. *Corporate Social Responsibility and Environmental Management*, 29(2), 367–384. DOI:10.1002/csr.2206

Pereira, I., & Oliveira, H. C. (2020). Public Sector Sustainability in the Balanced Scorecard – A Portuguese City Council Case. In W. Strielkowski, E. Animitsa, & E. Dvoryadkina (Eds.) *1st Conference on Sustainable Development: Industrial Future of Territories (IFT 2020). E3S Web Conferences, 208*(06017). DOI:10.1051/e3sconf/202020806017

Rösner, T., & Bredebach, C. (2022). Integrating the United Nations sustainable development goals into organizational strategy: A sustainability balanced scorecard approach using ANP and TOPSIS. *Journal of Sustainability Outreach*, 3(1), 1–18. DOI:10.37357/1068/jso/3.1.01

United Nations. (2015). Transforming Our World: The 2030 Agenda for Sustainable Development. Available online: https://www.undp.org/ukraine/publications/transforming-our-world-2030-agenda-sustainable-development?utm_ source=EN&utm_medium=GSR&utm_content=US_UNDP_PaidSearch_Brand_English&utm_campaign=CENTRAL&c_ src=CENTRAL&c_src2=GSR&gclid=EAIaIQobChMIvuLS5s_a_AIVBKuWCh2dgg8tEAAYASAAEgLW-g_D_BwE

APPENDIX A

Interview guide topics:

- What do you value most in each perspective of the Balanced Scorecard regarding sustainability?
- Regarding the SDGs the company prioritizes, give reasons why the group should focus on these and not others.
- Do the objectives align with the company's vision, mission and strategy?
- How are the SDGs communicated and shared within the company?
- Consider the SDGs on which the group focuses; what indicators do you propose to measure the underlying objectives?
- What initiatives were carried out by the company to achieve these objectives?
- What other initiatives do you suggest for the future?
- Consider the indicators suggested; how can they be affected by the BSC perspectives?

Chapter 3
Commitment to the Planet:
Explicit and Implicit Sustainable Corporate Reporting on SDGs

Federico Galán-Valdivieso
https://orcid.org/0000-0001-9632-2941
University of Almería, Spain

Isabel Cristina Mañas-Álvarez
University of Almería, Spain

María José Rodríguez-Martínez
University of Almería, Spain

María del Mar Gálvez-Rodríguez
https://orcid.org/0000-0002-3708-6229
University of Almería, Spain

ABSTRACT

Sustainable reporting implies that a company not only takes action to help meet the Sustainable Development Goals (SDGs), but also that it is transparent with its stakeholders to show its efforts and commitment. Previous literature is scarce in studies that focus on certain SDGs, particularly planet-related, and perhaps even more scarce in delving into specific actions taken to meet the targets. From a sample of the 51 biggest Spanish companies in terms of revenue, the authors analyse their 2022 sustainability reports. The results show that the most committed companies are also the most transparent when disclosing information about SDGs, and that, in line with previous research, SDGs 12 and 13 are the most addressed by compa-

DOI: 10.4018/979-8-3693-5663-0.ch003

nies. The analysis also allows us to conclude that firms lack real commitment and transparency, since the vast majority of them do not mention which specific actions are being taken to meet the sustainable goals.

1. INTRODUCTION

Sustainability is one of the pillars of modern economic development, and the achievement of the 17 Sustainable Development Goals (SDGs) has become the benchmark for countries, companies, and citizens to change current economic development for a more durable one in the long term. The Sustainable Development Goals (SDG) were adopted at the COP21 Sustainability Summit held in Paris in 2015, and their aim is to ensure the well-being of society by creating a sustainable development agenda for 2030. These are ambitious but achievable goals, as they are based on the Declaration of the elements set out in the United Nations. Although most of these goals must be put into practice by businesses and are a challenge for society, they serve as important tools to eradicate poverty, ensure a better quality of life for people, and protect the planet. There is no predominance of some goals over others, as they all seek to mitigate some problem that affects global sustainability. The United Nations offers a classification that divides reporting on the SDGs in companies' sustainability reports into five categories, called "The 5Ps of Development": People, Planet, Prosperity, Peace, and Partnerships (United Nations, 2015).

Corporations need to be transparent on their commitment to SDG (Liu et al., 2023), which implies granting access to information about their interest in contributing to the economic welfare of a country, as well as to ensure environmental quality, social cohesion and prosperity for future generations (García-Sánchez et al., 2020; Ferrero-Ferrero et al., 2023). The European Union has emerged as the main economic power to adapt its legislative environment and economic activity to the new demands in terms of sustainability (European Parliament, 2022).

As a response, UE companies have been anticipating these regulatory requirements, releasing sustainability information through their management reports, websites and social networks (Hummel, & Schlick, 2016; Setia et al., 2024), in an attempt to meet their stakeholders' needs for transparency. In this sense, transparency is defined as the disclosure of information that helps stakeholders in their understanding of the organization's commitment to sustainability and good governance practice (Kolk, 2008; Donner et al., 2024). How an organization demonstrates its commitment to sustainability is an open question, but researchers agree that quantity and/or quality of information, particularly in sustainability reports, can give clues about business commitment (Fernández-Feijoo et al., 2014).

Although the format and standards applicable to enforceable sustainability reporting are not yet clear, companies have generally been guided by the principles of the Global Reporting Initiative (GRI). GRI is an independent nongovernmental organisation that works to promote the preparation of sustainability reports to measure the economic, environmental, and social performance of their actions and as an instrument of transparency and accountability. The GRI standards are designed in such a way that they can be applicable to any company or public entity and, in addition, that they can be related to the different SDGs. In this way, the reports prepared following these standards will provide information to stakeholders, directly and indirectly, about the contribution to the achievement of the SDGs (Knut & Heß, 2023). In other words, corporate reports are a means for organisations to enhance transparency towards their stakeholders

Recent literature has focused primarily on the relationship between SDG disclosure and financial performance (Galeazzo et al., 2024), determinants of disclosure (Bose et al., 2024; Ferrero-Ferrero et al., 2023; Monteiro et al., 2024; Zampone et al., 2024) and SDG integration in sustainability reporting (Arena et al., 2023; Hamad et al., 2020, 2023; Kücükgül et al., 2022; Setia et al., 2024; Vallet-Bellmunt et al., 2023). Regarding the later, there is little evidence on how companies explicitly or implicitly show their commitment to SDGs in their reporting practices. Moreover, some studies focus on analysing the transparency of sustainable business practices to show commitment to a specific SDG related to the preservation of the Planet (i.e. Doni et al., 2020; Hakimdavar et al., 2020; Vallet-Bellmunt et al., 2023). However, to our knowledge, the number of studies that address such analysis considering all the five-planet related SDGs is still scarce.

Based on this research gap, our main aim is to analyse the degree of transparency on the firms' commitment to SDGs, particularly in SDGs related to the Planet (numbers 6, 12, 13, 14 and 15, according to the UN classification). GRI-specific standards and links with SDGs are used to deepen the achievement of each of the objectives. Thus, we posit the following research questions:

RQ1: What are the levels of transparency on direct and indirect commitment to SDGs?

RQ2: What are the levels of transparency on direct and indirect commitment to planet-related SDGs?

RQ3: What are the levels of transparency on the commitment to specific practices to meet the planet-related SDGs?

RQ4: Are there significant interactions among the level of transparency achieved on the commitment to each of the planet-related SDGs?

The posited research questions contribute to the main aim of the study, providing valuable information firstly regarding the transparency about the commitment of companies to achieving SDGs (RQ1), and then focusing on planet-related goals

(RQ2). This group of SDGs are of particular interest, since they represent the most critical goals to be achieved for the long-term survivorship of the humankind, and there is a real challenge for governments and companies to cover citizens and consumers' needs without causing or worsening environmental degradation (Xu et al., 2022). RQ3 and RQ4 are proposed to gain insight into the levels of transparency regarding which specific practices are being carried out, showing a real commitment to achieving the SDGs.

The analysis of the results shows that, in terms of transparency, a small number of companies show explicit or implicit information about how they cope with meeting SDGs. This behaviour persists when focusing on planet-related SDGs: companies disclose few information about the sustainable goals, and even less regarding which specific practices have been carried out. Despite the general lack of transparency, firms are more transparent when it comes to the SDG 12 about Responsible Consumption and Production.

This article contributes to both the academic and professional fields. From an academic perspective, it provides new insights about the extent to which companies disclose their commitment to the SDGs related to the planet and therefore the degree of commitment with each goal. Furthermore, it helps to unveil to what extent mentioning business practices and disclosing related information is symbolic or the practices are truly carried out and represent a real commitment to the goals. In the professional area, this study can serve as a guide for companies to find out which SDGs currently require more explicit disclosure and whether they are complying with the regulatory standards recently approved by the EU, and which will soon come into force.

The remainder of the manuscript is structured as follows. Section 2 reviews the previous literature on transparency, reporting, and SDGs; Section 3 describes the data sample and the methodology; Section 4 shows and discuss the results, and Section 5 concludes the work, providing limitations and future directions of research.

2. LITERATURE REVIEW

2.1. SDG and GRI Reporting Standards

SDGs were adopted by the United Nations in 2015, within the framework of the 2030 Agenda for Sustainable Development adopted at the XXI International Conference on Climate Change (COP21), with the aim of ending poverty, protecting the planet and ensuring peace and economic development. There are a total of 17 integrated objectives, that is, the actions undertaken in one of them will affect the outcome of the rest, so the balance between social, economic, and environmental sustainability must be sought. Specifically, the objectives are: (1) 'No poverty', (2) 'Zero hunger', (3) 'Good health and well-being', (4) 'Quality education', (5) 'Gender equality', (6) 'Clean water and sanitation', (7) 'Affordable and clean energy', (8) 'Decent work and economic growth', (9) 'Industry, innovation and infrastructure', (10) 'Reduced inequalities', (11) 'Sustainable cities and communities', (12) 'Responsible consumption and production', (13) 'Climate action', (14) 'Life below water', (15) 'Life on land', (16) 'Peace, justice and strong institutions' y (17) 'Partnerships for the goals' (UNDP, 2024). To ensure correct compliance and implementation of practices, a series of indicators was established for each specific target (17 objectives with a total of 169 targets). For this reason, the United Nations Statistical Commission established a list of 230 indicators (currently 231) that constitute the framework of global indicators of the 2030 Agenda by Resolution 71/313. Indicators are classified into three levels, depending on their methodological development and data availability (United Nations, 2024).

Among the different goals are the so-called SDGs Planet formed by objectives 6, 12, 13, 14 and 15. Specifically, SDG 6 'Clean Water and Sanitation' seeks to ensure universal access to safe and affordable drinking water by 2030, requiring adequate investments in infrastructure, provision of sanitation facilities and promotion of hygiene practices; SDG 12 'Responsible consumption and production' aims at efficient management of shared natural resources and proper disposal of toxic and polluting waste; SDG 13 'Climate action' supports developing countries in adapting to climate change and investing in low carbon development; SDG 14 'Life below water' aims to manage and sustainably protect marine and coastal ecosystems from land pollution, and confront the impacts of ocean acidification; and SDG 15 'Life on land', aims to undertake urgent actions aimed at reducing the loss of natural habitats and biodiversity; and supporting international food and water security, mitigation, and adaptation to climate change, peace and security (UNDP, 2024).

However, the United Nations Statistical Commission is not the only agency concerned with reporting and, therefore, monitoring the implementation and impact of the objectives. There are other organisations dedicated to reporting standards such as *Climate Disclosure Standards Board* (CDSB), *International Integrated Reporting Council* (IIRC), *Sustainability Accounting Standards Board* (SASB), and *Global Reporting Initiative* (GRI), the latter being the most relevant.

The *Global Reporting Initiative* (GRI), founded in 1997 in Boston (USA), is an independent international organisation that helps companies and other organisations take responsibility for their impacts, providing them with a series of items to include in their reports in order to achieve better communication (GRI, 2024). The GRI establishes global standards for impact reporting, achieving the most comprehensive sustainability reporting standards today thanks to the joint work of companies, investors, policymakers, members of civil society, labour organisations, and other experts. They offer, on the one hand, universal standards, which can be applicable by companies of any sector; and, on the other hand, thematic standards, either of economic, environmental, or social issues, each organisation selects the one that suits its form. These are regularly reviewed to ensure global best practices, as are these indicators for the SDGs, which, established in 2017, have been last revised in 2021 with the aim of maintaining an adequate update with international standards.

In order to promote and encourage the correct preparation of reports on the SDGs Planet, GRI proposes a total of 120 standards, focussing above all on specific targets that fully affect companies and need greater comprehensiveness in their report. For SDG 6, it sets 27 standards (8 for target 6.3, 5 for target 6.4, 10 for target 6.6, 2 for target 6.a and 2 for target 6.b); for SDG 12, includes 53 standards (8 for target 12.2, 27 for target 12.4, 17 for target 12.5, and 1 for target 12.8); for SDG 13, creates 11 standards, all related to target 13.1; for SDG 14, provides 11 standards (5 for target 14.2 and 6 for target 14.3); and for SDG 15, includes 18 standards (8 for target 15.1, 6 for target 15.2, and 4 for target 15.5).

The United Nations Statistical Commission and GRI, aware of the importance of the SDGs for the sustainability of the planet and the key actor that companies represent for their achievement, created the *Business Reporting on the SDGs* platform to encourage organisations to integrate SDG reporting. Likewise, the interaction of companies with this platform offers them a vision of the alignment of companies with the SDGs (Izzo et al., 2020).

2.2. Reporting and Disclosure in Organisations

Truly sustainable firms engage in sustainability not only take action to create value for the common good, but also are aware of the importance of being transparent in this regard (Dyllick & Muff, 2016). Transparency refers to the availability of information to all stakeholders in the company, such as directors, agents, and other stakeholders. The level of transparency achieved by corporations describes the extent to which a corporation's actions are observable, so this practice is an important internal and external accountability mechanism (Hebb, 2006; Parris et al., 2016).

In order to be transparent on their commitment to SDGs or their interest in integrating SDGs in their corporate strategies, corporations develop specific reports (Adedayo et al., 2021; Ferrero-Ferrero et al., 2023). In the SDG reporting, the company accounts for environmental, social, and economic practices aligned to SDGs, in a comprehensive report. It is or should be, the clear example of a corporate sustainability report for organisations (Adedayo et al., 2021) because they have indicators with which to measure their actions and are important at the organisational and global levels due to the nature of the objectives (Lanka et al., 2017).

SDGs reports facilitate planning, implementation, measurement, and communication of organisations' efforts to achieve them (Rosati & Faria, 2019a). The reasons for including them in their strategic planning are diverse: the integration of stakeholders' expectations, the development and design of sustainable business models that help provide solutions to social problems, managing global sustainability risks and creating opportunities for innovation and investment (Avrampou et al., 2019; Consolandi et al., 2020; Izzo et al., 2020; Vildåsen, 2018).

Academics who have previously analysed the determinants of non-financial disclosure primarily mention two theories to explain the voluntary behaviour of companies in non-financial reporting: the legitimacy theory and stakeholder theory (Cho & Patten, 2007; Christensen et al., 2019; Clarkson et al., 2008). Legitimacy and stakeholder theory explains that companies provide non-financial information to capital market participants and other non-financial stakeholders to actively influence their legitimacy. Organisations have a special interest for financial stakeholders compared to the rest (Guenther et al., 2016; Lai et al., 2018). This differs from the KPMG report (2020), which shows that the SDGs are driving the demand for impact data. Organisations, stakeholders, and civil society want to know how companies contribute to the SDGs and the real impact of those positive contributions.

Other authors also highlight several factors of the organisations that influence reporting on the SDGs, such as size, financial profitability, the level of intangible assets and corporate governance indicators, and even other sustainability-related factors, such as engaging in United Nations Global Compact and having previous experience in sustainability reporting (Krasodomska et al., 2022). This consolidates the connection established between the presentation of such reports and the theories of 'legitimacy, participation, and signalling' (Deegan, 2002; Freeman, 1994; Hahn & Kühnen, 2013) and highlights the fact that companies with proactive adoption of reporting respond better to stakeholder pressures (Izzo et al., 2020). In fact, there is a significant impact of SDG reporting on the performance of companies operating with high levels of social scrutiny and stakeholder pressure on ethical and environmental issues. Other organisational factors related to the disclosure of the SDG include commitment to sustainability frameworks, external assurance, proportion of female directors, and age of directors (Rosati & Faria, 2019b). Additionally, García-Sánchez et al. (2020) found that those companies that receive many 'sell' recommendations from financial analysts are particularly likely to adopt the disclosure of the SDG.

Transparency is a key factor for the correct evaluation of corporate reports. Despite this, most companies still present more symbolic than substantial information on SDGs to meet precisely the response to stakeholder pressure (García-Meca & Martínez-Ferrero, 2021). Although these reports could be an opportunity to improve the transparency of organisations, organisations can frequently make a significant mistake in the draughting of their reports, the so-called "rainbow washing". This practice consists of showing an aesthetic integration of the SDGs in the company, not specifying or properly developing the performance indicators to assess the monitoring of the objectives. For example, Hera-Saizarbitoria et al. (2022), after analysing reports from 1,370 organisations, perceive that, in most cases, the SDGs are used to add colour and icons to the document, following the trend of 'SDG icon picking' and '*SDG-washing*'. This behaviour makes it difficult to measure the level of the corporate disclosure of SDGs (Hummel & Szekely, 2022).

As noted above, the importance of organisations' compliance with reporting their actions toward achieving the SDGs is motivated by their contribution to economic growth and cooperation for a better future. With regulatory bodies prioritising mandatory or voluntary disclosure of sustainable initiatives, private entities have progressively increased their level of breakdown in sustainability reporting (Datta & Goyal, 2022). Studies show that there is no proper assessment of the SDGs due to the lack of a clear guideline on reporting sustainable development initiatives (Kornieieva, 2020). Lack of transparency is also a determining factor and the reason why innovations in accounting practices and technologies are proposed (Bebbington & Unerman, 2018; Díaz-Sarachaga, 2021; KPMG, 2020). In fact, the level of standardisation is different between countries: some of them disclose all SDG-related activities using the CSR report, while others disclose using the environmental report (Erin and Olojede, 2024). Although more developed countries report greater disclosure of nonfinancial information and correct adoption of the SDGs, this is due to the normative obligation to carry it out. In addition, companies in more sensitive industries that maintain a high level of legitimacy, are more likely to disclose the SDGs. As seen with this behaviour, companies adopt practices related to the SDGs and sustainability for reasons of legitimacy, social contract, and institutional factors. However, the way in which the SDGs are included through sustainability reporting often results in a discrepancy between sustainability disclosure and SDG disclosure. (Datta & Goyal, 2022).

Although companies will progressively increase the volume and quality of reporting under new non-financial reporting regulations, the more detailed analyses of these reports show that most companies specify the actions undertaken that are linked to the most relevant SDGs for their activity; while critical assessments of negative impacts, expectation statements and indicators together with quantitative targets are often not disclosed. Previous literature shows differences and similarities in SDG reporting depending on the country or industry (Krasodomska et al., 2023). For example, Ramos et al. (2022) conclude, for firms of different industries and countries (among those included in Corporate Knights' Sustainability ranking), that SDG numbers 5, 8, and 13 are the most widely adopted by firms from all industries, while SDGs 2, 6, and 14 tend to be the least mentioned. Industry and country are also determinants. For example, Italian companies disclose more information about SDGs 8 and 13, showing marked differences between industries (Izzo et al., 2020); European listed companies generally focus on SDGs 12 and 13 (Hummel & Szekely, 2022; Rizzato et al., 2023), while in Asian countries such as Philippines (Legaspi, (2023), Indonesia (Gutiérrez-Ponce et al., 2023) or Malaysia (Buniamin et al., 2022), SDGs numbers 2, 3, 4 and 8 (related to the welfare of the people) are the most important. However, although companies mention SDGs in their sustainability reports, they are not transparent on which practices, actions, and measures are set specifically to contribute to those goals (Costa et al., 2022; Di Vaio and Varriale (2020); Izzo et al., 2020).

For these reasons, a more in-depth work and research on SDG reporting is relevant to achieve a better understanding of how companies integrate the SDGs into their planning and decision making, how they communicate their contribution to stakeholders, and what practices they can adopt to improve implementation and corporate reporting.

3. DATA AND METHODOLOGY

The sample initially included the 60 Spanish companies with the highest level of sales income in 2022. Then we searched for sustainability reports in their websites, finding a total of 51 for the final sample (Table 1). The sample shows some industry concentration, since 21.56% of the firms belong to the automotive industry, 15.68% to the electric energy sector, and 11.76% to the food and textile industries.

Table 1. Companies in the sample and industry

Company	Industry	Company	Industry
Mercadona SA	Food Retailer	Vueling Airlines, SA	Transport
Repsol Petróleo SA	Hydrocarbons	Leroy Merlín España SL	Department Stores
Compañía Española De Petróleos SAU (Cepsa)	Electrical energy	Renfe Viajeros Sociedad Mercantil Estatal SA	Transport
Industria de Diseño Textil SA (Inditex)	Textile	Iveco España SL	Automotive
Endesa Energía SAU	Electrical energy	Nestlé España SAU	Food
El Corte Inglés SA	Department Stores	Santander Holding Internacional SA	Financial
SEAT SA	Automotive	Eroski SC	Department Stores
Sociedad Estatal Loterías y Apuestas Del Estado SA	Lottery	Samsung Electronics Iberia SA	Telecommunications
Telefónica de España SA	Telecommunications	Decathlon España SAU	Textile

continued on following page

Table 1. Continued

Company	Industry	Company	Industry
Ford España SA	Automotive	Toyota España SL	Automotive
Iberdrola SA	Electrical energy	Danone SA	Alimentación
Centros Comerciales Carrefour SA	Department Stores	Primark Tiendas SLU	Textile
Renault España SA	Automotive	Sprinter Megacentros del Deporte SL (Grupo ISRG)	Textile
BP Oil España SAU	Hydrocarbons	Enagás SA	Electrical energy
Mercedes Benz España SAU	Automotive	Lenovo Spain SL	Telecommunications
Gas Natural Comercializadora SA	Electrical energy	BMW Iberica SAU	Automotive
Peugeot Citroën Automóviles España SA	Automotive	Sanitas SA	Health
Iberia Líneas Aéreas De España Sociedad Anónima Operadora	Transport	El Pozo Alimentación SA	Food
Opel España SLU	Automotive	Grupo Cooperativo Cajamar	Financial
Orange España SAU	Telecommunications	Mango, S.L.	Textile
Aena S.M.E, SA	Transport	Movistar S.A.	Telecommunications
Lidl Supermercados SAU	Department Stores	Naturgy Aprovisionamientos SA	Electrical energy
Michelin España Portugal SA	Automotive	Loewe SA	Textile
Nissan Motor Ibérica SA	Automotive	Aluminio Español SL	Steel
Coca-Cola Europacific Partners Iberia SL	Food	Ferrovial SA	Transport
Consum SCoop	Food		

To analyse the level of transparency regarding the commitment to SDGs (RQ1 and RQ2), a content analysis was first performed to analyse if the company shows commitment to the SDGs by directly mentioning them in their reports (direct commitment) or not mentioning the SDGs, but implicitly carrying out business practices aligned to them (indirect commitment).

Coding was done individually by two researchers and then compared to check for inconsistencies, following a dichotomous system (0,1). Regarding direct commitment, 1 represents that the company discloses information regarding a particular SDG explicitly, and 0 otherwise; regarding indirect commitment, 1 means that the company mentions implicitly specific practices aligned to an SDG, although not mentioning the related goal explicitly (direct commitment) or implicitly), and 0 otherwise.

Regarding RQ3 and RQ4, a deeper content analysis is performed for the sustainable business practices aligned to SDGs related to the planet (numbers 6, 12, 13, 14 and 15). Given the large number of variables included in each target, they were grouped according to the types of practices carried out by the companies, according to the GRI (Table 2).

Table 2. SDG Planet and Categorisation of targets and variables

SDG 6 (Clean Water and Sanitation)	SDG6a. Implementation of practices aimed at mitigating water impacts by organisations
	SDG6b. Preparation of minimum regulations by companies to ensure the quality of effluent discharge
	SDG6c. Practices related to the assessment of significant and potential impacts of organisations in relation to waste
	SDG6d. Implementation of initiatives to prevent waste generation in organisations
	SDG6e. Practices aimed at controlling the extent to which the waste generated comes from third parties and how those third parties act in accordance with contractual obligations
	SDG6f. Total water consumption in companies
	SDG6g. Practices related to water preservation
	SDG6h. Practices for conducting a monitoring report on past impacts
SDG 12 (Responsible production and consumption)	SDG12a. Practices relating to the responsible consumption of materials used to produce and package the organisation's products and services
	SDG12b. Practices related to promoting the recycling of materials used to produce and package the organisation's products and services
	SDG12c. Practices related to the recovery of products and their packaging materials for each product category
	SDG12d. Responsible fuel consumption practices
	SDG12e. Sustainably management of the supply chain
	SDG12f. Practices relating to the assessment of the impacts of the organisation's waste/landfills
SDG 13 (Climate Action)	SDG13a. Climate change-related practices that generate risks and opportunities in organisations
	SDG13b. Reduction of the levels of consumption of fuels from non-renewable sources by companies
	SDG13c. Implementation of measures related to excessive energy consumption
	SDG13d. Initiatives relating to the rational use of energy as a result of its conservation and efficiency
	SDG13e. Reduction of harmful practices related to the emission of Greenhouse Gases

continued on following page

Table 2. Continued

SDG 14 (Life Below Water)	SDG14a. Practices carried out by organisations that have a direct or indirect impact on biodiversity
	SDG14b. Practices carried out with third parties aimed at protecting natural habitats
	SDG14c. Implementation of partnerships with third parties with a view to protecting or restoring areas of habitats where the organisation has carried out some of its work
	SDG14d. Implementation of initiatives that contribute, directly or indirectly, to reducing GHG emissions
	SDG14e. Practices related to the valuation of the emission of greenhouse gases propagated by the organisation
SDG 15 (Life On Land)	SDG15a. Practices aimed at accounting for the total number and volume of significant discharges that have an impact on the environment
	SDG15b. Practices to locate habitats most affected by water discharges
	SDG15c. Practices aimed at accounting for the nature of the impacts, direct and indirect, that organisations have on biodiversity
	SDG15d. Practices aimed at regulating significant air emissions

Transparency on business practices related to SDG 6 includes eight items (or categories), SDG 12 is made up of six items, both SDG 13 and SDG 14 include five items each, and, finally, SDG 15 has 4 items. Coding was performed following the above-mentioned process and resulted in dichotomous variables, where 1 represents that the firms carry out processes and actions (and disclose explicit information about them) to meet the target described by the item, and 0 otherwise. Therefore, the study includes the analysis of 51 variables, 3 for each SDG. For example, for SDG 6 we have SDG6T (1 if the firm mentions the SDG number 6 in its report, 0 otherwise), SDG6D (1 if the firm mentions the SDG number 6 directly and explicitly, 0 otherwise) and SDG6I (1 if the firm mention the SDG number 6 indirectly or implicitly, 0 otherwise).

4. RESULTS AND DISCUSSION

In order to answer RQ1, we explore the companies' level of transparency on their direct and indirect commitment to SDGs (Table 3). In average terms, considering both types of transparency (direct and indirect) companies integrate eight SDGs in their sustainability reports. From them, they directly mention their commitment to six SDGs, and in an indirect manner they show their commitment to other two SDGs. The companies that show greater engagement with SDGs are Gas Natural and Iberdrola, two companies in the energy sector (Figure 1).

Table 3. SDGs covered and mentioned in sustainability reports (total, direct and indirect commitments).

Firm	Firm total (SDGT)	Total Direct (SDGD)	Total Indirect (SDGI)
AENA S.M.E, SA	15	15	0
Aluminio Español SL	5	0	5
BMW Ibérica SAU	5	0	5
BP Oil España SAU	15	15	0
Centros Comerciales Carrefour SA	11	11	0
Coca-Cola Europacific Partners Iberia SL	14	6	8
Compañía Española de Petróleos SAU	13	11	2
Consum SC	13	13	0
Danone SA	13	13	0
Decathlón España SAU	9	0	9
El Corte Inglés SA	8	8	0
El Pozo Alimentación SA	9	9	0
Enagás SA	7	0	7
Endesa Energía SAU	4	4	0
Eroski SC	11	11	0
Ferrovial SA	3	3	0
Ford España SA	11	11	0
Gas Natural Comercializadora SA	17	3	14
Grupo Cooperativo Cajamar	14	14	0
Iberdrola SA	17	2	15
Iberia Líneas Aéreas de España SA	13	9	4
Industria de Diseño Textil SA	9	7	2
Iveco España SL	5	0	5
Lenovo Spain SL	2	0	2
Leroy Merlin España SL	6	6	0
LIDL Supermercados SAU	12	0	12
Loewe	2	0	2
Mango SL	10	10	0
Mercadona SA	9	9	0
Mercedes Benz España SAU	5	5	0
Michelin España Portugal SA	8	0	8
Movistar SA	6	6	0
Naturgy Aprovisionamientos SA	4	0	4

continued on following page

Table 3. Continued

Firm	Firm total (SDGT)	Total Direct (SDGD)	Total Indirect (SDGI)
Nestlé España SAU	6	6	0
Nissan Motor Ibérica SA	4	4	0
Opel España SLU	3	0	3
Orange España SAU	6	6	0
Peugeot Citroën Automóviles España SA	3	0	3
Primark Tiendas SLU	4	0	4
Renault España SA	16	16	0
RENFE Viajeros Sociedad Mercantil Estatal SA	13	13	0
Repsol Petróleo SA	11	11	0
Samsung Electronics Iberia SA	7	7	0
Sanitas SA	8	8	0
Santander Holding Internacional SA	10	10	0
Seat SA	9	9	0
Sociedad Estatal Loterías y Apuestas del Estado SA	9	9	0
Sprinter Megacentros del Deporte SL	4	0	4
Telefónica de España SA	11	10	1
Toyota España SL	5	0	5
Vueling Airlines SA	6	0	6

Figure 1. Direct, indirect, and total commitment to SDGs

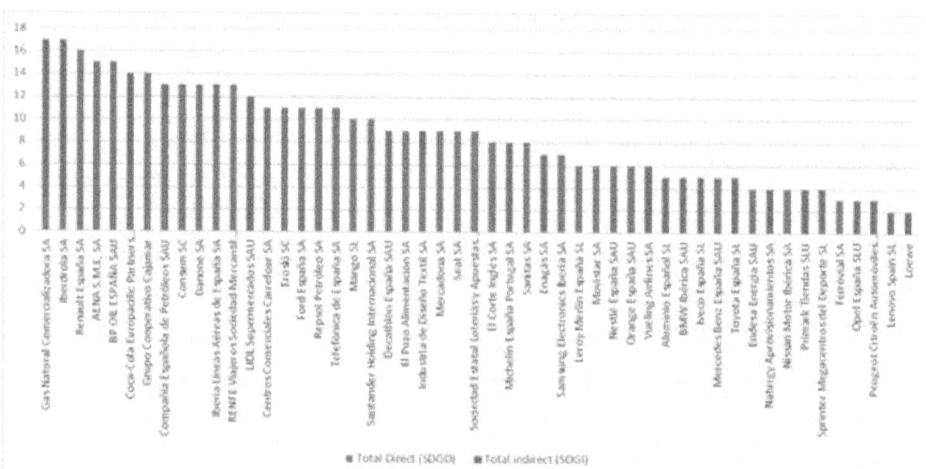

Delving further on the SDGs most mentioned and integrated in indirect manner, data highlight SDG 12 12 (Responsible Consumption and Production) and 13 (Climate Action (Table 4). On the opposite, companies seem to be less aware of the negative impacts of SDGs 1 (No Poverty), 2 (Zero Hunger), 14 (Life Below Water), 15 (Life on Land) and 16 (Peace, Justice and Strong Institutions).

Table 4. Percentage of firms with direct and indirect commitment to the SDGs

	% Direct	**% Indirect**	**% Total**
SDG 1	25,49%	9,80%	35,29%
SDG 2	15,69%	11,76%	27,45%
SDG 3	43,14%	11,76%	54,90%
SDG 4	33,33%	9,80%	43,14%
SDG 5	33,33%	19,61%	52,94%
SDG 6	27,45%	17,65%	45,10%
SDG 7	43,14%	13,73%	56,86%
SDG 8	52,94%	9,80%	62,75%
SDG 9	39,22%	13,73%	52,94%
SDG 10	31,37%	13,73%	45,10%
SDG 11	45,10%	7,84%	52,94%
SDG 12	54,90%	31,37%	86,27%
SDG 13	60,78%	25,49%	86,27%
SDG 14	13,73%	17,65%	31,37%
SDG 15	17,65%	19,61%	37,25%
SDG 16	21,57%	9,80%	31,37%
SDG 17	49,02%	11,76%	60,78%

Focusing on RQ2, that is, focusing on the transparency on the goals related to the planet (SDG 6; SDG 12; SDG 13; SDG 14; SDG 15), a similar analysis is performed. Only 12 firms in the sample cover the five planet-related goals (Table 5), mostly showing a direct commitment to the goals, particularly, as stated in the previous table, with goals 12 and 13.

Table 5. Planet-related SDGs covered and mentioned in sustainability reports (total, direct, and indirect commitments)

Firm	**Firm total (SDGT)**	**Total Direct (SDGD)**	**Total Indirect (SDGI)**
AENA S.M.E, SA	4	4	0

continued on following page

Table 5. Continued

Firm	Firm total (SDGT)	Total Direct (SDGD)	Total Indirect (SDGI)
Aluminio Español SL	2	0	2
BMW Ibérica SAU	2	0	2
BP OIL ESPAÑA SAU	5	5	0
Centros Comerciales Carrefour SA	3	3	0
Coca-Cola Europacific Partners Iberia SL	5	2	3
Compañía Española de Petróleos SAU	5	3	2
Consum SC	2	2	0
Danone SA	5	5	0
Decathlón España SAU	5	0	5
El Corte Inglés SA	3	3	0
El Pozo Alimentación SA	3	3	0
Enagás SA	2	0	2
Endesa Energía SAU	1	1	0
Eroski SC	5	5	0
Ferrovial SA	1	1	0
Ford España SA	3	3	0
Gas Natural Comercializadora SA	5	1	4
Grupo Cooperativo Cajamar	4	4	0
Iberdrola SA	5	1	4
Iberia Líneas Aéreas de España SA	3	2	1
Industria de Diseño Textil SA	3	2	1
Iveco España SL	4	0	4
Lenovo Spain SL	0	0	0
Leroy Merlin España SL	3	3	0
LIDL Supermercados SAU	4	0	4
Loewe	1	0	1
Mango SL	2	2	0
Mercadona SA	5	5	0
Mercedes Benz España SAU	2	2	0
Michelin España Portugal SA	2	0	2
Movistar SA	1	1	0
Naturgy Aprovisionamientos SA	2	0	2
Nestlé España SAU	2	2	0

continued on following page

Table 5. Continued

Firm	Firm total (SDGT)	Total Direct (SDGD)	Total Indirect (SDGI)
Nissan Motor Ibérica SA	2	2	0
Opel España SLU	2	0	2
Orange España SAU	2	2	0
Peugeot Citroën Automóviles España SA	2	0	2
Primark Tiendas SLU	2	0	2
Renault España SA	5	5	0
RENFE Viajeros S. Mercantil Estatal SA	3	3	0
Repsol Petróleo SA	3	3	0
Samsung Electronics Iberia SA	0	0	0
Sanitas SA	2	2	0
Santander Holding Internacional SA	1	1	0
Seat SA	3	3	0
S. Estatal Loterías y Apuestas del Estado SA	1	1	0
Sprinter Megacentros del Deporte SL	2	0	2
Telefónica de España SA	2	2	0
Toyota España SL	5	0	5
Vueling Airlines SA	5	0	5

With respect to RQ3 The results show that Mercadona is by far, the most committed firm to the planet SDGs, covering 23 of a total of 28 categories, followed by the subsidiaries in Spain of the big multinationals Renault (16) and Coca-Cola (15) (Figure 2). Interestingly, the next 8 firms only account for 10 to 13 items covered, while the vast majority only establish practices for certain targets (see Table 7 and Figures 2 and 3).

Table 6. Number of categories covered for each SDG (by firm)

Firms	SDG6 (8 cat.)	SDG12 (6 cat.)	SDG13 (5 cat.)	SDG14 (5 cat.)	SDG15 (4 cat.)	Total
AENA S.M.E, SA	3	3	4	0	1	11
Aluminio Español SL	0	0	0	0	0	0
BMW Ibérica SAU	0	0	0	0	0	0
BP OIL ESPAÑA SAU	3	1	3	2	1	10
Centros Comerciales Carrefour SA	0	4	3	1	0	8

continued on following page

Table 6. Continued

Firms	SDG6 (8 cat.)	SDG12 (6 cat.)	SDG13 (5 cat.)	SDG14 (5 cat.)	SDG15 (4 cat.)	Total
Coca-Cola Europacific Partners Iberia SL	0	6	5	4	0	15
Compañía Española de Petróleos SAU	0	2	3	0	0	5
Consum SC	0	4	3	0	0	7
Danone SA	2	5	3	2	1	13
Decathlón España SAU	0	0	0	0	0	0
El Corte Inglés SA	3	4	3	0	1	11
El Pozo Alimentación SA	0	5	4	0	0	9
Enagás SA	0	0	0	0	0	0
Endesa Energía SAU	0	0	5	0	0	5
Eroski SC	0	5	5	2	1	13
Ferrovial SA	6	0	0	0	0	6
Ford España SA	2	1	2	0	0	5
Gas Natural Comercializadora SA	0	1	4	0	0	5
Grupo Cooperativo Cajamar	5	1	0	0	1	7
Iberdrola SA	0	0	2	0	0	2
Iberia Líneas Aéreas de España SA	0	5	5	0	0	10
Industria de Diseño Textil SA	0	5	2	0	0	7
Iveco España SL	0	0	0	0	0	0
Lenovo Spain SL	0	0	0	0	0	0
Leroy Merlin España SL	0	4	4	0	1	9
LIDL Supermercados SAU	0	0	0	0	0	0
Loewe	0	0	0	0	0	0
Mango SL	0	5	4	0	0	9
Mercadona SA	7	6	4	3	3	23
Mercedes Benz España SAU	0	2	5	0	0	7
Michelin España Portugal SA	0	0	0	0	0	0
Movistar SA	0	0	2	0	0	2
Naturgy Aprovisionamientos SA	0	0	0	0	0	0
Nestlé España SAU	0	5	4	0	0	9
Nissan Motor Ibérica SA	0	2	5	0	0	7
Opel España SLU	0	0	0	0	0	0
Orange España SAU	0	2	3	0	0	5
Peugeot Citroën Automóviles España SA	0	0	0	0	0	0
Primark Tiendas SLU	0	0	0	0	0	0

continued on following page

Table 6. Continued

Firms	SDG6 (8 cat.)	SDG12 (6 cat.)	SDG13 (5 cat.)	SDG14 (5 cat.)	SDG15 (4 cat.)	Total
Renault España SA	4	2	5	2	3	16
RENFE Viajeros Sociedad Mercantil Estatal SA	4	2	5	0	0	11
Repsol Petróleo SA	4	3	5	0	0	12
Samsung Electronics Iberia SA	0	0	0	0	0	0
Sanitas SA	0	1	3	0	0	4
Santander Holding Internacional SA	0	0	5	0	0	5
Seat SA	2	1	2	0	0	5
Sociedad Estatal Loterías y Apuestas del Estado SA	0	3	0	0	0	3
Sprinter Megacentros del Deporte SL	0	0	0	0	0	0
Telefónica de España SA	0	4	3	0	0	7
Toyota España SL	0	0	0	0	0	0
Vueling Airlines SA	0	0	0	0	0	0

Figure 2. Planet SDG categories covered (by firm)

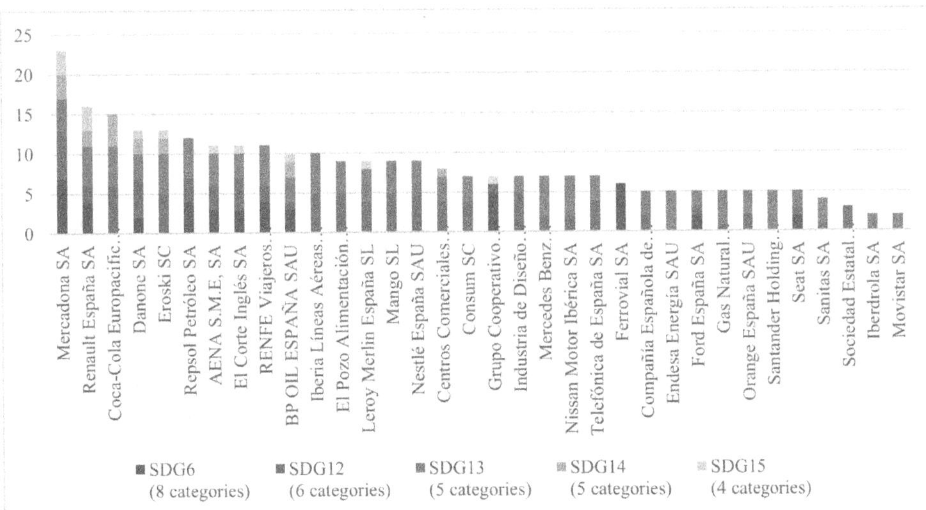

Figure 3. Intervals of categories covered (Pareto chart)

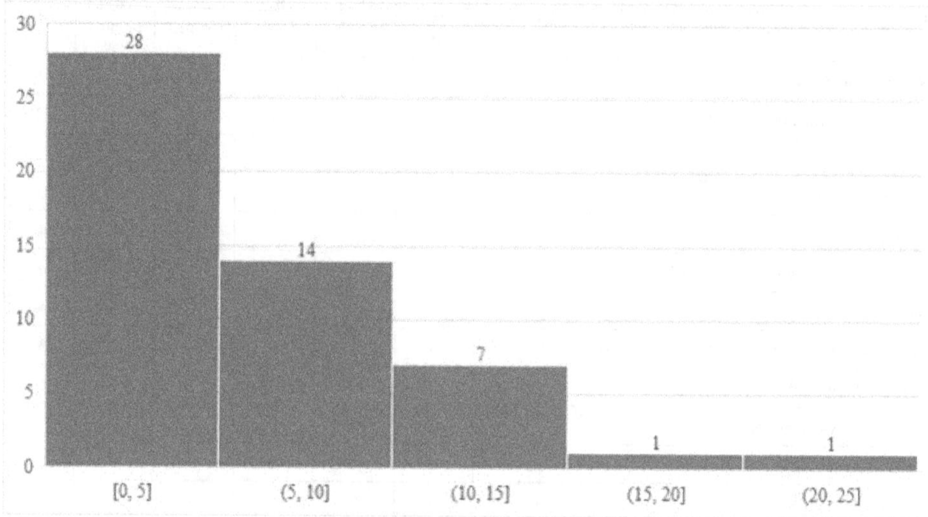

In some cases, results from Table 5 and Table 7 may differ in that a firm shows commitment with a specific goal in Table 5, but in Table 7 the corresponding categories may all be equal to zero. These results are not inconsistent, since a company can mention that a specific SDG is being addressed, but not mentioning which specific actions are being taken. In fact, a total of 17 companies do not explain sufficiently the type of practices set to contribute to the planet's SDGs.

Regarding RQ4, we want to analyse whether taking action to meet the targets of a specific goal has some relationship with other goals, implying that some SDGs are more frequent to be found with certain SDGs, so companies are more engaged with such SDGs and prioritize the disclosure of related practices. For that purpose, we first generate contingency tables for each pair of variables regarding total commitment with the planet's SDGs, and then we also perform the chi-square test for each pair of variables (Table 6). Results show that SDG 12 (Responsible Consumption and Production) exhibits a significant relationship with SDGs 6, 13, and 15 (all except number 14, Life Below Water). This result is reasonable since SDG 14 is the least addressed by companies in their sustainable practices.

Table 7. Chi-square test and p-values for contingency tables

Variables	Chi-square value	Degrees of Freedom	p-value (Asymptotic Significance)
SDG6T vs SDG12T	6.209	1	0.013*

continued on following page

Table 7. Continued

Variables	Chi-square value	Degrees of Freedom	p-value (Asymptotic Significance)
SDG6T vs SDG13T	0.385	1	0.535
SDG6T vs SDG14T	1.982	1	0.159
SDG6T vs SDG15T	0.325	1	0.569
SDG12T vs SDG13T	5.739	1	0.017*
SDG12T vs SDG14T	2.125	1	0.145
SDG12T vs SDG15T	5.257	1	0.022*
SDG13T vs SDG14T	0.632	1	0.427
SDG13T vs SDG15T	1.452	1	0.228
SDG14T vs SDG15T	0.079	1	0.779

* *Significant relationship at p=5%*

Finally, we perform an analysis using contingent tables between each pair of variables representing the different categories within each SDG, and calculate the chi-square test, thus exploring the joint presence of SDG categories in the reports. The higher the number of significant interactions, the higher the level of transparency regarding the commitment with those SDGs. Table 8 resumes the number of significant interactions of each variable with the rest, that is, the number of significant relationships with other categories. Of the total of 378 paired interactions, only 87 (23.01%) have a significant chi-square (p-value<5%). Results show that categories more involved in significant interactions are those related to SDG 12 (they are present in 53 significant interactions), SDG 13 (47), SDG 6 (39) and SDG 15 (15 interactions). This means that the SDG12-related categories (responsible consumption and production) are present more frequently together with other categories, that is, companies consider important to highlight their commitment to responsible consumption and production and how their practices exert an impact on other SDGs. Specifically, firms are strongly committed to practices related to the responsible consumption of materials used to produce and package the organisation's products and services (SDG12a), reduction of the levels of consumption of fuels from non-renewable sources (SDG13b) and reduction of harmful practices related to the emission of Greenhouse Gases (SDG13e).

Table 8. Number of significant interactions (chi-square test) between pairs of SDG categories

SDG 6	Int.	SDG 12	Int.	SDG 13	Int.	SDG 14	Int.	SDG 15	Int.
SDG6a	2	**SDG12a**	11	**SDG13a**	9	**SDG14a**	3	**SDG15a**	7
SDG6b	8	**SDG12b**	10	**SDG13b**	11	**SDG14b**	0	**SDG15b**	0

continued on following page

Table 8. Continued

SDG 6	Int.	SDG 12	Int.	SDG 13	Int.	SDG 14	Int.	SDG 15	Int.
SDG6c	6	SDG12c	10	SDG13c	6	SDG14c	6	SDG15c	8
SDG6d	4	SDG12d	10	SDG13d	10	SDG14d	4	SDG15d	0
SDG6e	3	SDG12e	3	SDG13e	11	SDG14e	7		
SDG6f	6	SDG12f	9						
SDG6g	1								
SDG6h	9								

5. CONCLUSION

Focusing on the SDGs and meeting the reporting standards has been the cornerstone of sustainability reports. This work aims to deepen the disclosure of SDG-related information, the strength of the commitment of firms, and particularly the SDGs closely related to improving our planet (6, 12, 13, 14 and 15). We finish the work exploring the real degree of commitment to SDGs and to transparency, analysing if companies declare which specific actions are being taken to meet these sustainability goals. For this purpose, a descriptive analysis of the non-financial reports of the biggest Spanish firms has been carried out.

Based on the results, some conclusions can be drawn. In general terms, the level of transparency regarding direct commitment to SDG is low, and the integration of actions that indirectly shows companies engagement with SDG is also scarce. However, there exists an important interest for firms are SDG 12 (Responsible Consumption and Production) and 13 (Climate Action). On the contrary, companies seem not to be interest in contributing to the achievement of the SDGs 2 (Zero Hunger) and 14 (Life Below Water) These results are in line with previous literature on European companies (Hummel & Szekely, 2022; Rizzato et al., 2023).

When focussing on planet-related SDGs (6, 12, 13, 14 and 15), only 10 firms from our sample take action to meet all five goals, while the rest are far below these commitments. Results prove a strong and significant relationship between SDGs 6, 12, 13 and 15, meaning that firms push themselves to take action to improve the situation of the planet. If we delve into the reports, searching for specific actions becomes a much more difficult task. Apart from one firm, most sampled companies present activities to cover less than five subcategories of specific actions to meet the sustainable targets. Companies do not provide a comprehensive breakdown of the actions undertaken during their activity to support the achievement of the SDGs. The mention of these is superfluous or even, in 17 of them, goes so far as to indicate only that measures are applied in relation to a specific objective, but without detailing any of them. The reason for this behaviour can be found in the greater cost assumed to make a detailed analysis of their actions (Christensen et al., 2019), or in the absence of concrete actions. In the latter case, we would be faced with the problem already presented 'Rainbow washing', so they add the mention of the SDGs to meet minimally the demands of stakeholders (García-Meca & Martínez-Ferrero, 2021), the recent legislation (especially from the European Union) and aesthetic issues in the reports (Hera-Saizarbitoria et al., 2022). We finally find that companies enhance transparency more frequently regarding responsible consumption and production, in an attempt to show to the stakeholders a true commitment to be sustainable from the depths of the company's activity.

The results shown are valuable to companies, especially as a reason to reflect on their current performance with respect to the SDG reporting and the level of transparency they offer. If they do not do it voluntarily, the growing activity of legislative initiatives will force them to implement solutions to their ambiguity and lack of transparency. The SDGs require effective cooperation between public institutions and private organisations, as they affect everyone worldwide. There is no Planet B.

This work presents some limitations which could lead to future lines of research. The authors have focused on the largest Spanish firms by sales revenue. The European legislation will force Public Interest Entities (PIEs) to disclose information following rules, guidelines, and regulations, so it will be interesting to explore the sustainability reporting of those companies. A second limitation is that the work only analyses information of one fiscal year (2022), so an interesting point of view could be exploring the evolution of reporting over the years. Of particular interest is, from our point of view, analysing the reporting behaviour of firms before and after the implementation of the European legislation.

REFERENCES

Arena, M., Azzone, G., Ratti, S., Urbano, V. M., & Vecchio, G. (2023). Sustainable development goals and corporate reporting: An empirical investigation of the oil and gas industry. *Sustainable Development (Bradford)*, 31(1), 12–25. DOI:10.1002/sd.2369

Avrampou, A., Skouloudis, A., Iliopoulos, G., & Khan, N. (2019). Advancing the sustainable develpment goals: Evidence from leading European banks. *Sustainable Development (Bradford)*, 27(4), 743–757. DOI:10.1002/sd.1938

Bebbington, J., & Unerman, J. (2018). Achieving the United Nations Sustainable Development Goals. *Accounting, Auditing & Accountability Journal*, 31(1), 2–24. DOI:10.1108/AAAJ-05-2017-2929

Bose, S., Khan, H. Z., & Bakshi, S. (2024). Determinants and consequences of sustainable development goals disclosure: International evidence. *Journal of Cleaner Production*, 434, 140021. DOI:10.1016/j.jclepro.2023.140021

Buniamin, S., Jaffar, R., Ahmad, N., & Johari, N. H. (2022). The role of corporate governance in achieving SDGs among Malaysian companies. *European Journal of Sustainable Development*, 11(3), 326–326. DOI:10.14207/ejsd.2022.v11n3p326

Cho, C. H., & Patten, D. M. (2007). The role of environmental disclosures as tools of legitimacy: A research note. *Accounting, Organizations and Society*, 32(7-8), 639–647. DOI:10.1016/j.aos.2006.09.009

Christensen, H. B., Hail, L., & Leuz, C. (2019). Adoption of CSR and sustainability reporting standards: economic analysis and review. *NBER Working Paper*.

Clarkson, P. M., Li, Y., Richardson, G. D., & Vasvari, F. P. (2008). Revisiting the relation between environmental performance and environmental disclosure: An empirical analysis. *Accounting, Organizations and Society*, 33(4-5), 303–327. DOI:10.1016/j.aos.2007.05.003

Consolandi, C., Phadke, H., Hawley, J., & Eccles, R. G. (2020). Material ESG outcomes and SDG externalities: Evaluating the health care sector's contribution to the SDGs. *Organization & Environment*, 33(4), 511–533. DOI:10.1177/1086026619899795

Costa, R., Menichini, T., & Salierno, G. (2022). Do SDGs really matter for business? Using GRI sustainability reporting to answer the question. *European Journal of Sustainable Development*, 11(1), 113. DOI:10.14207/ejsd.2022.v11n1p113

Datta, S., & Goyal, S. (2022). Determinants of SDG Reporting by Businesses: A Literature Analysis and Conceptual Model. *Vision (Basel)*. DOI:10.1177/09722629221096047

Deegan, C. (2002). Introduction: The legitimising effect of social and environmental disclosures: A theoretical foundation. *Accounting, Auditing & Accountability Journal*, 15(3), 282–311. DOI:10.1108/09513570210435852

Di Vaio, A., & Varriale, L. (2020). SDGs and airport sustainable performance: Evidence from Italy on organisational, accounting and reporting practices through financial and non-financial disclosure. *Journal of Cleaner Production*, 249, 119431. DOI:10.1016/j.jclepro.2019.119431

Díaz-Sarachaga, J. M. (2021). Shortcomings in reporting contributions towards the Sustainable Development Goals. *Corporate Social Responsibility and Environmental Management*, 28(4), 1–14. DOI:10.1002/csr.2129

Doni, F., Gasperini, A., & Soares, J. T. (2020). Monitoring, evaluation and reporting on SDG 13 implementation. In *SDG13–climate action: combating climate change and its impacts* (pp. 73–84). Emerald Publishing Limited. DOI:10.1108/978-1-78756-915-720201009

Donner, E. K., Meißner, A., & Bort, S. (2024). Moving from voluntary to mandatory sustainability reporting—Transparency in sustainable development goals (SDG) reporting: An analysis of Germany's largest MNCs. *Business Ethics, the Environment & Responsibility*, 00, 1–12. DOI:10.1111/beer.12687

Dyllick, T., & Muff, K. (2016). Clarifying the meaning of sustainable business: Introducing a typology from business-as-usual to true business sustainability. *Organization & Environment*, 29(2), 156–174. DOI:10.1177/1086026615575176

Erin, O. A., Bamigboye, O. A., & Oyewo, B. (2022). Sustainable development goals (SDG) reporting: An analysis of disclosure. *Journal of Accounting in Emerging Economies*, 12(5), 761–789. DOI:10.1108/JAEE-02-2020-0037

Erin, O. A., & Olojede, P. (2024). *Do nonfinancial reporting practices matter in SDG disclosure? An exploratory study*. Meditari Accountancy Research. DOI:10.1108/MEDAR-06-2023-2054

European Parliament. (2022). Directive (EU) 2022/2464 of the European Parliament and of the Council of 14 December 2022 amending Regulation (EU) No 537/2014, Directive 2004/109/EC, Directive 2006/43/EC and Directive 2013/34/EU, as regards corporate sustainability reporting. https://eur-lex.europa.eu/legal-content/EN/TXT/PDF/?uri=CELEX:32022L2464

Fernandez-Feijoo, B., Romero, S., & Ruiz, S. (2014). Commitment to corporate social responsibility measured through global reporting initiative reporting: Factors affecting the behavior of companies. *Journal of Cleaner Production*, 81, 244–254. DOI:10.1016/j.jclepro.2014.06.034

Ferrero-Ferrero, I., Muñoz-Torres, M. J., Rivera-Lirio, J. M., Escrig-Olmedo, E., & Fernández-Izquierdo, M. Á. (2023). SDG reporting: An analysis of corporate sustainability leaders. *Marketing Intelligence & Planning*, 41(4), 457–472. DOI:10.1108/MIP-07-2022-0332

Freeman, R. E. (1994). The politics of stakeholder theory: Some future directions. *Business Ethics Quarterly*, 4(4), 409–421. DOI:10.2307/3857340

Galeazzo, A., Miandar, T., & Carraro, M. (2024). SDGs in corporate responsibility reporting: A longitudinal investigation of institutional determinants and financial performance. *The Journal of Management and Governance*, 28(1), 113–136. DOI:10.1007/s10997-023-09671-y

García-Meca, E., & Martínez-Ferrero, J. (2021). Is SDG reporting substantial or symbolic? An examination of controversial and environmentally sensitive industries. *Journal of Cleaner Production*, 298, 126781. DOI:10.1016/j.jclepro.2021.126781

García-Sánchez, I. M., Aibar-Guzmán, B., Aibar-Guzmán, C., & Rodríguez-Ariza, L. (2020). "Sell" recommendations by analysts in response to business communication strategies concerning the Sustainable Development Goals and the SDG compass. *Journal of Cleaner Production*, 255, 1–12. DOI:10.1016/j.jclepro.2020.120194

García-Sánchez, I. M., Rodríguez-Ariza, L., Aibar-Guzmán, B., & Aibar-Guzmán, C. (2020). Do institutional investors drive corporate transparency regarding business contribution to the sustainable development goals? *Business Strategy and the Environment*, 29(5), 2019–2036. DOI:10.1002/bse.2485

GRI. (2024). *About GRI*. GRI. https://www.globalreporting.org/about-gri/

Guenther, E., Guenther, T., Schiemann, F., & Weber, G. (2016). Stakeholder relevance for reporting: Explanatory factors of carbon disclosure. *Business & Society*, 55(3), 361–397. DOI:10.1177/0007650315575119

Gutiérrez-Ponce, H., & Wibowo, S. A. (2023). Do sustainability activities affect the financial performance of banks? The case of Indonesian Banks. *Sustainability (Basel)*, 15(8), 6892. DOI:10.3390/su15086892

Hahn, R., & Kühnen, M. (2013). Determinants of sustainability reporting: A review of results, trends, theory, and opportunities in an expanding field of research. *Journal of Cleaner Production*, 59, 5–21. DOI:10.1016/j.jclepro.2013.07.005

Hakimdavar, R., Hubbard, A., Policelli, F., Pickens, A., Hansen, M., Fatoyinbo, T., & Schollaert Uz, S. (2020). Monitoring water-related ecosystems with earth observation data in support of Sustainable Development Goal (SDG) 6 reporting. *Remote Sensing (Basel)*, 12(10), 1634. DOI:10.3390/rs12101634

Hamad, S., Draz, M. U., & Lai, F.-W. (2020). The Impact of Corporate Governance and Sustainability Reporting on Integrated Reporting: A Conceptual Framework. *SAGE Open*, 10(2), 215824402092743. DOI:10.1177/2158244020927431

Hamad, S., Lai, F. W., Shad, M. K., Khatib, S. F. A., & Ali, S. E. A. (2023). Assessing the implementation of sustainable development goals: Does integrated reporting matter? *Sustainability Accounting. Management and Policy Journal*, 14(1), 49–74. DOI:10.1108/SAMPJ-01-2022-0029

Hebb, T. (2006). The Economic Inefficiency of Secrecy: Pension Fund Investors' Corporate Transparency Concerns. *Journal of Business Ethics*, 63(4), 385–405. DOI:10.1007/s10551-005-3968-9

Hera-Saizarbitoria, I. (2022). Organizations' engagement with sustainable development goals: From cherry-picking to SDG-washing? *Corporate Social Responsibility and Environmental Management*, 29(2), 316–328. DOI:10.1002/csr.2202

Hummel, K., & Schlick, C. (2016). The relationship between sustainability performance and sustainability disclosure reconciling voluntary disclosure theory and legitimacy theory. *Journal of Accounting and Public Policy*, 35(5), 455–476. DOI:10.1016/j.jaccpubpol.2016.06.001

Hummel, K., & Szekely, M. (2022). Disclosure on the sustainable development goals–Evidence from Europe. *Accounting in Europe*, 19(1), 152–189. DOI:10.1080/17449480.2021.1894347

Izzo, M. F., Ciaburri, M., & Tiscini, R. (2020). The challenge of Sustainable Development Goal reporting: The first evidence from Italian listed companies. *Sustainability (Basel)*, 12(8), 3494. DOI:10.3390/su12083494

Knut, B., & Heß, P. (2023). Stakeholder perceptions of the role of standards for addressing the sustainable development goals. *Sustainable Production and Consumption*, 37, 180–190. DOI:10.1016/j.spc.2023.02.016

Kolk, A. (2008). Sustainability, accountability and governance: Exploring multinational reporting practice. *Business Strategy and the Environment*, 17(1), 1–15. DOI:10.1002/bse.511

Kornieieva, Y. (2020). Non-financial reporting challenges in monitoring SDGs achievement: Investment aspects for transition economy. *International Journal of Economics and Business Administration*, VIII(1), 62–71. DOI:10.35808/ijeba/409

KPMG. (2020). *The time has come. The KPMG survey of sustainability reporting 2020*. KPMG. https://assets.kpmg.com/content/dam/kpmg/be/pdf/2020/12/The_Time_Has_Come_KPMG_Survey_of_Sustainability_Reporting_2020.pdf

Krasodomska, J., Zarzycka, E., & Zieniuk, P. (2023). Voluntary sustainability reporting assurance in the European Union before the advent of the corporate sustainability reporting directive: The country and firm-level impact of Sustainable Development Goals. *Sustainable Development*.

Krasodomska, J., Zieniuk, P., & Kostrzewska, J. (2022). Reporting on Sustainable Development Goals in the European Union: What drives companies' decisions? *Competitiveness Review*, 33(1), 120–146. DOI:10.1108/CR-12-2021-0179

Kücükgül, E., Cerin, P., & Liu, Y. (2022). Enhancing the value of corporate sustainability: An approach for aligning multiple SDGs guides on reporting. *Journal of Cleaner Production*, 333, 130005. DOI:10.1016/j.jclepro.2021.130005

Lai, A., Melloni, G., & Stacchezzini, R. (2018). Integrated reporting and narrative accountability: The role of preparers. *Accounting, Auditing & Accountability Journal*, 31(5), 1381–1405. DOI:10.1108/AAAJ-08-2016-2674

Lanka, S., Khadaroo, I., & Bohm, S. (2017). Agroecology accounting: Biodiversity and sustainable livelihoods from the margin. *Accounting, Auditing & Accountability Journal*, 30(7), 1592–1613. DOI:10.1108/AAAJ-12-2015-2363

Legaspi, J. L. R. (2023). The current state of sustainability reporting: Evidence from publicly listed financial institutions. *Corporate Governance and Sustainability Review*, 7(2), 18–28. DOI:10.22495/cgsrv7i2p2

Liu, Y., Heinberg, M., Huang, X., & Eisingerich, A. B. (2023). Building a competitive advantage based on transparency: When and why does transparency matter for corporate social responsibility? *Business Horizons*, 66(4), 517–527. DOI:10.1016/j.bushor.2022.10.004

Monteiro, S., Ribeiro, V., Vilhena, E., Lemos, K., & Molho, C. (2024). Determinants of online-reporting on sustainable development goals: The case of Portuguese Higher Education Institutions. *Social Responsibility Journal*, 20(3), 462–484. DOI:10.1108/SRJ-01-2023-0044

Parris, D. L., Dapko, J. L., Arnold, R. W., & Arnold, D. (2016). Exploring transparency: A new framework for responsible business management. *Management Decision*, 54(1), 222–247. DOI:10.1108/MD-07-2015-0279

Ramos, D. L., Chen, S., Rabeeu, A., & Abdul Rahim, A. B. (2022). Does SDG coverage influence firm performance? *Sustainability (Basel)*, 14(9), 4870. DOI:10.3390/su14094870

Rizzato, F., Tonelli, A., Fiandrino, S., & Devalle, A. (2024). Analysing SDG disclosure and its impact on integrated thinking and reporting. *Meditari Accountancy Research*, 32(3), 803–831. DOI:10.1108/MEDAR-07-2022-1751

Rosati, F., & Faria, L. G. (2019). Addressing the SDGs in sustainability reports: The relationship with institutional factors. *Journal of Cleaner Production*, 215, 1312–1326. DOI:10.1016/j.jclepro.2018.12.107

Setia, N., Abhayawansa, S., Joshi, M., & Wasantha Pathiranage, N. (2024). *Shifting perspectives: unveiling the dual nature of sustainability materiality in integrated reports*. Meditari Accountancy Research. DOI:10.1108/MEDAR-08-2023-2128

UNDP. (n.d.). *The SDGS in Action*. Sustainable Development Goals. https://www.undp.org/es/sustainable-development-goals

United Nations. (2015). *SDG Compass. The guide for business action on the SDG*s. https://sdgcompass.org/wp-content/uploads/2015/12/019104_SDG_Compass_Guide_2015.pdf

United Nations. (2024). *Tier Classification for Global SDG Indicators*. Sustainable Development Goals. https://unstats.un.org/sdgs/iaeg-sdgs/tier-classification/

Vallet-Bellmunt, T., Fuertes-Fuertes, I., & Flor, M. L. (2023). Reporting Sustainable Development Goal 12 in the Spanish food retail industry. An analysis based on Global Reporting Initiative performance indicators. *Corporate Social Responsibility and Environmental Management*, 30(2), 695–707. DOI:10.1002/csr.2382

Vildåsen, S. S. (2018). Corporate sustainability in practice: An exploratory study of the sustainable development goals (SDGs). *Business Strategy & Development*, 1(4), 256–264. DOI:10.1002/bsd2.35

Zampone, G., Nicolò, G., Sannino, G., & De Iorio, S. (2024). Gender diversity and SDG disclosure: The mediating role of the sustainability committee. *Journal of Applied Accounting Research*, 25(1), 171–193. DOI:10.1108/JAAR-06-2022-0151

Chapter 4
Assessing the Level and Determinants of Environmental Sustainability Disclosure in Portuguese and Brazilian Companies

Catarina Cepeda
https://orcid.org/0000-0002-3911-0894
ISCAP, CEOS, Polytechnic of Porto, Portugal

Albertina Paula Monteiro
ISCAP, CEOS, Polytechnic of Porto, Portugal

Amélia Cristina Ferreira da Silva
ISCAP, CEOS, Polytechnic of Porto, Portugal

Diana Silva
ISCAP, Polytechnic of Porto, Portugal

ABSTRACT

This study aims to analyze the level of environmental disclosure (ED) and its determinants. Employing a mixed-methods approach, this investigation employs content analysis in corporate reports spanning from 2016 to 2020. Furthermore, multiple regression analysis on panel data is utilized to identify the drivers of ED extent. Findings from this study indicate an upward trend in the ED index, which is

DOI: 10.4018/979-8-3693-5663-0.ch004

slightly higher in Brazil, with the sustainability report, the most widely used means of disclosure, showing the highest levels of ED. Global Reporting Initiative (GRI) indicators related to environmental compliance, emissions, and energy exhibit the highest levels of disclosure. Moreover, GRI standards adoption, CEO duality, and workers diversity are identified as significant influencers of ED extent in both countries. This research contributes valuable insights to both academic literature and practical application by scrutinizing the extent of ED in private and listed Portuguese companies and identifying influential factors.

1. INTRODUCTION

Corporate Social Responsibility (CSR) has become a central concern for companies, driven by growing awareness of social disparities and the need for more responsible development (Frey et al., 2008). This awareness is fueled by stakeholder demand for socially responsible business practices, reflecting the understanding that economic growth must be aligned with social and environmental sustainability (Unerman, 2000). The intersection between CSR and sustainable development is evident in literature. According to Monteiro (2022), CSR aims to contribute to sustainable development, covering the economic, social and environmental pillars.

With the globalization of concerns about sustainable development and the complexity of the business environment, companies have increased their focus on the CSR dimension and on communicating their performance to Stakeholders (Monteiro, 2022). The sustainable information disclosure contributes to greater transparency and accountability in business practices (Gray, 2010), with sustainability reports being considered the main means for this voluntary/mandatory information communication (Baker & Nazer, 2000; Monteiro et al., 2023).

However, despite the growing volume of information disclosed, the extent of Environmental Disclosure (ED) has been analyzed only mainly in listed companies, leaving aside other public interest companies (Monteiro et al., 2021; Monteiro et al., 2023). In addition, there are few studies that make a comparative analysis between different countries, to understand the differences between certain non-financial reporting policies/regulations and their application in practice.

Regarding the determinants of ED, previous studies are focused on corporate governance attributes (e.g., Gerged, 2021; Corvino et al., 2020; Shahab et al., 2020; Lagasio & Cucari, 2019), environmental certification (Monteiro et al., 2023), environmental determinants, as board, greenhouse gas (GHG) emissions, emission reduction initiatives (Giannaraki et al., 2014), financial indicators and industry profile (Giannaraki et al., 2014), among others. However, studies that analyze the effect of adopting Global Reporting Initiative (GRI) standards, workplace gender diversity and CEO duality are scarcer. In this regard, Ashraf et al.'s (2024) study reveals that Chinese listed firms CEOs with less experience tend to be less inclined to adopt GRI reporting standards for CSR reporting. Skouloudis et al. (2010) suggest that GRI standards contribute to non-financial reporting practices. Studies on workplace gender diversity are focused on effect of Board gender diversity (e.g., Cabeza-García et al., 2018; Al-Shaer and Zaman, 2016; Al Fadli et al., 2019), audit committee diversity (Bravo and Reguera-Alvarado, 2019), women managers (Monteiro et al., 2022), gender equality - women employees- (Monteiro et al., 2024) on sustainability/ESG reporting. Monteiro et al. (2024) found that gender diversity has a positive impact on ESG performance reporting in European Union (EU) listed entities. Monteiro et al. (2023) prove that corporate governance attributes, as number members and proportion of women on Board, positively affect the annual reporting ED index and the independent board members proportion positively influence the sustainability reporting ED index, in a sample of listed Portuguese companies. CEO duality is other variable that influenced the sustainability reporting. For instance, Felo (2010) verify that CEO duality contributes for corporate reporting transparency.

Given the above context and to fill the existing gap in the literature, this study aims to analyze the ED level by Portuguese and Brazilian companies (Listed and private companies), and its determinants. Specifically, it seeks to understand the (1) evolution of the Environmental Disclosure Extent Index (EDEI) over time, the documents (reports) most used to disclose environmental information, (2) the GRI 300 indicators with highest disclosure index and (3) the determinants of EDEI (GRI adoption, workplace gender diversity, board gender diversity, board independence members and CEO Duality).

We chose these two countries considering their difference in the implementation of non-financial reporting regulations, a country in the Eurozone (Portugal) and a country outside the Eurozone, South America (Brazil), to understand the differences. In this study, the "sample covers different geographic and socio-economic contexts" and "countries with the same national official language and cultural background, allowing an easier cross-comparison between the documents and data analyzed" (Ramos et al., 2015, p. 224).

Considering the study topic, this investigation focuses on ED, because both countries are in different environmental contexts. Brazil, as it is home to the largest tropical forest in the world, has a huge industry and is going through one of the worst phases of deforestation in the Amazon (Fearnside, 2005). On the other hand, Portugal, a small country with a much smaller industry, is at the forefront of renewable energy implementation (Carvalho et al., 2014). In addition, "environmental issues have become more and more important in recent years" to the business world, society at large and academic research (Gallego-Álvarez et al., 2018).

Based on the new institutional theory, we argue that the choice of ED topics varies according to different institutional pressures perceived by companies, in particular pressures from national institutions (Cormier et al., 2028). Scholars in this theory argue that coercive, mimetic, and normative forces lead many organizations to adopt organizational forms and policies that are considered legitimate in their field (DiMaggio & Powell, 1983). In line, legitimacy theory refers to a state or condition where the organization values align with the broader social system values (Lindblom, 1993).

The sustainability concept emerged to meet stakeholder demands (Herremans et al., 2016). Stakeholder theory presents two perspectives: moral and strategic (Frooman, 1999). The moral perspective asserts that those affected by an organization's actions have the right to be informed and to expect certain performance standards (Freeman, 1984; Mitchell et al., 1997), emphasizing a balance of interests and benefits (Herremans et al., 2016). On the other hand, the strategic perspective focuses on the advantages to the organization in achieving its goals (Freeman, 1984).

In this sense, considering that the stakeholder's interests are often not considered by their directors, this study also considers stewardship theory. This theory describes scenarios in which managers are driven not by personal objectives, but by the objectives of their directors (Davis et al., 1997, p. 21). According to management theory, these principles are not confined to a single group of stakeholders. Instead, "in diverse, loosely connected organizations, with multiple stakeholders and conflicting shareholder objectives, managers are motivated to make decisions that they believe are in the best interests of the group" (Davis et al., 1997, p. 25).

With institutional, legitimacy, stakeholder and stewardship theories lens, this study will investigate the evolution of EDEI, which GRI 300 indicators show the greatest extent of ED, as well as whether the extent varies between different types of business reports. Finally, research will identify the factors that influence EDEI, exploring the relationship between company GRI adoption, gender diversity and CEO duality, board of directors' attributes and country of origin.

Empirical evidence from this study can contribute to the literature as it compares ED and its determining factors that have yet to be explored in previous research. In terms of practical contributions, we hope that the results of this research will be relevant to company managers, by highlighting the importance of ED to stakeholders and identifying the factors that need to be developed in order to increase ED index, policymakers and regulators, in the sense that it can help them identify the measures needed to increase ED levels and promote companies' valorization/adoption of the factors influencing the disclosure of non-financial information.

The paper is structured as follows. The first part presents a review of the literature and research hypotheses. The third part addresses the research methodology, the fourth is dedicated to the results obtained and the last to the conclusions.

2. BACKGROUND AND RESEARCH HYPOTHESES

Sustainable development, which emerges from concern about the impact of human activities on the environment, prioritizes the harmonious interaction between human progress and environmental preservation (Mebratu, 1998). The most notable sustainable development definition was presented in 1987 by Gro Harlem Brundtland, in the report "Our Common Future", as a continuous process that meets the needs of the present without compromising future generations (Porter & Kramer, 2006).

The role of companies is crucial in sustainable development paradigm, and not just governments, as traditionally thought (Monteiro, 2022). Sustainable companies must not only seek profit but must also contribute to community well-being and minimize their environmental impacts (Savitz & Weber, 2007). Business sustainability encompasses economic, social and environmental aspects (Colglazier, 2015), as highlighted by the Triple Bottom Line concept (Monteiro et al., 2021). From this line, the European Commission identifies the "3 P's of sustainability" - People, Planet and Profit - as interconnected dimensions (Baden & Harwood, 2013). In addition to being profitable, companies must promote human development and mitigate their environmental impact (Porter & Kramer, 2006).

Sustainability, as mentioned above, is three-dimensional, comprising the economic, environmental and social pillars (Rainey, 2006). Regarding the environmental dimension, companies must efficiently manage natural resources and implement projects that minimize their environmental impact (Porter & Van der Linde, 1995). This not only benefits the environment, but also motivates employees and improves the company's reputation (Lee et al., 2017; Orazalin et al., 2020). The social dimension emphasizes the development of human capital and employee participation in business decisions (Alhaddi, 2015). The employee's involvement in sustainable practices also reinforces natural resources protection (Porter & Van der Linde, 1995). Ensuring social justice and equality is essential for social sustainability (Woodcraft, 2012). Regarding the economic dimension, companies must seek not only profit, but also create value in a sustainable way (Alhaddi, 2015). This involves the use of renewable resources, the waste and emissions reduction, which can generate additional business opportunities (Costa, 2019; Zhu et al., 2013). In short, business sustainability is fundamental to long-term economic success (Braccini & Margherita, 2018).

The CSR notion has evolved over time. While Friedman (1970) argued that companies' only social responsibility was to increase profits, CSR has become a global concern in recent decades, reflecting an important facet of contemporary business practices (Maon et al., 2009). The history of CSR dates to Howard Bowen, who in 1953 raised the question about the social responsibilities of businessmen, being considered the "father" of the CSR concept (Green et al., 2012). Today, CSR is defined as the voluntary integration of social and environmental concerns into companies' operations and interactions with stakeholders (European Commission, 2001). For Pinto (2014), CSR can be classified as responsive, focused on reducing negative impacts, and strategic, focused on combating social activities that compromise the environment. According to European Commission (2001), being socially responsible implies investing in human capital, relationships with stakeholders and environment protection (Green Book – Point 2.20). This behavior varies according to the responsibilities assumed by companies, which must meet stakeholders' expectations without compromising the local environment and the community (Bonson & Bednarova, 2015; Wolniak & Habek, 2016). Thus, CSR is a commitment by companies to contribute to sustainable development, engaging with stakeholders, such as employees, the local community and society in general (Rodriguez-Fernandez, 2016). In fact, CSR is a link between companies and society, requiring responsible actions that have positive impacts on stakeholders and minimize negative impacts on society and the environment (Šontaitė-Petkevičienė, 2015).

CSR must encompass internal and external strategies (Faria, 2015). Internally, it involves labor issues, training practices and human resource management to solve environmental problems and preserve natural resources (Moravcikova et al., 2015). Externally, it goes beyond the company's sphere and includes relationships with competitors, suppliers and customers and other stakeholders (Alcaraz-Quiles et al., 2017).

The CSR importance is widely recognized by business leaders, as stakeholders, including society in general, increasingly demand that organizations take a responsible stance (Adams & Zutshi, 2004). Companies that demonstrate social and environmental responsibility expect to reap a range of specific benefits, although not all of them can be quantified monetarily. Thus, integrating CSR into business strategies can lead to productivity gains, expansion into new markets and mitigation of pressure from stakeholders, resulting in business growth (Savitz & Weber, 2007). Furthermore, socially responsible companies are more financially attractive, as they have a greater capacity to create value and respond to external pressures (Steurer et al., 2018). Studies also suggest that CSR influences competitiveness, as it can generate significant competitive advantages (Kiroyan, 2015; Porter & Kramer, 2006). Furthermore, CSR can strengthen the company's reputation, improve relationships with employees and increase customer loyalty (Almeida & Coelho, 2019; Esen, 2013; European Commission, 2001; Le, 2022). These benefits reflect the CSR practices' positive impact on company's image and performance. Literature also recognizes CSR as a strategic variable that influences economic decisions and is crucial to identify, measure and disclose the social and environmental impacts of business activities (Epstein et al., 1976).

Increasing pressures from stakeholders, both internal and external, have led companies to become more socially and environmentally responsible and to communicate their performance through reports or other forms of disclosure (Monteiro, 2022). Both direct and indirect external influences lead organizations to be more attentive and responsive to their external constituents, according to institutional theory (Khan & Lockhart, 2022). However, the non-financial information disclosure is still limited, possibly due to a lack of legal requirements, associated costs or poor business performance (Michelon et al., 2013).

Although non-financial information disclosure is currently optional for most companies, it is in the interest of everyone involved with the organization (Monteiro, 2010). To promote this disclosure and guarantee its quality and extent, several frameworks were developed, the most widely used being that of the GRI (Halkos & Mamikos, 2021).

The GRI, a non-profit body founded in 1997, aims to provide guidelines to improve the quality, rigor and usefulness of companies' sustainability reports for stakeholders (Halkos & Mamikos, 2021). Over time, these guidelines have undergone several evolutions (Monteiro, 2022). In 2000, the first version of the guidelines (GRI-G1) was released, with almost 50 companies adopting them immediately, requiring rigorous audits and updates to ensure guidelines credibility (GRI, 2011). A year later, in 2001, GRI was transformed into an autonomous, non-profit foundation by CERES, and in 2002, it was officially recognized as an organization cooperating with the United Nations environment program, introducing the GRI-G2 guidelines (GRI, 2011). During the 21st century, the guidelines evolved with versions GRI-G3 in 2006, GRI-G3.1 in 2010 and GRI-G4 in 2013, adding new content and strategic structures for sustainability reports (GRI, 2011). More recently, in 2018, the organization launched the GRI standards, an updated version of the previous guidelines, providing modular and interrelated global standards (Lima, 2021). The GRI standards are made up of four series: GRI 100, GRI 200, GRI 300 and GRI 400. The GRI 100 series covers basic principles and requirements of sustainability reporting, while GRI 200 deals with economic standards, GRI 300 with environmental standards and the GRI 400 of social standards.

Previous studies verify that most companies that prepare sustainability reports follow the GRI standards (Luo and Tang, 2023; del Mar Alonso-Almeida et al., 2014), which address the three pillars of sustainability: economic, environmental and social. GRI Standards allow companies to use a common language in sustainability reports, contributing to a better understanding of their content by users.

The voluntary disclosure of social and environmental information is explained by several theoretical approaches, with emphasis on Legitimacy and Stakeholder theories. These theories are closely interconnected, as both have focus on communication with stakeholders and influence companies' activities in different ways (Burgwal & Vieira,

2014). Legitimacy theory emphasizes the importance of companies being aligned with the values and norms of society to be legitimized by it. This implies adopting a reliable organizational structure and responding to the interests of stakeholders in social and environmental issues to improve reputation and legitimacy (Tilling, 2004; Caetano & Eugénio, 2014). However, there are debates about whether legitimacy should be determined exclusively by society or whether companies should have an active voice in this process (Mobus & Tacoma, 2005). On the other hand, Stakeholder theory highlights the importance of companies establishing favorable relationships with interested parties, considering their diverse interests, such as shareholders, suppliers, customers and society in general. These relationships can influence companies' actions and the need to disclose more information increases with the company's size and exposure to society (Ahmad et al., 2003; Freeman, 1984). Thus, Stakeholder and Legitimacy theories explore interactions between companies and their stakeholders, highlighting the importance of communication and consideration of stakeholders' interests to achieve organizational objectives and preserve reputation and legitimacy (Lettieri, 2003; Slack & Shrives, 2008).

In mandatory non-financial reporting research tend to use institutional theory to prove that companies explore that stricter regulations result in more environmental activities (Li et al., 2018). Despite this, the adoption of environmental actions can cause decoupling practices in response to external regulations (Tang et al., 2023). Institutional theory has the assumptions on the role of inconsistency between organizational and institutional goals, institutional uncertainty, and oversight in determining the organizational policy-practice alignment (Bromley & Powell, 2012). In this line, Stewardship theory suggests that managers' and CEO's interests naturally align with those of the principals (Pastoriza & Arinio, 2008). Additionally, it argues that an organization needs a structure that facilitates efficient alignment between directors and shareholders. Therefore, concepts such as motivation, goal congruence, trust, and organizational identification are encompassed within the framework of stewardship theory (Van Puyvelde et al., 2013).

According to GRI (2011), sustainability reports aim to disclose quality information to stakeholders about the companies economic, social and environmental performance. Those that follow the GRI guidelines and disclose transparent environmental information, aligned with their values and principles, tend to demonstrate adequate performance and, therefore, can present better levels of ED (Gomes & Eugénio, 2012). Luo and Tang (2023, p. 2985), based on a sample of large international companies finding that "firms that follow GRI standards when preparing their ESG reports are more likely to achieve greater carbon mitigation". According to Galani et al. (2012), companies adopting GRI reporting tend to disclose a higher level of information. In line, Skouloudis et al., 2010 state that GRI standards contributes to the company's accountability promoting fair and transparent non-financial reporting practices. Based on these premises, the first research hypothesis is formulated:

H1: Companies that adopt GRI standards in their reports have a higher EDEI.

In sociology's institutional theory, businesses conform to external influences and societal norms to gain social acceptance and legitimacy (Meyer & Rowan 1977). Regulations and guidelines can shape behaviors and mindsets, potentially prompting companies to promote greater gender equality within their management structures (Allemand et al., 2014). CSR actions increase the legitimacy of the firm in the eyes of its members, external stakeholders and the public (Helm, 2013). In line, Stakeholder theory highlights that an organization operates within a larger social framework, where it both influences and is influenced by various societal groups (Freeman & Reed, 1983). According to Torchia et al. (2011), low female representation in companies can limit women's ability to influence decisions and, consequently, affect the information disclosure. However, Orazalin et al. (2020) highlight that women bring human and relational capital to companies, contributing to a diverse management perspective that can benefit the disclosure of information.

Study of Monteiro et al. (2022, p. 523) reveal the "that gender diversity in management teams is positively associated with performance in relation to labour and human rights, and that such a performance acts as a mediating factor by fostering a higher disclosure of information regarding these issues". In relation to studies developed within the scope of workplace gender diversity influence on sustainability reporting level, literature appears to be little explored. In this regard, Monteiro et al. (2024) show that gender diversity is positively associated with ESG performance reporting to a sample of EU listed entities. In this context, the following hypothesis are proposed:

H2: Companies with workplace gender diversity have the highest EDEI.

Nordberg (2008), with stakeholder theory lens, state that corporate boards have a duty to oversee operations for the welfare of all stakeholders. According to stakeholder theory, when employees perceive that the company provides favorable working conditions and equitable incentives, they are more likely to be actively involved and committed to the organization (Lii et al., 2013). Furthermore, companies with diverse boards are believed to be more capable of comprehending wider societal demands and cultivating a favorable corporate image, which ultimately improves outcomes for stakeholders. Recent literature has brought attention to the significant aspect of board diversity, particularly emphasizing gender diversity (Yasser et al., 2017). As evidenced by Bear et al. (2010), the presence of women on boards of directors is essential to positively influence CSR. Furthermore, Tiron-Tudor et al. (2020) highlight that women tend to adopt different moral reasoning, characterized by a more careful and protective approach. This diversity of thought can positively impact the quality and extent of information disclosed in business reports (Frias-

Aceituno et al., 2013; Tiron-Tudor et al., 2020). Monteiro et al. (2023) found that that the number of women on the board has a positive influence on the extent to which environmental information is disclosed in the reports and accounts of listed companies. Considering these aspects, the following hypothesis is formulated:

H3: Companies with gender diversity on the board of directors have the highest EDEI.

In stewardship theory lens, Brickley et al. (1997) pointed out that independent board chairs face agency challenges. Keay (2017) argued that there are in fact a variety of reasons why board accountability is necessary and appropriate in a corporate setting, under stewardship theory. For Haniffa and Cooke (2002), the effective performance of the board of directors is closely linked to the role played by independent members. The presence of these members is crucial, as they safeguard the interests of shareholders against any management opportunistic behavior with their experience to improve the company's operations (Barros et al., 2013). Previous research also suggests that the presence of independent board is positively related to the extent and quality of environmental information disclosure (Monteiro et al. 2023; Majeed et al., 2015). Based on this premise, the following hypotheses are formulated in this study:

H4: Companies with a greater number of independent members on the board of directors have the highest EDEI.

Adding complexity to the CEO duality understanding, Brickley et al., (1997) illuminated the disadvantages/advantages of CEO non-duality that expanded beyond the conventional boundaries of stewardship theory. They pointed out splitting the CEO and chairman roles raises costs while diminishing the efficacy of communication between the two positions. Moreover, they underscored that the separation of roles (non-duality) has implications for CEO succession, reinforcing also that while separation brings costs, it also yields benefits. Drawing from this nuanced perspective, the authors examined the relationship between CEO duality and corporate performance. Their analysis revealed evidence supporting the stewardship theory prediction of a positive correlation across various performance metrics.

Several empirical studies have investigated the relationship between CEO duality and firm ESG performance. For instance, a study by Kiel and Nicholson (2003) found a negative correlation between CEO duality and corporate social performance, indicating that firms with CEO duality tend to have lower levels of social responsibility. Other research has shown that the CEO duality also has negative effects on ESG performance (e.g., Naciti, 2019; Velte, 2020). Conversely, studies such as that of Filatotchev et al. (2013) have provided mixed evidence, indicating that the relationship between CEO duality and ESG performance may be contingent on various factors such as industry context, firm size, and institutional settings. Uyar et al. (2021) found that CEO duality moderates the association between board gender diversity and corporate social performance. Felo (2010) states that "audit committee composition, board composition and CEO duality are related to various measures of corporate reporting transparency". Following these presupposes we formulate the following research hypothesis:

H5: Companies with a CEO duality have the highest EDEI.

3. METHODOLOGY

This study adopts a methodological approach that combines qualitative and quantitative techniques. The qualitative part involves analyzing the content reports (such as financial, integrated and sustainability reports) of Portuguese and Brazilian companies in the period from 2016 to 2020.

The company's selection was carried out using the GRI website (https://www.globalreporting.org), focusing on companies that registered reports in the GRI database during the period studied. When reports for a given year or period were missing from the GRI database, they were collected directly from the company's website, if available.

The final sample consists of 120 companies, 49% of which are Portuguese and 51% Brazilian. Table 1 presents details about the companies included in the sample.

Table 1. Companies sample

Portuguese companies		Brazilian companies	
• **Águas de Lisboa e Vale do Tejo** • **Águas de Portugal** • **Altri** • **ANA Aeroportos** • **APDL** • **APS** • **APSS** • **Atlântico Europa Bank** • **Auchan** • **BoEDLlti** • **Brisa** • **Caixa Geral de Depósitos** • **Carris** • **Celbi** • **Correios de PT - CTT** • **Corticeira Amorim** • **CP - Comboios de PT** • **Delphi Automotive** • **EDP** • **EPAL** • **Galp** • **Gestamp Aveiro** • **Hovione** • **Huf Portuguesa** • **INCM** • **Jerónimo Martins** • **José de Mello Saúde** • **Lidl Portugal** • **Lipor** • **Logoplaste**	• Luís Simões • Metro do Porto • Metro de Lisboa • Millennium BCP • Mota-Engil SGPS • Nestlé Portugal • NOS • Novo Banco • REN • Resíduos do Nordeste • RTP • Santa Casa da Misericórdia de Lisboa • Santa Casa da Misericórdia do Porto • Santander Totta • Secil • Simarsul • Sonae • Sonae Indústria • Sonae Sierra • Sovena • Sumol + Compal • TAP Group • Teixeira Duarte • The Navigator Company • TMG Automotive • Tratolixo • Trivalor • Unicer • Vodafone	• A. C. Camargo Cancer Center • Aegea • AES Tietê • AmBev • B2W Companhia Digital • Banco do Brasil • Biosev • BRF S.A. • BSBIOS Energia Renovável • CEEE-D • CEEE-GT • Celulose Irani • Cenibra • Centrais Elétricas do Pará (Celpa) • CESP • CHESF • Copagaz • Copel • CTG Brasil • Duratex • Eletrobrás Furnas • Embraer • ENGIE • Fitesa • GOL • Grupo Energisa • Instituto da Oportunidade Social • Itaipu Binacional • Light • Lojas Renner	• Neoenergia • Nexa Resources • Ocyan • OuroFino - Saúde Animal • Petrobras • Racional Engenharia • Rede D'OR São Luiz • Renault Brasil • Sabesp • Sanasa • Sanofi Brasil • São Martinho • SETA Engenharia • Sicredi • Sirio Libanes Hospital • Sistema Federação das Indústrias Estado do Paraná • Suzano Papel e Celulose • TAESA • Toyota do Brasil • Triunfos Participações e Investimentos • Unimed Circuito das Águas • Unimed Cuiabá • Unimed Sorocaba • Unimed Vales do Taquari e Rio Pardo • Vale • Veracel • Volkswagen do Brasil • Votorantim Cimentos • Votorantim Energia • WEG • Wilson Sons

This study involves analyzing a total of 288 reports from Portuguese companies based and 291 reports from Brazilian companies. Within this research, an environmental reporting index was developed to measure the EDEI.

The following formula is used to determine EDEI:

EDEI =

- ej – Number of $\sum_{n=1}^{e} ej/e$ indicators included in the report
- e – Total number of indicators

The environmental sustainability reporting evaluation is based on the indicators belonging to GRI 300 Environmental Category (2020). The extent of environmental reporting measurement follows the criteria previously applied in preceding studies (Monteiro et al., 2021; Monteiro et al., 2023). In this regard, a dichotomous dummy variable is adopted, where the value "1" indicates the presence of information reporting, while the value "0" denotes the absence of information reporting.

To analyze the factors that influence EDEI the following regression is used to test the research hypotheses:

$$IEDAn= \beta 0+\beta 1GRIn+\beta 2DIVERn+\beta 3WBDn+\beta 4INDBn+\beta 5CEOdualityn+\beta 6DJSIn+\beta 7SIZEn+\beta 8ROAn+\beta 9ROEn+\beta 10SENIO$$

The explanatory variables are defined as follows (table 2):

Table 2. Sample variables meaning.

Variables	Meaning	Scale	Source/literature
Independent variables			
GRI	"Is the company's CSR report published in accordance with the GRI guidelines? - in focus on CSR report or data published within the framework or guidelines of GRI principles" Yes:1; No:0	0-1	Refinitiv (2020)
DIVER	Gender Diversity – represents the proportion of women among the company's total employees.	0-100	Ardito et al, (2021); Birindelli et al, (2019); Frías-Aceituno et al, (2013); García-Sánchez et al, (2020a, 2020b); Monteiro et al, (2022); Wasiuzzaman & Subramaniam (2023); Williams (2003)
WBD	Number of women on the board of directors – number of women on the board of directors.	Number	Refinitiv (2020)
INDB	Percentage of independent board members as reported by the company.	0-100	Refinitiv (2020)
CEOduality	(CEO duality) – Number of CEO's that is CEO has both the presidency of the company as the chairman of its Board of Directors.	Number	Refinitiv (2020)
Control variables			
DJSI	Dow Jones Sustainability Index - The DJSI introduces a number of indicators that allow us to see what the firm is doing, such as the evaluation of intangible assets, development of human capital, organizational issues, strategic plans, corporate governance and investor relations.	0-100	López et al. (2007).
SIZE	Natural logarithm of assets.	Logarithm	Aluchna et al, (2022); Amorelli & García-Sánchez (2020); Bowrin (2018); Cahaya & Hervina (2019); McGuinness et al, (2016); Monteiro et al, (2022); Orazalin & Baydauletov (2020)

continued on following page

Table 2. Continued

Variables	Meaning	Scale	Source/literature
ROA	Financial performance measured by return on assets - Net income/Total assets.	0-100	Aluchna et al, (2022); Amorelli & García-Sánchez (2020); Aydoğmuş et al, (2022); Baraibar-Diez & Odriozola (2019); Bifulco et al, (2023); Issa & Zaid (2021); Monteiro et al, (2022); García-Sánchez et al, (2020a); Orazalin & Baydauletov (2020); Parra-Domínguez et al, (2021); Wasiuzzaman & Wan Mohammad (2020); Wasiuzzaman & Subramaniam (2023).
ROE	Measure of the profitability of a business in relation to its equity; where: ROE = Net Income/Average Shareholders' Equity.	0-100	Aluchna et al, (2022); Amorelli & García-Sánchez (2020)
SENIO	Companies' seniority (years).	Number	

In addition, this study examines the impact of the introduction of Decree-Law 89/2017, of 28 /07 (in Portugal) and Resolution No. 4557/2017, of February 23 (in Brazil) in environmental information disclosure, reports before and after 2018 were analyzed.

Regarding the descriptive statistics from both countries, we highlight that Brazilian companies had, in medium, a major EDEI (51%) and GRI adoption (93%), when compared to Portuguese companies (41% and 77%, respectively); however, the difference is relatively small. Regarding the workplace gender diversity (DIVER), the opposite is true. On average, this indicator was 37% in Portuguese companies and 28% in Brazilian companies. Regarding the number of women on board of directors (WBD), we find that, on average, Portugal has 1 woman on the board and in Brazil approximately 2 women, considering that in both countries the minimum is 0 and the maximum is 5 of women on the board.

In fact, both countries have somewhat low gender diversity. Brazilian companies may have a lower average in gender diversity because its regulatory framework is not as robust as the EU's. Furthermore, a study by Spencer Stuart (2017), based on 176 Brazilian companies, found that women comprised only 8.2% of board members and 1.7% of CEOs, indicating minimal progress in gender diversity. Regarding CEO duality, this indicator is higher in Brazilian than Portuguese companies. This value is normal considering that Portugal (small country) has few listed companies, and these do not reach the proportion of Brazilian listed companies. As for the percentage of independent board members, the average is similar in Portugal and Brazil (97% and 98%, respectively).

Table 3 presents the research variables descriptive statistics.

continued on following page

Table 3. Continued

Table 3. Descriptive statistics

VARIABLE	OBS	MEAN	STD. DEV.	MIN	MAX
PORTUGAL(PT)					
EDEI	288	.4115835	.2552774	0	.8533654
GRI	288	.7708333	.4210283	0	1
DIVER	288	.3711858	.1710184	.0861742	.9370985
WBD	288	1.305755	1.295662	0	5
INDBD	288	.9756944	.1754026	0	2
CEODUALITY	278	.7841727	1.938635	0	9
CONTROL VARIABLES					
DJSI	288	.6875	.4643192	0	1
SENIO	288	.4193056	.3424907	0	1
ROA	288	3541334	1.44e+07	11.49476	1.38e+08
SIZE	288	3766695	1.50e+07	71.15771	1.38e+08
ROE	288	3.15e+08	1.37e+09	9583.25	8.79e+09
BRAZIL(BR)					
EDEI	291	.5080376	.1714876	0	.8533654
GRI	291	.9312715	.2534277	0	1
DIVER	291	.2825149	.1953665	.0074384	.7693718
WBD	291	1.646048	1.03814	0	5
INDBD	291	.9862543	.1166341	0	1
CEODUALITY	291	1.742268	1.737686	0	8
CONTROL VARIABLES					
DJSI	291	.5051546	.5008347	0	1
SENIO	291	.273488	.2838588	0	.98
ROA	291	1736351	9481557	98.15134	9.23e+07
SIZE	291	1281309	6000295	0	7.53e+07
ROE	291	2.43e+08	1.59e+09	365.56	1.27e+10

4. RESULTS ANALYSIS AND DISCUSSION

This study aims to analyze the ED level by Portuguese and Brazilian companies. Specifically, it seeks to understand the (1) evolution of the EDEI over time, the documents (reports) most used to disclose environmental information, (2) the GRI 300 indicators with highest disclosure index and (3) the EDEI determinants (GRI adoption, workplace gender diversity, board gender diversity, board independence members and CEO Duality).

Regarding the first objective, as can be seen in table 3, EDEI averages is 41% and 51% for Portuguese and Brazilian companies, respectively. Its evolution has not been uniforming over the years for companies in both countries, specifically:

- From 2016 to 2017: in Portugal it increased by 20.36% and in Brazil by 1.61%;
- From 2017 to 2018: in Portugal it increased by 6.33% and in Brazil by 9.67%;
- From 2018 to 2019: in Portugal it increases by 0.05% and in Brazil by 2,31%;
- From 2019 to 2020: in Portugal it increases by 0.33% and in Brazil by 6.62%.

Figure 1 presents EDEI per country from 2016 to 2020.

Figure 1. EDEI per country from 2016 to 2020

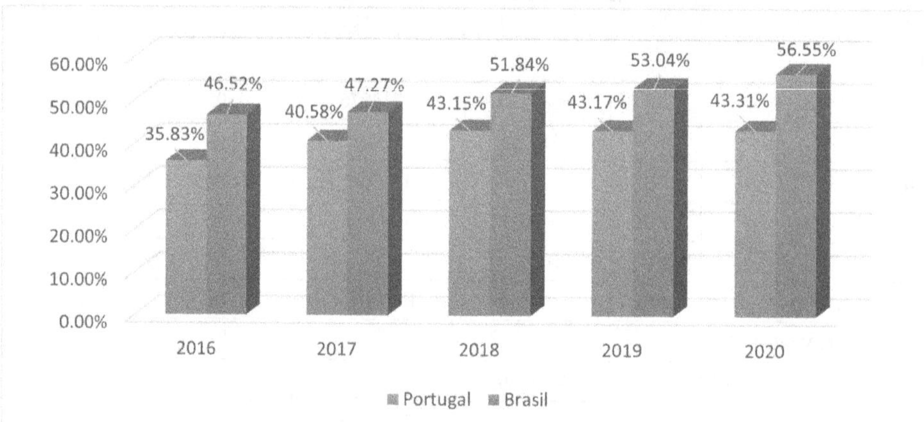

In this study it was found that the introduction of sustainable disclosure information regulations (Resolution no. 4557/2017, of February 23, in Brazil and Decree-Law no. 89/2017, of July 28, in Portugal), had a positive impact on the companies analyzed EDEI, given the increase seen from 2017 to 2018.

Regarding the EDEI per reporting type to analyze the reports most used to disclose environmental information, Table 4 presents the documents analyzed in the study (annual, integrated and sustainability report). On average, most companies disclose non-financial information using sustainability reports (59%), followed by annual reports (18%) and, finally, integrated reports (8%).

Table 4. Frequency of environmental information disclosure in different types of reports

Type	Level	2016		2017		2018		2019		2020		Mean	
		n	%	n	%	n	%	n	%	n	%	n	%
Annual	N.D.	20	17	12	10	12	10	14	12	11	11	13	11
	D	16	13	23	19	22	18	21	18	22	21	21	18
Integrated	N.D.	0	0	1	1	1	1	1	1	0	0	1	1
	D	5	4	3	2,5	9	7	12	10	15	15	9	8
Sustainability	N.D.	2	2	3	2,5	2	2	3	3	4	4	3	3
	D	77	64	78	65	74	62	66	56	50	49	69	59
Total		120	100	120	100	120	100	117	100	102	100	116	100

Legend: N.D. - Does not disclose; D – Disclose

Figure 2 and 3 shows that, for both countries, EDEI is more expressive in the sustainability reports, followed by the integrated report and then the annual report.

Figure 2. EDEI of Portuguese companies by report type, from 2016 to 2020

Figure 3. EDEI of Brazilian companies by report type, from 2016 to 2020

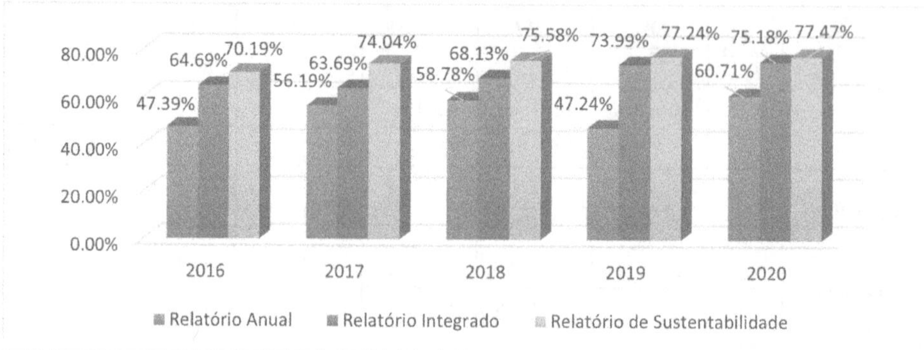

The second study objective is to identify in which GRI 300 indicator there is the greatest extent of environmental information disclosure. Table 5 shows the percentage averages by indicator for the period from 2016 to 2020. Considering the indicator 307 – Environmental Compliance, it is the one with the best ED rates, with disclosure rates above 73% in Portugal and 93% in Brazil. Subsequently, indicators 305 – Emissions, 302 – Energy, 303 – Water and effluents, 304 – Biodiversity, 306 – Effluents and waste have disclosure rates between 40% and 79. Thus, in this study it is possible to conclude that companies from both countries have better disclosure rates in the following indicators: GRI 307 - Environmental Compliance, GRI 305 - Emissions and GRI 302 – Energy.

Table 5. EDEI for GRI 300 indicators

		301	302	303	304	305	306	307	308
EDEI	**PT**	29,25%	61,74%	59,49%	41,80%	68,56%	40,08%	73,01%	23,33%
	BR	54,72%	77,80%	71,50%	59,89%	79,46%	40,00%	93,07%	33,46%

Finally, regarding the last research objectives, in this study we estimated 2 models, one for Portuguese companies and one for Brazilian companies (Table 6). The models are statistically significant ($p<0.001$; R^2-PT=68% and R^2- BR 32%). Regarding R^2, results suggest that a significant part of the dependent variable EDEI is explained by the explanatory variables.

Empirical evidence reveals that GRI adoption (β= 0.49; $p<0.001$), workplace gender diversity (β= 0.078; $p<0.001$) and CEO duality (β= 0.013; $p<0.01$) are positively associated with EDEI in Portuguese Companies. In Brazilian companies' case, we verified that GRI adoption (β= 0.51; $p<0.001$) and CEO duality (β= 0.023;

p<0.001) are positively associated with EDEI, however a work gender diversity is negatively associated with EDEI (β= -0.027; p<0.01).

Regarding H1, it is supported by our study. This empirical evidence is in line with Skouloudis *et al.* (2010), who suggest that companies tend to follow the GRI standards and disclose transparent environmental information and Galani *et al.* (2012), which states that companies that follow GRI standards tend to provide better sustainability disclosure levels.

Workplace gender diversity has a positive relationship with EDEI in Portuguese companies. The same does not apply to Brazilian companies, so H2 is partially supported in this research. In this respect, Tiron-Tudor *et al.* (2020) emphasize that women, on average, tend to adopt a more cautious and protective approach to decision-making, which can have profound implications for CSR strategies. Moreover, research conducted by Frias-Aceituno *et al.* (2013) and further by Tiron-Tudor *et al.* (2020) underscores gender diversity impact on the quality and extent of information disclosed in business reports. Monteiro *et al.* (2024) show also that gender diversity has a positive impact on ESG performance reporting to a sample of EU listed entities. This inclination towards transparency can enhance the credibility of corporate reports and foster greater trust among stakeholders. In line, all stakeholders have the responsibility to promote gender diversity (Helm, 2013) and the institutional pressures related to non-financial reporting are crucial to these achievements (Allemand *et al.,* 2014). Moreover, it should be noted that the country where companies are headquartered is considered an important determinant of the company's non-financial disclosure level (Cepeda, 2024). In this sense, these results are exactly the opposite in Brazilian companies, showing that higher levels of ED are associated with companies with gender inequality.

Our results don't support H3 and H4. In this respect, Monteiro *et al.* (2023) found that the number of women on the board has a positive influence on the extent of environmental information disclosure in the annual reports of Portuguese listed companies. However, for the disclosure of sustainability reports, no significant relationship was found. The same authors found that the independent board members proportion was correlated with ED only in sustainability reports. Although H3 is not supported, it is noteworthy that in 2011, Dani *et al.* (2019), verify that 66.3% of Brazilian listed companies had no women on their boards. On the other hand, those companies include the presence of women 20% of the chairs of boards. When comparing the percentage among countries, among the companies that have at least one woman on the board, Brazil found itself behind countries like China, India and Russia (IBGC, 2011). Recently, data from 2022 indicate that out of every 100 companies with shares traded on the stock exchange in Brazil, 61 do not have women in statutory management positions, and 37 do not have female participation on the board of directors (B3, 2022).

Finally, H5 were supported in both countries, following the Felo (2010), who finds that CEO duality contributes positively to corporate transparency.

Table 6. Explanatory model

EDEI	Coef. PT	Coef. BR	Hypothesis	Results
GRI	0.4923423***	0.5179255***	H1	Supported
DIVER	0.0785778***	-0.0276986**	H2	Partially supported
WBD	0.0040021	-0.0234938	H3	Not supported
INDBD	-0.0853876	0.1157083	H4	Not supported
CEOduality	0.0134689**	0.0235588***	H5	Supported
Control Variables				
DJSI	0.0092333	0.0237053		
SENIO	-0.1743306	0.3680079**		
ROA	-2.85e-10	-1.08e-09		
SIZE	-1.62e-09	-1.04e-09		
ROE	7.12e-12	-2.00e-13		
_cons	0.0865482	-0.1059482		
sigma_u	0.12447256	0.1550122		
sigma_e	0.094126	0.07558169		
rho	0.63619844	0.80792442		
R^2	68%	32%		

Legend: ***p<0.001; **p<0.01;*p<0.05

5. CONCLUSION

Sustainability disclosure has been a hot topic in the literature due to the pressure exerted by the company's internal and external stakeholders.

This study, based on a sample of Portuguese and Brazilian companies (listed and private) supported by a content analysis of corporate reports, develops the EDEI, analyzes its evolution, from 2016 to 2020, and identifies which communication tools are most used to disseminate environmental information. The study also identifies the most disclosed matters within the scope of GRI 300. Finally, the EDEI determinants were analyzed using the multiple linear regression technique with panel data.

In the analysis of EDEI's evolution, the results indicate a growing trend in ED rates, which are slightly higher in Brazilian companies. This result agrees with most studies developed in this field, such as Barbosa *et al.* (2021), in Portuguese case. Among the different report types analyzed, the sustainability reports are the most used and the ones that show better ED levels. In this study, it was possible to assess the positive impact of Decree-Law 89/2017, of 07/28 and Resolution No. 4557/2017, of February 23, on EDEI, due to the increase in environmental disclosure from 2017 to 2018 in both countries.

Regarding the GRI indicators, the results indicate that the indicators related to environmental compliance (GRI 307), emissions (GRI 305) and energy (GRI 302) are the ones with higher EDEI.

Our study ensures robustness by employing two models, yielding significant results ($p<0.001$) with notable explanatory power, both for the model that analyzes Portuguese companies (R^2-PT=68%) and for Brazilian companies (R^2-BR=32%). In Portuguese firms, positive associations between GRI adoption, work gender diversity and CEO duality with EDEI, are found in this study, according to previous research, highlighting the importance of ED and diverse factors in enhancing CSR strategies. Conversely, in Brazilian firms, while GRI adoption and CEO duality positively impact EDEI, gender diversity reveals a negative association. Surprisingly, our findings support a positive link between CEO duality and EDEI, challenging prior research. Nonetheless, some hypotheses were unsupported, namely those related to the relationship with board of directors diversity and the number of board of directors members with EDEI.

Sustainability reports, as defined by GRI, serve to furnish stakeholders with comprehensive insights into a company's economic, social, and environmental performance. Companies that comply with GRI guidelines and transparently disclose environmental information tend to demonstrate enhanced performance and greater accountability. Influenced by institutional theory, businesses often adhere to societal norms and regulations, potentially fostering gender equality within management structures. Gender diversity not only enhances corporate social responsibility but also facilitates information dissemination, in line with stakeholder theory. CEO duality, examined within the context of stewardship theory, influences communication efficacy and organizational performance. Empirical evidence revealed a positive relationship between CEO duality and ESG performance/reporting.

Overall, our study advances a better understanding of the disclosure of environmental information, the effect of corporate strategies on ED in different contexts, proving some differences. This research exposes specific challenges that companies, in each country, face to implement robust ED practices. In this context, Brazilian companies needed to improve the workplace gender diversity and Portuguese companies should improve the EDEI.

The study results are relevant to the literature, as it explores ED levels and their determinants in two countries in different geographic, regulatory, environmental and socio-economic contexts and with the same national official language and cultural background. In addition, both countries share a historical past. Regarding practical contributions, research results can make company managers aware of the need to disclose environmental information to stakeholders, given that one of the major challenges is related to the extent and accountability of environmental reporting. Furthermore, managers must value/adopt the issues identified in this study as driving ED. On the other hand, the results are also useful for policymakers and institutions in improving ED standards. The results are also useful for political decision-makers and regulatory institutions, as they can provide guidance to companies to promote increased sustainability disclosure, specifically in the environmental dimension.

This study analyzes the extent of ED and not its quality, which restricts the analysis to this type of measure. For future research, it is suggested to analyze the ED quality. Also, future studies can be applied to European companies and companies that are subject to the new European Directive 2022/2464 to obtain empirical evidence on the effect of the Directive on EDEI.

REFERENCES

Al Fadli, A., Sands, J., Jones, G., Beattie, C., & Pensiero, D. (2019). Board gender diversity and CSR reporting: Evidence from Jordan. *Australasian Accounting. Business and Finance Journal*, 13(3), 29–52.

Al-Shaer, H., & Zaman, M. (2016). Board gender diversity and sustainability reporting quality. *Journal of Contemporary Accounting & Economics*, 12(3), 210–222. DOI:10.1016/j.jcae.2016.09.001

Allemand, I., Brullebaut, B., & Raimbault, S. (2014). Recommendations for boards of directors of investor owned firms from the co-operative model. In *Research Handbook on Sustainable Co-operative Enterprise* (pp. 206–220). Edward Elgar Publishing. DOI:10.4337/9781783472024.00019

Ashraf, A., Qi, B., Meile, Z., & Marie, M. (2024). CEO career horizons, foreign experience, and state ownership impact on the adoption of the Global Reporting Initiative standards for corporate social responsibility reporting. Business Ethics, the Environment & Responsibility. DOI:10.1111/beer.12673

Ashraf, M. Z., Wei, W., Usman, M., & Mushtaq, S. (2024). How can natural resource dependence, environmental-related technologies and digital trade protect the environment: Redesigning SDGs policies for sustainable environment? *Resources Policy*, 88, 104456. DOI:10.1016/j.resourpol.2023.104456

Azzam, M., AlQudah, A., Abu Haija, A., & Shakhatreh, M. (2020). The association between sustainability disclosures and the financial performance of Jordanian firms. *Cogent Business & Management*, 7(1), 1859437. DOI:10.1080/23311975.2020.1859437

Baden, D., & Harwood, I. (2013). Terminology matters: A critical exploration of corporate social responsibility terms. *Journal of Business Ethics*, 116(3), 615–627. DOI:10.1007/s10551-012-1498-9

Baker, N., & Nazer, K. (2000). Empirical evidence on corporate social disclosure (CSD) practices in Jordan. *International Journal of Commerce and Management*, 10(3&4), 18–34. DOI:10.1108/eb047406

Barros, C., Boubakar, S., & Hamrouni, A. (2013). Corporate governance and voluntary disclosure in France. *Journal of Applied Business Research*, 29(2), 561–578. DOI:10.19030/jabr.v29i2.7657

Bear, S., Rahman, N., & Post, C. (2010). The impact of board diversity and gender composition on corporate social responsibility and firm reputation. *Journal of Business Ethics*, 97(2), 207–221. DOI:10.1007/s10551-010-0505-2

Bravo, F., & Reguera-Alvarado, N. (2019). Sustainable development disclosure: Environmental, social, and governance reporting and gender diversity in the audit committee. *Business Strategy and the Environment*, 28(2), 418–429. DOI:10.1002/bse.2258

Brickley, J. A., Coles, J. L., & Jarrell, G. (1997). Leadership structure: Separating the CEO and chairman of the board. *Journal of Corporate Finance*, 3(3), 189–220. DOI:10.1016/S0929-1199(96)00013-2

Bromley, P., & Powell, W. W. (2012). From smoke and mirrors to walking the talk: Decoupling in the contemporary world. *The Academy of Management Annals*, 6(1), 483–530. DOI:10.5465/19416520.2012.684462

Brown, B. J., Hanson, M. E., Liverman, D. M., & Merideth, R. W.Jr. (1987). Global sustainability: Toward definition. *Environmental Management*, 11(6), 713–719. DOI:10.1007/BF01867238

Burgwal, D., & Vieira, R. (2014). Environmental disclosure determinants in dutch listed companies. *Revista de Contabilidade e Finanças de São Paulo*, 25(64), 60–78. DOI:10.1590/S1519-70772014000100006

Burhan, A. H. N., & Rahmanti, W. (2012). The impact of sustainability reporting on company performance. *Journal of Economics, Business, &Accountancy Ventura*, 15(2), 257–272. DOI:10.14414/jebav.v15i2.79

Cabeza-García, L., Fernández-Gago, R., & Nieto, M. (2018). Do board gender diversity and director typology impact CSR reporting? *European Management Review*, 15(4), 559–575. DOI:10.1111/emre.12143

Caetano, D., & Eugénio, T. (2014). Relato de Sustentabilidade de Empresas da Construção Civil em Portugal e Espanha. *Revista Ambiente Contábil, 10(1)*, 273-290.

Carvalho, A., Schmidt, L., Santos, F. D., & Delicado, A. (2014). Climate change research and policy in Portugal. *Wiley Interdisciplinary Reviews: Climate Change*, 5(2), 199–217. DOI:10.1002/wcc.258

Cepeda, C. (2024). Can Crisis Periods Affect the ESG Reporting Scope? The Portuguese Euronext Entities Case. *Journal of Risk and Financial Management*, 17(5), 191. DOI:10.3390/jrfm17050191

Colglazier, W. (2015). Sustainable development agenda: 2030. *Science*, 349(6252), 1048–1050. DOI:10.1126/science.aad2333 PMID:26339011

Cormier, D., & Gomez-Gutierrez, L. (2018). On the search for mimetic patterns in environmental disclosure: An international perspective. *International Journal of Sustainable Development and World Ecology*, 25(7), 655–671. DOI:10.1080/13504509.2018.1439849

Corvino, A., Doni, F., & Bianchi Martini, S. (2020). Corporate governance, integrated reporting and environmental disclosure: Evidence from the South African context. *Sustainability (Basel)*, 12(12), 4820. DOI:10.3390/su12124820

Dani, A. C., Picolo, J. D., & Klann, R. C. (2019). Gender influence, social responsibility and governance in performance. *RAUSP Management Journal*, 54(2), 154–177. DOI:10.1108/RAUSP-07-2018-0041

Davis, J. H., Schoorman, F. D., & Donaldson, L. (1997). Towards a stewardship theory of management. *Academy of Management Review*, 22(1), 20–47. DOI:10.2307/259223

Decree-Law n.º 89/2017, from 28 de july. Retrived from Diário da República Eletrónico: https://dre.pt/dre/detalhe/decreto-lei/89-2017-107773645

del Mar Alonso-Almeida, M., Llach, J., & Marimon, F. (2014). A closer look at the 'Global Reporting Initiative'sustainability reporting as a tool to implement environmental and social policies: A worldwide sector analysis. *Corporate Social Responsibility and Environmental Management*, 21(6), 318–335. DOI:10.1002/csr.1318

DiMaggio, P. J., & Powell, W. W. (1983). The Iron Cage Revisited: Institutional Isomorphism and Collective Rationality in Organizational Fields. *American Sociological Review* 48:147–60. Crossref. ISI. Directive 2014/95/UE from European Parliament and the Council, from 22 October. Retrived from Official Journal of the European Union: https://eur-lex.europa.eu/legal-content/PT/TXT/?uri=CELEX:32014L0095

Directive 2022/2464/EU of the European Parliament and of the Council of 14 December 2022 amending Regulation (EU) No 537/2014, Directive 2004/109/EC, Directive 2006/43/EC and Directive 2013/34/EU as regards corporate sustainability reporting. https://eur-lex.europa.eu/legal-content/PT/TXT/PDF/?uri=CELEX:32022L2464

Eccles, R. G., & Spiesshofer, B. (2015). Integrated reporting for a re-imagined capitalism. *Harvard Business School General Management Unit Working Paper*, (16-032).

Epstein, M., Flamholtz, E., & McDonough, J. J. (1976). Corporate social accounting in the United States of America: State of the art and future prospects. *Accounting, Organizations and Society*, 1(1), 23–42. DOI:10.1016/0361-3682(76)90005-2

Evangelinos, K., Fotiadis, S., Skouloudis, A., Khan, N., Konstandakopoulou, F., Nikolaou, I., & Lundy, S. (2018). Occupational health and safety disclosures in sustainability reports: An overview of trends among corporate leaders. *Corporate Social Responsibility and Environmental Management*, 25(5), 961–970. DOI:10.1002/csr.1512

Fearnside, P. M. (2005). Deforestation in Brazilian Amazonia: History, rates, and consequences. *Conservation Biology*, 19(3), 680–688. DOI:10.1111/j.1523-1739.2005.00697.x

Federal Law 13.303, from 30 june 2016. https://legislacao.presidencia.gov.br/atos/?tipo=LEI&numero=13303&ano=2016&ato=264ETT650dZpWT936. (accessed on 05 May 2024).

Felo, A. J., & Transparency, C. R.Board Independence and Expertise, and CEO Duality. (2010). DOI:10.2139/ssrn.1373942

Filatotchev, I., Jackson, G., & Nakajima, C. (2013). Corporate governance and national institutions: A review and emerging research agenda. *Asia Pacific Journal of Management*, 30(4), 965–986. DOI:10.1007/s10490-012-9293-9

Fonseca, A., McAllister, M. L., & Fitzpatrick, P. (2014). Sustainability reporting among mining corporations: A constructive critique of the GRI approach. *Journal of Cleaner Production*, 4, 70–83. DOI:10.1016/j.jclepro.2012.11.050

Freeman, R. E. (1984). *Strategic management: A stakeholder approach.* Pitman.

Freeman, R. E., & Reed, D. L. (1983). Stockholders and stakeholders: A new perspective on corporate governance. *California Management Review*, 25(3), 93–94. DOI:10.2307/41165018

Frias-Aceituno, J. V., Rodriguez-Ariza, L., & Garcia-Sanchez, I. M. (2013). The role of the board in the dissemination of integrated corporate social reporting. *Corporate Social Responsibility and Environmental Management*, 13(20), 219–233. DOI:10.1002/csr.1294

Frooman, J. (1999). Stakeholder influence strategies. *Academy of Management Review*, 24(2), 191–205. DOI:10.2307/259074

Galani, D., Gravas, E., & Stavropoulos, A. (2012). Company characteristics and environmental policy. *Business Strategy and the Environment*, 21(4), 236–247. DOI:10.1002/bse.731

Gallego-Álvarez, I., Lozano, M. B., & Rodríguez-Rosa, M. (2018). An analysis of the environmental information in international companies according to the new GRI standards. *Journal of Cleaner Production*, 182, 57–66. DOI:10.1016/j.jclepro.2018.01.240

Gerged, A. M. (2021). Factors affecting corporate environmental disclosure in emerging markets: The role of corporate governance structures. *Business Strategy and the Environment*, 30(1), 609–629. DOI:10.1002/bse.2642

Giannarakis, G., Konteos, G., & Sariannidis, N. (2014). Financial, governance and environmental determinants of corporate social responsible disclosure. *Management Decision*, 52(10), 1928–1951. DOI:10.1108/MD-05-2014-0296

Gray, R. (2010). A Re-Evaluation of Social, Environmental and Sustainability Accouning: An Exploration of an Emerging Trans-Disciplinary Field? *Sustainability Accounting. Management and Policy Journal*, 1(1), 11–32.

Guesser, T., Hein, N., Pfitscher, E. D., & Lunkes, R. J. (2015). Environmental impact management of Brazilian companies: Analyzing factors that influence disclosure of waste, emissions, effluents, and other impacts. *Journal of Cleaner Production*, 96, 148–160. DOI:10.1016/j.jclepro.2013.10.035

Halkos, G., & Nomikos, S. (2021). Corporate social responsibility: Trends in global reporting initiative standards. *Economic Analysis and Policy*, 69, 106–117. DOI:10.1016/j.eap.2020.11.008

Haniffa, R., & Cooke, T. (2002). Culture, corporate governance and disclosure in Malaysian corporations. *Abacus*, 38(3), 317–349. DOI:10.1111/1467-6281.00112

Helm, S. (2013). A matter of reputation and pride: Associations between perceived external reputation, pride in membership, job satisfaction and turnover intentions. *British Journal of Management*, 24(4), 542–556. DOI:10.1111/j.1467-8551.2012.00827.x

Herremans, I. M., Nazari, J. A., & Mahmoudian, F. (2016). Stakeholder relationships, engagement, and sustainability reporting. *Journal of Business Ethics*, 138(3), 417–435. DOI:10.1007/s10551-015-2634-0

Hussain, M. J., Tian, G., Ashraf, A., Khan, M. K., & Ying, L. (2023). Chief executive officer ability and corporate environmental sustainability information disclosure. *Business Ethics, the Environment & Responsibility*, 32(1), 24–39. DOI:10.1111/beer.12485

IBGC Instituto brasileiro de Governança Corporativa (IBGC) (2011). Relatório de mulheres na administração das empresas brasileiras listadas – 2010 e 2011. *Available at:*http://hotsite.mma.gov.br/redemulheres/wpcontent/uploads/Pesquisa_Mulheres_no_Conselho.pdf

IIRC. (2013). The International Integrated Reporting Framework. Available at https://integratedreporting.org/wpcontent/uploads/2013/12/13-12-08-the-international-ir-framework-2-1.pdf

Keay, A. (2017). Stewardship theory: Is board accountability necessary? *International Journal of Law and Management*, 59(6), 1292–1314. DOI:10.1108/IJLMA-11-2016-0118

Khan, M., & Lockhart, J. (2022). Corporate social responsibility decoupling in developing countries: Current research and a future agenda. *Business and Society Review*, 127(1), 127–143. DOI:10.1111/basr.12254

Kiel, G. C., & Nicholson, G. J. (2003). Board composition and corporate performance: How the Australian experience informs contrasting theories of corporate governance. *Corporate Governance*, 11(3), 189–205. DOI:10.1111/1467-8683.00318

Kiroyan, N. (2015). NCSR Sustainability Reporting. *SKK Migas Indonesian Petroleum Association 39th Convention, 11.*

Kouloukoui, D., Sant'Anna, Â. M. O., da Silva Gomes, S. M., de Oliveira Marinho, M. M., de Jong, P., Kiperstok, A., & Torres, E. A. (2019). Factors influencing the level of environmental disclosures in sustainability reports: Case of climate risk disclosure by Brazilian companies. *Corporate Social Responsibility and Environmental Management*, 26(4), 791–804. DOI:10.1002/csr.1721

Lagasio, V., & Cucari, N. (2019). Corporate governance and environmental social governance disclosure: A meta-analytical review. *Corporate Social Responsibility and Environmental Management*, 26(4), 701–711. DOI:10.1002/csr.1716

Lazzaretti, K., Godoi, C. K., Camilo, S. P. O., & Marcon, R. (2013). Gender diversity in the boards of directors of Brazilian businesses. *Gender in Management*, 28(2), 94–110. DOI:10.1108/17542411311303239

Lee, E., Walker, M., & Zeng, C. (2017). Do Chinese state subsidies affect voluntary corporate social responsibility disclosure? *Journal of Accounting and Public Policy*, 36(3), 179–200. DOI:10.1016/j.jaccpubpol.2017.03.004

Lettieri, C. (2003). Quem realmente interessa às empresas? Contribuições analíticas da teoria dos stakeholders ao estudo da responsabilidade corporativa.

Li, D., Huang, M., Ren, S., Chen, X., & Ning, L. (2018). Environmental legitimacy, green innovation, and corporate carbon disclosure: Evidence from CDP China 100. *Journal of Business Ethics*, 150(4), 1089–1104. DOI:10.1007/s10551-016-3187-6

Lii, Y., Wu, K., & Ding, M. (2013). Doing good does good? sustainable marketing of CSR and consumer evaluations. *Corporate Social Responsibility and Environmental Management*, 20(1), 15–28. DOI:10.1002/csr.294

Lindblom, C. K. (1993). The implications of organizational legitimacy for corporate social performance and disclosure. *Paper presented at the Critical Perspectives on Accounting Conference*, New York, NY.

López, M. V., Garcia, A., & Rodriguez, L. (2007). Sustainable development and corporate performance: A study based on the Dow Jones sustainability index. *Journal of Business Ethics*, 75(3), 285–300. DOI:10.1007/s10551-006-9253-8

Luo, L., & Tang, Q. (2023). The real effects of ESG reporting and GRI standards on carbon mitigation: International evidence. *Business Strategy and the Environment*, 32(6), 2985–3000. DOI:10.1002/bse.3281

Majeed, S., Aziz, T., & Saleem, S. (2015). The Effect of Corporate Governance Elements on Corporate Social Responsibility (CSR) Disclosure: An Empirical Evidence from Listed Companies at KSE Pakistan. *International Journal of Financial Studies*, 3(4), 530–556. DOI:10.3390/ijfs3040530

Mebratu, D. (1998). Sustainability and sustainable development: Historical and conceptual review. *Environmental Impact Assessment Review*, 18(6), 493–520. DOI:10.1016/S0195-9255(98)00019-5

Meyer, H. D., & Rowan, B. (2006). Institutional analysis and the study of education. *The new institutionalism in education*, 113.

Michelon, G. (2011). Sustainability disclosure and reputation: A comparative study. *Corporate Reputation Review*, 14(2), 79–96. DOI:10.1057/crr.2011.10

Michelon, G., Boesso, G., & Kumar, K. (2013). Examining the link between strategic corporate social responsibility and company performance: An analysis of the best corporate citizens. *Corporate Social Responsibility and Environmental Management*, 20(2), 81–94. DOI:10.1002/csr.1278

Mitchell, R. K., Agle, B. R., & Wood, D. J. (1997). Toward a theory of stakeholder identification and salience: Defining the principle of who and what really counts. *Academy of Management Review*, 22(4), 853–886. DOI:10.2307/259247

Mobus, J., & Tacoma, T. (2005). Mandatory environmental disclosures in a legitimacy theory context. *Accounting, Auditing & Accountability Journal*, 18(4), 492–517. DOI:10.1108/09513570510609333

Monteiro, A. P. (2022). *Social Accounting: Analysis of the disclosure on labor practices and human rights and its determinants*. Phd in Economics and Business. Universidade de Santiago de Compostela.

Monteiro, A. P., Cepêda, C., Borges, A. P., & Vieira, E. (2024). Does CSR committee presence, stakeholder engagement, gender equality (SDG 5) and firm value influence ESG performance reporting? An EU pre and during Covid-19 analysis. *Measuring Business Excellence*. DOI:10.1108/MBE-03-2024-0034

Monteiro, A. P., García-Sánchez, I. M., & Aibar-Guzmán, B. (2022). Labour practice, decent work and human rights performance and reporting: The impact of women managers. *Journal of Business Ethics*, 180(2), 523–542. DOI:10.1007/s10551-021-04913-1

Monteiro, A. P., Pereira, C., & Barbosa, F. M. (2023). Environmental disclosure on mandatory and voluntary reporting of Portuguese listed firms: the role of environmental certification, lucratively and corporate governance. *Meditari accountancy research, 31*(3), 524-553.

Monteiro, A. P., Pereira, C., & Silva, A. (2021). *Corporate Social Responsailty Reporting*. Ponte Editora.

Monteiro, S. M., & Guzmán, B. A. (2010). The influence of the Portuguese environmental accounting standard on the environmental disclosures in the annual reports of large companies operating in Portugal - A first view (2002-2004). *Management of Environmental Quality*, 21(4), 414–435. DOI:10.1108/14777831011049070

Naciti, V. (2019). Corporate governance and board of directors: The effect of a board composition on firm sustainability performance. *Journal of Cleaner Production*, 237, 117727. DOI:10.1016/j.jclepro.2019.117727

Navarro-Galera, A., Ruiz-Lozano, M., Tirado-Valencia, P., & de los Ríos-Berjillos, A. (2017). Promoting sustainability transparency in European local governments: An empirical analysis based on administrative cultures. *Sustainability (Basel)*, 9(3), 432. DOI:10.3390/su9030432

Orazalin, N., & Baydauletov, M. (2020). Corporate social responsibility strategy and corporate environmental and social performance: The moderating role of board gender diversity. *Corporate Social Responsibility and Environmental Management*, 27(4), 1664–1676. DOI:10.1002/csr.1915

Pastoriza, D., & Ariño, M. A. (2008, June). When agents become stewards: Introducing learning in the stewardship theory. In *1st IESE Conference, Humanizing the Firm & Management Profession*, Barcelona, IESE Business School. DOI:10.2139/ssrn.1295320

Porter, M., & Kramer, M. (2006). *Strategy & Society: The link between Competitive Advantage and Corporate Social Responsibility, Harvard Business Review (HBR), Estados Unidos da América*. Harvard Business Publishing.

Rainey, D. (2006). *Sustainable Business Development: Inventing the Future Through Strategy, Innovation, and Leadership*. Cambridge University Press. DOI:10.1017/CBO9780511617607

Ramos, T. B., Montano, M., De Melo, J. J., Souza, M. P., de Lemos, C. C., Domingues, A. R., & Polido, A. (2015). Strategic Environmental Assessment in higher education: Portuguese and Brazilian cases. *Journal of Cleaner Production*, 106, 222–228. DOI:10.1016/j.jclepro.2014.12.088

Resolution nº 2014/4.327, from 25 April, https://www.bcb.gov.br/pre/normativos/res/2014/pdf/res_4327_v1_O.pdf

Rosa, F. S., Guesser, T., Hein, N., Pfitscher, E. D., & Lunkes, R. J. (2015). Environmental impact management of Brazilian companies: Analyzing factors that influence disclosure of waste, emissions, effluents, and other impacts. *Journal of Cleaner Production*, 96, 148–160. DOI:10.1016/j.jclepro.2013.10.035

Savitz, A. W., & Weber, K. (2007). The sustainability sweet spot. *Environmental Quality Management*, 17(2), 17–28. DOI:10.1002/tqem.20161

Shahab, Y., Ntim, C. G., Chen, Y., Ullah, F., Li, H. X., & Ye, Z. (2020). Chief executive officer attributes, sustainable performance, environmental performance, and environmental reporting: New insights from upper echelons perspective. *Business Strategy and the Environment*, 29(1), 1–16. DOI:10.1002/bse.2345

Skouloudis, A., Evangelinos, K., & Kourmousis, F. (2010). Assessing non-financial reports according to the Global Reporting Initiative guidelines: Evidence from Greece. *Journal of Cleaner Production*, 18(5), 426–438. DOI:10.1016/j.jclepro.2009.11.015

Slack, R., & Shrives, P. (2008). Social disclosure and legitimacy in Premier League football clubs: The first ten years. *Journal of Applied Accounting Research*, 9(1), 17–28. DOI:10.1108/09675420810886105

Steurer, R., Martinuzzi, A., & Margula, S. (2018). Public policies on CSR in Europe: Themes, instruments, and regional differences. *Corporate Social Responsibility and Environmental Management*, 19(4), 206–227. DOI:10.1002/csr.264

Stuart, S. (2017), Brasil Board Index 2017, available at: https://www.spencerstuart.com/-/media/pdf%20files/research%20and%20insight%20pdfs/bi-brazil-2017.pdf

Tang, P., Wang, C., Jiang, Q., Liu, X., & Wang, J. (2023). Symbol or substance? Environmental regulations and corporate environmental actions decoupling. *Journal of Environmental Management*, 346, 118950. DOI:10.1016/j.jenvman.2023.118950 PMID:37696070

Tilling, M. (2004). *Refinements to legitimacy theory in social and environmental accounting*. Flinders University.

Tiron-Tudor, A., Hurghis, R., Lacurezeanu, R., & Podoaba, L. (2020). The Level of European Companies' Integrated Reports Alignment to the< IR> Framework: The Role of Boards' Characteristics. *Sustainability (Basel)*, 12(21), 8777. DOI:10.3390/su12218777

Unerman, J. (2000). Methodological issues – reflections on quantification in corporate social reporting content analysis. *Accounting, Auditing & Accountability Journal*, 13(5), 667–681. DOI:10.1108/09513570010353756

Uyar, A., Kuzey, C., Kilic, M., & Karaman, A. S. (2021). Board structure, financial performance, corporate social responsibility performance, CSR committee, and CEO duality: Disentangling the connection in healthcare. *Corporate Social Responsibility and Environmental Management*, 28(6), 1730–1748. DOI:10.1002/csr.2141

Van Puyvelde, S., Caers, R., Du Bois, C., & Jegers, M. (2013). Agency problems between managers and employees in nonprofit organizations: A discrete choice experiment. *Nonprofit Management & Leadership*, 24(1), 63–85. DOI:10.1002/nml.21081

Vaz, N., Fernandez-Feijoo, B., & Ruiz, S. (2016). Integrated reporting: An international overview. *Business Ethics (Oxford, England)*, 25(4), 577–591. DOI:10.1111/beer.12125

Velte, P. (2020). Does CEO power moderate the link between ESG performance and financial performance? A focus on the German two-tier system. *Management Research Review*, 43(5), 497–520. DOI:10.1108/MRR-04-2019-0182

Williams, B. (2015). Reporting on sustainability by Australian Councils - A Communication Perspective. *Asian Review of Accounting*, 23(2), 186–203. DOI:10.1108/ARA-12-2013-0079

Yasser, Q. R., Al Mamun, A., & Ahmed, I. (2017). Corporate social responsibility and gender diversity: Insights from Asia Pacific. *Corporate Social Responsibility and Environmental Management*, 24(3), 210–221. DOI:10.1002/csr.1400

Zeng, S. X., Xu, X. D., Dong, Z. Y., & Tam, V. W. (2010). Towards corporate environmental information disclosure: An empirical study in China. *Journal of Cleaner Production*, 18(12), 1142–1148. DOI:10.1016/j.jclepro.2010.04.005

Zhou, D., Saeed, U. F., & Agyemang, A. O. (2024). Assessing the Role of Sustainability Disclosure on Firms' Financial Performance: Evidence from the Energy Sector of Belt and Road Initiative Countries. *Sustainability (Basel)*, 16(2), 930. DOI:10.3390/su16020930

Chapter 5
Key Audit Matters: An Analysis of the Disclosed Categories in the Water and Sanitation Sector

Natália Lemos
https://orcid.org/0000-0003-2382-0645
Research Centre on Accounting and Taxation, Polytechnic University of Cávado and Ave, Portugal

Sara Serra
https://orcid.org/0000-0003-3107-1752
Research Centre on Accounting and Taxation, Polytechnic University of Cávado and Ave, Portugal

Lurdes R. Silva
Research Centre on Accounting and Taxation, Polytechnic University of Cávado and Ave, Portugal

Patrícia Quesado
Research Centre on Accounting and Taxation, Polytechnic University of Cávado and Ave, Portugal

Kátia Lemos
https://orcid.org/0000-0002-3961-5964
Research Centre on Accounting and Taxation, Polytechnic University of Cávado and Ave, Portugal

ABSTRACT

This study focuses on the companies of the Águas de Portugal Group, which operate in the water and sanitation sector, and aims to perform a content analysis of the

DOI: 10.4018/979-8-3693-5663-0.ch005

auditor's reports and, specifically, of the key audit matters (KAM) disclosed from 2017 to 2021. Although it is not mandatory to disclose KAM, 57% of companies disclosed KAM in the period under review. Content analysis shows a high similarity in the number and content of KAM disclosed by companies in the period in which the same firm audits them. The categories of KAM disclosed are investment - recognition and measurement; impairment of investments; impairment of debts; revenue - recognition of downward activity; revenue - expense recovery deviations; and process of split. Audit responses to disclosed KAM mainly included inspections, followed by analytical procedures and inquiries, with reperformance being the least common procedure.

INTRODUCTION

Access to water, the most precious of resources, as well as sanitation, are human rights enshrined by the United Nations, with the Sustainable Development Goal (SDG) 6 - Clean Water and Sanitation – assuming a transversal importance in the framework of the SDGs of the 2030 Agenda (BCSD Portugal, 2024). Given the essential role of water for human life, managing water supply and sanitation services is a core mission performed in the Portuguese context by the Águas de Portugal Group. The Águas de Portugal Group is a business group of exclusively public capital that acts as a business instrument of the state for the pursuit of public policies in water supply and wastewater sanitation (Águas de Portugal, 2024).

The Águas de Portugal Group ensures public services essential to public health and the preservation of the environment, and its role is relevant to the local economy, regional cohesion, and sustainable development. The Group's governance model is guided by the highest ethical standards, transparency, responsibility, and excellence in public management practices and is a governance model endorsed by all Group companies. Águas de Portugal, SGPS, S.A. is the Group's holding company that, through regional-based companies, enhances value creation for all stakeholders and progressively contributes to achieving the SDG (Águas de Portugal, 2024).

Law 12/2008 of 26th February, which consists of the first amendment to Law 23/96 of 26th July, establishes the collection and treatment services of wastewater (point f of art.º 1, n.º 2) and municipal solid waste management services (point g of art.º 1, n.º 2) and as essential public services. Águas de Portugal, SGPS is the largest and most influential group in the Portuguese water and sanitation sector since it covers a vast geographical area and serves millions of people, representing a significant sample of the sector (Águas de Portugal, 2024), which is critical for public health and environmental sustainability. In sum, the selection of the Águas de Portugal group is justified by their pivotal role in providing essential public services, the complexity of the audit environment in the water and sanitation sector, and the broader implications for stakeholders and industry best practices. This study focuses on the holding of the Group and on the thirteen companies whose mission is related to water supply, sanitation, and reuse (Conselho das Finanças Públicas, 2024). According to Yalcin (2022), auditor report content analysis is needed to contribute to research on audit quality. In this sense, this investigation aims to perform a content analysis of the auditor's reports and, specifically, an analysis of KAM disclosed in the auditor's reports from 2017 to 2021. The content analysis' purpose is to identify the extent of boilerplate language given its impact on the informational value of KAM disclosures, being the primary focus is on the 'most significant material distortion risks identified' and the 'audit approach synthesis' sub-sections of the KAM disclosure section of the auditor report.

The Group's holding and the thirteen companies made available the accountability documents and, specifically, the auditor's reports on their websites, facilitating the quick data collection of the auditor's reports for the fourteen companies from 2017 to 2021. This content analysis was crucial in determining which companies disclose KAM, as it is not mandatory for companies in the water and sanitation sector. However, Law 58/2005 of 29th December – also known as Water Law – still establishes the regulatory framework for companies like Águas de Portugal, SGPS to ensure that they uphold high standards of transparency and accountability in their financial reporting practices even if specific disclosures like KAM are not mandatory. Additionally, the identification of the audit firms that audit the companies under analysis was a key step, especially for the subsequent discovery of high levels of similarity in both the number and content of the KAM disclosed when comparing company auditor reports in the period in which the same audit firm audits them.

The identification of the disclosed KAM categories, as well as the detailed content analysis of the 'most significant material distortion risks identified' and the 'audit approach synthesis' - two sub-sections present in the KAM disclosure section - allowed a better understanding of the matters that require special attention from the auditor in the water and sanitation sector. Even though companies in this sector voluntarily disclose KAM, disclosure should still aim to improve the value of the auditor's report by providing relevant and specific information. A common criticism of the traditional auditor's report was that it provided little entity-specific information because its form was standardized, with a dichotomous opinion using boilerplate language. To enhance the value of the auditor report and improve audit quality, the International Auditing and Assurance Standards Board (IAASB) argued that KAM should differ from entity to entity and encouraged auditors to be as entity-specific and audit-specific as possible in the description of a KAM. However, in the specific context of the water and sanitation sector, we found that this objective outlined by

IAASB is not fully achieved, given that the disclosure of KAM exhibits high levels of similarity when comparing the KAM disclosures in the different auditor's reports.

The remainder of the investigation is structured as follows. In the next section, we present the background in terms of KAM literature. Then, the methodology is introduced, namely, the data collection process. Subsequently, the results and discussion of these are addressed. Finally, we present the conclusions of this study.

BACKGROUND

Auditor reports have a long history of debate among the scientific community regarding their usefulness to users of financial statements (Church et al., 2008; Manoel & Quel, 2017) since users do not perceive such reports to have information value. There has been a significant audit' expectation gap' between what financial statement users expect an audit to deliver and what the audit profession believes it provides (Hegazy & Kamareldawla, 2021; Iwanowicz & Iwanowicz, 2019). This became especially true after the financial failures where auditors were held accountable for such failures (Iwanowicz &Iwanowicz, 2019; Mock et al., 2013).

Vanstraelen et al. (2012) suggested that the usefulness of the auditor report would depend on the inclusion of relevant information presented to users. Users expect to receive information to help them better understand the financial statements (Yalcin, 2022), while auditors, on the other hand, tend to minimize the risk of litigation by providing the minimum level of information required by the auditing standards (Hegazy & Kamareldawla, 2021).

Given the criticism of the standardized auditor report, the IAASB took initiatives regarding the additional reporting requirements that would help reduce the audit expectation gap created by the traditional reporting framework (Iwanowicz & Iwanowicz, 2019). These initiatives also intended to reduce the information gap, that is, the gap between the information users' desire and the information available through the audited financial statements, other corporate disclosures, and the auditor's report (Bedard et al., 2016; Manoel & Quel, 2017).

The IAASB revised some of its traditional audit reporting standards, providing additional disclosure to improve the value of communication and decision-usefulness of the audit reports. The introduction of the new audit report standard, ISA 701 - Communicating Key Audit Matters in the Independent Auditor's Report, which became effective on December 15, 2016, was a consequence of the IAASB revision of the audit standards. It relates to the communication of KAM, which should significantly improve audit report decisions (Hegazy & Kamareldawla, 2021; Iwanowicz & Iwanowicz, 2019).

The revision of ISA 700 - Forming an Opinion and Reporting on Financial Statements, the standard that addresses the auditor's responsibility to form an opinion on the financial statements and the form and content of the auditor's report issued, according to paragraphs 1 and 4 of ISA 700, was precisely due to the need to increase the value of the report making the information provided in the report more relevant to stakeholders (Bedard et al., 2016).

This enhancement was a direct result of the auditor's efforts to make the information provided in the report more relevant to stakeholders (Vanstraelen et al., 2012), with the introduction of the concept of KAM, enshrined in paragraphs 30 and 31 of ISA 700, that establish that auditors must report KAM in their report following ISA 701.

The communication of KAM is mandatory for listed entities and, additionally, when required by law or regulation as is the case for public interest entities. Further informs ISA 700 (Revised) that when the auditor decides to report KAM in their report (even if they are not obliged to do so and decide to do so voluntarily), they must follow ISA 701 (Manoel & Quel, 2017). This is the case of the audit firms of some of the companies of Águas de Portugal Group, that disclose KAM even though it is not mandatory under art. 3º of Law 148/2015, of 9th September. This decision follows Águas de Portugal Group mission to consistently balance technical, economic, and financial rigor with environmental sustainability to meet stakeholders' expectations (Águas de Portugal, 2024).

ISA 701 addresses the auditor's responsibility to communicate KAM in their report, further specifying the form and content of the communication. Paragraph 8 of ISA 701 defines KAM as "those matters that, in the auditor's professional judgment, were of most significance in the audit of the financial statements of the current period [with these being] selected from matters communicated with those charged with governance" (p. 3).

According to paragraph 9 of ISA 701, the auditor shall consider the "(a) areas of higher assessed risk of material misstatement, or significant risks identified per ISA 315 (Revised) - Identifying and Assessing the Risks of Material Misstatement; [as well as] (b) significant auditor judgments relating to areas in the financial statements that involved significant management judgment, including accounting estimates that have been identified as having high estimation uncertainty; [and] (c) the effect on the audit of significant events or transactions that occurred during the period" (p. 3) to determine the matters which require particular attention in the execution of the audit (Hegazy & Kamareldawla, 2021; Yalcin, 2022).

According to ISA 701, the decision-making process for determining KAM is designed to select a smaller number of matters from the communications with those charged with governance based on the auditor's judgment about which matters were of most significance. Determining which and how many of those matters that required significant auditor attention were of most significance in the current period's audit is a matter of professional judgment (Iwanowicz & Iwanowicz, 2019).

The number of KAM to be included in the auditor's report may be affected by the size and complexity of the entity, the nature of its business and environment, and the facts and circumstances of the audit engagement (Lennox et al., 2023). In general, the greater the number of matters initially determined to be KAM, the more the auditor may need to reconsider whether each matter meets the definition of a KAM. Lengthy lists of KAM may be contrary to the notion that such matters are most significant in the audit.

The standard also describes how each KAM should be presented in the respective section of the auditor's report (Iwanowicz & Iwanowicz, 2019; Lennox et al., 2023). According to Gambetta et al. (2023), in addition to including a reference for related disclosures, if any, in the financial statements, the auditor shall also indicate, following paragraph 13 of ISA 701: "(a) why the matter was considered to be one of most significance in the audit and therefore determined to be a key audit matter; and (b) how the matter was addressed in the audit" (p. 4).

Gambetta et al. (2023) establishes that audit firms use different techniques to describe in the audit report the matters of most significance identified as KAM and the procedures performed to address them. In some cases, the auditor uses a single column, starting with the KAM title, followed by the content description, then an explanation of how the matter is addressed in the audit, and finally a brief conclusion. Other auditors use a two-column format, using the first column to describe the KAM and the second to describe the procedures used to address them. In some cases, the auditor uses graphs or tables to summarize the KAM and to show how they have evolved over time. Irrespective of the layout used, it is clear that to comply with ISA 701, the auditor must describe the KAM and the procedures used to address them. Regarding the audit procedures employed to address the disclosed KAM, ISA 500 - Audit Evidence - lists the following procedures: inspection, observation, confirmation, recalculation, reperformance, analytical procedures, and inquiry.

While determining KAM is a matter of professional judgment (Iwanowicz & Iwanowicz, 2019), prior research has considered different predictors of the number and type of KAM reported (Duboisée de Ricquebourg & Maroun, 2023). These can be categorized broadly as either entity or audit-specific.

Starting with entity features, the complexity of business models and operations goes hand-in-hand with the auditor's assessment of the KAM at both the overall and assertion levels since, for example, the use of more precise or rules-based accounting requirements may lower the use of professional judgment among preparers and contribute to a reduction in the number of KAM (Pinto et al., 2020). Turning to the content of financial statements, Sierra-García et al. (2019) finds that higher revenue, inventory, goodwill, and intangible asset balances are associated with more KAM.

The type of industry is also found to influence the number of KAM by Pinto et al. (2020) and Sierra-García et al. (2019). For the latter, results are sensitive to classifying KAM as either entity- or account-level issues. The empirical results are mixed, but there is, at least, some evidence to support the general position that entity features contribute to the complexity of engagements and the associated KAM determination.

Regarding the audit-specific features, Sierra-García et al. (2019) find that neither audit nor non-audit fees are associated with the total number of KAM reported. Still, audit fees are inversely related to the number of account-level KAM. The opposite is true for entity-level KAM. Pinto et al. (2020) confirm that audit fees are not driving KAM determination, while Abdelfattah et al. (2021) report a positive association between audit fees and the number of KAM. According to Abdullatif & Al Rahahleh's (2020), Big 4 audit firms often disclose more KAM than non-Big 4 audit firms. These outcomes are anticipated since the major four audit companies are thought to employ highly skilled personnel who are more financially stable, have greater access to information technology, and adhere to KAM disclosure laws (Velte, 2019).

Focusing on specific firms, Deloitte, EY and KPMG report fewer entity and account-level KAM than PwC. This may be the result of PwC's clients being more complex and regulated than those audited by other professional firms (Sierra-García et al., 2019). Rousseau and Zehms (2020) test the relative importance of the unobservable audit partner and audit firm decision styles. Controlling for audit partner fixed effects led to a significant increase in the explanatory power of a KAM determinants model compared to the model with audit firm fixed effects, suggesting that the decision-making styles of audit partners were 'the primary force behind KAM reporting outcomes.

The Financial Reporting Council expects auditor report disclosures to be entity-specific and audit-specific (Financial Reporting Council, 2015). However, the auditing standards do not require the auditor to modify substantial year-to-year auditor reports. Nonetheless, the regulator has expressed concerns about the lack of changes in auditor reports over time, especially concerning disclosed KAM from one year to the next, since the new audit report objectives are unlikely to be achieved if the auditor's choice of disclosures is unchanged mainly across years (Zhang & Shailer, 2021). While some degree of year-to-year changes is evident (Lennox et al., 2023), auditors' reports generally need more explanation for changing or retaining KAM.

Gambetta et al. (2023) identified the audit firm and the type of KAM as determinants of KAM description and KAM audit procedures' informative value and showed that the audit firm impacts in different ways the quality of the additional information provided to stakeholders via KAM disclosure. Their findings indicate that the audit firm specifically influences the informative value of the descriptions made, both of the KAM and of the audit procedures used to describe them. Additionally, they uncovered that the informative value of the KAM audit procedures description depends on whether the type of KAM disclosed is related to entity-level or accounting-level risk.

Lin (2023) warns that if KAM disclosures are homogenized, namely following the same pattern or a mere formality, and are not corrected and guided in time, then the strength and effectiveness of the KAM disclosure will undoubtedly be significantly reduced, which will also deviate from the original intention of the audit report reform. Therefore, whether KAM disclosures enhance the personalization, readability and practicality of audit reports, improve the information communication and decision support value of audit reports, and promote the improvement of audit quality are some of the key issues in current audit research.

Within this context, our research stands out with its unique approach. We aim to conduct a comprehensive content analysis of the auditor's reports, focusing specifically on the KAM disclosed in the reports from 2017 to 2021. The novelty of our study lies in the in-depth analysis of the KAM content, and the audit procedures adopted by reading the auditor reports longitudinally. We seek to determine whether the KAM disclosures are merely a formality to meet normative requirements or if they truly reflect the unique realities of each company.

METHODOLOGY

This research focuses on the holding of the Águas de Portugal Group and the thirteen companies (presented in Table 1) whose mission is related to water supply, sanitation, and reuse, given that Law 12/2008 of 26th February established their services as essential public services. However, the disclosure of KAM is not mandatory and is under art. 3º of Law 148/2015, of 9th September, for the companies of Águas de Portugal Group, some of them still disclose KAM on their auditor reports.

Table 1. Águas de Portugal Group and subsidiaries

Águas de Portugal Group and subsidiaries	
AdP, SGPS	**AdP - Águas de Portugal, SGPS, S.A.**
AdNorte, S.A.	AdNorte - Águas do Norte, S.A.
AdAM, S.A.	AdAM - Águas do Alto Minho, S.A.
AdDP, S.A.	AdDP - Águas do Douro e Paiva, S.A.
SIMDOURO, S.A.	SIMDOURO, S.A.
AdRA, S.A.	AdRA - Águas da Região de Aveiro, S.A.

continued on following page

Table 1. Continued

Águas de Portugal Group and subsidiaries	
AdP, SGPS	**AdP - Águas de Portugal, SGPS, S.A.**
AdCL, S.A.	AdCL - Águas do Centro Litoral, S.A.
EPAL, S.A.	EPAL, S.A.
AdVT, S.A.	AdVT - Águas do Vale do Tejo, S.A.
AdTA, S.A.	AdTA - Águas do Tejo Atlântico, S.A.
SIMARSUL, S.A.	SIMARSUL, S.A.
AgdA, S.A.	AgdA - Águas Públicas do Alentejo, S.A.
AdSA, S.A.	AdSA - Águas de Santo André, S.A.
AdA, S.A.	AdA - Águas do Algarve, S.A.

ISA 700 (Revised) states that auditors who decide to report KAM in their report (even if they are not obliged to do so and decide to do so voluntarily) must follow ISA 701. This research aims to perform a content analysis of the auditor's reports and, specifically, an analysis of Key Audit Matters (KAM) disclosed in the auditor's reports from 2017 to 2021.

The content analysis will allow us to identify which companies disclose KAM and which audit firms audit the companies under analysis. However, the focus of the content analysis will be on the 'most significant material distortion risks identified' and the 'audit approach synthesis' sub-sections of the KAM disclosure section of the auditor report. Since the novelty draws precisely from the longitudinal analysis of these sub-sections to verify if there is a similarity in writing as a way only to meet the normative requirements, or if they are consistent with the reality of each company.

According to paragraph 13 of ISA 701 of the KAM disclosure section, this detailed analysis will allow a better understanding of the matters that require special attention from the water and sanitation sector auditor and will provide insights about the mandatory elements.

The data collection was carried out efficiently in October 2023 since the Group's holding and the thirteen companies made available the accountability documents and, specifically, the auditor's reports on their websites. The data collection process entailed accessing these websites and search, within the website structure, for the accountability documents, being these subsequently downloaded to conduct the content analysis. The researchers had no influence over the unavailability of the auditor's report for certain companies, which led to a smaller sample size. This is the main difficulty with the data collection process. Table 2 presents the data collection summary, demonstrating instances in which we did not obtain the auditor's report as it was unavailable online at the date of data collection (identified as w/o Auditor Report), as well as indicating, in advance, the auditor reports that have (indicated as w/KAM) or not (indicated as w/o KAM) a KAM disclosure section. Comprehensively, the auditor reports that don't have a KAM disclosure section (identified as w/o KAM) will not be used in the KAM content analysis, so companies that don't have a KAM disclosure section throughout the period under analysis are excluded. We can thus determine that sixty-five auditor reports were the final sample of the content analysis initiated in the scope of this investigation, of which thirty-four reports (52% of the initial sample) have a section dedicated to the dissemination of KAM.

Table 2. Auditor Reports and KAM sections of Águas de Portugal companies

Company\ Year	**2017**	**2018**	**2019**	**2020**	**2021**
AdP, SGPS	w/o Auditor Report	w/ KAM	w/ KAM	w/ KAM	w/ KAM
AdNorte	w/ KAM	w/ KAM	w/ KAM	w/ KAM	w/ KAM
AdAM	w/o Auditor Report	w/o Auditor Report	w/o KAM	w/o KAM	w/o KAM
AdDP	w/o KAM	w/o KAM	w/o KAM	w/o KAM	w/o KAM
SIMDOURO	w/o KAM	w/o KAM	w/o KAM	w/o KAM	w/o KAM
AdRA	w/o KAM	w/o KAM	w/ KAM	w/ KAM	w/ KAM
AdCL	w/ KAM	w/ KAM	w/ KAM	w/ KAM	w/ KAM
EPAL	w/ KAM	w/ KAM	w/ KAM	w/ KAM	w/ KAM
AdVT	w/ KAM	w/ KAM	w/ KAM	w/ KAM	w/ KAM
AdTA	w/o KAM	w/o KAM	w/ KAM	w/ KAM	w/ KAM
SIMARSUL	w/o KAM	w/o KAM	w/o KAM	w/o KAM	w/o KAM
AgdA	w/o Auditor Report	w/o KAM	w/o KAM	w/o KAM	w/o KAM
AdSA	w/o KAM	w/o KAM	w/o KAM	w/o Auditor Report	w/o KAM
AdA	w/ KAM	w/ KAM	w/ KAM	w/ KAM	w/o Auditor Report
Total Stats	**2017**	**2018**	**2019**	**2020**	**2021**
w/o Auditor Report	21%	7%	0%	7%	7%
w/o KAM	43%	50%	43%	36%	43%
w/KAM	36%	43%	57%	57%	50%

Note: **w/o Auditor Report = Auditor's Report not available online at the time of data collection; w/o KAM = Auditor's Report does not have a KAM section; w/ KAM = Auditor's Report has a KAM section.**

The data analysis encompassed a general overview of the auditor reports specifying which audit firms developed these documents as well as the number of KAM reported. The content analysis was performed manually without any textual analysis tools (Chang et al., 2024) or eye-tracking approaches (Sirois et al., 2018). This approach was only possible given the small sample size that did not justify a heavy expense in tools such as NVivo, Leximancer, or similar. The process of analyzing the content in detail begins with identifying the KAMs presented in the audit reports. The next step involves reading the descriptions of each KAM to gain a deeper understanding of the issues disclosed. We identified similar issues, previously categorized under various subheadings, and consolidated them into six "final" KAM categories. Considering the defined objectives, the data was processed using descriptive analyses of the results. An in-depth analysis is made of the disclosures presented in the audit reports, identifying the most disclosed KAM, highlighting the most significant material distortion risks identified in the audit reports and the audit approach to these matters. By employing this detailed content analysis methodology, the study ensures a robust and thorough examination of KAM disclosures in the Águas de Portugal Group's audit reports.

RESULTS AND DISCUSSION

Since the companies of Águas de Portugal Group are not required to disclose KAM, under art. 3º of Law 148/2015, of 9th September, so the first step is precisely to determine which companies voluntarily reported KAM in an appropriate KAM section. Based on Table 2, we can identify that fifty-seven percent of companies disclose KAM in the period under review. Águas de Portugal, SGPS, S.A. (hereinafter AdP, SGPS), Águas do Norte, S.A. (hereinafter AdNorte), Águas do Centro Litoral, S.A. (hereinafter AdCL), Empresa Portuguesa das Águas Livres, S.A. (hereinafter EPAL), Águas do Vale do Tejo, S.A. (hereinafter AdVT), and Águas do Algarve, S.A. (hereinafter AdA) are six companies that disclose KAM in an appropriate KAM section during all the years under review (except when the auditor's report is unavailable in specific years, as in the case of AdP, SGPS and AdA).

In addition, we can also verify that, as a percentage, the years with more auditor reports with KAM section were 2019 and 2020 (both with 57%), 2017 being the year with less auditor reports with the KAM section, and this percentage is also due to the high percentage of unavailable reports.

The other two companies - Águas da Região de Aveiro, S.A. (hereinafter AdRA) and Águas do Tejo Atlântico, S.A. (hereinafter AdTA) - only disclosed KAM from 2019 to 2021, when the audit firm responsible for its auditor's report became PricewaterhouseCoopers & Associates, SROC. The definition of this relationship is made possible by the joint analysis of Table 2 and Table 3, which presents the audit firms responsible for the auditor's reports.

Table 3. Audit Firms of Águas de Portugal companies

<table>
<tr><th></th><th>2017</th><th>2018</th><th>2019</th><th>2020</th><th>2021</th></tr>
<tr><td>**AdP, SGPS**</td><td>w/o Auditor Report</td><td colspan="4">Non-Big4 Grant</td></tr>
<tr><td>**AdNorte**</td><td>Non-Big4 Esteves</td><td>Big 4 EY</td><td colspan="3">Big 4 PwC</td></tr>
<tr><td>**AdRA**</td><td colspan="2">Big 4 EY</td><td colspan="3">Big 4 PwC</td></tr>
<tr><td>**AdCL**</td><td>Non-Big4 Esteves</td><td>Big 4 EY</td><td colspan="3">Big 4 PwC</td></tr>
<tr><td>**EPAL**</td><td colspan="2">Big 4 EY</td><td colspan="3">Big 4 PwC</td></tr>
<tr><td>**AdVT**</td><td>Non-Big4 Esteves</td><td>Big 4 EY</td><td colspan="3">Big 4 PwC</td></tr>
<tr><td>**AdTA**</td><td colspan="2">Big 4 EY</td><td colspan="3">Big 4 PwC</td></tr>
<tr><td>**AdA**</td><td>Non-Big4 Esteves</td><td>Big 4 EY</td><td colspan="2">Big 4 PwC</td><td>w/o Auditor Report</td></tr>
</table>

Note: **w/o Auditor Report = Auditor's Report not available online at the time of data collection; Big 4 EY = Ernst & Young Audit & Associates - SROC; Big 4 PwC = PricewaterhouseCoopers & Associates, SROC; Non-Big4 Grant = Grant Thornton & Associates, SROC; Non.Big4 Esteves = Esteves, Pinho & Associates, SROC.**

Based on Table 3, we can identify, regarding audit firms, that four audit firms audit companies in the water and sanitation sector. Of these audit firms, two are Big 4 audit firms - Ernst & Young Audit & Associates, SROC, and PricewaterhouseCoopers & Associates, SROC - and two are non-Big 4 audit firms - Grant Thornton & Associates, SROC, and Esteves, Pinho & Associates, SROC.

Grant Thornton & Associates was solely responsible for the auditor's report of the Group's holding during the period under review (except 2017, for which we have no information considering the unavailability of the auditor's report). In turn, PricewaterhouseCoopers & Associates was responsible for all auditor reports from 2019 to 2021 for the thirteen other companies (except for two instances where we could not assess the audit firm due to the unavailability of the auditor's report).

For 2017 and 2018, Ernst & Young Audit & Associates audited the thirteen companies. The exception to this conclusion, in 2018, is AdAM due again to the unavailability of the auditor's report. As for 2017, AdAM and AgdA do not have auditor reports available, so we cannot infer anything about the audit firm. Additionally, in 2017, Esteves, Pinho & Associates was responsible for the reports of four companies, namely AdNorte, AdCL, AdVT and AdA, and Ernst & Young Audit & Associates was responsible only for the reports of the remaining companies.

Since previous studies (e.g. Abdullatif & Al Rahahleh's, 2020) uncover that Big 4 audit firms often disclose more KAM than non-Big 4 audit firms and that, regarding specific Big 4 audit firms, EY discloses fewer KAM than PwC (Sierra-García et al., 2019), we present in Table 4 the number of KAM disclosed.

Table 4. Number of KAM of Águas de Portugal companies

	2017	2018	2019	2020	2021
AdP, SGPS	w/o Auditor Report	1	1	1	1
AdNorte	3	3	4	4	4
AdRA	w/o KAM	w/o KAM	3	3	3
AdCL	2	3	3	3	3
EPAL	2	2	1	1	1
AdVT	3	3	3	3	3
AdTA	w/o KAM	w/o KAM	2	2	2
AdA	2	2	3	3	w/o Auditor Report

Note: **w/o Auditor Report = Auditor's Report not available online at the time of data collection; w/o KAM = Auditor's Report does not have a KAM section.**

Table 4 provides a comprehensive overview of the range of KAM disclosed. This range spans from a single disclosed KAM, as in the case of the holding audited by Grant & Thornton & Associates, to four KAM disclosed, as in the case of AdNorte in the period from 2019 to 2021, audited by PricewaterhouseCoopers & Associates.

Analyzing the number of KAM reported in 2017 by Esteves, Pinho & Associates, SROC for AdNorte, AdCL, AdVT, and AdA and comparing to the number of KAM reported in 2018 by Ernst & Young Audit & Associates for the same companies allowed to identify that the number of KAM reported remained the same for AdNorte and AdVT (3 KAM reported in both years for both companies) as well as for AdA (2 KAM reported in both years). Only AdCL verified an increase from 2 to 3 KAM reported when changing from Esteves, Pinho & Associates, SROC to Ernst & Young Audit & Associates aligning to results of Abdullatif & Al Rahahleh's, 2020) that Big 4 audit firms disclose more KAM than non-Big 4 audit firms. Regarding the comparison made between EY and PwC, AdCL and AdVT had both 3 KAM reported in 2018 (when audited by Ernst & Young Audit & Associates) and in 2019 (when audited by PricewaterhouseCoopers & Associates, SROC), while AdNorte and AdA registered an increase from 3 to 4 or from 2 to 3 KAM reported, respectively. However, EPAL verified a decrease from 2 to 1 KAM reported when comparing 2018 (when audited by Ernst & Young Audit & Associates) and 2019 (when audited by PricewaterhouseCoopers & Associates, SROC). Therefore, the results from Sierra-García et al. (2019) that EY discloses fewer KAM than PwC does not fully align with the water and sanitation sector reality.

As previously stated, the decision-making process in determining KAM, according to ISA 701, is designed to select a smaller number of matters from the matters communicated with those charged with governance based on the auditor's judgment. The standard also establishes the possibility of determining that there are no KAM to communicate, with paragraph 16 of ISA 701 stating that "if the auditor determines, depending on the facts and circumstances of the entity and the audit, that there are no key audit matters to communicate [...], the auditor shall include a statement to this effect in a separate section of the auditor's report under the heading "Key Audit Matters" (p. 4). Thus, we make it clear that the absence of a KAM section stems from the companies' decision not to disclose KAM since disclosure is voluntary, not the determination that there is no KAM to disclose.

As mentioned earlier, the primary focus of the content analysis is on the 'most significant material distortion risks identified' and the 'audit approach synthesis' sub-sections of the KAM disclosure section of the auditor report. The next section will delve into a detailed analysis, providing a deeper understanding of the matters that demand special attention from the auditor in the water and sanitation sector. It will also shed light on the mandatory elements, as outlined in paragraph 13 of ISA 701, of the KAM.

The content analysis is based on the sub-sections of the KAM disclosure in the auditor's report, which derive from the standard guidance established in paragraph 13 of ISA 701 of how each KAM should be presented. The standard refers that, in addition to including a reference for related disclosures in the financial statements, the auditor shall also indicate: "(a) why the matter was considered to be one of most significance in the audit and therefore determined to be a key audit matter; and (b) how the matter was addressed in the audit" (p. 4).

Focusing primarily on KAM, the first part of the content analysis is dedicated to identifying the KAM categories disclosed and subsequent analysis of the 'most significant material distortion risks identified', the name given to the sub-section where it presents precisely why the matter was considered to be one of the most significant in the audit and, therefore, determined to be a KAM.

In addition to paragraph 13, paragraph 11 of ISA 701 also states that the auditor shall describe each KAM, using an appropriate sub-heading, in a separate section of the auditor's report under the heading 'Key Audit Matters'. The first step of the detailed content analysis begins with the identification of the following sub-headings. The second step consisted of reading the description of each KAM, which enabled a deeper understanding of the disclosed KAM. We uncover the same matters, previously sorted into KAM with distinct sub-heading nomenclatures, and grouped various sub-headings with similar matters into six 'final' KAM categories: (1) Investment - recognition, and measurement; (2) Impairment of Investments; (3) Impairment of Debts; (4) Revenue - recognition of downward activity; (5) Revenue - expense recovery deviations; (6) Process of Split. Table 5 shows the KAM categories disclosed and which companies disclosed these categories.

Table 5. KAM Categories of Águas de Portugal companies

Category \ Company	AdP	AdNorte	AdRA	AdCL	EPAL	AdVT	AdTA	AdA
Investment - recognition, and measurement		5x	3x	5x		5x	3x	4x
Impairment of Investments	4x							
Impairment of Debts		5x		5x	2x	5x		4x
Revenue - recognition of downward activity		3x	3x		5x			
Revenue - expense recovery deviations		4x	3x	4x		4x	3x	2x
Process of split		1x				1x		

Note: **w/o Auditor Report = Auditor's Report not available online at the time of data collection; w/o KAM = Auditor's Report does not have a KAM section.**

It can be concluded that the categories that appear most frequently are those related to Investment - recognition, and measurement Impairment of debts and Revenue - expense recovery deviations.

The following sub-section is devoted precisely to the content analysis of the 'most significant material distortion risks identified', where the reason why the matters were determined as KAM is presented. This sub-section will be better understood by the following sub-section dedicated to the 'audit approach synthesis', where it will be presented how these matters were dealt with in the audit, identifying the audit procedures adopted for each category of KAM.

KAM Content Analysis: Most Significant Material Distortion Risks Identified

In the light of ISA 701, the significance of a matter can be described as its relative importance considering the context. Moving on to the description of each KAM, according to ISA 701, the adequacy of the description of a KAM is a matter of professional judgment. The description of a KAM is intended to provide a brief and balanced explanation to enable intended users to understand why the matter was one of the most significant in the audit and how the matter was addressed in the audit. Limiting the use of highly technical auditing terms also helps intended users who need a reasonable knowledge of auditing to understand the basis for the auditor's focus on particular matters during the audit.

ISA 701 states that the description of KAM is not a mere reiteration of what is disclosed in the financial statements. Relating a matter directly to the entity's specific circumstances may also help minimize the potential for such descriptions to become overly standardized and less valuable over time. For example, certain matters may be determined as KAM in a particular industry across several entities due to the industry's circumstances or the underlying complexity in financial reporting. In describing the reasons why the auditor considered the matter to be one of the most significant, it may be helpful for the auditor to highlight aspects specific to the entity (e.g., circumstances that affected the underlying judgments made in the financial statements of the current period) to make the description more relevant for intended users. This also may be important when describing a KAM that recurs over periods.

That being said, we present the description of each KAM category identified based on the content analysis of the auditor's report.

(1) Investment - Recognition and Measurement

The first KAM category, *Investment - recognition, and measurement*, relates to infrastructure usage rights tied to concessions, registered as Intangible Assets, and amortized systematically based on economic benefits as approved by regulatory authorities (ERSAR) (for upward activities) and partnership commissions (for downward activities).

Amortizations are calculated using invoiced water and effluent flows for the year and projected flows until the concession ends, as outlined in the Economic and Financial Feasibility Study (EVEF). An estimated expense amount is registered to cover liabilities for contractual or expansion investments, calculated based on the Economic and Financial Feasibility Study. The Economic and Financial Feasibility Study and Tariff Project Budget (OPT) include assumptions about future activity levels and required investments, making this a high-judgment area.

This matter's relevance arises from the materiality of the amounts involved in infrastructure usage rights and contractual investments, affecting financial statements through amortization and increased investment expenses. The materiality and complexity justify its classification as a KAM.

(2) Impairment of Investments

The second KAM category, *Impairment of Investments*, concerns potential impairments in financial investments and is disclosed only in auditor reports of the Group's holding, audited by Non-Big4 Grant Thornton & Associates. This KAM addresses possible impairments in financial investments, measured at cost less impairment losses, and the recognition of provisions for additional liabilities in negative equity holdings.

This matter is relevant because these investments are important to the entity's assets and the complex process of assessing impairment losses. The assessment involves a high degree of judgment and the use of estimates.

Given the complexity and judgment required in impairment assessments, this matter is significant due to its potential impact on the entity's financial condition. The materiality and complexity justify its classification as a KAM.

(3) Impairment of Debts

The third KAM category is *Impairment of Debts*. This KAM deals with the impairment of debts from both municipal clients (from upward activities) and final consumers (from downward activities). The entity evaluates this matter promptly, with payment agreements being made regularly and legal measures taken when necessary. Public entities are generally not subject to impairment losses due to low perceived insolvency risk. In their assessment, the Management Boards consider the adoption of possible measures to ensure the recoverability of balances, such as activating the mechanism associated with credit privilege, executing debt settlement agreements, and filing injunctions/lawsuits.

This matter's relevance is that the non-recovery of outstanding amounts could jeopardize the concession's economic and financial balance, making it critical. The need for accurate judgment in assessing debts impairment and the potential impact on financial stability justify its classification as a KAM.

(4) Revenue - Recognition of Downward Activity

The fourth KAM category, Revenue - recognition of downward activity, relates to recognizing revenue from sales of water and sanitation services (in the context of downward activity). Revenue is recognized at water delivery, including (1) effective consumption sales, (2) estimated consumption based on customer history, and (3) estimated unbilled water supply.

Estimated consumption for invoicing is calculated using Aquamatrix, an algorithm based on average daily consumption and historical profiles tested against actual consumption samples. The valuation of estimated quantities is based on defined tariffs, making this a significant judgment area.

This matter's relevance relates to the complexity of estimating water consumption and associated tariffs. Accurate judgment in recognizing revenue from downward activity is crucial for reflecting the entity's financial performance, which justifies its classification as a KAM.

(5) Revenue - Expense Recovery Deviations

The fifth KAM category, *Revenue - Expense Recovery Deviations*, involves correcting revenue for regulated activities to ensure full expense recovery and guaranteed shareholder remuneration. The estimation of the Expense Recovery Deviations is based on the best available information at the date, namely on the Budget and Tariff Project (OPT). It must be approved by regulatory authorities (for upward activity) or partnership committees (for downward activity).

Estimating the Expense Recovery Deviation is complex and judgment-intensive, involving significant uncertainty about its approval. This matter's relevance stems from the need for accurate judgment in assessing revenue corrections to ensure compliance with contractual agreements.

The complexity and judgment required in estimating expense recovery deviations make this matter crucial for understanding the entity's financial performance and compliance with regulatory requirements, which justifies its classification as a KAM.

(6) Process of Split

The sixth KAM category, Process of Split, pertains to the 2017 split processes of AdNorte, S.A. and AdVT, S.A. following new legislation. These splits created new systems, transferring assets, liabilities, and capital to newly formed entities.

The impact of the split processes, assumptions for calculating split-off balances, and their complexity make this matter significant. Accurate judgment in managing these processes is crucial for reflecting their accurate impact on financial statements.

This matter is relevant not only because of the significant changes in the entities' structure but also because of the financial impact of the splits. The complexity and judgment involved justify its classification as a KAM.

Once the presentation of the description of each KAM category is finished, some remarks need to be identified and highlighted before moving on to the 'audit approach synthesis'. The significant discovery of the content analysis of the KAM description, present in 'more significant material distortion risks identified', is related to the high degree of similarity in the descriptions analyzed. Similarities between companies in the same sector, as is the context of this sample, is not uncommon. However, in this content analysis, the high level of similarity found reaches a degree of equal disclosure in terms of description used, often with the exact same words (especially in the case of reports belonging to PricewaterhouseCoopers & Associates).

When we compare the description of KAM in the appropriate section in auditor reports of a company prepared by the same audit firm (as is the case with Ernst & Young Audit & Associated and PricewaterhouseCoopers & Associates in several years), there is an 'almost absolute' similarity with differences referring to the notes to the financial statements identified and the concrete values associated with the matters mentioned. As is understandable, this information should be amended according to the period under review. However, the rest of the KAM description is 'practically' the same. In the case of PricewaterhouseCoopers & Associates, it is also noteworthy that this similarity occurs not only between reports from the same company over the period under analysis but also when comparing reports from the auditor of different companies.

ISA 701 established that the auditor's determination of KAM is limited to the matters of most significance in the audit of the financial statements for the current period. However, the standard states that although the ISA does not require the auditor to update the KAM included in the auditor's report from previous periods, it may be helpful for the auditor to consider whether issues that were KAM in auditing the financial statements of prior periods remain a KAM in auditing the financial statements of the current period. Specifically in this context, where there is such a high degree of similarity in the KAM released in several periods, users of information from a single auditor's report are not aware that these matters are considered relevant not only in a given audit but considered appropriate to the entity over several periods. In other words, the KAM disclosure is not audit-specific but rather entity-specific. Even to mention that the disclosure of KAM is entity-specific, regardless of the specific audit, is only partially true, since, especially in the case of PricewaterhouseCoopers & Associates, the disclosure of KAM is similar across several entities, being only sector-specific at most.

KAM Content Analysis: Audit Approach Synthesis

The standard established that the amount of detail provided in the auditor's report to describe how a KAM was addressed in the audit is a matter of professional judgment. Following paragraph 13(b) of ISA 701, the auditor may represent aspects of the auditor's response or approach that were most relevant to the matter or specific to the assessed risk of material misstatement, a brief overview of procedures performed, an indication of the outcome of the auditor's procedures; or key observations concerning the matter, or some combination of these elements.

The standard also defines that the description of aspects of the auditor's response or approach to a matter when the audit approach required significant tailoring to the facts and circumstances of the entity may assist intended users in understanding unusual circumstances and significant auditor judgment needed to address the risk of material misstatement. In addition, the audit approach in a particular period may have been influenced by entity-specific circumstances, economic conditions, or industry developments. It may also be helpful for the auditor to refer to the nature and extent of communications with those charged with governance.

Moving on to the description of the audit approach, according to ISA 701, there may be challenges in describing the auditor's procedures, particularly in complex, judgmental areas of the audit. It may be challenging to summarize the procedures performed concisely that adequately communicate the nature and extent of the auditor's response to the assessed risk of material misstatement and the significant auditor judgments involved. Nonetheless, the auditor may consider it necessary to describe specific procedures performed to communicate how the matter was addressed in the audit. Such description may typically be at a high level rather than include a detailed description of procedures.

According to paragraphs 1 and 2 of the ISA 500, the standard explains what constitutes audit evidence in an audit of financial statements and deals with the auditor's responsibility to design and perform audit procedures to obtain sufficient appropriate audit evidence to draw reasonable conclusions on which to base the auditor's opinion. It applies to all the audit evidence obtained during the audit.

The standard states that most of the auditor's work in forming the auditor's opinion consists of obtaining and evaluating audit evidence. Audit procedures to obtain audit evidence can include inspection, observation, confirmation, recalculation, reperformance, and analytical procedures, often in some combination, in addition to inquiry.

The description of the audit approach in this section of the content analysis will again follow the defined KAM categories as the audit procedures used to obtain audit evidence on KAM depended on the category of KAM in question. Since most auditor reports present the audit approach with a brief overview of the audit procedures performed, we will adopt the same presentation below. The overview presentation of the audit procedures will be followed by its classification under ISA 500.

ISA 500 outlines a comprehensive set of audit procedures essential for gathering evidence. Inspection involves examining documentation, records, or tangible assets to corroborate financial information. Observation entails witnessing processes or activities firsthand to validate their accuracy and completeness. Confirmation involves obtaining written or oral responses directly from third parties to corroborate financial details, such as balances or terms of agreements.

Recalculation involves independently verifying mathematical accuracy, ensuring figures are correctly totaled, computed, or summarized. Reperformance requires the auditor to redo procedures or tests originally performed by management, ensuring consistency and accuracy. Analytical procedures involve assessing relationships and trends within financial data to identify inconsistencies or unusual patterns that may warrant further investigation. Inquiry entails seeking explanations or clarifications from management or personnel regarding financial information, transactions, or processes to gain a deeper understanding and corroborate evidence. Table 6 presents the audit procedures, meticulously applied following ISA 500, that enabled auditors to obtain sufficient and appropriate evidence regarding the KAM disclosed.

Table 6. Audit Response by KAM Categories of Águas de Portugal companies

Response \ Category	Investment - recognition, and measurement	Impairment of Investments	Impairment of Debts	Revenue - recognition of downward activity	Revenue - expense recovery deviations	Process of split
Inspection	3x	2x	3x	4x	5x	7x
Observation	1x			1x		
Confirmation	1x		2x			
Recalculation	1x			1x	1x	
Reperformance			3x			
Analytical Procedures	1x	1x	2x	4x		1x
Inquiry	1x	2x	2x	1x		

Based on Table 6, we can verify that the most recurrent audit procedure, applied within all categories of KAM disclosed, is the inspection. Common audit responses are analytical procedures and inquiries, employed in most KAM categories. On the other hand, observation and reperformance are the least used audit procedures considering the content analysis performed, especially reperformance that was only used against KAM of debt impairment.

CONCLUSION

The investigation focused on the holding of the Group and on the thirteen companies (whose mission is related to water supply, sanitation, and reuse) and entailed performing a content analysis of the auditor's reports and, specifically, an analysis of KAM disclosed in the auditor's reports from 2017 to 2021.

Findings from the content analysis allowed to determine which companies disclose KAM - eight of fourteen companies in the sector - since disclosure is not mandatory for companies in the sector of water and sanitation. In addition, the identification of the four audit firms that audit the companies under analysis was crucial, especially for the subsequent discovery of high levels of similarity in both the number and content of the KAM disclosed when comparing company auditor reports in the period in which they are audited by the same audit firm.

Results uncovered six disclosed KAM categories after the analysis of the subheadings, namely: 1) Investment - recognition, and measurement; (2) Impairment of Investments; (3) Impairment of Debts; (4) Revenue - recognition of downward activity; (5) Revenue - expense recovery deviations; (6) Process of Split. The identification of the disclosed KAM categories, as well as the detailed content analysis of the 'most significant material distortion risks identified' and the 'audit approach synthesis' - two sub-sections present in the KAM disclosure section - allowed a better understanding of the matters that require special attention from the auditor in the water and sanitation sector.

As for the audit response, the content analysis allowed uncovering inspection as the most common audit procedure, applied to all categories of KAM, followed by analytical procedures and inquiries. In the context of water and sanitation companies, on the other hand, reperformance and observation were the less common responses.

Given that the novel purpose of this research was precisely to verify if there was a similarity in writing as a way to only meet the normative requirements, the results of the content analysis show that the goal of KAM disclosure in the extended auditor's report is not fully met in the auditor's report of companies in the water and sanitation sector. Even though companies in this sector voluntarily disclose KAM, disclosure should still aim to improve the value of the auditor's report by providing relevant and specific information. A common criticism of the traditional auditor's report was that it provided little entity-specific information because its form was standardized, with a dichotomous opinion using boilerplate language. To enhance the value of the auditor report and improve audit quality, the International Auditing and Assurance Standards Board (IAASB) argued that KAM should differ from entity to entity and encouraged auditors to be as entity-specific and audit-specific as possible in the description of a KAM. However, in the specific context of the water and sanitation sector, we found that this objective outlined by IAASB is not fully achieved, given that the disclosure of KAM exhibits high levels of similarity when comparing the KAM disclosures in the different auditor's reports.

Thus, this research contributes to the auditing literature related to the audit profession and the informational value of the auditor report, as well as for regulators by presenting an unbiased analysis of the content evidenced in the sub-sections of KAM description and audit procedures. This analysis is, hopefully, a first step towards the possibility of improvement of the auditor's report. In addition, it contributes to society given the impact that the KAM disclosure assessed by the auditor's professional judgment may cause.

Notwithstanding, the present study has its limitations specially since it only analyses companies in the water and sanitation sector, which can affect the level and content of KAM disclosure. Further limitations draw from the investigator's judgment used in the categorization of the KAM. Thus, it is suggested for future research the analysis of auditor reports from different industries and the comparison between them. Additionally, in the context of entities that are not required to disclose KAM, a study of the determining factors of voluntary disclosure of KAM would be innovative in view of the current state of the art in the field of auditing.

Methodologically, the present study is also constrained by data availability problems that significantly reduced the sample under analysis. This is a common obstacle for investigations that rely on accountability documents. Finally, given that the content analysis was performed manually, the subjective judgment of the researchers also played a part in determining the 'most significant material distortion risks identified' and the 'audit approach'. Nonetheless, the subjectivity inherent to the researcher's role does not tarnish the findings regarding the boilerplate language considering the succinct and clear-cut nature of disclosures in the KAM section.

REFERENCES

Abdelfattah, T., Elmahgoub, M., & Elamer, A. A. (2021). Female audit partners and extended audit reporting: UK evidence. *Journal of Business Ethics*, 174(1), 177–197. DOI:10.1007/s10551-020-04607-0

Abdullatif, M., & Al-Rahahleh, A. S. (2020). Applying a New Audit Regulation: Reporting Key Audit Matters in Jordan. *International Journal of Auditing*, 24(2), 268–291. DOI:10.1111/ijau.12192

Águas de Portugal. (2024). *Relatório de Sustentabilidade 2021*. https://www.adp.pt/pt/sustentabilidade/relatorios-de-sustentabilidade/downloads/file507_pt.pdf

Bedard, J., Coram, P., Esphbodi, R., & Mock, T. J. (2016). Does recent academic research support changes to audit reporting standards? *Accounting Horizons*, 30(2), 255–275. DOI:10.2308/acch-51397

Business Council for Sustainable Development (BCSD) Portugal. (2024). *Objetivos de Desenvolvimento Sustentável - Objetivo 6: Água Potável e Saneamento*. https://ods.pt/objectivos/6-agua-e-saneamento/

Chang, Y.-T., Chi, W., & Stone, D. N. (2024). Is Client-Specific Information Useful to Investors? Evidence From Key Audit Matter Reports. *Journal of Accounting, Auditing & Finance*, 39(3), 786–806. DOI:10.1177/0148558X221091804

Church, B., Davis, S., & McCracken, S. (2008). The auditor's reporting model: A literature overview and research synthesis. *Accounting Horizons*, 22(1), 69–90. DOI:10.2308/acch.2008.22.1.69

Conselho das Finanças Públicas. (2024). *Relatório nº 2 de 2023 Setor Empresarial do Estado 2020-2021*. https://www.cfp.pt/uploads/publicacoes_ficheiros/cfp_rel-02-2023.pdf

Duboisée de Ricquebourg, A., & Maroun, W. (2023). How do auditor rotations affect key audit matters? Archival evidence from South African audits. *The British Accounting Review*, 55(2), 101099. DOI:10.1016/j.bar.2022.101099

Financial Reporting Council. (2015). *Extended auditors' reports: A review of experience in the first year*. https://frc.org.uk/Extended-auditors-reports.pdf

Gambetta, N., Sierra-García, L., García-Benau, M. A., & Novejarque-Civera, J. (2023). The Informative Value of Key Audit Matters in the Audit Report: Understanding the Impact of the Audit Firm and KAM Type. *Australian Accounting Review*, 104(33), 114–134. DOI:10.1111/auar.12396

Hegazy, M. A. A., & Kamareldawla, N. M. (2021). Key audit matters: Did IAASB unravel the knots of confusion in audit reports decisions? *Managerial Auditing Journal*, 36(8), 1025–1052. DOI:10.1108/MAJ-11-2019-2464

International Auditing and Assurance Standards Board. (2018a). *ISA 315 (Revised) - Identifying and Assessing the Risks of Material Misstatement through Understanding the Entity and Its Environment*. https://www.ifac.org/_flysystem/azure-private/publications/files/A017%202013%20IAASB%20Handbook%20ISA%20315%20Revised.pdf

International Auditing and Assurance Standards Board. (2018b). *ISA 500 - Audit Evidence*. https://www.ifac.org/_flysystem/azure-private/publications/files/A023%202012%20IAASB%20Handbook%20ISA%20500.pdf

International Auditing and Assurance Standards Board. (2018c). *ISA 700 (Revised) - Forming an Opinion and Reporting on Financial Statements*. https://www.iaasb.org/publications/international-standard-auditing-isa-700-revised-forming-opinion-and-reporting-financial-statements

International Auditing and Assurance Standards Board. (2018d). *ISA 701 - Communicating Key Audit Matters in the Independent Auditor's Report*. https://www.iaasb.org/publications/international-standard-auditing-isa-701-new-communicating-key-audit-matters-independent-auditors

Iwanowicz, T., & Iwanowicz, B. (2019). ISA 701 and Materiality Disclosure as Methods to Minimize the Audit Expectation Gap. *Journal of Risk and Financial Management*, 12(4), 1–20. DOI:10.3390/jrfm12040161

Law 12/2008 of Assembly of the Republic (2008). Republic Diary No. 40/2008, Series I of 2008-02-26. https://diariodarepublica.pt/dr/detalhe/lei/12-2008-247453

Law 148/2015 of Assembly of the Republic (2015). Republic Diary No. 176/2015, Series I of 2015-09-09. https://diariodarepublica.pt/dr/legislacao-consolidada/lei/2015-74094268

Law 23/96 of Assembly of the Republic (1996). Republic Diary No. 172/1996, Series I-A of 1996-07-26. https://diariodarepublica.pt/dr/detalhe/lei/23-1996-408366

Law 58/2005 of Assembly of the Republic (2005). Republic Diary No. 249/2005, Series I-A of 2005-12-29. https://diariodarepublica.pt/dr/detalhe/lei/58-2005-469068

Lennox, C. S., Schmidt, J. J., & Thompson, A. M. (2023). Why are expanded audit reports not informative to investors? Evidence from the United Kingdom. *Review of Accounting Studies*, 28(2), 497–532. DOI:10.1007/s11142-021-09650-4

Lin, J. (2023). Does the disclosure of key audit matters improve the audit quality for sustainable development: Empirical evidence from China. *PLoS One*, 18(5), e0285340. DOI:10.1371/journal.pone.0285340 PMID:37141326

Manoel, J., & Quel, L. F. (2017). Innovation in the International Standards for the New Independent Audit Report. *Journal on Innovation and Sustainability*, 8(1), 130–143. DOI:10.24212/2179-3565.2017v8i1p130-143

Mock, T. J., Bedard, J., Coram, J. P., Davis, S. M., Esphabodi, R., & Wrane, R. C. (2013). The audit reporting model: Current research synthesis and implications. *Auditing*, 32(1, Supplement 1), 323–351. DOI:10.2308/ajpt-50294

Pinto, I., Morais, A. I., & Quick, R. (2020). The impact of the precision of accounting standards on the expanded auditor's report in the European Union. *Journal of International Accounting, Auditing & Taxation*, 40, 100333. DOI:10.1016/j.intaccaudtax.2020.100333

Rousseau, L. M., & Zehms, K. M. (2020). Audit partner style in key audit matter reporting decisions. SSRN *Electronic Journal*. http://dx.doi.org/DOI:10.2139/ssrn.3625651

Sierra-García, L., Gambetta, N., García-Benau, M. A., & Orta-Pérez, M. (2019). Understanding the determinants of the magnitude of entity-level risk and account-level risk key audit matters: The case of the United Kingdom. *The British Accounting Review*, 51(3), 227–240. DOI:10.1016/j.bar.2019.02.004

Sirois, L. P., Bédard, J., & Bera, P. (2018). The informational value of key audit matters in the auditor's report: Evidence from an eye-tracking study. *Accounting Horizons*, 32(2), 141–162. DOI:10.2308/acch-52047

Vanstraelen, A., Schelleman, C., Meuwissen, R., & Hofmann, I. (2012). The audit reporting debate: Seemingly intractable problems and feasible solutions. *European Accounting Review*, 21(2), 193–215. DOI:10.1080/09638180.2012.687506

Velte, P. (2019). Associations between the Financial and Industry Expertise of Audit Committee Members and Key Audit Matters within Related Audit Reports. *Journal of Applied Accounting Research*, 21(1), 185–200. DOI:10.1108/JAAR-10-2018-0163

Yalcin, N. (2022). Content analysis of audit reports in stock indices EURONEXT 100 vs BIST 100. *Istanbul Business Research*, 51(2), 433–458. DOI:10.26650/ibr.2022.51.938151

Zhang, P. F., & Shailer, G. (2021). Changes in audit effort and changes in auditors' disclosures of risks of material misstatement. *The British Accounting Review*, 53(3), 100970. DOI:10.1016/j.bar.2020.100970

ADDITIONAL READING

European Commission (EC). (2011). *Proposal for a regulation of the European parliament and of the council on specific requirements regarding statutory audit of Public-Interest entities*, https://op.europa.eu/en/publication-detail/-/publication/6de7d1dc-7261-4eb8-ae57-5e9afbda7463/language-en

European Parliament and Council of the European Union. (2014). *Regulation of the European Parliament and of the Council on specific requirements regarding statutory audit of Public-Interest entities and repealing commission decision 2005/909/EU*, https://eur-lex.europa.eu/legal-content/EN/TXT/?uri=celex:32014R0537

Financial Reporting Council (FRC). (2012). *Consultation paper - proposed revisions to international standards on auditing (UK and Ireland) to give effect to the FRC effective company stewardship proposals.* www.frc.org.uk/getattachment/cf1f2c07-b64e-40bbbcbb51f639760978/Consultation-Paper-Proposed-Revisions-to-International-Standards-on-Auditing(UK-and-Ireland).aspx

Financial Reporting Council (FRC). (2016). *Extended auditor's reports. A further review of experience.*www.frc.org.uk/getattachment/76641d68-c739-45ac-a251-cabbfd2397e0/Report-on-the-Second-Year-Experienceof-Extended-Auditors-Reports-Jan-2016.pdf

International Auditing and Assurance Standards Board (IAASB). (2015). *The New Auditor's Report: Greater Transparency into the Financial Statement Audit.* IFAC.

International Auditing and Assurance Standards Board (IAASB). (2015). *New and revised auditor reporting standards and related conforming amendments.* www.ifac.org/system/files/uploads/IAASB/Audit%20Reporting-At%20a%20Glance-final.pdf

The Association of Chartered Accountants. (2018). *Key audit matters: unlocking the secrets of the audit.*https://www.accaglobal.com/gb/en/professional-insights/global-profession/key-audit-matters.html

KEY TERMS AND DEFINITIONS

Analytical Procedures: Consist of evaluations of financial information through analysis of plausible relationships among both financial and non-financial data.

External Confirmation: Represents audit evidence obtained by the auditor as a direct written response to the auditor from a third party (the confirming party), in paper form, or by electronic or other medium.

Inquiry: Consists of seeking information of knowledgeable persons, both financial and non-financial, within the entity or outside the entity. Inquiry is used extensively throughout the audit in addition to other audit procedures.

Inspection: Involves examining records or documents, whether internal or external, in paper form, electronic form, or other media, or a physical examination of an asset.

Observation: Consists of looking at a process or procedure being performed by others, for example, the auditor's observation of inventory counting by the entity's personnel, or of the performance of control activities.

Recalculation: Consists of checking the mathematical accuracy of documents or records. Recalculation may be performed manually or electronically.

Reperformance: Involves the auditor's independent execution of procedures or controls that were originally performed as part of the entity's internal control.

Chapter 6
Impact of Sustainability Strategies on ESG Performance Disclosure

Albertina Paula Monteiro
CEOS, Polytechnic of Porto, Portugal

Catarina Cepeda
https://orcid.org/0000-0002-3911-0894
CEOS, Polytechnic of Porto, Portugal

Cristina Macedo
ISCAP, Polytechnic of Porto, Portugal

Carla Cardoso
ISCAP, Polytechnic of Porto, Portugal

Catarina Oliveira
ISCAP, Polytechnic of Porto, Portugal

ABSTRACT

With signaling lens, this study aims to analyze whether the environmental, social, and governance (ESG) performance disclosure is influenced by sustainability strategies and global reporting initiative (GRI) standards adoption. The data obtained from the Refinitiv Eikon database, for Chinese listed companies, are subject to correlation and regression analysis for panel data. The findings reveal that the presence of business ethics and human rights policies have a positive impact on ESG performance disclosure. Additionally, stakeholder engagement level and GRI standards adoption are predictive variables for ESG performance disclosure. Exclusive analysis in the

DOI: 10.4018/979-8-3693-5663-0.ch006

China's industrial sector restricts the results generalization. This study explores the effect of sustainability strategies on ESG performance disclosure.

INTRODUCTION

Issues related to the sustainability environmental dimension have been widely debated in the literature as a result of natural disasters and climate change (Lopez-Gamero *et al.*, 2009). People have begun to realize that the existence of human societies is "ultimately dependent on the services provided by the Earth's physical, chemical and biological systems" (Shield *et al.*, 2002, p. 150). However, recently, there has been a redirection of concerns towards economic and social issues, in the Corporate Social Responsibility (CSR) context (Villiers & Sharma, 2020).

CSR has become increasingly important as it gives organizations responsibility for the impact of their operations on society and the environment (European Commission, 2012). Integrating sustainability policies into business strategies is an imperative response to growing environmental and social concerns (Latapí Agudelo *et al.,* 2019).

In fact, sustainable strategies are essential for achieving long-term economic, environmental, and social goals (e.g., KsiężaK and Fischbach, 2017; Shahzad *et al.,* 2020). Companies choose to adopt certain strategies such as the Triple Bottom Line (TBL), circular economy, sustainable supply chain management, green Innovation and stakeholder engagement. For instances, TBL approach considers three performance dimensions: social, environmental, and economic (KsiężaK & Fischbach, 2017). Companies adopting TBL aim to achieve a balance between these three pillars, ensuring that business practices contribute positively to society and the environment while maintaining profitability (KsiężaK & Fischbach, 2017). The circular economy is a concept related to sustainable strategies, which is focused on designing out waste and pollution, keeping products and materials in use, and regenerating natural systems (Esken *et al.,* 2018). It contrasts with the traditional linear economy of "take, make, dispose" and encourages practices like recycling, reusing, and refurbishing (Stoyanova, 2019). Other concept associated to sustainable strategies is green innovation. This concept involves developing new products, processes, or services that reduce environmental impacts (Shahzad *et al.,* 2020). It can include advancements in renewable energy, energy efficiency, sustainable agriculture, and eco-friendly manufacturing processes (Shahzad *et al.,* 2020). Lastly, engaging with stakeholders is crucial for implementing sustainable strategies (Freeman, 1984). Effective engagement ensures that the interests and concerns of all parties are considered, leading to more inclusive and sustainable decision-making (e.g., Freeman, 1984; Freeman and Mcvea, 2001).

In fact, the literature shows that the growing importance of developing sustainability at a global level, the business environment complexity and the need for additional information, have led companies to place greater value on CSR and to communicate their performance to stakeholders (Monteiro, 2022). According to Monteiro and Aibar-Guzmán (2010), the reasons that drive towards environmental disclosure are the social pressures and legal requirements. Therefore, the sustainability information disclosure plays a crucial role in promoting organizations greater transparency (Gray, 2010).

About sustainability strategies, sustainability policies indicate to stakeholders a company's commitment to ESG issues. By implementing comprehensive sustainability policies, companies can communicate their dedication to ethical practices, through corporate reports, reducing stakeholder uncertainty about their real intentions (Pinelli & Maiolini, 2017). In fact, according to Dragomir and Dragomir (2020) and Armstrong (2020), corporate ethics and human rights policies are fundamental to a company's sustainability strategy and significantly influence the ESG performance disclosure. Another sustainability strategy is the stakeholder's engagement on company's ESG issues. To establish a dialogue with various stakeholders, companies have released sustainability reports to communicate their CSR/sustainability practices (Campra *et al.,* 2020). It is expected that the stakeholder's involvement has an impact on the sustainability disclosure performance. However, the sustainability strategies literature on sustainability reporting is under-explored.

On the one hand, various frameworks have emerged with the aim of promoting Non-Financial Information (NFI) reporting and guaranteeing its quality. In this regard, Global Reporting Initiative (GRI) standards stands out, as it has been the most widely used in the sustainability reports preparation on a global scale (Halkos & Nomikos, 2021). In line, Lu and Cheng (2023) found that the environmental regulation impact on Environmental, Social, and Governance (ESG) performance of Chinese companies improves the ESG performance of state-owned companies. Other studies have been carried out to analyze the level (extent and quality) of sustainability disclosure, the companies determining factors and their impacts on ESG disclosure (e.g., Dai *et al.*, 2019; Dong *et al.,* 2023; Lu *et al.*, 2017). However, studies that analyses the relationship between the level of GRI Standards adoption and CSR/ESG disclosure is still limited (Jain *et al.*, 2024).

In terms of theoretical perspectives, the signaling theory has been widely applied across disciplines like finance, strategic management, and marketing but has seen limited development in business ethics, where its empirical support is inconsistent (Zerbini, 2017). Recently introduced to business ethics, the theory's foundations need further refinement (Zerbini, 2017). This theory helps explain how companies communicate their commitment to social and environmental responsibilities to stakeholders, such as investors, customers, and employees (Conte *et al.,* 2023). Some studies highlight its role in signaling ethical standards to stakeholders, while others question the market's ability to identify false claims (Martin Curran & Moran 2007).

In view of the above, the paper proposes signaling theory, as a framework supportive of a strategic CSR approach, to analyze whether the Chinese companies´ESG performance disclosure is influenced by the sustainability strategies (sustainability policies and the level of stakeholder engagement) and the GRI standards adoption.

The study contributes to academics, companies, regulators entities and stakeholder by demonstrating how CSR strategies, ESG reporting standards like GRI, and signaling theory enhance corporate transparency, build stakeholder trust, and support strategic decision-making in ESG practices to attract socially responsible investors. In this way, this study contributes to: (1) the literature development, with new empirical evidence; (2) for practice, namely for company managers and stakeholders, as it shows the need for companies to give importance to these sustainability strategies and the transparency of information for strategic decision-making, and for regulators, as it is essential to define standards that guide and promote quality sustainability reporting.

The article is structured in six parts. After this introduction, the second part is dedicated to the literature review, which explores the main theoretical concepts related to the topics under study and presents the research hypotheses. The third part identifies the research methodology. Then, in parts four and five, the results are presented and the results are analyzed and discussed, respectively. Finally, the last part is devoted to the conclusion, the contributions and limitations of the study, as well as suggestions for future research.

LITERATURE REVIEW

Over the years, there has been a growing awareness of company's broader role in society, demanding that they not only fulfil legal obligations, but also act responsibly, creating value for society (Latapí Agudelo *et al.*, 2019). In fact, environmental and social aspects, contribute to the life quality and create meaningful jobs, being a crucial part of the worldwide business agenda (Jain *et al.*, 2024; Zwetsloot, 2003). To this extent, Zwetsloot (2003) point out that the challenges facing companies transcend the mere profits maximization, pushing them to reflect on their values, principles, corporate identity and business partners choice.

In recent decades, organizations and governments have developed a responsibility agenda, which includes measures for corporate sustainability, CSR or ESG initiatives, including standards and instruments, that aim to promote sustainability development and performance disclosure (Jain *et al.*, 2024).

To meet the stakeholders' strains and promote the sustainability disclosures standardization, transparency and relevance at a global level, in 2021, the International Financial Reporting Standards (IFRS) foundation underwent significant changes related to the sustainability topic. The creation of a new standard-setting board, the International Sustainability Standards Board (ISSB), stands out (Street & Gordon, 2023). Therefore, there are now two regulatory bodies in the IFRS Foundation: 1) the International Accounting Standards Board (IASB), which maintains the objectives of promoting the adoption of international accounting standards; 2) the ISSB, which aims to provide standards on sustainability at a global level (IFRS Foundation, 2021).

On the other hand, the European Financial Reporting Advisory Group (EFRAG), a private association, created in 2001 with the European Commission encouragement, extended its mission in 2022, following the new role assigned to it in the Corporate Sustainability Reporting Directive (CSRD), to provide technical advice to the European Commission in the form of draft European Union (EU) Sustainability Reporting Standards. This association carries out activities that are organized into two pillars: (1) Financial Reporting, to influence the development of IFRS Standards from a European perspective and how they contribute to the efficiency of capital markets and provide endorsement advice on (amendments to) IFRS Standards to the European Commission; (2) sustainability reporting to develop draft EU sustainability reporting standards and related amendments for the European Commission.

In this way, EFRAG contributes to the sustainability accounting standards development in the EU, which help organizations to integrate ESG information into their reports. There is an imperative need to establish a body, such as the GRI, responsible for defining guidelines and standards for sustainability reporting, covering a wide range of indicators (Global Sustainability Standards Board, 2023).

To this extent, Street and Gordon (2023) state that sustainability standards are based on the substantial changes that sustainability standards are causing in companies financial reports, driving the need to incorporate ESG issues into organizational strategies, processes and reports.

The non-financial reports requirement can boost organizations interest in adopting more sustainable practices, causing positive impacts on communities, environment and economy (Permatasari & Gunawan, 2023). However, Permatasari and Gunawan (2023) point out that reporting must be carried out carefully, i.e. it must consider different stakeholders' interests and avoid excessive burdens on companies, especially for small and medium-sized enterprises which often have limited resources. According to Braam and Peeters (2018), the increase in published reports number by companies reflects the growing concern or awareness of providing information relevance to stakeholders about their efforts to promote a more sustainable world. In turn, Callado and Fensterseifer (2010) point out that sustainability indicators reflect organizational performance in ESG dimensions. ESG performance indicators are crucial for investment decision-making in the financial markets, highlighting the corporate ethics policy relevance (Bianchi *et al.*, 2010).

According to Akanwa and Agu (2005) (cited by Ugoani, 2019), business ethics are essential to avoid irrationality, irresponsibility, and corruption, contributing to business sustainability and good business leadership. The authors point out that the sustainability or business ethics policies application promotes compliance with environmental regulations, improves management practices and CSR reports. Weiss (2021) indicates that there is a need to clarify moral obligations and social responsibilities in decision-making, underlining the interconnection between sustainability policies and ESG performance.

By improving socio-economic and socio-environmental practices, companies are simultaneously aligning themselves with Human Rights (HR) policies, demonstrating social responsibility and adding value to this commitment (Engelmann & Nascimento, 2021). Hence, this behaviour contributes to greater inclusion and diversity in companies, promoting equity in opportunities, development conditions and people recognition (Engelmann & Nascimento, 2021). According to Liu and Nemoto (2021) and Alvares and Souza (2016), achieving positive ESG performance not only confers a competitive advantage, but also attracts and retains talent in organizations. According to Liu and Nemoto (2021), these practices promote workforce integration, financial performance, social capital and employee satisfaction.

Literature suggests that sustainability policies positively contribute to ESG performance. On the other hand, Rajesh and Rajendran (2020) state that companies with high ESG performance tend to have better sustainability disclosure levels. High-profile CSR initiatives not only attract media attention but also serve as a robust mechanism to demonstrate the company's dedication to ethical practices and community well-being (Hahn & Kühnen, 2013). In fact, companies can signal their commitment to sustainability by adopting policies aimed at reducing carbon footprints, minimizing waste, and enhancing energy efficiency. For example, committing to science-based targets for reducing greenhouse gas emissions or transitioning to 100% renewable energy sources are strong signals (Hahn & Kühnen, 2013). Sustainability policies serve as signals to stakeholders about a company's commitment to environmental and social responsibilities. By adopting comprehensive sustainability policies, companies can demonstrate their dedication to ethical practices, reducing stakeholders' uncertainty about their true intentions (Pinelli & Maiolini, 2017). This is particularly effective when the policies are stringent and require significant resources to implement, making them credible signals (Pinelli & Maiolini, 2017). In this context, within the signalling theory, we formulate the first research:

H1. The company's sustainability policies positively influence ESG performance disclosure.

Specifically, business ethics policies are a critical component of a company's overall sustainability strategy, and they play a significant role in influencing ESG performance disclosure (Dragomir & Dragomir, 2020). These policies, which outline the ethical standards and principles guiding a company's operations, can significantly affect how the company communicates its ESG efforts to stakeholders. Business ethics policies help establish a company's commitment to ethical conduct, which is fundamental in building credibility and trust with stakeholders (Dragomir & Dragomir, 2020). When companies adhere to high ethical standards, they signal their integrity and accountability, which enhances stakeholder confidence in the information disclosed. This is crucial for ESG performance disclosure, as stakeholders rely on the accuracy and reliability of these reports to make informed decisions (Schwartz, 2013). In view of the above, we formulate the following sub-hypothesis:

H1.1 The companies business ethics policy positively influences ESG performance disclosure.

Human rights policies play a crucial role on sustainability and companies can enhance their ESG reporting, demonstrating their dedication to ethical practices and social responsibility (Armstrong, 2020). A robust human rights policy signals a company's commitment to respecting and protecting the rights of all individuals affected by its operations (Engelmann & Nascimento, 2021). This commitment builds trust and credibility among stakeholders, including employees, customers, investors, and the communities in which the company operates. In turn, trustworthy companies are more likely to be transparent in their ESG disclosures, providing stakeholders with accurate and reliable information about their ESG practices and performance (Engelmann & Nascimento, 2021). Therefore, in this study it is hoped that the existence of human rights policies in the company will contribute positively to greater disclosure of ESG performance. Thus, this research has the following sub-hypothesis:

H1.2 The company's human rights policy positively influences ESG performance disclosure.

Companies' active involvement with stakeholders is another sustainability strategy, as it allows them to meet their needs and expectations (Freeman & Mcvea, 2001). Stakeholder theory highlights the importance of considering not just internal stakeholders, but also other groups such as customers, suppliers, local communities, and others, with an interest in the organization (Freeman & Mcvea, 2001). Stakeholder theory, from of organizational management perspective, is strategically geared towards continued business success (Gray *et al.*, 1995). Thus, Freeman and Mcvea (2001) point out that management must develop methods that meet the needs of all stakeholders and the social responsibility dissemination because it's an instrument of communication between the organization and its stakeholders.

In this context, the ESG disclosure practices, driven by the growing interest in sustainability, denotes that active stakeholder's engagement not only strengthens relationships with all stakeholders, but also aims to reduce information asymmetries (Li *et al.*, 2018). According to Fernandez-Feijoo *et al.* (2014), the pressure exerted by stakeholders can significantly influence the transparency/accountability level required in corporate reporting. In this way, Moneva and Llena (2000) stat that, under the stakeholders influence to satisfy their information needs, companies disclose more environmental information in their reports.

Hahn *et al.* (2023) state that corporate disclosure involves practices in which companies provide non-financial information, such as sustainability/CSR/ESG to stakeholders. In this respect, Romero *et al.* (2019) found that Spanish companies with greater dialogue with stakeholders stand out from the rest in terms of the information disclosed quality on ESG performance. The companies NFI report gives them public visibility. This public visibility helps build trust and credibility with stakeholders (Porter & Kramer, 2006). According to the signalling theory, when stakeholders see consistent and meaningful CSR efforts, they are more likely to perceive the company as responsible and trustworthy, which can enhance stakeholder loyalty and support. Thus, within the signalling theory, this study aims to analyse whether stakeholder involvement has a positive impact on ESG performance disclosure, so the second research hypothesis is formulated:

H2. Greater stakeholder involvement positively influences ESG performance disclosure.

Frameworks related to sustainability reporting play a key role in standardizing and disclosing ESG information by organizations (Khakimovna & Oktyamovna, 2022). According to Khakimovna and Oktyamovna (2022), the best-known framework is GRI, which establishes guidelines/standards for sustainability reporting, promoting transparency and accountability, in a comprehensive format that encompasses economic, environmental and social dimensions, known as the three pillars of sustainability. Globally, most CSR/sustainability reports adopt the principles and indicators established by the GRI standards to address quantitative aspects related to performance in the ESG dimensions (Paun, 2018). According to Paun (2018), this adoption prevalence highlights the GRI significant influence in standardizing disclosure practices on sustainability performance at a global level.

The predominance GRI standards use is also evident in European companies, which consider them to be the best option available for the sustainable information disclosure (Lock & Seele, 2016). Disclosing sustainability performance following the GRI guidelines/standards not only ensures consistency, but also makes it possible to analyse the data in relation to the company's performance over time, as well as enabling intra- and inter-industry comparisons (Paun, 2018).

The GRI established structure provides a standard by requiring participants to communicate three categories of sustainability indicators (economic, environmental and social) (Landrum & Ohsowski, 2018). Within these dimensions, the authors point out that the GRI matrix gives each company the flexibility to disclose the topics it considers most relevant to itself and its stakeholders.

On the other hand, Luo and Tang (2023) found that companies that follow GRI standards when preparing their ESG reports are more likely to achieve greater carbon emissions mitigation. This means that companies that adopt the GRI standards tend to achieve better performance and therefore better disclosure rates (Luo andTang 2023; Romero *et al.*, 2019). In fact, companies publish ESG reports to signal their commitment to transparency and accountability in their CSR practices. These reports often follow recognized frameworks like the GRI, which adds to the signal credibility (Hahn & Kühnen, 2013). From this point of view, we formulate the third research hypothesis:

H3. The GRI standards adoption positively influences ESG performance disclosure.

METHODOLOGY

This study takes a quantitative approach, applying the multivariate regression technique for panel data, to analyse whether the ESG performance disclosure depends on sustainability strategies (business ethics and human rights policy, stakeholder involvement level and the GRI standards adoption).

The study's target population consists of Chinese listed companies whose corporate information is available on the Refinitiv Eikon database. Companies that disclose NFI in an integrated report or in any other statement format were identified. The final sample consists of an unbalanced panel of data, which includes 193 listed companies in China's industrial sector. For the period 2017 to 2021, 965 observations resulted.

This study analysed Chinese companies because they belong to a country facing serious environmental and social problems.

Refinitiv Eikon is a provider of important data, which is used by many academics and investors (e.g. Berg *et al.*, 2021; Monteiro *et al.*, 2022b). The data was statistically analyzed using STATA software version 16.

The variables used are shown in Table 1.

Table 1. Research variables

Variable	Description	Scale	Source
Dependent variable			
ESG performance disclosure	Overall score of the company based on the information communicated in the environmental, social and corporate governance pillars (ESG Score)	0-100 (%)	Aluchna *et al.*, (2022); Aydoğmuş *et al.*, (2022); Baraibar-Diez and Odriozola (2019); Refinitiv (2020); Wasiuzzaman and Subramaniam (2023)
Independent variables			
Business ethics policy	Does the company describe in its code of conduct that it strives to maintain the highest level of general business ethics?	0-1 (0-no; 1-yes)	Refinitiv (2020)
Human rights policy	Does the company have a policy to ensure respect for human rights in general?	0-1 (0-no; 1-yes)	Refinitiv (2020)
GRI Standards	Is the company's CSR report published in accordance with the GRI guidelines/ standards?	0-1 (0-no; 1-yes)	Refinitiv (2020)
Stakeholder involvement	Does the company explain how it relates to its stakeholders? - information on how the company relates to its stakeholders, how it involves them in its decision-making process; what procedures are in place for involvement. - emphasis on establishing two-way communication between the company and its various stakeholders.	0-100 (%)	Refinitiv (2020)
Control variables:			
Company size	Total assets	€	Refinitiv (2020)
ROA	Financial performance measured by return on assets – net profit/total assets	0-100 (%)	Aluchna *et al.*, (2022); Aydoğmuş *et al.*, (2022); Baraibar-Diez and Odriozola (2019); Bifulco *et al.*, (2023); Monteiro *et al.*, (2022); García-Sánchez *et al.*, (2020a); Wasiuzzaman and Subramaniam (2023).

Source: Refinitiv (2017-2021)

The models presented in Equations [1] were designed to test the proposed hypotheses. Thus, Equation [1] was developed to identify the independent variables effect, Business Ethics Policy (BEP), Human Rights Policy (HRP), GRI Standards (GRIS) and Stakeholder Engagement (E_Stakeholder) on the dependent variable, ESG performance disclosure (ESGSperf_discl), including the control variables to avoid biased results (Size and ROA).

Equations [1] $ESGSperf\_dicl_{it} = \beta 0 + \beta 1 BEP_{it} + \beta 2\ HRP_{it} + \beta 3\ GRIS_{it} + \beta 4\ E\_Stakeholder_{it} + \beta 5\ Size_{it} + \beta 6\ ROA_{it} + \varepsilon_{it}$

RESULTS

Descriptive Analysis

Table 2 shows the sample descriptive statistics. The ESG performance disclosure (ESGSperf_discl) average is 32.64%. Regarding the business ethics policies (BEP) existence, the average is very low (12%), i.e., of the 193 companies studied, only 12% have this type of policy (23 companies). Similarly, the human rights policies (HRP) existence recorded an average of 38%, indicating that, on average, 73 of the 193 companies have this type of policy. The stakeholder engagement level recorded average around 36.53%, indicating that, on average, their score is 36.53% out of 100%. The GRI standards (GRIS) adoption registered an average value of 29.30%, indicating that most Chinese industrial companies do not apply GRI standards.

Table 2. Descriptive statistics of the variables

Variable	N. Obs.	Average	Standard deviation	Minimum	Maximum
ESGperf_discl	603	32.64	15.56	1.02	83.35
BEP	596	0.12	0.32	0	1
HRP	603	0.38	0.48	0	1
GRIS	589	29.30	39.47	0	90.80
E_Stakeholders	603	36.53	37.58	0	79.25
Size	965	11892127340	30219341361	23629659	330732706691
ROA	965	0.04	0.06	0	0.33

Source: Refinitiv (2017-2021)

Table 3 shows the sustainability reports number published between 2017 and 2021. The data reveal that over the years, the sustainability reports number has increased significantly.

Table 3. Number of reports per year

Year	N. Reports
2017	60
2018	71
2019	117
2020	162
2021	193
Total	**603**

Source: Refinitiv (2017-2021)

Regression Analysis

In this study, we examined the strength of the correlation between independent variables, using the Spearman test. The correlation values are low (< 0.60), which indicate the absence of the multicollinearity (table 4).

Table 4. Correlation matrix between variables

	ESGperf_discl	BEP	HRP	GRIS	E_Stakeholders	Size	ROA
ESGperf_discl	1.0000						
BEP	0.6025***	1.0000					
HRP	0.3967***	0.2505***	1.0000				
GRIS	0.5620***	0.4058***	0.1844***	1.0000			
E_Stakeholders	0.4900***	0.4622***	0.1518***	0.5353***	1.0000		
Size	0.2181***	0.2437	0.0515***	0.2385***	0.1956***	1.0000	
ROA	-0.0465	-0.0270	-0.0374	-0.1640***	-0.1043***	-0.1270***	1.0000

Legend: ***p<0.001

Before analysing the multiple regression, we performed the Hausman test to check whether we should use a fixed effects estimator or a random effects estimator. The test indicates that it is indifferent whether to use fixed or random effects [Prob>chi2 = (V_b-V_B is not positive definite)]. As Prob > F = 0.0000, it is more advisable to use the fixed effects estimator (Table 5).

The regression analysis for fixed effects reveals that all the model variables have a positive and significant impact on ESG performance disclosed by the Chinese companies analysed. Only, one control variable (ROA) was not found to have a significant influence on the dependent variable. Thus, the results support all the research hypothesis (see table 5). Specifically, our results indicate that sustainability policies related to business ethics ($p<0.001$; $\beta=10.25895$) and human rights ($p<0.001$; $\beta=14.26094$) have a positive impact on ESG performance disclosure, which supports H1. Moreover, Stakeholder engagement proves to be a predictive variable of the dependent variable ($\beta=0.482798$; $p<0.001$), showing that when companies act with stakeholders, they tend to disclose better ESG performance levels. Regarding GRI standards adoption, our results prove that they can guide companies towards better sustainability performance disclosure ($\beta=0.0877391$; $p<0.000$).

The model variables explain 58% of the variance in ESG performance disclosure.

Table 5. Linear regression results

Fixed-effects (witin) regression			**Number of observations**	**=**	**581**
Group Variable: ID			**Number of groups**	**=**	**191**
R-sq:			Obs. per group:		
Within	=	0.5450	min	=	1
Between	=	0.5760	avg	=	3.0
Overall	=	0.5836	max	=	5
curr(u_i, Xb)	=	-0.1007	F(6,384)	=	76.66
			Prob > F	=	0.0000

Table 5b. (continued)

ESG performance disclosure (ESGperf_discl)	**Coef.**	**Std. Err.**	**t**	**P>|t|**	**[95% Coef. Interval]**	
BEP	**10.25895**	**1.712174**	**5.99**	**0.000**	**6.89254**	**13.62536**
HRP	14.26094	1.271089	11.22	0.000	11.76177	16.7601
GRIS	0.0877391	0.013284	6.60	0.000	0.0616207	0.1138575
E_Stakeholders	0.482798	0.0144402	3.34	0.001	0.0198881	.0766715
Size	9.98e-11	3.11e-11	3.21	0.001	3.86e-11	1.61e-10
ROA	135.9689	926.9946	0.15	0.883	-1686.652	1958.59
_Cons	20.09181	.8999279	22.33	0.000	18.3224	21.86121
sigma_u	8.8464127					
sigma_e	5.7111624					
rho	.70582218	(fraction of variance due to u_i)				
F test that all u_i=0: F(190, 384) = 6.42 Prob > F = 0.0000						

Table 6 presents the hypotheses test summary.

Table 6. Hypothesis summary results

Hypothesis	**Results**
H1- The company's sustainability policies positively influence ESG performance disclosure	Supported
H1.1- The companies business ethics policy positively influences ESG performance disclosure.	Supported
H1.2 - The company's human rights policy positively influences ESG performance disclosure.	Supported
H2 - Greater stakeholder involvement positively influences ESG performance disclosure.	Supported
H3- The GRI standards adoption positively influences ESG performance disclosure.	Supported

Discussion

Our research found that sustainability policies related to business ethics and human rights significantly enhance ESG performance disclosure, supporting the H1.1 and H1.2. These results are in line with the foundations of Dragomir and Dragomir (2020) and Armstrong (2020), who state that companies with sustainability policies tend to have better ESG disclosure levels. Hence, according to the signaling theory, is possible to verify that corporate actors can address information asymmetry through the implementation of corporate actions and policies (Papoutsi & Sodhi, 2020). We can conclude that ccompanies that value ethical practices and respect for human rights are likely to disclose their ESG efforts more comprehensively. From a signalling theory perspective, these policies serve as signals to stakeholders about the company's commitment to responsible business practices (Papoutsi & Sodhi, 2020). This signalling helps to reduce information asymmetry by providing stakeholders with information on the company's ethical values and social responsibilities.

Still within the scope of sustainability strategies, this research also identifies stakeholder involvement as another significant predictor of ESG performance disclosure. Companies that actively engage with stakeholders tend to more transparently. This proactive stakeholder engagement helps companies to build trust and enhances the credibility of the disclosed ESG information to them. These results statistically support H2, following the Hahn *et al.* (2023) and Romero *et al.* (2019) studies. These authors highlight that ESG disclosure involves practices that provide information on non-financial issues, such as sustainability or CSR, to stakeholders, which have a positive impact on the companies' non-financial performance. Thus, according to signaling theory, this involvement in ESG reporting is valuable for exploring how different parties, each with varying levels of information, interpret signals (Connelly *et al.*, 2011; Khanchel *et al.*, 2023).

Regarding GRI standards adoption, also positively influence ESG performance disclosure. Our results are in line with Luo and Tang (2023) and Romero *et al.* (2019) presupposes, who state that the GRI standards adoption tend to achieve better performance and therefore better ESG disclosure rates. In this sense, according to signaling theory, green norms, like GRI standards, engage symbolic actions that can be effective at signaling to external stakeholders the firms' values regarding green issues (Ramus & Montiel, 2005). Companies' adhering to GRI guidelines tend to provide more comprehensive and standardized ESG disclosures, thereby signaling their commitment to transparency and accountability in sustainability reporting (Ramus & Montiel, 2005). This adherence aligns with stakeholder expectations and enhances the comparability of ESG performance across different companies (Shen *et al.,* 2023).

CONCLUSION

In the last decade, the sustainability reports publication, or other documents as a tool for disclosing NFI on companies' sustainability performance has led to a growing awareness of their importance for business development. By focusing on listed companies in China's industrial sector, this study provides a comprehensive quantitative and analytical analysis of the between relationship sustainability strategies (sustainability policies, stakeholders engagement and GRI standards adoption) and ESG performance disclosure, with signaling theory lens, for the 2017 to 2021 period.

The results point to a moderate average for ESG performance disclosure (32.64%), showing the companies' commitment to ESG performance disclosure practices. However, the lower averages for the existence of business ethics and human rights policies indicate opportunities for improvement in these areas. Despite the active involvement of stakeholders, the GRI standards adoption remains low, suggesting that Chinese companies are not aligned with internationally recognized standards for sustainability reporting, losing accountability and comparability of ESG reporting.

The regression analysis highlights the sustainability policies, stakeholder involvement, and GRI standards adoption relevance in the ESG performance disclosure. Business ethics policies and human rights policies show a positive and significant impact, supporting hypothesis H1. Furthermore, stakeholder involvement manifests itself as a predictive variable of the dependent variable (ESG performance), supporting hypothesis H2. The GRI standards adoption is also positively related to ESG performance disclosure, supporting hypothesis H3. The model variables explain 58% of the dependent variable variance.

This study, by offering valuable insights into sustainability strategies in the specific context of Chinese companies in the manufacturing sector, contributes to the understanding of the dynamics related to this business context and alerts to the effort of these companies to improve their ESG-related practices and transparency. Furthermore, considering the signalization theory, it highlights the stakeholder involvement relevance to achieve better ESG performance and collaborate in companies' social policies.

Empirical evidence highlights the sustainability policies relevance, stakeholder engagement and GRI standards adoption in the ESG disclosure reporting, providing useful guidance for academics, companies, regulators and stakeholders seeking to promote sustainability in the Chinese business sector.

However, it is important to recognize the research limitations since the exclusive focus on China's industrial sector may limit the results generalizability. There may be imperfections in the way ESG scores are measured, since they are measured quantitatively (Monteiro *et al.*, 2024). Future research suggests expanding the analysis to different sectors and additional regions, as well as further investigation into the specific determinants that influence the GRI standards adoption among Chinese companies. To provide a more complete understanding of sustainability dynamics in the Chinese business landscape, it may also be important to explore contextual and cultural influences on the sustainable practices adoption and ESG performance disclosure, as well as to assess the government policies impact.

REFERENCES

Aluchna, M., Roszkowska-Menkes, M., & Kamiński, B. (2022). From talk to action: The effects of the non-financial reporting directive on ESG performance. *Meditari Accountancy Research*, 31(7), 1–25. DOI:10.1108/MEDAR-12-2021-1530

Alvares, K. P., & de Souza, I. M. (2016). Sustentabilidade na gestão de pessoas: Práticas e contribuições às organizações. *Revista Gestão Organizacional*, 9(2), 24–38. DOI:10.22277/rgo.v9i2.3285

Armstrong, A. (2020). Ethics and ESG. Australasian Accounting. *Business and Finance Journal*, 14(3), 6–17.

Aydoğmuş, M., Gülay, G., & Ergun, K. (2022). Impact of ESG performance on firm value and profitability. *Borsa Istanbul. RE:view*, 22, S119–S127.

Baraibar-Diez, E., & Odriozola, , M. (2019). CSR committees and their effect on ESG performance in UK, France, Germany, and Spain. *Sustainability*, 11(18), 5077. DOI:10.3390/su11185077

Berg, F., Fabisik, K., & Sautner, Z. (2021). Is History Repeating Itself? The(un) predictable Past of ESG Ratings. *European Corporate Governance Institute–Finance Working Paper*: 708. DOI:10.2139/ssrn.3722087

Bianchi, R. J., Drew, M. E., & Walk, A. N. (2010). On the responsible investment disclosure practices of the world's largest pension funds. *Accounting Research Journal*, 23(3), 302–318. DOI:10.1108/10309611011092619

Bifulco, G. M., Savio, R., Paolone, F., & Tiscini, R. (2023). The CSR committee as moderator for the ESG score and market value. *Corporate Social Responsibility and Environmental Management*, 30(6), 3231–3241. DOI:10.1002/csr.2549

Braam, G., & Peeters, R. (2018). Corporate sustainability performance and assurance on sustainability reports: Diffusion of accounting practices in the realm of sustainable development. *Corporate Social Responsibility and Environmental Management*, 25(2), 164–181. DOI:10.1002/csr.1447

Callado, A. L. C., & Fensterseifer, J. E. (2010). Indicadores de sustentabilidade: uma abordagem empírica a partir de uma perspectiva de especialistas. *Simpósio de administração da produção, logística e operações internacionais*, 13, 2010.

Campra, M., Esposito, P., & Lombardi, R. (2020). The engagement of stakeholders in nonfinancial reporting: New information-pressure, stimuli, inertia, under short-termism in the banking industry. *Corporate Social Responsibility and Environmental Management*, 27(3), 1436–1444. DOI:10.1002/csr.1896

Conte, F., Sardanelli, D., Vollero, A., & Siano, A. (2023). CSR signaling in controversial and noncontroversial industries: CSR policies, governance structures, and transparency tools. *European Management Journal*, 41(2), 274–281. DOI:10.1016/j.emj.2021.12.003

Cui, J., Dai, J., Wang, Z., & Zhao, X. (2022). Does environmental regulation induce green innovation? A panel study of Chinese listed firms. *Technological Forecasting and Social Change*, 176, 121492. DOI:10.1016/j.techfore.2022.121492

Dai, J., Lu, C., & Qi, J. (2019). Corporate social responsibility disclosure and stock price crash risk: Evidence from China. *Sustainability (Basel)*, 11(2), 448. DOI:10.3390/su11020448

Dong, S., Xu, L., & McIver, R. P. (2023). Sustainability reporting quality and the financial sector: Evidence from China. *Meditari Accountancy Research*, 31(5), 1190–1214. DOI:10.1108/MEDAR-05-2020-0899

Dragomir, V. D., & Dragomir, V. D. (2020). Ethical aspects of environmental strategy. *Corporate Environmental Strategy: Theoretical, Practical, and Ethical Aspects*, 75-113.

Engelmann, W., & Nascimento, H. C. P. (2021). O desenvolvimento dos direitos humanos nas empresas por meio do ESG como forma de qualificar as relações de trabalho. *Revista da Escola Judicial do TRT4,3*(6).

Esken, B., Franco-García, M. L., & Fisscher, O. A. (2018). CSR perception as a signpost for circular economy. *Management Research Review*, 41(5), 586–604. DOI:10.1108/MRR-02-2018-0054

European Commission. (2012). Communication from the commission to the european parliament, the council, the european economic and social committee and the committee of the regions a Roadmap for moving to a competitive low carbon economy in 2050. https://eur-lex.europa.eu/legal-content/EN/TXT/?uri=celex:52011DC0112

European Union (2014). Directive 2014/95/EU of the european parliament and of the council of 22 october 2014 amending Directive 2013/34/EU as regards disclosure of non-financial and diversity information by certain large undertakings and groups. *Official Journal of the European Union, 2014,* L 330, 1–9. https://eur-lex.europa.eu/legal-content/EN/TXT/HTML/?uri=CELEX:32014L0095

European Union (2022). Directive 2022/2464/EU of the european parliament and of the council of 14 December 2022 amending Regulation (EU) No 537/2014, Directive 2004/109/EC, Directive 2006/43/EC and Directive 2013/34/EU, as regards corporate sustainability reporting. *Official Journal of the European Union, 2022*, L 322, 15–80. https://eur-lex.europa.eu/legal-content/EN/TXT/HTML/?uri=CELEX:32022L2464

Fernandez-Feijoo, B., Romero, S., & Ruiz, S. (2014). Effect of Stakeholders' Pressure on Transparency of Sustainability Reports within the GRI Framework. *Journal of Business Ethics*, 122(1), 53–63. DOI:10.1007/s10551-013-1748-5

Freeman, R., & Mcvea, J. (2001). A Stakeholder Approach to Strategic Management. SSRN *Electronic Journal*. https://doi.org/DOI:10.2139/ssrn.263511

García-Sánchez, I. M., Hussain, N., Khan, S. A., & Martínez-Ferrero, J. (2020). Managerial entrenchment, corporate social responsibility, and earnings management. *Corporate Social Responsibility and Environmental Management*, 27(4), 1818–1833. DOI:10.1002/csr.1928

Global Sustainability Standards Board. (2023). GRI: Foundation 2021. https://globalreporting.org/

Gray, R. (2010). A re-evaluation of social, environmental and sustainability accounting: An exploration of an emerging trans-disciplinary field? *Sustainability Accounting. Management and Policy Journal*, 1(1), 11–32. DOI:10.1108/20408021011059205

Gray, R., Kouhy, R., & Lavers, S. (1995). Corporate social and environmental reporting: A review of the literature and a longitudinal study of UK disclosure. *Accounting, Auditing & Accountability Journal*, 8(2), 44–47. DOI:10.1108/09513579510146996

Hahn, R., & Kühnen, M. (2013). Determinants of sustainability reporting: A review of results, trends, theory, and opportunities in an expanding field of research. *Journal of Cleaner Production*, 59, 5–21. DOI:10.1016/j.jclepro.2013.07.005

Hahn, R., Reimsbach, D., & Wickert, C. (2023). Nonfinancial Reporting and Real Sustainable Change: Relationship Status-It's Complicated. *Organization & Environment*, 36(1), 3–16. DOI:10.1177/10860266231151653

Halkos, G., & Nomikos, S. (2021). Corporate social responsibility: Trends in global reporting initiative standards. *Economic Analysis and Policy*, 69, 106–117. DOI:10.1016/j.eap.2020.11.008

Hepburn, C. (2006). Regulation by prices, quantities, or both: A review of instrument choice. *Oxford Review of Economic Policy*, 22(2), 226–247. DOI:10.1093/oxrep/grj014

IFRS Foundation. (2021). IFRS Advisory Council Update International Sustainability Standards Board. https://www.ifrs.org/content/dam/ifrs/meetings/2021/november/advisory-council/ap4-update-on-international-sustainability-standards-board.pdf

Jain, A., Ripa, D., & Torres, L. (2024). Have companies arisen to the challenge of promoting sustainable work? The role of responsible business practices in the context of evolving employment and working conditions. *Safety Science*, 170, 106364. DOI:10.1016/j.ssci.2023.106364

Khakimovna, N. F., & Oktyamovna, S. A. (2022). Sustainability Reporting Towards Common Standards. *European Journal of Innovation In Nonformal Education*, 2(4), 236–239.

Kramer, M. R., & Porter, M. E. (2006). Strategy and society: The link between competitive advantage and corporate social responsibility. *Harvard Business Review*, 84(12), 78–92. PMID:17183795

Księżak, P., & Fischbach, B. (2017). Triple bottom line: The pillars of CSR. *Journal of corporate responsibility and leadership, 4*(3), 95-110.

Landrum, N. E., & Ohsowski, B. (2018). Identifying Worldviews on Corporate Sustainability: A Content Analysis of Corporate Sustainability Reports. *Business Strategy and the Environment*, 27(1), 128–151. DOI:10.1002/bse.1989

Latapí Agudelo, M. A., Jóhannsdóttir, L., & Davídsdóttir, B. (2019). A literature review of the history and evolution of corporate social responsibility. *International Journal of Corporate Social Responsibility*, 4(1), 1–23. DOI:10.1186/s40991-018-0039-y

Li, X., Zheng, C., Liu, G., & Sial, M. S. (2018). The effectiveness of internal control and corporate social responsibility: Evidence from Chinese capital market. *Sustainability (Basel)*, 10(11), 4006. DOI:10.3390/su10114006

Liu, L., & Nemoto, N. (2021). Environmental, social and governance (ESG) evaluation and organizational attractiveness to prospective employees: Evidence from Japan. *Journal of Accounting and Finance*, 21(4), 14–29. DOI:10.33423/jaf.v21i4.4522

Lock, I., & Seele, P. (2016). The credibility of CSR (corporate social responsibility) reports in Europe. Evidence from a quantitative content analysis in 11 countries. *Journal of Cleaner Production*, 122, 186–200. DOI:10.1016/j.jclepro.2016.02.060

López-Gamero, M. D., Molina-Azorín, J. F., & Claver-Cortés, E. (2009). The whole relationship between environmental variables and firm performance: Competitive advantage and firm resources as mediator variables. *Journal of Environmental Management*, 90(10), 3110–3121. DOI:10.1016/j.jenvman.2009.05.007 PMID:19482410

Lu, F., Kozak, R., Toppinen, A., D'Amato, D., & Wen, Z. (2017). Factors influencing levels of CSR disclosure by forestry companies in China. *Sustainability (Basel)*, 9(10), 1800. DOI:10.3390/su9101800

Lu, S., & Cheng, B. (2023). Does environmental regulation affect firms' ESG performance? Evidence from China. *MDE. Managerial and Decision Economics*, 44(4), 2004–2009. DOI:10.1002/mde.3796

Luo, L., & Tang, Q. (2023). The real effects of ESG reporting and GRI standards on carbon mitigation: International evidence. *Business Strategy and the Environment*, 32(6), 2985–3000. DOI:10.1002/bse.3281

Martin Curran, M., & Moran, D. (2007). Impact of the FTSE4 Good Index on firm price: An event study. *Journal of Environmental Management*, 82(4), 529–537. DOI:10.1016/j.jenvman.2006.02.010 PMID:16678334

Moneva, J. M., & Llena, F. (2000). Environmental disclosures in the annual reports of large companies in Spain. *European Accounting Review*, 9(1), 7–29. DOI:10.1080/096381800407923

Monteiro, A. P. (2022). *Social Accounting: analysis of the disclosure on labor practices and human rights and its determinants* [Doctoral dissertation]. University of Santiago de Compostela, Spain.

Monteiro, A. P., García-Sánchez, I. M., & Aibar-Guzmán, B. (2022). Labour practice, decent work and human rights performance and reporting: The impact of women managers. *Journal of Business Ethics*, 180(2), 523–542. DOI:10.1007/s10551-021-04913-1

Monteiro, S., & Aibar-Guzmán, B. (2010). Organizational and accounting change within the context of the environmental agenda: Evidence from Portugal. *Journal of Accounting & Organizational Change*, 6(4), 404–435. DOI:10.1108/18325911011091800

Papaj, E. (2017). *Non-financial information regarding the amended accounting act bill.* https://api.semanticscholar.org/CorpusID:169622468

Papoutsi, A., & Sodhi, M. S. (2020). Does disclosure in sustainability reports indicate actual sustainability performance? *Journal of Cleaner Production*, 260, 121049. DOI:10.1016/j.jclepro.2020.121049

Paun, D. (2018). Corporate sustainability reporting: An innovative tool for the greater good of all. *Business Horizons*, 61(6), 925–935. DOI:10.1016/j.bushor.2018.07.012

Permatasari, P., & Gunawan, J. (2023). Sustainability policies for small medium enterprises: Who are the actors? *Cleaner and Responsible Consumption*, 9, 100122. DOI:10.1016/j.clrc.2023.100122

Pham, C. V., Liu, S. F., & Chen, S. H. (2024). *Corporate ESG performance and intellectual capital: International evidence.* Asia Pacific Management Review. DOI:10.1016/j.apmrv.2023.12.003

Pinelli, M., & Maiolini, R. (2017). Strategies for sustainable development: Organizational motivations, stakeholders' expectations and sustainability agendas. *Sustainable Development (Bradford)*, 25(4), 288–298. DOI:10.1002/sd.1653

Rajesh, R., & Rajendran, C. (2020). Relating environmental, social, and governance scores and sustainability performances of firms: An empirical analysis. *Business Strategy and the Environment*, 29(3), 1247–1267. DOI:10.1002/bse.2429

Ramus, C. A., & Montiel, I. (2005). When are corporate environmental policies a form of green-washing? *Business & Society*, 44(4), 377–414. DOI:10.1177/0007650305278120

Refinitiv. (2020). Environmental, Social and Governance (ESG) Scores from Refinitiv. Refinitiv.

Ren, S., Hu, Y., Zheng, J., & Wang, Y. (2020). Emissions trading and firm innovation: Evidence from a natural experiment in China. *Technological Forecasting and Social Change*, 155, 119989. DOI:10.1016/j.techfore.2020.119989

Romero, S., Ruiz, S., & Fernandez-Feijoo, B. (2019). Sustainability Reporting and stakeholder engagement in Spain: Different instruments, different quality. *Business Strategy and the Environment*, 28(1), 221–232. DOI:10.1002/bse.2251

Schwartz, M. S. (2013). Developing and sustaining an ethical corporate culture: The core elements. *Business Horizons*, 56(1), 39–50. DOI:10.1016/j.bushor.2012.09.002

Shahzad, M., Qu, Y., Javed, S. A., Zafar, A. U., & Rehman, S. U. (2020). Relation of environment sustainability to CSR and green innovation: A case of Pakistani manufacturing industry. *Journal of Cleaner Production*, 253, 119938. DOI:10.1016/j.jclepro.2019.119938

Shen, H., Lin, H., Han, W., & Wu, H. (2023). ESG in China: A review of practice and research, and future research avenues. *China Journal of Accounting Research*, 100325(4). Advance online publication. DOI:10.1016/j.cjar.2023.100325

Shields, D. J., Šolar, S. V., & Martin, W. E. (2002). The role of values and objectives in communicating indicators of sustainability. *Ecological Indicators*, 2(1-2), 149–160. DOI:10.1016/S1470-160X(02)00042-0

Stoyanova, T. (2019). CSR strategies applied in terms of circular economy. *Economic Alternatives*, 2, 263–274.

Street, D. L., & Gordon, E. A. (2023). An interview with IASB Chair Dr. Andreas Barckow. *Journal of International Financial Management & Accounting*, 34(2), 358–377. DOI:10.1111/jifm.12171

Ugoani, J. (2019). Business ethics and its effect on organizational sustainability. *Global Journal of Social Sciences Studies*, 5(2), 119–131. DOI:10.20448/807.5.2.119.131

Villiers, C., & Sharma, U. (2020). A critical reflection on the future of financial, intellectual capital, sustainability and integrated reporting. *Critical Perspectives on Accounting*, 70, 101999. DOI:10.1016/j.cpa.2017.05.003

Wang, L., Liu, B., Zhu, Y., Yang, M., Du, C., Han, Z., & Cao, C. (2022). General metal–organic framework-derived strategy to synthesize yolk-shell carbon-encapsulated nickelic spheres for sodium-ion batteries. *Journal of Colloid and Interface Science*, 613, 23–34. DOI:10.1016/j.jcis.2021.12.157 PMID:35032774

Wasiuzzaman, S., & Subramaniam, V. (2023). Board gender diversity and environmental, social and governance (ESG) disclosure: Is it different for developed and developing nations? *Corporate Social Responsibility and Environmental Management*, 30(5), 2145–2165. Advance online publication. DOI:10.1002/csr.2475

Weiss, J. W. (2021). *Business ethics: A stakeholder and issues management approach*. Berrett-Koehler Publishers.

Zerbini, F. (2017). CSR initiatives as market signals: A review and research agenda. *Journal of Business Ethics*, 146(1), 1–23. DOI:10.1007/s10551-015-2922-8

Zheng, Z., Li, J., Ren, X., & Guo, J. M. (2023). Does corporate ESG create value? New evidence from M&As in China. *Pacific-Basin Finance Journal*, 77, 101916. DOI:10.1016/j.pacfin.2022.101916

Zhou, G., Liu, L., & Luo, S. (2022). Sustainable development, ESG performance and company market value: Mediating effect of financial performance. *Business Strategy and the Environment*, 31(7), 3371–3387. DOI:10.1002/bse.3089

Zwetsloot, G. I. (2003). From management systems to corporate social responsibility. *Journal of Business Ethics*, 44(2), 201–208. DOI:10.1023/A:1023303917699

Chapter 7
Exploring the Impact of Cultural and Gender Diversity on ESG Performance Reporting of EU Healthcare Corporations

Catarina Cepeda
https://orcid.org/0000-0002-3911-0894
ISCAP, Polytechnic of Porto, Portugal

Amélia Silva
CEOS.PP, ISCAP, Polytechnic of Porto, Portugal

Francisco Carreira
https://orcid.org/0000-0001-9913-4698
CICE, School of Business and Administration, Polytechnic of Setúbal, Portugal

ABSTRACT

The primary research objective is to analyze the influence of cultural and gender diversity (board cultural diversity and board gender diversity and executive's member gender diversity) on the companies Environmental, Social, and Governance (ESG) performance reporting and the mediating effect of workforce and human rights policies. This study utilizes data sourced from healthcare listed companies within the European Union (EU). Structural Equation Modelling (SEM) is employed to examine the interplay among various constructs. Results show that board cultural

DOI: 10.4018/979-8-3693-5663-0.ch007

and gender diversity has a positive impact on ESG performance reporting. However, the workforce only improves the relationship between board gender diversity and ESG performance reporting. This study contributes to the literature by incorporating multidimensional perspectives of diversity into one general framework that stresses the mediating role of workforce in the interactive effect of cultural and gender diversity initiatives with ESG reporting practices. Moreover, by promoting ESG measures that apply global gender diversity and equality, the findings have practical implications for human resource policies and development at the organizational level.

INTRODUCTION

In today's fast-paced business environment, establishing a sustainable organizational framework is not merely a suggestion but a critical imperative (Crane *et al.*, 2014). Achieving sustainability requires an active and unwavering commitment to social responsibility, which is essential for building value-centric connections with stakeholders (Arayakarnkul *et al.*, 2022). Under this perspective, sustainability practices should be reported to enhance communication between companies and their stakeholders (Cepeda, 2024).

As guardians of corporate governance, boards of directors are expected to guide companies along a path where social responsibility is not just an afterthought but an integral component of the overall corporate strategy (Stiles, 2001). In fact, boards of directors are central figures in strategic planning, management oversight, and vigilant monitoring of companies (Kapri, 2023), particularly regarding social causes and environmental preservation (Langevoort, 2000). This multifaceted commitment, rooted in the fiduciary duties of boards, forms the foundation for building a sustainable organization—a delicate balancing act between economic goals and broader social welfare (Harjoto *et al.*, 2015).

In the current scenario, diversity policies and equal opportunities are essential pillars for implementing an effective ESG strategy (De Lucia *et al.*, 2020). It's not just about signaling norms of non-discrimination; it's about proactively promoting diverse work environments and inclusive cultures, and empowering individuals to reach their full potential (De Lucia *et al.*, 2020). Previous studies have largely overlooked the empirical effects of gender diversity on ESG components, which poses a notable challenge for companies and stakeholders (Johnston & Samanta, 2023; Monteiro *et al.*, 2022, 2023, 2024a, 2024b).

The influence of corporate governance attributes on ESG practices' performance and disclosure has been a focal point of scholarly inquiry. For Arayssi *et al.* (2020) and Van Hoang *et al.* (2021), the transparency, accountability, and board engagement in ESG issues emerge as critical factors influencing ESG performance

(Arayssi *et al.,* 2020; Van Hoang *et al.,* 2021). Furthermore, several authors state that the board characteristics, such as gender and cultural diversity, are significant determinants of ESG performance outcomes (e.g. Al-Hiyari *et al.,* 2023; Monteiro *et al.,* 2023; Monteiro *et al.,* 2024a; Monteiro *et al.,* 2024b). Literature suggests that the relationship between Board Gender Diversity, Board Cultural Diversity, and ESG performance is a subject of growing interest and research within the realm of corporate governance and sustainable business practices (Beji *et al.,* 2021; Monteiro *et al.,* 2022). In fact, numerous studies have delved into the impact of board diversity, both in terms of gender and cultural background, on various aspects of corporate performance, including ESG metrics. For instance, Ioannou and Serafeim (2017) found a positive association between board gender diversity and the extent of ESG reporting, suggesting that boards gender diversity is more inclined to prioritize and disclose information related to environmental and social responsibility. For instance, Shahbaz *et al.* (2020) found that female directors wield more influence on environmental and governance indicators, while Al-Shaer and Zaman (2016) demonstrated that board gender diversity is associated with higher sustainability report quality. Monteiro *et al.* (2024b) also found that gender equality, with focus on Sustainable Development Goal (SDG 5) are positively associated with ESG performance reporting.

On the other hand, Håkanson *et al.* (2016) emphasized the importance of integration and multiculturalism in leveraging cultural diversity for positive business outcomes. In this respect, Al-Hiyari *et al.* (2023) founds that boards with diverse cultural backgrounds are better equipped to address the complex social and environmental challenges faced by organizations, leading to improved ESG performance through enhanced stakeholder engagement and strategic decision-making. However, the combined effect of board gender diversity and board cultural diversity presents nuanced challenges (Paolone *et al.,* 2024).

Most studies on board gender diversity have focused on its impact on financial performance, neglecting its crucial role in non-financial performance (Manyaga *et al.,* 2020). To address these gaps, this study aims to dissect the direct impact of board gender and cultural diversity on ESG performance reporting, as well as the mediating effect of workforce and human right policies. Certain policies can leverage corporate governance and enhance companies' ESG performance (Johnston & Samanta, 2023). However, the mediating effect of workforce and human rights policies in connection with gender and cultural diversity and ESG performance remains underexplored terrain. Understanding these variables' crucial role in shaping the nexus between diversity, governance, and corporate transparency is essential in advancing the global pursuit of SDGs.

The ensuing sections of this study follow a structured framework. Section 2 elucidates the theoretical underpinnings, conducts a meticulous review of pertinent literature, and formulates hypotheses. Section 3 delineates the research methodology employed. Subsequent sections present empirical findings, discuss their implications, and conclude with recommendations for future research endeavors.

LITERATURE REVIEW

ESG indicators such as global gender diversity and equality are expected to improve social performance (Boulouta, 2013), financial performance (Cho *et al.,* 2021), reputation (Brammer, Millington, and Pavelin, 2009), ESG reporting (Liang, *et al.,* 2023). Bravo, and Reguera-Alvarado, 2019) and diversity initiatives (Glass and Cook, 2018). Recent studies have shed light on the correlation between board cultural diversity and ESG performance reporting (Ouyang *et al.,* 2022). Scholars have delved into the impact of cultural diversity within board compositions on the effectiveness of ESG reporting practices, aiming to discern how diverse cultural perspectives influence a company's sustainability disclosures.

Al-Hiyari *et al.* (2023) examined the relationship between board cultural diversity and ESG performance reporting, revealing significant associations. Their findings suggest that a more culturally diverse board contributes positively to the quality and comprehensiveness of ESG disclosures, thereby enhancing transparency and accountability.

Similarly, Shahbaz *et al.* (2020) conducted a comprehensive analysis of board cultural diversity and its implications for ESG reporting. Their research unveiled a robust positive correlation between the degree of cultural diversity on corporate boards and the sophistication of ESG performance reporting mechanisms. Moreover, they emphasized the pivotal role of diverse cultural perspectives in fostering a holistic approach to sustainability reporting (Shahbaz *et al.,* 2020).

Paolone *et al.* (2024) explored the impact of board cultural diversity on ESG performance reporting specifically within the European banking sector. Their study demonstrated that companies with culturally diverse boards tend to exhibit more robust ESG reporting practices, aligning with global sustainability standards and regulatory requirements.

Overall, these studies underscore the significance of board cultural diversity in shaping the quality, accuracy, and comprehensiveness of ESG performance reporting initiatives. They highlight the importance of embracing diverse cultural perspectives within corporate governance structures to enhance transparency, accountability, and stakeholder trust in sustainability disclosures.

Following these foundations, we formulate the first hypothesis:

H1: Board Cultural Diversity is positively associated with ESG Performance Reporting

Considering the relevance of gender diversity, it is important to understand how workforce dynamics influence the impact of cultural diversity on corporate boards regarding the effectiveness of sustainability reporting practices. Johnston and Samanta (2023) investigated the interplay between board cultural diversity and workforce dynamics, highlighting the potential moderating effect of the workforce on ESG performance reporting. Their research revealed that companies with culturally diverse boards experienced enhanced ESG reporting outcomes when supported by a proactive and engaged workforce committed to sustainability objectives. Similarly, Schleich (2022) conducted empirical research on the relationship between board cultural diversity, workforce policies, and ESG reporting quality. The findings suggested that workforce involvement and diversity initiatives serve as crucial moderators, amplifying the positive influence of board cultural diversity on the comprehensiveness and transparency of ESG disclosures. Moreover, Radu *et al.* (2023) explored the mediating and moderating effects of the workforce on the relationship between board cultural diversity and ESG performance reporting. Their study emphasized the significance of effective communication channels and inclusive organizational cultures in maximizing the impact of cultural diversity within boards on sustainability reporting outcomes.

Overall, these studies underscore the importance of considering workforce dynamics as a moderating factor in the relationship between board cultural diversity and ESG performance reporting. Following these foundations, we formulate the first hypothesis:

H1a: Workforce moderates the effect of Board Cultural Diversity on ESG Performance Reporting.

Not only do workforce policies reinforce ESG performance, but human rights policies can also do so. For instance, Lee and Kim (2023) investigated the role of human rights standards and certifications in moderating the effect of board cultural diversity on ESG performance reporting. Their study highlighted the importance of aligning corporate governance practices with internationally recognized human rights principles to enhance the credibility and transparency of sustainability disclosures. Hence, we formulate the second hypothesis:

H1b: Human Rights moderate the effect of Board Cultural Diversity on ESG Performance Reporting.

The literature indicates a strong correlation between board diversity (both gender and cultural) and ESG performance. Diverse boards bring a variety of perspectives and experiences, which can lead to more comprehensive and effective strategies for addressing ESG concerns (Monteiro *et al.*, 2022). As organizations continue to recognize the importance of sustainability in their operations, fostering diversity at the board level emerges as a critical factor in driving long-term success and stakeholder value (Monteiro *et al.,* 2024b).

Wu *et al.* (2022) conducted a comprehensive meta-analysis of studies examining the relationship between board gender diversity and ESG performance reporting. Their findings consistently demonstrated a positive correlation between higher representation of women on corporate boards and enhanced sustainability reporting quality across various industries and regions. Similarly, Manita *et al.* (2018) investigated the impact of board gender diversity on ESG reporting practices in a longitudinal study spanning multiple years. Their research revealed a significant positive relationship between the proportion of female directors on boards and the comprehensiveness and transparency of ESG disclosures, highlighting the role of gender diversity in fostering corporate transparency and accountability. Monteiro *et al.* (2024a, b) also found a positive relation between board gender diversity and ESG performance reporting in their research on EU companies.

Moreover, Ouni *et al.* (2020) explored the mediating mechanisms through which board gender diversity influences ESG performance reporting, focusing on factors such as stakeholder engagement, board dynamics, and corporate governance practices. Their study underscored the importance of gender-inclusive decision-making processes in promoting sustainability-oriented behaviors and disclosures.

Overall, these studies underscore the significant association between Board Gender Diversity and ESG Performance Reporting, highlighting the role of gender diversity in promoting corporate transparency, accountability, and sustainability-oriented practices. Following these findings, we formulate the second hypothesis:

H2: Board Gender Diversity is positively associated with ESG Performance Reporting.

For instance, Johnston and Samanta (2024) explored how workforce policies can act as a moderator between board gender diversity and ESG performance. Their research found that companies with robust workforce inclusion initiatives tend to amplify the positive impact of gender-diverse boards on ESG performance reporting. This suggests that supportive and diverse workforce policies can enhance the effectiveness of gender-diverse boards in driving sustainable practices and transparency.

Additionally, Sharma *et al.* (2020) investigated the role of the workforce in moderating the relationship between board gender diversity and ESG performance. Their study revealed that organizations with gender-diverse workforce policies exhibit stronger ESG performance, particularly in areas related to social responsibility and governance reporting. This underscores the importance of aligning workforce diversity efforts with broader corporate sustainability goals to maximize their impact on ESG performance.

Furthermore, Radu *et al.* (2023) examined how workforce engagement and participation can moderate the influence of board gender diversity on ESG performance reporting. Their findings suggest that companies fostering an inclusive and participatory work environment tend to experience greater synergy between gender-diverse boards and ESG performance outcomes. This implies that active workforce involvement in sustainability initiatives can amplify the positive effects of gender diversity on ESG reporting practices. In this line, we formulate the hypothesis H2a: H2a: Workforce moderates the effect of Board Gender Diversity on ESG Performance Reporting.

Regarding board gender diversity, Beji *et al.* (2021) found that board gender diversity is positively associated with human rights and corporate governance dimensions. On the other hand, Branco *et al.* (2022) found that within their sample, companies accorded minimal significance to reporting information related to human rights issues. Interestingly, their research suggests that the diversity of nations represented on the board of directors emerged as the sole significant factor influencing such reporting practices. This implies a potential connection between board diversity, particularly in terms of national representation, and the consideration given to human rights reporting within corporate governance frameworks (Branco *et al.,* 2022).

Following these findings, we formulate the hypothesis H2b:

H2b: Human Rights moderate the effect of Board Gender Diversity on ESG Performance Reporting.

An insightful connection between Board Gender Diversity and Executive Members Gender Diversity can be observed in the study by Catalyst (2004). They found that companies with greater gender diversity on their boards are more likely to have diverse executive teams as well. This suggests that the push for gender diversity at the board level may permeate throughout the organization, leading to increased diversity among executive members. The study highlights the interconnectedness of gender diversity initiatives at different levels of corporate leadership and their potential impact on organizational dynamics and performance (Catalyst, 2004).

One pertinent study on the association between Executive Members Gender Diversity and ESG Performance Reporting was conducted by Carter *et al.* (2010). They discovered a positive relationship between gender diversity among executive team members and the extent of ESG reporting in firms. This finding suggests that companies with greater gender diversity in their executive ranks tend to prioritize and disclose more comprehensive information related to ESG aspects. This study sheds light on the potential impact of gender diversity at the executive level on enhancing corporate transparency and accountability regarding ESG matters. Given the above, we formulate the third hypothesis: H3: Executive Members Gender Diversity is positively associated with ESG Performance Reporting.

Regarding gender diversity, Oboreh *et al.* (2022) explored how workforce diversity and human rights initiatives can amplify the impact of gender diversity among executive members on ESG performance reporting. The findings suggest that companies with more diverse workforces tend to exhibit stronger correlations between executive gender diversity and ESG reporting quality. This underscores the importance of aligning diversity efforts across different organizational levels to enhance overall sustainability practice. On the other hand, Monteiro *et al.* (2022) found that gender diversity in management teams is positively associated with performance in relation to labor and human rights, and that such performance acts as a mediating factor by fostering higher disclosure of information regarding these issues. In this line, we formulate the following hypotheses:

H3a: Workforce moderates the effect of Executive Members Gender Diversity on ESG Performance Reporting.

H3b: Human Rights moderate the effect of Executive Members Gender Diversity on ESG Performance Reporting.

Figures 1 presents research models. It illustrates how cultural and gender diversity influences ESG performance reporting and the moderating roles of workforce (Model 1) and human rights policies (Model 2) in this relationship.

Figure 1. Research models

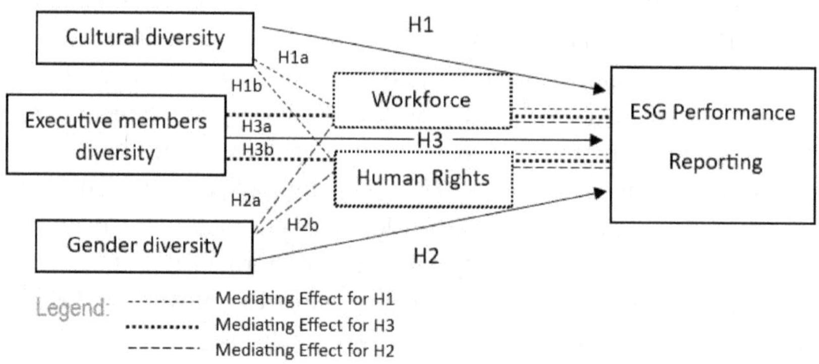

METHODOLOGY

Our study focuses on healthcare firms listed in the EU. We gathered data from the Refinitiv database, now known as LSEG Data & Analytics, for the year 2021, comprising 207 companies. We identified organizations disclosing non-financial data through sustainability reports, integrated reports, or alternative formats, following the methodology outlined by Monteiro *et al.* (2022). Employing a quantitative approach rooted in positivism, this study explores the impact of Board cultural and gender diversity, as well as the executive's member diversity on ESG performance reporting with a particular focus on how workforce and human rights considerations mediate this relationship.

Table 1 provides a detailed overview of the variables under study. The table outlines the type of data collected for each variable, whether measured as a percentage or score, and specifies their classification as independent, mediating, or dependent variables. This classification providing a clear framework for understanding their respective functions within the research models.

Table 1. Variables under study

Variable	Meaning	Scale	Source	The role of the variable
Board Cultural Diversity (%)	Percentage of board members that have a cultural background different from the location of the corporate headquarters.	0-100	Refinitiv (2020)	Independent
Board Gender Diversity (%)	Percentage of female on the board.	0-100		Independent
Executive Members Gender Diversity (%)	Percentage of female executive members.	0-100		Independent
Workforce (%)	Workforce category score measures a company's effectiveness towards job satisfaction, healthy and safe workplace, maintaining diversity and equal opportunities, and development opportunities for its workforce.	0-100		Mediating
Human Rights (%)	Human rights category score measures a company's effectiveness towards respecting the fundamental human rights conventions.	0-100		Mediating
ESG Performance Reporting (%)	Refinitiv ESG Score is an overall company score based on the reported information in the environmental, social and corporate governance pillars (ESG Score)	0-100		Dependent

Statistical analysis was performed using Partial Least Squares based Structural Equation Modeling (PLS-SEM), according to Hair *et al.* (2017) recommendations. PLS choice, instead of covariance based Structural Equation Modeling (CB-SEM) was supported by our sample size, low to the standards of CB-SEM, and to the absence of need to satisfy normality assumption of variables (e.g. Silva *et al.,* 2017). Statistical software was SmartPLS, version 4.0.

Some of our data was panelled, but we choose to treat each record as a different firm because a large part of the repeated records was missing.

In this study we included moderation analysis to investigate the potential damping or strengthening of moderators into the associations of explanatory variables and dependent variable.

Data was analysed according to Hair *et al.* (2018) recommendations. We did not assess reliability, convergent and discriminant validity because our analysis fell in the category of path analysis, with a single variable per construct.

Regarding the explanatory power of the models, we analysed endogenous latent variables' coefficient of determination (R^2). Model fit was assessed with Standardized Root Mean Square Residual (SRMR), considering values below 0.10 as threshold to accept model specification and prevent the bias of estimates (Henseler *et al.,* 2014). Tuker-Lewis index (TLI) was calculated and threshold for good adjustment was set at >0.90.

Collinearity diagnostics were verified by calculating Variance Inflation Factor (VIF), accepting results below 5. The contribute of each construct to explanatory power of the latent variables was assessed with f squared (f^2), an effect size measure. Thresholds recommendations for f^2 followed Hair *et al.* (2017) recommendations, namely 0.02, 0.15 and 0.35 for low, medium e high effect size, respectively.

Predictive relevance was assessed according to Shmueli *et al.* (2016) recommendations. So, we calculated root mean square error (RMSE) and mean absolute error (MAE) with PLS Predict algorithm with a 10-fold validation.

A bootstrap method for 1000 samples was used to calculate p-values and confidence intervals for the calculated estimates. Strength of association was assessed with non-standardized coefficients (β); T-student's statistics were calculated dividing β by the standard deviation (e.g. Hair *et al.,* 2019).

Model 1: Mediator Effect of Workforce

H1: Board Cultural Diversity is associated with ESG Performance Reporting

H1a: Workforce moderate the effect of Board Cultural Diversity on ESG Performance Reporting

H2: Board Gender Diversity is associated with ESG Performance Reporting

H2a: Workforce moderate the effect of Board Gender Diversity on ESG Performance Reporting

H3: Executive Members Gender Diversity is associated with ESG Performance Reporting

H3a: Workforce moderate the effect of Executive Members Gender Diversity on ESG Performance Reporting

Model 2: Mediator Effect of Human Rights

H1: Board Cultural Diversity is associated with ESG Performance Reporting

H1b: Human Rights moderate the effect of Board Cultural Diversity on ESG Performance Reporting

H2: Board Gender Diversity is associated with ESG Performance Reporting

H2b: Human Rights moderate the effect of Board Gender Diversity on ESG Performance Reporting

H3: Executive Members Gender Diversity is associated with ESG Performance Reporting

H3.b: Human Rights moderate the effect of Executive Members Gender Diversity on ESG Performance Reporting

RESULTS

In relation to descriptive statistics (Table 2), it is possible to verify that companies in the healthcare sector have on average, relatively low cultural and gender diversity (Cultural Diversity Council=31.49%; Gender Diversity Council=29.28%; Executive Members Gender Diversity=25.44%). Despite this, the effectiveness of these companies in relation to job satisfaction, healthy and safe workplace, maintaining diversity and equal opportunities and development opportunities for their workforce, on average, is high at 62.01%. Despite this, a company's effectiveness in respecting fundamental human rights conventions is reduced by 37.58%.

Finally, regarding general ESG performance, there is an average ESG performance relative to pressure and with moderate transparency in the public disclosure of relevant ESG data (42.78%) according to Refinitiv criteria (2020).

Table 2. Descriptive statistics

Variable	Obs	Mean	Std. Dev.	Min	Max
Board Cultural Diversity (%)	227	31.48689	12.55199	0	60
Board Gender Diversity (%)	79	29.27558	20.46779	5.882353	66.66667
Executive Members Gender Diversity (%)	227	25.44129	16.36257	0	70
Workforce (%)	226	62.01895	23.93017	.8503401	98.71324
Human Rights (%)	226	37.57784	35.31849	0	96
ESG Performance Reporting (%)	227	42.78022	19.46293	1.666799	88.20785

A total of 217 complete records were included in the study considering all variables studied, namely the independent variables of Gender Diversity (Board Gender Diversity, Board Cultural Diversity, and Executive Members Gender Diversity the dependent variable of ESG performance reporting and the moderators Workforce score and Human Rights score.

Table 3 shows results for research models and the corresponding hypothesis, concerning the association of exploratory variables with the dependent variable of ESG performance reporting and the moderator effects of Workforce score and Human rights score in the association of each gender diversity variable (Board Gender Diversity, Board Cultural Diversity, and Executive Members Gender Diversity) with the dependent variable of ESG performance reporting. R-squared results were all close or higher to 0.60. SRMR was lower than 0.10 for all models. TLI was higher than 0.90 for all models. These results suggest good fit. Considering all models, between 41% and 58% of the indicators in each model had lower RMSE and lower MAE when compared to linear regression model. So, we concluded for medium do good prediction power.

R-squared results were all close or higher than 0.60. SRMR was lower than 0.10TLI was always higher than 0.90. These results suggest good fit. Considering all models, between 39% and 56% of the indicators in each model had lower RMSE and lower MAE when compared to linear regression model. So, we concluded for medium do good prediction power.

Direct positive associations of gender diversity variables with ESG performance reporting were confirmedfor Board Cultural Diversity on model 1 (β=0.055, p=0.020, f^2=0.007), and model 2 (β=0.100, p<0.001, f^2=0.026). These results confirm the H1 and the fundaments ofShahbaz et al. *(2020)andPaolone* et al. *(2024)that reveals a strong link between board cultural diversity and robust ESG reporting, emphasizing its pivotal role in aligning with global standards. This underscores the importance of embracing diverse cultural perspectives for enhancing transparency and stakeholder trust in sustainability disclosures.*

Regarding the moderate effect of workforce (H1a) and Human right policies (H1b) the results do not indicate that these policies influence the connection between the cultural board diversity and ESG performance reporting. Hence, our results aren't in line with the fundaments of Johnston and Samanta (2024), Schleich (2022) and Lee and Kim (2023) that highlight the role of workforce and human rights dynamics in the impact of board cultural diversity on ESG reporting emphasizing the importance of engaged and inclusive workforce and human rights practices.

Regarding H2, our results indicate that Board Gender Diversity is directly related to ESG performance reporting (β=0.141, p<0.001, f2=0.043) in Model 1 and (β=0.182, p<0.001, f2=0.082) in Model 2. Thus, board diversity, encompassing both gender dimensions, is strongly correlated with ESG performance, providing *diverse perspectives and expertise crucial for sustainable success and transparency (Wu* et al., *2022;Manita* et al., *2018;Ouni* et al., *2020). These findings align with those ofMonteiro* et al. *(2024a), demonstrating that board gender diversity influences ESG performance reporting. Furthermore, our results support the notion presented byMonteiro* et al. *(2022), as these authors assert that gender diversity in management teams is positively associated with performance related to labor and human rights; in this study, performance acts as a mediating factor by fostering greater disclosure of information on these issues.*

In the same hypothesis (H2a), Model 1 found a moderating effect of Workforce Score on the association between Board Gender Diversity and ESG performance reporting ($\beta=0.062$, $p<0.001$, $f2=0.016$). The moderation effect shows that at +1 SD of Workforce Score, the slope is higher, suggesting that the relationship between Board Gender Diversity and ESG performance reporting is strengthened with higher Workforce Scores. These results support the findings of Johnston and Samanta (2024), Sharma *et al.* (2020), and Radu *et al.* (2023), who argue that robust workforce policies enhance the positive impact of gender-diverse boards on ESG performance. This underscores the role of a diverse and supportive workforce in maximizing the synergy between gender-diverse boards and ESG performance, advocating for an inclusive work environment aligned with sustainability goals. However, our findings contradict the results of Liang, *et al* (2023) who found that disclosure is more prevalent in industries with low gender diversity, suggesting that that investor demand for disclosure is higher when firms operate in a poor gender diversity.

Regarding Human Rights, they did not moderate the relationship between gender diversity and ESG performance reporting. These results are consistent with the empirical findings of Branco *et al.* (2022), which suggest that companies place little importance on reporting information related to Human Rights issues. However, this contradicts the findings of Beji *et al.* (2021), who found evidence that board gender diversity is positively associated with human rights and corporate governance dimensions.

Finally, hypothesis 3 was not proven in both models (H3a and H3b), these results do not meet the results of Carter *et al.* (2010) that found a positive association between Executive Members Gender Diversity and ESG Performance Reporting, indicating that greater gender diversity among executives correlates with enhanced disclosure of ESG-related information. In addition, Oboreh *et al.* (2022) highlight the role of workforce diversity in amplifying the impact of executive gender diversity on ESG reporting.

Table 3. PLS-SEM for effects on dependent variable of ESG performance reporting for models 1 and 2.

Model 1 (Mediator variable: Workforce)	**B**	**SD**	**p-value**	**f^2**	**R^2 for DV**	**SRMR/ NFI**
H1: Board Cultural Diversity - ESG performance reporting	0.055	0.024	0.020*	0.007	0.589	0.001/ 1.000
H1a: Mediator effect: Workforce	0.034	0.019	0.073	0.004		
H2: Board Gender Diversity - ESG performance reporting	0.141	0.027	<0.001*	0.043	0.603	0.010/ 0.994
H2a: Mediator effect: Workforce	0.062	0.017	<0.001*	0.016		
H3: Executive Members Gender Diversity - ESG performance reporting	-0.006	0.026	0.814	0.000	0.584	0.001/ 1.000
H3a: Mediator effect: Workforce	-0.014	0.019	0.437	0.001		
Model 2 (Mediator variable: Human Rights)						
H1: Board Cultural Diversity - ESG performance reporting	0.100	0.026	<0.001*	0.026	0.614	0.000/ 1.000
H1b: Mediator effect: Human Rights	0.033	0.019	0.084	0.004		
H2: Board Gender Diversity - ESG performance reporting	0.182	0.032	<0.001*	0.082	0.634	0.000/ 1.000
H2b: Mediator effect: Human Rights	-0.002	0.025	0.927	0.000		
H3: Executive Members Gender Diversity - ESG performance reporting	0.004	0.025	0.854	0.000	0.604	0.001/ 1.000
H3b: Mediator effect: Human Rights	0.024	0.022	0.252	0.002		

Legend: $*p<0.05$

CONCLUSION

In contemporary society, there has been a discernible shift towards prioritizing sustainable development and corporate social responsibility. A pivotal dimension of CSR is encapsulated within ESG factors, which have emerged as fundamental metrics for evaluating comprehensive non-financial performance within organizations. The significance of gender diversity in the context of ESG performance is increasingly acknowledged as an integral element of corporate sustainability endeavors. Workplace gender diversity denotes the equitable representation and involvement of individuals from diverse gender identities, fostering an inclusive organizational environment. The implications of gender diversity on transparency, accountability and global sustainability are profound, especially with the SDG 5 application, as Monteiro *et al.´s* (2024b) study proved for a sample European companies

Transparent disclosure concerning gender diversity practices manifests a commitment to participatory decision-making processes, thereby fostering sustainable and innovative business approaches. On the other hand, organizations that prioritize gender diversity in their workplaces often experience heightened levels of employee engagement and well-being. Thus, gender diversity assumes a relevant role in social responsibility initiatives, with companies embracing diverse and inclusive policies, encompassing both workforce and human rights considerations.

This study analyses the relationship between gender diversity and ESG performance reporting and the mediating effect of workforce and human's rights policies. The study supports a direct positive correlation between board cultural diversity and ESG performance reporting, aligning with prior research (Ouyang *et al.,* 2022; Al-Hiyari *et al.,* 2023; Shahbaz *et al.,* 2020; Paolone *et al.,* 2024). These results emphasize the critical role of embracing diverse cultural perspectives within corporate governance structures to enhance transparency and stakeholder trust in sustainability disclosures. However, the moderating effects of human rights policies on this association were not supported by the findings.

Furthermore, the study confirms a strong positive association between board gender diversity and ESG performance reporting, consistent with existing research (Wu *et al.,* 2022; Manita *et al.,* 2018; Monteiro *et al.,* 2024 a,b; Monteiro *et al.,* 2022; Ouni *et al.,* 2020). Additionally, the moderation effect of workforce diversity on the relationship between board gender diversity and ESG performance reporting was supported, indicating that robust workforce policies amplify the positive impact of gender-diverse boards on sustainability reporting. However, human rights policies did not moderate this relationship as hypothesized.

Interestingly, the hypothesized association between executive members' gender diversity and ESG performance reporting was not supported by the findings, contrary to previous research (Carter *et al.,* 2010; Oboreh *et al.,* 2022). This suggests that while board gender diversity influences ESG reporting practices, the impact of executive members' gender diversity on sustainability outcomes may not be as significant.

In conclusion, the research contributes valuable insights into the complex interplay between board diversity, executives' members diversity, workforce dynamics, human rights policies, and ESG performance reporting. While confirming the importance of board diversity in driving and reporting sustainable practices, the study highlights the need for further exploration into the moderating effects of workforce and human rights dynamics on this relationship. Additionally, the contrasting findings regarding executive members' gender diversity underscore the need for nuanced approaches in understanding the influence of diversity at different levels of corporate leadership on sustainability outcomes.

The findings of the article carry significant managerial implications. Companies seeking to improve their ESG disclosure scores and establish a sustainable, responsible image with stakeholders should prioritize board-related factors in their strategies. The results underscore the necessity for companies to enhance gender diversity on their boards and to effectively increase female representation at the board level. By highlighting the importance of implementing ESG measures that emphasize global gender diversity, the findings provide practical insights for human resource policies and organizational development.

This study has certain limitations. First, it treated each of the five years of each case, as unique and independent of one another. Therefore, a panel data analysis would be appropriate to examine year-to-year differences and observe the evolution of ESG performance reporting. Additionally, it would be valuable to analyze other regions around the world and compare developed and developing countries, as well as to apply this study to different sectors. It would also be important to investigate decoupling practices in ESG disclosure related to gender and cultural diversity.

REFERENCES

Adams, R. B., & Ferreira, D. (2009). Women in the boardroom and their impact on governance and performance. *Journal of Financial Economics*, 94(2), 291–309. DOI:10.1016/j.jfineco.2008.10.007

Al-Hiyari, A., Ismail, A. I., Kolsi, M. C., & Kehinde, O. H. (2023). Environmental, social and governance performance (ESG) and firm investment efficiency in emerging markets: The interaction effect of board cultural diversity. Corporate Governance. *Corporate Governance (Bradford)*, 23(3), 650–673. DOI:10.1108/CG-03-2022-0133

Al-Shaer, H., & Zaman, M. (2016). Board gender diversity and sustainability reporting quality. *Journal of Contemporary Accounting & Economics*, 12(3), 210–222. DOI:10.1016/j.jcae.2016.09.001

Arayakarnkul, , Chatjuthamard, P., & Treepongkaruna, S. (2022). Arayakarnkul, P., Chatjuthamard, P., and Treepongkaruna, S. (2022). Board gender diversity, corporate social commitment and sustainability. *Corporate Social Responsibility and Environmental Management*, 29(5), 1706–1721. DOI:10.1002/csr.2320

Arayssi, M., Jizi, M., & Tabaja, H. H. (2020). The impact of board composition on the level of ESG disclosures in GCC countries. Sustainability Accounting. *Management and Policy Journal*, 11(1), 137–161.

Beji, R., Yousfi, O., Loukil, N., & Omri, A. (2021). Board diversity and corporate social responsibility: Empirical evidence from France. *Journal of Business Ethics*, 173(1), 133–155. DOI:10.1007/s10551-020-04522-4

Boulouta, I. (2013). Hidden connections: The link between board gender diversity and corporate social performance. *Journal of Business Ethics*, 113(2), 185–197. DOI:10.1007/s10551-012-1293-7

Brammer, S., Millington, A., & Pavelin, S. (2009). Corporate reputation and women on the board. *British Journal of Management*, 20(1), 17–29. DOI:10.1111/j.1467-8551.2008.00600.x

Branco, A. P. C., Bianchi, M. T., & Castelo Branco, M. (2022). Board demographic diversity and human rights reporting in Western Europe. *PSU Research Review*, 6(3), 158–174. DOI:10.1108/PRR-06-2020-0018

Campbell, K., & Mínguez-Vera, A. (2008). Gender diversity in the boardroom and firm financial performance. *Journal of Business Ethics*, 83(3), 435–451. DOI:10.1007/s10551-007-9630-y

Carter, D. A., D'Souza, F., Simkins, B. J., & Simpson, W. G. (2010). The gender and ethnic diversity of US boards and board committees and firm financial performance. *Corporate Governance*, 18(5), 396–414. DOI:10.1111/j.1467-8683.2010.00809.x

Catalyst. (2004). The bottom line: Connecting corporate performance and gender diversity. Catalyst.

Cepeda, C. (2024). Can Crisis Periods Affect the ESG Reporting Scope? The Portuguese Euronext Entities Case. *Journal of Risk and Financial Management*, 17(5), 191. DOI:10.3390/jrfm17050191

Cho, Y., Kim, S., You, J., Moon, H., & Sung, H. (2021). Application of ESG measures for gender diversity and equality at the organizational level in a Korean context. *European Journal of Training and Development*, 45(4/5), 346–365. DOI:10.1108/EJTD-05-2020-0090

Crane, A., Matten, D., & Spence, L. (2014). *Corporate Social Responsibility: Readings and Cases in a Global Context.* Routledge.

De Lucia, C. D., Pazienza, P., & Bartlett, M. (2020). Does good ESG lead to better financial performances by firms? Machine learning and logistic regression models of public enterprises in Europe. *Sustainability (Basel)*, 12(13), 5317. DOI:10.3390/su12135317

Glass, C., & Cook, A. (2018). Do women leaders promote positive change? Analyzing the effect of gender on business practices and diversity initiatives. *Human Resource Management*, 57(4), 823–837. DOI:10.1002/hrm.21838

Hair, J., Hult, G., Ringle, C., & Sarstedt, M. (2017). *A Primer on Partial Least Squares Structural Equation Modeling (PLS-SEM)* (2nd ed.). Sage.

Hair, J., Risher, J., Sarstedt, M., & Ringle, C. (2019). When to use and how to report the results of PLS-SEM. *European Business Review*, 31(1), 2–24. DOI:10.1108/EBR-11-2018-0203

Hair, J. F., Sarstedt, M., Ringle, C. M., & Gudergan, S. P. (2018). *Advanced Issues in Partial Least Squares Structural Equation Modeling (PLS-SEM).* Sage., DOI:10.3926/oss.37

Håkanson, L., Ambos, B., Schuster, A., & Leicht-Deobald, U. (2016). The psychology of psychic distance: Antecedents of asymmetric perceptions. *Journal of World Business*, 51(2), 308–318. DOI:10.1016/j.jwb.2015.11.005

Haniffa, R., & Hudaib, M. (2007). Locating audit expectations gap within a cultural context: The case of Saudi Arabia. *Journal of International Accounting, Auditing & Taxation*, 16(2), 179–206. DOI:10.1016/j.intaccaudtax.2007.06.003

Harjoto, M., Laksmana, I., & Lee, R. (2015). Board diversity and corporate social responsibility. *Journal of Business Ethics*, 132(4), 641–660. DOI:10.1007/s10551-014-2343-0

Henseler, J., Dijkstra, T. K., Sarstedt, M., Ringle, C. M., Diamantopoulos, A., Straub, D. W., Ketchen, D. J.Jr, Hair, J. F., Hult, G. T. M., & Calantone, R. J. (2014). Common Beliefs and Reality About PLS: Comments on Ronkko and Evermann (2013). *Organizational Research Methods*, 17(2), 182–209. DOI:10.1177/1094428114526928

Ioannou, I., & Serafeim, G. (2017). The consequences of mandatory corporate sustainability reporting. *Harvard Business School research working paper*, (11-100).

Johnston, A., & Samanta, N. (2024). ESG and workforce engagement: Experiences in the UK. In Research Handbook on Environmental, Social and Corporate Governance (pp. 158-178). Edward Elgar Publishing.

Kapri, S. S. (2023). The role of corporate governance in mitigating financial risk: An Indian experiences. *Journal of Cardiovascular Research*, 12(6), 2114–2121.

Langevoort, D. C. (2000). The human nature of corporate boards: Law, norms, and the unintended consequences of independence and accountability. *Geological Journal*, 89, 797.

Lee, J., Lee, J., Lee, C., & Kim, Y. (2023). Identifying ESG trends of International container shipping companies using semantic network analysis and multiple case theory. *Sustainability (Basel)*, 15(12), 9441. DOI:10.3390/su15129441

Liang, C., Lourie, B., Nekrasov, A., & Yoo, I. S. (2023). Voluntary disclosure of workforce gender diversity. *Available atSSRN* 3971818.

Manita, R., Bruna, M. G., Dang, R., & Houanti, L. H. (2018). Board gender diversity and ESG disclosure: Evidence from the USA. *Journal of Applied Accounting Research*, 19(2), 206–224. DOI:10.1108/JAAR-01-2017-0024

Manyaga, C. B., Muturi, W., & Oluoch, O. (2020). Board gender diversity and financial performance of commercial banks in Kenya. *Journal of Finance and Accounting*, 8(1), 1–10.

Monteiro, A. P., Cepêda, C., Borges, A. P., & Vieira, E. (2024b). Does CSR committee presence, stakeholder engagement, gender equality (SDG 5) and firm value influence ESG performance reporting? An EU pre and during Covid-19 analysis. *Measuring Business Excellence. Vol. ahead-of-print No. ahead-of-print. https://doi.org/*DOI:10.1108/MBE-03-2024-0034

Monteiro, A. P., Cepêda, C., & da Silva, A. F. (2024a). Does the Workforce and Sustainability Reports Strengthen the Relationship between Gender Diversity and Sustainability Performance Reporting? *Administrative Sciences*, 14(6), 105. DOI:10.3390/admsci14060105

Monteiro, A. P., Cepêda, C., Pereira, C., & Silva, A. (2023). Social Performance Disclosed by European Companies: The Role of the Board Attributes and the Country's Legal System. *Journal of Risk and Financial Management*, 16(6), 284. DOI:10.3390/jrfm16060284

Monteiro, A. P., García-Sánchez, I. M., & Aibar-Guzmán, B. (2022). Labour practice, decent work and human rights performance and reporting: The impact of women managers. *Journal of Business Ethics*, 180(2), 523–542. DOI:10.1007/s10551-021-04913-1

Oboreh, M., Justina, D. E., & Agbarha, K., Egberi, M., & Onyeyime, E. (2022). Workforce gender diversity and performance of multinational companies in Nigeria. *Journal of Positive School Psychology*, 1582–1590.

Ouni, Z., Ben Mansour, J., & Arfaoui, S. (2020). Board/Executive gender diversity and firm financial performance in Canada: The mediating role of environmental, social, and governance (ESG) orientation. *Sustainability (Basel)*, 12(20), 8386. DOI:10.3390/su12208386

Ouyang, Y., Zhang, Y., & Xue, X. (2022, April). The impact of board cultural diversity on company ESG performance under different risk backgrounds. In Proceedings of the 5th International *Conference on Financial Management*, Education and Social Science, Hohhot, China (pp. 9-10).

Paolone, F., Pozzoli, M., Chhabra, M., & Di Vaio, A. (2024). Cultural and gender diversity for ESG performance towards knowledge sharing: Empirical evidence from European banks. *Journal of Knowledge Management*, 28(11), 106–131. DOI:10.1108/JKM-05-2023-0445

Radu, O. M., Dragomir, V. D., & Ionescu-Feleagă, L. (2023). The Conceptual Link between Country Competitiveness and Corporate ESG Performance. *InProceedings of the International Conference on Business Excellence, 17*(1),763-775. DOI:10.2478/picbe-2023-0071

Schleich, M. V. (2022). What are the human resources policies and practices most used by companies with the best ESG ratios in Brazil? *RAE*, 62(5), e2021–e0370. DOI:10.1590/s0034-759020220511x

Shahbaz, M., Karaman, A. S., Kilic, M., & Uyar, A. (2020). Board attributes, CSR engagement, and corporate performance: What is the nexus in the energy sector? *Energy Policy*, 143, 111582. DOI:10.1016/j.enpol.2020.111582

Shmueli, G., Ray, S., Estrada, J. M. V., & Chatla, S. B. (2016). The elephant in the room: Predictive performance of PLS models. *Journal of Business Research*, 69(10), 4552–4564. DOI:10.1016/j.jbusres.2016.03.049

Silva, G. M., Styles, C., & Lages, L. F. (2017). Breakthrough innovation in international business: The impact of tech-innovation and market-innovation on performance. *International Business Review*, 26(2), 391–404. DOI:10.1016/j.ibusrev.2016.10.001

Stiles, P. (2001). The impact of the board on strategy: An empirical examination. *Journal of Management Studies*, 38(5), 627–650. DOI:10.1111/1467-6486.00252

Van Hoang, T. H., Przychodzen, W., Przychodzen, J., & Segbotangni, E. A. (2021). Environmental transparency and performance: Does the corporate governance matter? *Environmental and Sustainability Indicators*, 10, 100123. DOI:10.1016/j.indic.2021.100123

Wu, Q., Furuoka, F., & Lau, S. C. (2022). Corporate social responsibility and board gender diversity: A meta-analysis. *Management Research Review*, 45(7), 956–983. DOI:10.1108/MRR-03-2021-0236

Chapter 8

The Disclosure of Social Responsibility Information on the Websites of Non-Profit Organizations:

The Case of Portuguese Mercies

Corneliu Zabolotnic
School of Management and Technology, Polytechnic Institute of Santarém, Portugal

Rui Manuel da Costa Robalo
School of Management and Technology, Polytechnic Institute of Santarém, Portugal

ABSTRACT

This study analyses the social responsibility (SR) information disclosed by the Portuguese mercies that are part of the Union of Portuguese Mercies and that had a website. These non-profit organizations prefer to disclose SR information on their homepage, adopting mainly a text format balanced with images. Around half of them disclose between four and ten pages of SR information, with larger mercies disclosing more SR information pages than the smaller ones. The SR information disclosed mainly refers to their activities, rather than environment and/or human resources, and few disclose codes of conduct and/or ethics. This study contributes to the literature of SR disclosure in three ways. First, it adds empirical evidence related to a different type of non-profit organization that has not been studied.

DOI: 10.4018/979-8-3693-5663-0.ch008

Second, it provides evidence that the Portuguese mercies use their websites mainly to disclose SR information about their work area and activities. Third, it shows that the disclosure of SR information depends a lot on the characteristics of each type of non-profit organization.

INTRODUCTION

The themes of social responsibility (SR), and in particular corporate social responsibility, have attracted the interest of researchers from several scientific fields over the last few decades (Gray et al., 1995; Ebrahim, 2003; Monteiro & Aibar-Guzmán, 2009; Bebbington & Unerman, 2018). This has happened because social and environmental concerns have been increasing at different institutional levels. As far as the organizational level is concerned, it should be noted that it began by implying growing practices of voluntary disclosure of SR information by for-profit organizations (e.g., Branco & Rodrigues, 2008, Dincer & Dincer, 2010; Guziana & Dobers, 2013), SR disclosure practices that have been growing in non-profit organizations (e.g., Dainelli et al., 2013; Nie et al., 2016; Rossi et al., 2020).

Information asymmetries between organizations and their stakeholders, or at least the perception of such asymmetries, can give rise to doubts about the performance of organizations. In the context of non-profit organizations, funders, whether private or public, seek greater transparency in the SR information disclosed to ensure the best use of the resources they provide directly or indirectly to these organizations. Some non-profit organizations meet the needs of specific social groups that are the responsibility of public sector entities and are subject to showing how they use government funds (Knott & Wilson, 2024). In turn, organizations that receive little government funding rely more on donations and are more likely to voluntarily disclose SR information (Nie et al., 2016).

Organizations, whether for-profit or not-for-profit, disclose SR information using various instruments. Traditional accountability is one of the instruments adopted to disclose the work done by organizations in this field. This includes management reports, ease of access for stakeholder participation in dialogue with the organization, both external and internal performance evaluation and responding to stakeholder concerns (Tremblay-Boire & Prakash, 2014). In addition, for-profit and non-profit organizations have sought to disclose SR information on their websites (Dincer & Dincer, 2010; Dainelli et al., 2013; Robalo & Patrocínio, 2019; Monteiro et al., 2024). Websites are an important means of reporting SR practices because organizations' stakeholders increasingly rely on the Internet for their information needs.

Although there are more and more studies exploring the disclosure of SR information on websites of non-profit organizations, there is still a need to include a greater diversity of this type of organization. Mercies are social economy organizations recognized as private social solidarity institutions and are present in several countries (e.g., Portugal, Brazil, Spain, France, Italy, Luxembourg, Ukraine). The disclosure of SR information on mercies' websites has not been explored. Therefore, the aim of this study is to analyze the quantity and content of SR information disclosed by Portuguese mercies on their websites, as well as the ways and places in which it is disclosed on the websites.

The next section, the literature review, will look at the disclosure of SR information and stakeholder theory, the context of Portuguese mercies, as well as the formulation of the research questions. The third section, the research methodology, will present the procedures used to collect and analyze the empirical data. The fourth section presents and discusses the empirical results in relation to similar studies. Finally, the conclusions section will present the contributions and limitations of this study, as well as suggestions for future research.

LITERATURE REVIEW

Disclosure of SR Information and Stakeholder Theory

The concept of SR began to be understood by researchers as the part of the universe of language symbols, signs, meanings, norms, beliefs, perceptions and values by which individuals and organizations define themselves and are defined by others (Gray et al., 1995). In this context, SR information serves to rationalize and justify organizations' management practices. SR information can also be understood as a means by which individuals and organizations are held accountable for their actions (Ebrahim, 2005). The disclosure of SR information by organizations has thus emerged as a response to the concerns of their stakeholders and the possibility for them to assess their performance.

Several studies have identified different factors that influence the disclosure of SR information by organizations (e.g., Gray et al., 1995; Monteiro & Aibar-Guzmán, 2009; Ribeiro et al., 2016; Monteiro et al., 2024). These factors include time, the country of the organization, capital intensity, the age of the organization, the existence of a SR department, the attitude of executives, the size of the organization, the type of industry the organization is in, profitability, foreign ownership of the organization, stock exchange listing, the existence of environmental certificates, the accounting context and the degree of environmental management practices.

In turn, researchers have used different theoretical perspectives to understand the degree to which organizations disclose SR information. Early on, some researchers argued that economic issues cannot be studied in isolation from social, political and institutional issues, within which the economic issues are embedded (e.g. Gray et al., 1995). It is in this context that stakeholder theory takes on relevance, given its potential to interpret and explain organizations' SR disclosure practices (Gray et al, 1995; Dainelli et al., 2013; Ortega-Rodríguez et al., 2020; Rossi et al., 2020). This theory assumes that organizations are dependent on the support of their stakeholders. The stronger the power of the stakeholders, the more adaptive the organization must be. Thus, the disclosure of SR information is seen as a dialogue between the organization and its stakeholders.

Both for-profit and non-profit organizations depend heavily on the communication they adopt with their stakeholders. In turn, non-profit organizations are particularly vulnerable to SR difficulties, given the nature of their "products" and services, and the institutional context in which they operate. The study by Dhanani and Connolly (2014) shows that the non-governmental organizations analyzed felt a responsibility to disclose SR information, with annual reports and their reviews being a fundamental part of this process. The actions taken were an attempt to make the information accessible to various stakeholder groups. However, these organizations tried to emphasize the reporting requirements and expectations of the most powerful funders. There have been attempts to make documents more appealing to make them more accessible and, in some cases, to disclose SR information in an "entrepreneurial" way to maximize financial support. Competition for limited financial resources is one of the explanations for SR disclosure practices being aligned with the expectations of the most powerful stakeholders to secure financial support.

Websites are an instrument through which non-profit organizations reduce information asymmetries. Through websites, non-profit organizations voluntarily provide their stakeholders with additional information about their activities and increase their participation in the governance of these organizations. Websites can serve as a tool for fundraising or as an active policy for mobilizing supporters to reach potential clients. There are studies of online disclosure of SR information that propose two functions for websites - providing information and engaging in dialogue/interaction with stakeholders - but note that, in general, organizations have only used them for informational purposes (Kang & Norton 2004; Waters 2007; Gandía, 2009; Saxton & Guo 2011).

Websites make it possible to disclose SR information to a wider range of stakeholders at a relatively low cost. However, feeding information into websites can be costly for organizations with little experience, and resources may have to be diverted from tasks related to their missions. Each organization can be strategic when making its disclosures because its stakeholders may want proof that the organization is carrying out what was previously communicated and may even ask for more information on internal policies, and resisting such requests can create doubts about the quality of the information previously disclosed.

Research related to the disclosure of SR information by non-profit organizations has also produced evidence that more transparent organizations, i.e. those that disclose financial and non-financial information that exceeds mandatory legal requirements, attract more funds and donations than those that disclose simpler information on their websites. In addition to the amount of information disclosed on organizations' websites, the depth of the information, i.e. the level of detail of the content disclosed, is an important factor. For example, the study by Rossi et al. (2020) on 204 foundations in the UK and Italy showed how the depth of disclosure on websites affects donations. It showed that foundations that were more dependent on funds were more sensitive to the disclosure of detailed content about their performance. Also, the study by Dainelli et al. (2013) showed that SR disclosure practices on websites are influenced by the number and power of different stakeholders.

Context of the Portuguese Mercies

Within the scope of this study are the Portuguese mercies. The objectives of these organizations include the provision of goods, services and other initiatives to promote well-being and quality in the field of social solidarity. The Holy House of Mercy of Lisbon was the first Portuguese mercy, founded in 1498 by Friar Miguel Contreiras, with the support of Queen Leonor, widow of King João II. Queen Leonor devoted herself intensely to the sick, the poor, orphans, prisoners and artists, and sponsored the foundation of this mercy, establishing the first legitimate non-governmental organization in the world, at a time when it would have been unthinkable for a social institution to exist that declared itself to be lay and non-governmental (Holy House of Mercy of Passos, 2016). The Holy House of Mercy of Lisbon served as an inspiration for the creation of other mercies in Portugal and in the Portuguese diaspora, and mercies were the Portuguese Crown's main instrument of social action.

Currently, the Portuguese mercies are recognized as private social solidarity institutions (Decree-Law no. 172-A/2014), are considered social economy entities (Law no. 30/2013) and are a legal person of public utility (Law no. 36/2021). The mercies are active throughout Portugal and have a vast network of facilities that ensure adequate responses to the communities in which they operate and carry out their activities near citizens. They respond to social needs through different sources of funding. More specifically, funding for Portuguese mercies comes from several sources: (1) from the central administration of the Portuguese state, on a regular and occasional basis, to support specific needs; (2) from Portuguese municipalities, through protocols aimed at specific areas of intervention and priorities; (3) from contributions from users and families, in return for providing services in the several social responses; (4) from membership fees; (5) and from donations, inheritances and other income from activities carried out on the institutions' own initiative.

In turn, Portuguese mercies can be members of the Union of Portuguese Mercies (UPM). This organization was created in 1976 to guide, coordinate, stimulate and represent the Portuguese mercies, defending their interests and organizing services of common interest. According to articles 5 and 8 of the UPM's statutes, all of Portugal's current mercies and future brotherhoods constitute the UPM and will be admitted as UPM members by the fact of their existence (Union of Portuguese Mercies, 2015).

The UPM currently has around 360 mercies, which are present in 308 Portuguese municipalities. To support the mercies, the UPM has several service lines that accompany the leaders and technicians of the Portuguese mercies in areas that are decisive for their activities. In addition, the UPM manages facilities in areas such as profound disability, old age and health (Union of Portuguese Mercies, 2018).

In addition to its ongoing dialogue with the Portuguese mercies, the UPM has also acted in dialogue with a wide range of institutional partners. It has also represented the interests of the mercies in various forums. In turn, with a view to partnership and internationalization, the UPM is a member of structures such as the European Union of Mercies and the International Confederation of Mercies.

Formulation of the Research Questions

Non-profit organizations tend not to make enough use of the disclosure of SR information on their websites. For example, Saxton and Guo (2009) looked at the disclosure of SR information on the websites of 117 community foundations in the United States and concluded that these organizations do not use the full capacity of the Internet to engage with stakeholders. In this context, although 78 per cent of these foundations had basic resources for contacting stakeholders, only 7 per cent had more developed resources for soliciting the preferences and needs of interested parties. In turn, in the European context, the study by Rodríguez et al. (2011), based on information gathered from the websites of 130 Spanish non-governmental organizations, highlighted the scarcity of use of the Internet for disclosing SR information, despite the increase in its use. This study also points out that the websites were mainly used by these organizations to disclose SR information about their area of work and their activities.

The location of the websites where SR information is disclosed can vary between for-profit and non-profit organizations. For example, studies analyzing the location of SR information on the websites identify three locations: on the website's homepage, in a section of the website entitled “about us” or in a different section (Dincer &

Dincer, 2010; Rodriguez et al., 2011; Branco et al., 2014, Robalo & Patrocínio, 2019). According to these authors, when SR information is disclosed on the homepage, it indicates greater recognition and effort in the quality of disclosure. Disclosing SR information in the "about us" (or "who we are") section indicates an intention to make this information stand out. Organizations that have a specific section for the disclosure of SR information are more prominent than those that opt for the previous situations. However, the results differ between for-profit organizations (e.g., Dincer & Dincer, 2010; Branco et al., 2014) and non-profit organizations (e.g., Rodriguez et al., 2011; Robalo & Patrocínio). Therefore, based on the diversity of results from previous studies, the following research question is justified:

Q1: Do the Portuguese mercies disclose SR information on the homepage of their websites or on other pages?

The way in which SR information is disclosed on organizations' websites should also be studied to find out, for example, what kind of strategies they may be using to communicate with their stakeholders. According to Dincer & Dincer (2010), the three categories used to divide the disclosure of SR information on websites are: mainly text, mainly images, and text balanced with images. Here too, there appear to be differences between studies exploring this topic (e.g., Dincer & Dincer, 2010; Branco et al., 2014; Robalo & Patrocínio, 2019), which may be related to the specific context of the organizations studied. The following research question is therefore formulated:

Q2: What are the formats (text, image, and text balanced with image) for disclosing SR information adopted by the Portuguese mercies?

The number of pages of SR information disclosed on websites can show how committed organizations are to communicating this type of information to their stakeholders. Here too, there are major differences between for-profit organizations (e.g., Dincer & Dincer, 2010; Branco et al., 2014), and between for-profit and non-profit organizations (e.g., Robalo & Patrocínio, 2019). Non-profit organizations disclose fewer SR information pages than for-profit organizations. This can also vary depending on the type of non-profit organization. Therefore, for the context of the Portuguese mercies, the following research question is formulated:

Q3: How many pages do the Portuguese mercies have for disclosing SR information on their websites?

The size of the organization is also one of the factors that could influence the disclosure of SR information on the websites of Portuguese mercies. Generally, studies on the influence of the size of non-profit organizations on the disclosure of SR information have reported an association between these two aspects (e.g., Rodríguez et al., 2011; Leardini et al., 2020; Rossi et al., 2020). This tends to be explained by the fact that larger non-profit organizations are aware of the need to communicate online with their stakeholders (Rodríguez et al., 2011), and have more financial and technical resources to do so. However, there are also studies that do not confirm this association between greater organizational size and a higher level of disclosure of SR information (e.g., Tremblay-Boire & Prakash, 2014; Ribeiro et al., 2016; Robalo & Patrocínio, 2019). This study therefore poses the following research question:

Q4: Do the larger Portuguese mercies disclose more SR information on their websites than the smaller ones?

It is also relevant to study in greater detail the content of SR information disclosed on the websites of for-profit and non-profit organizations. In the context of for-profit organizations, Branco and Rodrigues (2008) divided the disclosure of SR information into four categories: (1) environmental, (2) human resources, (3) products and consumers, and (4) community involvement. The authors report that the information most disclosed on websites was more related to products and consumers, followed by information related to human resources. In the context of non-profit organizations, Tremblay-Boire and Prakash (2014) analyzed the disclosure of SR information on the websites of 200 non-governmental organizations in the United States of America in four sectors: (a) arts, culture and humanity, (b) education, (c) health and (d) religion. Religious organizations had a low level of disclosure because the trust between donors and these organizations is already established by the religious bond. Organizations in the health sector disclosed more information on their websites in order to combat the asymmetries underlying the type of goods they provide, as well as due to the government requirements in the country. In the European context, Rodríguez et al. (2011) showed that the 123 Spanish non-governmental organizations disclosed little about economic and organizational aspects, while they disclosed more information related to social objectives, such as areas of work and beneficiaries. Therefore, given the diversity of the type of disclosures presented in previous studies, the following research question is formulated:

Q5: Do Portuguese mercies disclose information related to the environment, human resources, products/services and users on their websites?

Finally, codes of conduct and/or ethics also tend to show the commitment that for-profit and non-profit organizations may have to adopting socially responsible activities and practices. Codes of conduct and/or ethics are documents that work as an instrument containing rules, guidelines and standards based on the organization's values and principles to influence decisions, guide relations with internal and external stakeholders and encourage the behaviors that is intended to be instilled in employees. For-profit and non-profit organizations tend to have high levels of disclosure of these codes (e.g. Branco et al., 2014; Robalo & Patrocínio, 2019). However, this is not always the case in non-profit organizations (Tremblay-Boire & Prakash, 2014). The following research question is therefore formulated for the Portuguese mercies:

Q6: Do Portuguese mercies disclose codes of conduct and/or ethics on their websites?

The methodological steps followed in this study to answer the formulated research questions are described in the next section.

RESEARCH METHODOLOGY

Data on the disclosure of SR information was collected via the websites of the Portuguese mercies belonging to the UPM, and links to these websites are available at the following electronic address: https://www.ump.pt/Home/misericordias/misericordias-em-portugal/. Data was collected between 21 October 2020 and 30 March 2021. This collection followed a geographical criterion, starting in the north-west of the country and ending in the south-east. Thus, during the total data collection period, SR information content was collected from the UPM member organizations that had a website.

A form was created to collect data on the disclosure of SR information by Portuguese mercies. The structure of this form followed the research questions formulated in section 2.3 of this study, and an Excel sheet was created for each of the mercies. Thus, in relation to each mercy's website, we first visualized where the initial link for disclosing SR information was, with the options available according to research question Q1 (“home page” or “other”).

In relation to research question Q2 concerning the presentation format of the SR information pages on the websites of the UPM's mercies, data was collected to analyze whether these mercies presented this information mainly in “text” format, in “image” format or in “text balanced with images” format. The distinction between these three types of SR information disclosure was made as follows: (i) if the pages presented no images or not very relevant images and presented text, then it was considered “mainly text”; (ii) if the pages presented mainly images and some text in which there was only a description of the image, then it was considered “mainly images”; (iii) and if the pages presented images and text describing the images plus additional text about SR information on the page under analysis, then it was considered “text balanced with images”.

In relation to research question Q3, the number of pages on which the UPM's mercies disclose SR information was defined based on the reference of the size of an A4 physical page. In turn, the information collected on this item was based on three levels of disclosure (between 1 and 3 pages, between 4 and 10 pages, and more than 10 pages), to be comparable with other studies that have adopted this benchmark of disclosure levels.

To answer research question Q4, it was necessary to collect data on the value of the financial assets and the number of employees of each of the mercies belonging to the UPM. Thus, for each mercy, information was collected on its financial assets contained in the financial statements for 2019 in their management reports and/or accounts disclosed on their website. In cases where this information was not available for 2019, the information from the most recent year available was inserted. In turn, the number of employees was also obtained from the information in the management reports available on the websites. The mercies were grouped by different dimensions according to the criteria adopted by Robalo & Patrocínio (2019), i.e. the criteria established by Decree-Law 98/2015, of 2 June, in relation to the total balance sheet of the entities and the number of employees.

To answer research question Q5, data was collected on the SR information content disclosed on the mercies' websites relating to the environment, human resources, and products/services and users. The data on products/services and users was searched for in the following focus areas (valences): food, culture, worship, employment, ageing, children, young people, precariousness, disability, health, heritage, volunteering, environment, refugees, home support, domestic violence, education, senior education and other areas of social responsibility.

Finally, to answer research question Q6 on codes of ethics and/or conduct, we searched the websites of the mercies belonging to the UPM for documents with rules, guidelines and standards based on the values and principles of these organizations, which were intended to guide the behavior of their employees towards the various stakeholders.

Presentation and Discussion of Results

This research included the population of 360 mercies, of which 298 (83%) had a website and the remaining 62 (17%) did not have a website. In turn, and in relation to the first research question, around 71.5% of mercies with a website disclose SR information on their homepage, while 28.5% disclose it on other pages of their websites.

These results are surprisingly similar to those of the study by Branco et al. (2014) on Swedish and Spanish companies listed on capital markets, but different from those of the study by Robalo & Patrocínio (2019), which focuses on Portuguese foundations, i.e. non-profit organizations. However, it should also be noted that there are different behaviors among Portuguese mercies and that the use of the "home page" may be related to the fact that these mercies are mostly small and medium-sized, using the home page to communicate with their stakeholders. In turn, and as Rodriguez et al. (2011) point out, the size of non-profit organizations affects the disclosure of SR information on their websites, and these smaller organizations tend to disclose mainly information about their areas of work and their activities. Thus, the results obtained in this study can be interpreted as meaning that the mercies carry out certain standard activities for social support, which are presented right on the home page to disclose their purpose.

Regarding the format in which SR information is disclosed (research question Q2), there is a clear preference among Portuguese mercies for a text format balanced with images. Around 70% of the mercies adopt a balanced disclosure format between text and images, while 23% choose to disclose their SR information almost exclusively through text and 7% adopt the image format. The results obtained regarding the presentation format of SR information continue to differ from the results obtained by Robalo & Patrocínio (2019) on Portuguese foundations, which mainly disclose SR information in text format. Portuguese mercies mainly disclose this information in text format balanced with images. This is an important result of this study. This may be because the foundations have more pages with their projects and their explanations than the mercies. In this sense, the mercies had fewer pages dedicated to projects. This may also be because the mercies have protocols with municipalities and financial support from the Portuguese state to support and fulfil social needs. One of the mercies' objectives seems to present and inform about the "services" they provide, seeking to communicate more effectively with their stakeholders.

Regarding the number of pages of SR information that Portuguese mercies disclose (research question Q3), there are different practices. Excluding the pages dedicated to information about the Covid-19 pandemic, around half of the mercies disclose between four and ten pages of SR information (see Table 1).

Table 1. Levels of disclosure of SR information of Portuguese mercies

Levels of disclosure	*Number of mercies*	*Percentage*
Between 1 and 3 pages	44	15%
Between 4 and 10 pages	152	51%
More than 10 pages	77	26%
Not disclosed	25	8%
Total	**298**	**100%**

The results obtained regarding the number of pages of SR information disclosed on the websites of Portuguese mercies differ significantly from the patterns shown in studies on for-profit organizations (e.g., Branco et al., 2014; Dincer & Dincer, 2010) and studies on non-profit organizations (e.g., Robalo & Patrocínio, 2019). Once again, these results seem to show that this type of non-profit organization has its own specificities in terms of its social mission and institutional context.

To explore the effect of size on the disclosure of SR information, the criteria defined by Decree-Law 98/2015 of 2 June were used for the Portuguese context. These criteria were based on the value of financial assets and the number of employees. Of the 298 mercies that had a website, 100 of them did not disclose information on the value of their financial assets and/or the number of employees on their website. As a result, of the 198 Portuguese mercies that cumulatively disclosed this information, most of them are classified as medium or small mercy. Only 2 per cent are classified as large mercy and 3 per cent as micro mercy (see Table 2).

Table 2. Number of mercies by type of size

Type of size	*Number of mercies*	*Percentage*
Big	4	2%
Average	100	51%
Small	89	45%
Micro	5	3%
Total	**198**	**100%**

With regard to research question Q4, this study shows that larger mercies disclose more SR information pages than smaller ones (see Table 3), which is consistent with the majority of studies on for-profit and non-profit organizations, with the exception of some studies on non-profit organizations (e.g., Trimblay-Boire & Prakash, 2014; Robalo & Patrocínio, 2019). In turn, large Portuguese mercies disclose more pages related to heritage, followed by topics related to ageing. In fact, ageing is the content most disclosed by mercies the other sizes.

Table 3. Average number of pages disclosed by type of size

Type of size	*Total number of disclosed pages*	*Number of mercies*	*Average number of pages per mercy*
Big	86	4	22
Average	1028	100	10
Small	541	89	6
Micro	16	5	3
Total	**1671**	**198**	---

Regarding research question Q5 on the content of the information disclosed on the mercies' websites, only 1 page on the environment was published by a mercy that did not disclose information on assets and the number of employees. Considering only those mercies that disclosed information on assets and the number of employees, regarding human resources only 4% of the pages disclosed on the websites were related to volunteering. Compared to the study by Robalo & Patrocínio (2019) on Portuguese foundations, the results were similar in the sense that the information disclosed on human resources and the environment was also low.

The SR information disclosed by the mercies refer mainly to their activities (see Table 4). This situation is similar to that reported in the study by Rodríguez et al. (2011) on Spanish non-governmental organizations, which disclosed more about their areas of work and beneficiaries. Ageing is the content most disclosed by the Portuguese mercies, followed by childhood and health. These mercies act as organizations to meet the needs of the community. As Portugal is an ageing country, it is the mercies that act in care for the elderly, fulfilling a specific need in the country. With health content being the third most disclosed, most of the time this content also referred to care for the elderly.

Table 4. Number of SR pages disclosed by valence and dimension

Valence	*Large size*	*Medium size*	*Small size*	*Micro size*	*Total*
Food	3	45	35	1	**84**
Home support	3	86	57	3	**149**
Trade	1	8	3	0	**12**
Covid-19	4	48	30	1	**83**
Worship	0	14	15	1	**30**
Culture	4	47	22	0	**73**
Disability	3	12	5	2	**22**
Education	0	2	0	0	**2**
Senior education	0	1	2	0	**3**
Employment	0	12	2	0	**14**
Ageing	15	238	146	4	**403**
Childhood	7	158	63	0	**228**
Young people	5	10	7	0	**22**
Other areas of social responsibility	2	11	2	0	**15**
Heritage	20	83	56	0	**159**
Precarity	4	63	35	2	**104**
Refugees	0		1	0	**1**
Health	11	146	42	1	**200**
Domestic violence	1	1	0	0	**2**
Volunteering	3	43	18	1	**65**
No information	0	3	7	1	**11**
Total	**86**	**1028**	**541**	**16**	**1671**

In addition, the mercies also work for children and young people, through crèches and youth homes, to eliminate, in the latter case, risk factors for young people who are more marginalized by society. The mercies are long-lived organizations with a valuable historical heritage, and this content is widely disclosed. Given the mercies' connection to religion, it is interesting that the content related to religious worship was only ranked eleventh. The result obtained for the disclosure of religious information may be justified by the trust that donors and these organizations have in the religious link, as argued by Tremblay-Boire & Prakash (2014).

Regarding codes of conduct and/or ethics (research question Q6), this study shows that these codes were disclosed by 29 mercies, far less than expected. Few mercies have disclosed this type of document, contrary to the results of Branco *et al.* (2014) and Robalo & Patrocínio (2019), which once again reinforces the specificities of this type of non-profit organization. This may indicate that this type of organization already has a good reputation and does not consider it relevant to disclose a code of conduct and/or ethics to increase its legitimacy with its stakeholders (Tremblay-Boire & Prakash, 2014).

CONCLUSION

This study analyzed the quantity, form and content of SR information disclosed on the websites of the Portuguese mercies belonging to the UPM (Union of Portuguese Mercies), as well as the location of the website where it is disclosed. Portuguese mercies prefer to disclose SR information on their homepage, adopting mainly a text format balanced with images. Excluding the pages dedicated to information about the Covid-19 pandemic, around half of the Portuguese mercies disclose between four and ten pages of SR information. The larger mercies disclose more SR information pages than the smaller ones, and the SR information disclosed mainly refers to their activities, rather than environment and/or human resources. Few mercies disclose codes of conduct and/or ethics.

The study on the websites of Portuguese mercies contributed to the issue of the disclosure of SR information by non-profit organizations in different ways. The first contribution of this study is that it is a pioneer in exploring the disclosure of SR information in mercies, a type of non-profit organization that has not captured the attention of researchers, and there is still no accumulated knowledge.

The second contribution of this study stems from the fact that Portuguese mercies use their websites mainly to disclose information about their area of work and their activities, as has happened in other types of non-profit organizations reported in other studies (e.g., Rodríguez *et al.,* 2011; Tremblay-Boire & Prakash, 2014).

The third and final contribution of this study is related to the specific nature of this type of non-profit organization (mercy), in terms of its history, its social mission and its organizational management. These specificities may help to explain why many of the results obtained in this study differ significantly from the results of other studies that have looked at the disclosure of SR information in both for-profit and non-profit organizations.

This study also has its limitations. One of these is related to the fact that it only looked at a specific type of non-profit organization and in just one country. It is therefore suggested that future research could look at mercies located in other countries or other types of non-profit organizations, whether in a national or international context.

REFERENCES

Bebbington, J., & Unerman, J. (2018). Achieving the United Nations sustainable sevelopment goals: An enabling role of accounting research. *Accounting, Auditing & Accountability Journal*, 31(1), 2–24. DOI:10.1108/AAAJ-05-2017-2929

Bo, H., Li, T., & Toolsema, L. (2009). Corporate social responsibility investment and social objectives: An examination on social welfare investment of Chinese state owned enterprises. *Scottish Journal of Political Economy*, 56(3), 267–295. DOI:10.1111/j.1467-9485.2009.00484.x

Branco, M. C., Delgado, C. J., Sá, M., & Sousa, C. (2014). Comparing CSR communication on corporate websites in Sweden and Spain. *Baltic Journal of Management*, 9(2), 231–250. DOI:10.1108/BJM-10-2013-0151

Branco, M. C., & Rodrigues, L. L. (2008). Factors influencing social responsibility disclosure by Portuguese companies. *Journal of Business Ethics*, 83(4), 685–701. DOI:10.1007/s10551-007-9658-z

Carvalho, F., Santos, G., & Gonçalves, J. (2018). The disclosure of information on sustainable development on the corporate website of the certified Portuguese organisations. *International Journal of Qualitative Research*, 12(1), 253–276. DOI:10.18421/IJQR12.01-14

Dainelli, F., Manetti, G., & Sibilio, B. (2013). Web-Based Accountability Practices in Non-profit Organisations: The Case of National Museums. *Voluntas*, 24(3), 649–665. DOI:10.1007/s11266-012-9278-9

Decree-Law no. 119/83. *Official Journal of the Portuguese Republic*, no. 46 - Series I, of 25 February.

Decree-Law no. 172-A/2014. *Official Journal of the Portuguese Republic*, no. 221 - Series I, of 14 November.

Decree-Law no. 89/2017. *Official Journal of the Portuguese Republic*, no. 145 - Series I, of 28 July.

Decree-Law no. 98/2015. *Official Journal of the Portuguese Republic*, no. 106 - Series I, of 2 June.

Dhanani, A., & Connolly, C. (2014). Non-governmental organisational accountability: Talking the talk and walking the walk? *Journal of Business Ethics*, 129(3), 613–637. DOI:10.1007/s10551-014-2172-1

Dincer, C., & Dincer, B. (2010). An investigation of Turkish small and medium-sized enterprises online CSR communication. *Social Responsibility Journal*, 6(2), 197–207. DOI:10.1108/17471111011051711

Ebrahim, A. (2005). Accountability myopia: Losing sight of organisational learning. *Nonprofit and Voluntary Sector Quarterly*, 34(1), 56–87. DOI:10.1177/0899764004269430

Ebrhahim, A. (2003). Accountability in practice: Mechanisms for NGOs. *World Development*, 31(5), 813–829. DOI:10.1016/S0305-750X(03)00014-7

Fu, W., & Deshpande, S. (2012). Factors impacting ethical behaviour in a Chinese state-owned steel company. *Journal of Business Ethics*, 105(2), 231–237. DOI:10.1007/s10551-011-0962-2

Gandía, L. J. (2009). Internet disclosure by nonprofit organisations: Empirical evidence of nongovernmental organisations for development in Spain. *Nonprofit and Voluntary Sector Quarterly*, 40(1), 57–78. DOI:10.1177/0899764009343782

Garde-Sanchez, R., López-Pérez, M. V., & López-Hernández, A. M. (2018). Current trends in research on social responsibility in state-owned enterprises: A review of the literature from 2000 to 2017. *Sustainability (Basel)*, 10(2403), 2403. Advance online publication. DOI:10.3390/su10072403

Gray, R., Kouhy, R., & Lavers, S. (1995). Corporate social and environmental reporting: A review of the literature and a longitudinal study of UK disclosure. *Accounting, Auditing & Accountability Journal*, 8(2), 44–47. DOI:10.1108/09513579510146996

Gunningham, K. N., & Thornton, D. (2003). *Shades of green*. Stanford University.

Guziana, B., & Dobers, P. (2013). How sustainability leaders communicate corporate activities of sustainable development. *Corporate Social Responsibility and Environmental Management*, 20(4), 193–204. DOI:10.1002/csr.1292

Habermas, J. (1987). *The theory of communicative action: Lifeworld and systems, a critique of functionalist reason*. Polity Press.

Hansmann, H. B. (1980). The role of nonprofit enterprise. *The Yale Law Journal*, 89(5), 835–902. http://hdl.handle.net/20.500.13051/4588. DOI:10.2307/796089

Holy House of Mercy of Passos. (2016). *The history of the Holy Houses*. Imprensa. Retrieved June 3, 2021, from http://www.scmp.org.br/materia/61/a-historia-das-santas-casas

Kang, S., & Norton, H. E. (2004). Nonprofit organisations' use of the world wide web: Are they sufficiently fulfilling organisational goals? *Public Relations Review*, 30(3), 279–284. DOI:10.1016/j.pubrev.2004.04.002

Knott, S., & Wilson, J. P. (2024). Core charitable purpose and voluntary CSR activities in charity organisations: Do they conflict? *Social Responsibility Journal*, 20(6), 1056–1071. DOI:10.1108/SRJ-09-2023-0498

Law no. 30/2013. *Official Journal of the Portuguese Republic*, no. 88 - Series I, of 8 May.

Leardini, C., Rossi, G., & Landi, S. (2020). Organisational factors affecting charitable giving in the environmental nonprofit context. *Sustainability (Basel)*, 12(21), 8947. DOI:10.3390/su12218947

Monteiro, S., & Aibar-Guzmán, B. (2009). Determinants of environmental disclosure in the annual reports of large companies operating in Portugal. *Corporate Social Responsibility and Environmental Management*, 17(4), 185–204. DOI:10.1002/csr.197

Monteiro, S., Ribeiro, V., Vilhena, E., Lemos, K., & Molho, C. (2024). Determinants of online-reporting on sustainable development goals: The case of Portuguese higher education institutions. *Social Responsibility Journal*, 20(3), 462–484. DOI:10.1108/SRJ-01-2023-0044

Ortega-Rodríguez, C., Licerán-Gutiérrez, A., & Moreno-Albarracín, A. L. (2020). Transparency as a key element in accountability in non-profit organisations: A systematic literature review. *Sustainability (Basel)*, 12(14), 5834. DOI:10.3390/su12145834

Ribeiro, V. P., Aibar-Guzman, B., Aibar-Guzmán, C., & Monteiro, S. (2016). Determinants of environmental accounting and reporting practices in Portuguese local entities. *Corporate Communications*, 21(3), 352–370. DOI:10.1108/CCIJ-11-2015-0071

Robalo, R., & Patrocínio, W. (2019). Disclosure of corporate social responsibility on the websites of Portuguese foundations. In A. Ferreira, R. Marques, G. Azevedo, H. Inácio, & C. Santos (Eds.), *Modernisation and accountability in the social economy sector* (pp. 176-195). DOI:10.4018/978-1-5225-8482-7.ch010

Rodríguez, M. D., Pérez, M. D., & Godoy, M. L. (2011). Determining factors in online transparency of NGOs: A Spanish case study. *Voluntas*, 23(3), 661–683. DOI:10.1007/s11266-011-9229-x

Rossi, G., Leardini, C., & Landi, S. (2020). The more you know, the more you give: Influence of online disclosure on European community foundations' donations. *Nonprofit Management & Leadership*, 31(1), 81–101. DOI:10.1002/nml.21412

Saxton, G. D., & Guo, C. (2009). Accountability online: Understanding the web-based accountability practices of nonprofit organisations. *Nonprofit and Voluntary Sector Quarterly*, 40(2), 270–295. DOI:10.1177/0899764009341086

Tremblay-Boire, J., & Prakash, A. (2014). Accountability.org: Online disclosures by U.S. nonprofits. *Voluntas*, 26(2), 693–719. DOI:10.1007/s11266-014-9452-3

Union of Portuguese Mercies. (2015). *Statutes of the Union of Portuguese Mercies*. Union of Portuguese Mercies. https://cdn.ump.pt/files/files/Estatutos.pdf

Union of Portuguese Mercies. (2018). *Presentation of the UPM*. Retrieved March 1, 2021, from Union of Portuguese Mercies. https://www.ump.pt/Home/uniao/apresentacao/

Waters, R. D. (2007). Nonprofit organisations' use of the internet: A content analysis of communication trends on the internet sites of the Philanthropy 400. *Nonprofit Management & Leadership*, 18(1), 59–76. DOI:10.1002/nml.171

Chapter 9
The Quality of Sustainability Reporting of the Largest Portuguese Companies

Sónia Monteiro
CICF, Polytechinc University of Cávado and Ave, Portugal

Vanda Roque
https://orcid.org/0000-0001-6038-1851
UNIAG, Polytechnic University of Cávado and Ave, Portugal

Márcia Faria
Polytechnic University of Cávado and Ave, Portugal

ABSTRACT

This study aims to identify whether regulation and sector of activity influence the quality of sustainability reporting. By analysing the content of 2021 sustainability reports of 66 large Portuguese companies, the authors construct a sustainability reporting quality index based on the 2016 GRI standards. By means of a univariate and multivariate analysis, they test the influence of regulation and sector of activity on the quality of sustainability reporting. The results suggest that the requirement for non-financial reporting, imposed by the European directive, does not influence the quality of Portuguese companies' sustainability reporting, except in the environmental dimension. Although the quality index is low (19.6%), the results show that there are statistically significant differences between the quality of environmental reporting and the type of sector. According to the analysis, companies belonging to environmentally sensitive sectors report environmental information with higher

DOI: 10.4018/979-8-3693-5663-0.ch009

quality.

INTRODUCTION

Sustainability reporting has become crucial for companies. Sustainability is becoming an increasingly important issue in society, forcing companies to demonstrate and be accountable for their impact on the economy, the environment, and society. To address the pressures from stakeholders, companies publish sustainability reports (SRs), which outline their policies and initiatives concerning the economy, the environment, and society (Carvajal & Nadeem, 2022).

Within the European Union (EU), Directive 2014/95/EU of 22 October 2014 (transposed into Portugal by Decree-Law 89/2017 of 28 July) established mandatory non-financial reporting for certain types of entities. The disclosure of non-financial information can be included in the management report or presented separately (for example, through SRs).

Authors such as Romero et al. (2019) argue that the quality of non-financial information is higher when presented in SRs. Balluchi et al. (2020) consider that the use of separate reports is more beneficial for companies, allowing them to aggregate more information and delve deeper into the topics covered. In fact, there is empirical evidence (e.g. Pereira et al., 2020; Caputo et al., 2020; Ottenstein et al., 2022) of a positive relationship between the use of separate reports and the quality of non-financial information disclosed, suggesting that the EU Directive has contributed to improve the quality of information.

Several studies have investigated the factors that influence sustainability reporting. Some authors (e.g. Dienes et al. 2016; Farisyi et al., 2022; Benvenuto et al., 2023) have identified a common set of factors linked to companies' characteristics, such as size, sector of activity, corporate governance, among others, which can affect sustainability reporting. However, there are still few studies that focus on the quality of sustainability reporting (Minutiello & Tettamanzi, 2022), especially in the Portuguese context.

In this context, this study aims to evaluate the quality of sustainability reporting in Portugal and explore its determinant factors. Focusing on a sample comprising the "500 Largest & Best Portuguese Companies", our objective is to assess the comprehensiveness of their SRs and determine if they meet the disclosure requirements of the most important international framework for sustainability reporting, namely the Global Reporting Initiative (GRI) standards. Additionally, this study investigates whether the quality of sustainability reporting is affected by the mandatory non-financial reporting requirements of Directive 2014/95/EU and/or the involvement of companies in environmentally sensitive sectors.

This study contributes to the scarce empirical literature on sustainability reporting quality by developing a detailed sustainability reporting quality index, based on the disclosure requirements of 2016 GRI standards, which can be useful for researchers who wish to replicate it in different geographical contexts and develop comparative studies.

The remainder of the paper is structured as follows: the next section presents the theoretical background and research hypotheses. Following that, the methodology is presented, namely the sample and methods, and the results are discussed. Finally, the main conclusions are presented as well as the main limitations and the suggestions for future research.

BACKGROUND AND RESEARCH HYPOTESIS

In recent years, there has been an increase in international efforts to develop common principles to guide companies preparing their SRs. These principles underscore the relationship between organisations' environmental and social behaviour and their strategy, governance, and performance. The aim is to assist companies in making more sustainable decisions and enabling stakeholders to understand the organisation's operations accurately (Bachoo et al., 2013).

The GRI standards are recognised as the most important framework for preparing SRs and widely used internationally (KPMG, 2020). In Portugal, the GRI Standards were the most widely used among listed companies in 2017 (Carmo & Ribeiro, 2022). Moreover, companies adhering to GRI Standards for preparing SRs are more likely to report more detailed information (Carmo & Ribeiro, 2022).

Over the years, several countries, such as Denmark, Australia, France, and the United Kingdom, have initiated mandatory sustainability disclosures for public interest companies (Hoffmann et al., 2018). The EU has also intensified efforts to enhance corporate transparency concerning sustainability issues (Posadas et al., 2022). The Directive 2014/95/EU requires large undertakings (i.e., public-interest entities exceeding, on average, 500 employees) to disclose a non-financial statement containing information of its activities related to environmental and social issues, as well as human rights, anti-corruption and anti-bribery efforts. Non-financial information should be included in the management report or presented separately in a financial statement, with some companies opting to use SRs.

Several studies have analysed the relationship between mandatory sustainability reporting and the quality of the information disclosed, yielding inconclusive results. Tudor et al. (2019) argue that the decision to disclose sustainability information is not influenced by legal obligations imposed on companies. In the Portuguese context, Carmo and Ribeiro (2022) observed that companies subject to mandatory disclosure continue to report non-financial information in a limited manner, with crucial information often undisclosed. According to Posadas et al. (2022), the introduction of Directive 2014/95/EU had no impact on enhancing the quality of non-financial reporting. Thus, non-financial reporting still exhibits several shortcomings, indicating room for improvement (Hoffmann et al., 2018).

Conversely, Monteiro et al. (2023) concluded that large Portuguese companies obliged to report non-financial information by the Decree-Law 89/2017, which transposed the EU directive, had higher average disclosures compared to those reporting non-financial information voluntarily. In the Italian and German contexts, Mion and Adaui (2019) found that Directive 2014/95/EU contributed to increase the quality of the non-financial information disclosed, demonstrating ta positive relationship between mandatory non-financial information disclosure and the quality of information provided to stakeholders.

In light of the above, we have defined the following research hypothesis:

H1: The quality of sustainability information is higher for companies subject to mandatory non-financial reporting than for companies disclosing non-financial information voluntarily.

Several studies have examined whether the quality of non-financial information disclosed differs between companies in environmentally sensitive sectors or those that are not. Companies in sensitive industries often exhibit greater environmental vulnerabilities, attracting increased attention from stakeholders (Reverte, 2016). Thus, companies in environmentally sensitive sectors may provide higher-quality non-financial information compared to those outside such sectors (Tudor et al., 2019; Posadas et al., 2022).

In light of the above, we propose the following research hypothesis:

H2: The quality of sustainability information is higher for companies in environmentally sensitive sectors than for companies not in environmentally sensitive sectors.

These hypotheses are supported by DiMaggio and Powell's Institutional Theory (1983). Institutional Theory posits that organisations are influenced by the institutional context in which they operate (Posadas et al., 2022). According to DiMaggio and Powell (1983), there are three types of institutional pressure: coercive, mimetic, and normative. Coercive pressure emanates from legal systems and societal expectations, leading companies to adjust their behaviour to comply with applicable laws and societal norms. Mimetic pressure prompts companies to imitate best practices of successful peers in response to uncertainty. Normative pressure is associated with professional norms and values in specific fields.

This theory incorporates the term "isomorphism" to describe companies operating within the same institutional context, that are compelled to make similar decisions to attain legitimacy (Bartolacci et al., 2022). Coercive isomorphism arises from the pressure exerted on companies by other organisations and societal expectations. This pressure prompts companies to adjust their behaviour to comply with the prevailing laws and norms of the society in which they operate (DiMaggio & Powell, 1983). Studies by Posadas et al. (2022) and Tudor et al. (2019) support the institutional theory (mimetic isomorphism). They demonstrate that mimetic institutional mechanisms are more effective in enhancing the quality of non-financial information disclosed. In this study, coercive isomorphism may explain the mandatory non-financial information disclosures and mimetic isomorphism may be related to similarities in sustainability reporting within sectors, if existent.

METHODOLOGY

Sample

The study focuses on the "500 Largest & Best Portuguese Companies" of 2021, as identified in the special edition of Exame magazine. Of these 500 companies, 203 were excluded because their reports included the activities of other companies within the same group that either do not operate solely in Portugal or disclose sustainable information through other types of reports (e.g. integrated report, annual report and accounts). This exclusion resulted in a sample of 297 companies. Among these 297 companies, only 66 companies (22%) disclosed SRs in 2021, which constitutes our final sample. Within the group of companies disclosing SRs, 54 (82%) did so voluntarily, while 12 companies (18%) disclosed SRs to comply with the obligation imposed by Directive 2014/95/EU. Regarding the sector of activity, 20 companies (30%) belong to environmentally sensitive sectors, while 46 (70%) do not belong to environmentally sensitive sectors (see Table 1).

Table 1. Sample characterisation

Type of Disclosure		Type of Sector	
Mandatory	**Voluntary**	**Environmentally sensitive**	**Non-Environmentally sensitive**
12 (18%)	54 (82%)	20 (30%)	46 (70%)

Source: Own elaboration

Methods

To assess the quality of sustainability disclosures, we conducted a content analysis of the 2021 SRs published by the companies in the sample. We analyse a total of 502 disclosure requirements based on 2016 GRI Standards (see Appendix I), covering:

- Universal Standards: General Disclosures (GRI 102) and Management Approach (GRI 103), totalling 166 disclosure requirements;
- Specific Standards: focused on Economic Performance (GRI 200), Environmental Performance (GRI 300) and Social Performance (GRI 400), totalling 336 disclosure requirements.

Based on these 502 disclosure requirements, we created a Sustainability Reporting Quality Index to gauge the quality of information of SRs. For each requirement (i_n), we assigned a value of 1 if it was disclosed by the company (0 otherwise). The final value of the Index is determined by the quotient between the total number of requirements disclosed by the company and the total number of disclosure requirements comprising the Index (i), as per the formula below:

$$Index = \frac{\sum_{n=1} 1_n}{j}$$

Furthermore, based on GRI specific standards, we developed three sub-indices: Economic, Environmental and Social, considering the maximum number of disclosure requirements in each topic (59, 146 and 131, respectively).

In an initial stage, we conducted a univariate analysis to examine the differences in the quality of sustainability reporting based on the obligation to disclose non-financial information (H1) and on the environmental sensitive sector (H2).

To test the first research hypothesis, companies disclosing SRs were categorised into two groups: 1) companies obligated to report non-financial information; and 2) companies voluntarily reporting non-financial information. This categorisation followed the rule imposed by Directive 2014/95/EU.

To test the second research hypothesis, companies disclosing SRs were categorised into two groups: 1) companies in environmentally sensitive sectors; and 2) companies in non-environmentally sensitive sectors. This categorisation was based on previous studies, namely Fernandez-Feijoo et al. (2014) and Monteiro & Aibar-Guzmán (2010). The environmentally sensitive sectors are: Forestry, Pulp and Paper, Mining, Oil and Gas, Construction, Pharmaceuticals and Transport.

We then employed a t-test for independent samples or the respective non-parametric test, if the conditions for applying the parametric test (normal distribution and homogeneity of variance) were not met.

In a second stage, we conducted a multivariate analysis using multiple linear regression, wherein the quality of SRs (as measured by the Index) served as the dependent variable and the type of disclosure (mandatory vs. voluntary) and the type of sector (environmentally sensitive vs. non- environmentally sensitive) were the independent variables. Additionally, size and profitability were introduced as control variables. Size was measured by the natural logarithm of assets in 2021, whereas profitability was measured by return on assets (ROA) in 2021. The equation below outlines the multiple linear regression model considered:

INDEX = $\alpha_0 + \beta_1$.(Type of disclosure) + β_2.(Type of sector)+ β_3.(Size)+ β_4.(-Profitability) + e

RESULTS DISCUSSION

Descriptive Analysis

Table 2 presents the descriptive statistics for the Sustainability Reporting Quality Indices.

Table 2. Sustainability reporting quality indices

Index	Minimum	Maximum	Average	Standard deviation
Global	0.017	0.368	0.196	0.099
Economic	0.000	0.254	0.120	0.080
Environmental	0.000	0.230	0.093	0.063
Social	0.000	0.282	0.112	0.076

Source: Own elaboration

As observed, the Global Index ranges from 0.017 to 0.368, with an average of 0.196. SRs disclosure satisfies only a small portion of the disclosure requirements outlined in the 2016 GRI Standards, indicating a relatively low quality of SRs among Portuguese companies. This finding aligns with the conclusions drawn by Carmo and Ribeiro (2022) and Hoffmann et al. (2018), who noted significant gaps in non-financial information reporting, suggesting ample room for improvement.

Comparing the three sub-indices, the Economic Index exhibits the highest average value, while the Environmental Index displays the lowest average value. Thus, companies in the sample tend to disclose more information pertaining to economic issues.

Table 3 shows the quality of SRs for companies obligated to disclose non-financial information under Decree-Law 89/2017 and for companies that do so voluntarily.

Table 3. SR quality index by type of disclosure (compulsory vs. voluntary)

Index	Type of Disclosure	N	Min	Max	Median	Mean	Standard deviation
Global	1) Mandatory	12	0.082	0.320	0.221	0.213	0.096
	2) Voluntary	54	0.017	0.368	0.184	0.192	0.0999
Economic	1) Mandatory	12	0.017	0.237	0.119	0.123	0.072
	2) Voluntary	54	0.000	0.254	0.153	0.119	0.082
Environmental	1) Mandatory	12	0.033	0.230	0.145	0.132	0.078
	2) Voluntary	54	0.000	0.191	0.099	0.085	0.056
Social	1) Mandatory	12	0.061	0.177	0.134	0.119	0.049
	2) Voluntary	54	0.000	0.282	0.092	0.111	0.081

Source: Own elaboration

Regarding the Global Index, its average value is higher for companies obligated to disclose sustainability information (0.213) compared to companies disclosing sustainability information voluntarily (0.192). Upon analysing the various sub-indices (economic, environmental, social), we infer that companies obligated to disclose non-financial information tend, on average, to publish higher-quality SRs than those that do so voluntarily.

Table 4 shows the values of the Indices for companies belonging to an environmentally sensitive sector and for those not belonging to such sectors.

Table 4. SR quality index by type of sector

Index	Type of Sector	N	Min	Max	Median	Mean	Standard deviation
Global	1) Environmentally sensitive	20	0.017	0.276	0.179	0.170	0.085
	2) Non-environmentally sensitive	46	0.022	0.368	0.191	0.207	0.103
Economic	1) Environmentally sensitive	20	0.000	0.203	0.153	0.110	0.072
	2) Non-environmentally sensitive	46	0.000	0.254	0.119	0.124	0.083
Environmental	1) Environmentally sensitive	20	0.013	0.191	0.138	0.111	0.064
	2) Non-environmentally sensitive	46	0.000	0.230	0.079	0.086	0.062
Social	1) Environmentally sensitive	20	0.000	0.244	0.092	0.110	0.062
	2) Non-environmentally sensitive	46	0.000	0.282	0.095	0.113	0.083

Source: Own elaboration

Regarding the Global Index, its average value is lower for companies operating in environmentally sensitive sectors (0.170) compared to companies that do not operate in such sectors (0.207). Surprisingly, companies in environmentally sensitive sectors exhibit, on average, lower quality SRs than those outside such sectors. This trend is also evident in the Economic and Social Indices, although the difference is almost negligible in the latter. However, when considering the Environmental Index, companies in environmentally sensitive sectors disclose higher-quality environmental information (0.111) than those not in such sectors (0.086). This finding aligns with expectations, as companies in environmentally sensitive sectors typically have a more pronounced negative impact on the environment. Thus, these companies tend to provide more detailed environmental information. However, it's crucial to note that the average disclosure in both types of sectors is relatively low, indicating a failure to meet most requirements outlined in 2016 GRI Sustainability Reporting Standards.

Univariate Analysis

To test whether the quality of SRs exhibits statistically significant differences depending on whether disclosure is compulsory or voluntary (H1), we employed a non-parametric test, as the conditions for applying the t-test for independent samples were not met. The results are presented in Table 5. The results indicate that the median quality of SRs does not differ significantly between companies obligated to report non-financial information and those that do so voluntarily. Therefore, it is not possible to validate H1.

Table 5. Median Test Results on H1

Index	Type of Disclosure	N	Median	Difference (1-2)	Sig[a]
Global	1) Mandatory	12	0.221	0.021	0.750
	2) Voluntary	54	0.184		
Economic	1) Mandatory	12	0.119	0.004	0.400
	2) Voluntary	54	0.153		
Environmental	1) Mandatory	12	0.145	0.047	0.247
	2) Voluntary	54	0.099		
Social	1) Mandatory	12	0.134	0.008	0.663
	2) Voluntary	54	0.092		

a. Asymptotic significance, corrected for Yates Continuity

Source: Own elaboration

To test whether the quality of SRs exhibits statistically significant differences between environmentally sensitive sectors and non-environmentally sensitive sectors (H2), we employed a non-parametric test, as the conditions for applying the t-test for independent samples were not met. The results are shown in Table 6.

Table 6. Median Test Results on H2

Index	Type of Sector	N	Median	Difference (1-2)	Sig[a]
Global	1) Environmentally sensitive	20	0.179	-0.012	0.181
	2) Non-environmentally sensitive	46	0.191		
Economic	1) Environmentally sensitive	20	0.153	0.034	0.334
	2) Non-environmentally sensitive	46	0.119		
Environmental	1) Environmentally sensitive	20	0.138	0.059	0.047
	2) Non-environmentally sensitive	46	0.079		
Social	1) Environmentally sensitive	20	0.092	-0.003	0.916
	2) Non-environmentally sensitive	46	0.095		

a. Asymptotic significance, corrected for Yates Continuity
Source: Own elaboration

For a 95% confidence level, the quality of SR does not differ significantly between companies in environmentally sensitive sectors and those in non-environmentally sensitive sectors. Thus, the H2 cannot be validated. However, when we consider the sub-indices, we find that the median quality of environmental reporting is higher for companies in environmentally sensitive sectors than for companies not in such sectors. This suggests that companies with a greater negative impact on the environment tend to disclose more environmental information in their SRs than other companies.

Multivariate Analysis

Table 7 provides the results from the linear regression models.

Table 7. Linear regression models results

	Global		Economic		Environmental		Social	
	Coef.	*t-stat*	*Coef.*	*t-stat*	*Coef.*	*t-stat*	*Coef.*	*t-stat*
Constant	0.005	0.041	-0.032	-0.342	-0.049	-0.716	0.068	0.749
Type of disclosure	0.002	0.054	-0.011	-0.390	0.020	1.894*	0.006	0.234
Type of sector	-0.033	-1.280	-0.011	-0.532	0.016	1.832*	-0.001	-0.066
Size	0.015	1.673*	0.012	1.604	0.010	1.754*	0.003	0.392
Profitability	0.002	2.016**	0.002	1.525	0.001	1.806*	0.001	1.398
N	66		66		66		66	
Z	1.886		1.003		3.468**		0.529	
R^2	0.110		0.062		0.185		0.034	
R^2_a	0.052		0.000		0.132		-0.030	

continued on following page

Table 7. Continued

	Global		Economic		Environmental		Social	
	Coef.	*t-stat*	*Coef.*	*t-stat*	*Coef.*	*t-stat*	*Coef.*	*t-stat*
Mean VIF	1.151		1.151		1.151		1.151	

Level of significance: *p<0,1; **p<0,05; *** p<0,01

Source: Own elaboration

When considering the Global Index, the variables relating to mandatory disclosure and belonging to an environmentally sensitive sector do not appear to be statistically significant, consistent with the previous univariate analysis. Company size and profitability have a positive and statistically significant effect on the quality of sustainability disclosures at a significance level of 10% and 5% respectively.

When analysing the Environmental Index, all the considered variables positively and significantly affect environmental reporting, at a significance level of 10%. Thus, companies subject to mandatory disclosures and those in environmentally sensitive sectors have better quality environmental reporting. Moreover, larger companies with better profitability tend to present higher-quality environmental information.

For the Economic and Social Indices, none of the independent variables is statistically significant, and both models have very low coefficients of determination (6.20% and 3.40% respectively).

From the results obtained, it can be concluded that H1 cannot be validated, indicating no significant differences in the quality of sustainability reporting between companies subject to mandatory disclosure (by Directive 2014/95/EU) and those reporting non-financial information voluntarily. These findings align with Carmo and Ribeiro (2022) and Posadas et al. (2022), who also conclude that the quality of sustainability reporting is not influenced by mandatory disclosure. So, contrary to Mion and Adaui (2019), our findings suggest that the coercive mechanism resulting from Directive 2014/95/EU has no impact on the quality of sustainability reporting.

Moreover, the results indicate that operating in an environmentally sensitive sector does not influence the quality of non-financial reporting, except for environmental reporting. This result is consistent with Krivačić (2017), but contrary to Posadas et al. (2022) and Tudor et al. (2019). Thus, overall, H2 cannot be validated, except when considering the quality of environmental reporting. In fact, in the univariate analysis, for a 5% significance level, it was found that the quality of environmental reporting is higher in companies belonging to environmentally sensitive sectors. This result was corroborated in the multivariate analysis, albeit only at a 10% significance level. This result suggests that companies with a more negative environmental impact are more prone to disclose environmental information, consistent with the extensive literature on environmental information disclosure.

SOLUTIONS AND RECOMMENDATIONS

This study contributes to the existing literature on sustainability reporting by focusing on the contextual factors that may affect sustainability reporting, i.e., factors which contextualize the environment in which a company operates and may affect the depth in which it addresses sustainability issues in its reports. Regulation and the sector in which a company operates are examples of contextual factors considered in this study.

Moreover, we contribute to the literature by providing empirical evidence on the quality of sustainability reporting of Portuguese companies. The results obtained could benefit academia, companies and their stakeholders, as well as regulatory bodies.

We also believe that the detailed nature of our Sustainability Reporting Quality Index represents an innovative tool for assessing the degree of compliance with GRI standards, the most widely used framework worldwide. Therefore, our Index may be valuable for researchers wishing to replicate it in other geographical contexts, enabling comparative studies. The low value of the Index obtained in our study may prompt reflection by regulatory bodies (such as the GRI itself), as it highlights that the quantity and detail of disclosure requirements could potentially compromise the quality of information disclosed by companies.

FUTURE RESEARCH DIRECTIONS

Despite its contributions, this study has limitations related to sample size and the analysis period. In fact, it only includes companies that disclose non-financial information in a separate report and focuses solely on the year 2021. Some Portuguese companies disclose sustainability information in integrated reports or in financial statements, which could alter the results if included in the sample.

For future research, we recommend including an analysis of the non-financial information contained in integrated reports and management reports. Additionally, extending the analysis for more than one period, would allow for a larger number of observations, as well as enable an examination of the evolution of sustainability reporting practices over time.

CONCLUSION

In recent years, the reporting of non-financial information has gained increased importance in business activities. Companies view sustainability as essential for preserving their existence, and understand that their actions must reflect economic, environmental, and social responsibilities (Ece & Sari, 2020).

Consequently, more companies are inclined to report non-financial information, whether voluntarily or mandatorily due to Directive 2014/95/EU. However, sustainability reporting remains a relatively underexplored topic in Portugal, with limited research on the disclosure of sustainable practices and the quality of reporting.

To evaluate the quality of sustainability reporting among large Portuguese companies, we conducted a content analysis of their SRs and developed a Sustainability Reporting Quality Index based on 2016 GRI Standards. The detailed nature of the Index revealed a low average quality of SRs published by Portuguese companies, with an average compliance of 20% with the disclosure requirements. This finding suggests that many of the disclosure requirements outlined in 2016 GRI Standards are not met.

The motivation for organisations to disclose higher quality sustainability information may stem from the influence of existing regulations on non-financial information disclosure (coercive isomorphism) and/or the desire to adopt disclosure practices akin to those considered successful by society or by larger groups within the same industry or sector (mimetic isomorphism). It was within this framework of institutional theory that we formulated our research hypotheses.

The overall conclusion is that the results did not meet expectations. The quality of reporting by Portuguese companies is notably low, indicating a lack of comprehensive sustainability information available to stakeholders to assess corporate practices.

Nevertheless, our results reveal the importance of contextual factors for environmental reporting. Notably, companies operating within environmentally sensitive sectors demonstrate better environmental reporting practices, consistent with the mimetic isomorphism advocated by institutional theory. In comparison, the role of legislative pressure (and coercive isomorphism) appears to be limited.

ACKNOWLEDGMENT

The authors acknowledge the financial support of FCT - Foundation for Science and Technology, I.P., within the scope of multi-annual funding UIDB/04043/2020

REFERENCES

Bachoo, K., Tan, R., & Wilson, M. (2013). Firm Value and the Quality of Sustainability Reporting in Australia: Firm Value and the Quality of Sustainability Reporting. *Australian Accounting Review*, 23(1), 67–87. DOI:10.1111/j.1835-2561.2012.00187.x

Balluchi, F., Lazzini, A., & Torelli, R. (2020). Credibility of environmental issues in non-financial mandatory disclosure: Measurement and determinants. *Journal of Cleaner Production*, 288, 25744.

Bartolacci, F., Bellucci, M., Corsi, K., & Soverchia, M. (2022). A Systematic Literature Review of Theories Underpinning Sustainability Reporting in Non-financial Disclosure. In Cinquini, L., & De Luca, F. (Eds.), *Non-financial Disclosure and Integrated Reporting* (pp. 87–113). Springer International Publishing. DOI:10.1007/978-3-030-90355-8_4

Benvenuto, M., Aufiero, C., & Viola, C. (2023). A systematic literature review on the determinants of sustainability reporting systems. *Heliyon*, 9(4), e14893. DOI:10.1016/j.heliyon.2023.e14893 PMID:37064487

Caputo, F., Leopizzi, R., Pizzi, S., & Milone, V. (2020). The non-financial reporting harmonization in Europe: Evolutionary pathways related to the transposition of the directive 95/2014/EU within the italian context. *Sustainability (Basel)*, 12(1), 92. DOI:10.3390/su12010092

Carmo, C., & Ribeiro, C. (2022). Mandatory Non-Financial Information Disclosure under European Directive 95/2014/EU: Evidence from Portuguese Listed Companies. *Sustainability (Basel)*, 14(8), 4860. DOI:10.3390/su14084860

Carvajal, M., & Nadeem, M. (2022). Financially material sustainability reporting and firm performance in New Zealand. *Meditari Accountancy Research*, 31(4), 938–969. DOI:10.1108/MEDAR-06-2021-1346

Dienes, D., Sassen, R., & Fisher, J. (2016). What are the drivers of sustainability reporting? A systematic review. *Sustainability Accounting. Management and Policy Journal*, 7(2), 154–189.

DiMaggio, P. J., & Powell, W. W. (1983). The Iron Cage Revisited: Institutional Isomorphism and Collective Rationality in Organizational Fields. *American Sociological Review*, 48(2), 147. DOI:10.2307/2095101

Ece, O., & Sari, S. S. (2020). Relationship between corporate sustainability reporting and firm efficiency, productivity, and profitability and firm value: Evidence from Turkey. *Academic studies in economics and administrative sciences*. 83-113

Farisyi, S., Musadieq, M., Utami, H., & Damayanti, C. (2022). A Systematic Literature Review: Determinants of Sustainability Reporting in Developing Countries. *Sustainability (Basel)*, 14(16), 10222. DOI:10.3390/su141610222

Fernandez-Feijoo, B., Romero, S., & Ruiz-Blanco, S. (2014). Women on Boards: Do They Affect Sustainability Reporting? *Corporate Social Responsibility and Environmental Management*, 21(6), 351–364. DOI:10.1002/csr.1329

Hoffmann, E., Dietsche, C., & Hobelsberger, C. (2018). Between mandatory and voluntary: Non-financial reporting by German companies. *Sustainability Management Forum*, 26(1–4), 47–63.

Krivačić, D. (2017). Sustainability Reporting Quality: The Analysis of Companies in Croatia. *Journal of Accounting and Management*, 07(01).

Minutiello, V., & Tettamanzi, P. (2022). The quality of nonfinancial voluntary disclosure: A systematic literature network analysis on sustainability reporting and integrated reporting. *Corporate Social Responsibility and Environmental Management*, 29(1), 1–18. DOI:10.1002/csr.2195

Mion, G., & Adaui, C. R. (2019). Mandatory Nonfinancial Disclosure and Its Consequences on the Sustainability Reporting Quality of Italian and German Companies. *Sustainability (Basel)*, 11(17), 4612. DOI:10.3390/su11174612

Monteiro, S., & Aibar-Guzmán, B. (2010). Determinants of environmental disclosure in the annual reports of large companies operating in Portugal. *Corporate Social Responsibility and Environmental Management*, 17(4), 185–204. DOI:10.1002/csr.197

Monteiro, S., Marques, R., & Lemos, K. (2023). Fatores determinantes do relato não financeiro obrigatório vs voluntário em grandes empresas portuguesas. International Workshop on Accounting and Taxation - IWAT2023, Oporto, 17 february

Ottenstein, P., Erben, S., Jost, S., Weuster, C., & Zulch, H. (2022). From voluntarism to regulation: Effects of directive 2014/95/EU on sustainability reporting in the EU. *Journal of Applied Accounting Research*, 23(1), 55–98. DOI:10.1108/JAAR-03-2021-0075

Pereira, L., Lemos, K., Monteiro, S., & Ribeiro, V. (2020), The Determinants of Non-Financial Reporting in Portuguese Listed Companies, Proceedings 35th International Business Information Management Association Conference (IBIMA)-Education Excellence and Innovation Management, 1-2 April 2020 Seville, Spain.

Posadas, S., Ruiz-Blanco, S., Fernandez-Feijoo, B., & Tarquinio, L. (2022). Institutional isomorphism under the test of Non-financial Reporting Directive. Evidence from Italy and Spain. *Meditari Accountancy Research*, 31(7), 26–48. DOI:10.1108/MEDAR-02-2022-1606

Reverte, C. (2016). Corporate social responsibility disclosure and market valuation: Evidence from Spanish listed firms. *Review of Managerial Science*, 10(2), 411–435. DOI:10.1007/s11846-014-0151-7

Romero, S., Ruiz, S., & Fernandez-Feijoo, B. (2019). Sustainability reporting and stakeholder engagement in Spain: Different instruments, different quality. *Business Strategy and the Environment*, 28(1), 221–232. DOI:10.1002/bse.2251

Tudor, A., Silvia, N., Ştefănescu, C., & Zanellato, G. (2019). Encompassing Non-Financial Reporting in a Coercive Framework for Enhancing Social Responsibility: Romanian Listed Companies Case. *Amfiteatru Economic*, 21(52), 590. DOI:10.24818/EA/2019/52/590

APPENDIX I

Table 8. Disclosure requirements under analysis

Standards GRI 2016	Disclosures	Nº of Disclosure Requirements
Universal Standards		
GRI 102 General Disclosures	GRI 102-1 a 102-56	115
GRI 103 Management Approach (for each specific standard)	GRI 103-1 a 103-3	51
166		
Specific Standards		
GRI 200 Economic Performance	GRI 201-1 a 201-4	25
	GRI 202-1 a 201-2	8
	GRI 203-1 a 203-2	5
	GRI 204-1	3
	GRI 205-1 a 205-3	16
	GRI 206-1	2
		59
GRI 300 Environmental Performance	GRI 301-1 a 301-3	5
	GRI 302-1 a 302-5	27
	GRI 303-1 a 303-3	14
	GRI 304-1 a 304-4	17
	GRI 305-1 a 305-7	43
	GRI 306-1 a 306-5	39
	GRI 307-1	1
	GRI 308-1 a 308-2	6
		146

continued on following page

Table 8. Continued

Standards GRI 2016	Disclosures	Nº of Disclosure Requirements
Universal Standards		
GRI 400 Social Performance	GRI 401-1 a 401-3	19
	GRI 402-1	2
	GRI 403-1 a 403-4	24
	GRI 404-1 a 404-3	6
	GRI 405-1 a 405-2	8
	GRI 406-1	9
	GRI 407-1	1
	GRI 408-1	5
	GRI 409-1	3
	GRI 410-1	2
	GRI 412-1 a 412-3	7
	GRI 413-1 a 413-2	10
	GRI 414-1 a 414-2	6
	GRI 415-1	2
	GRI 416-1 a 416-2	5
	GRI 417-1 a 417-3	13
	GRI 418-1	4
	GRI 419-1	5
		131

336

Chapter 10
ESG Dynamics as a Dialogical Process: A Case Study

Ilaria Martino
https://orcid.org/0009-0009-4987-137X
University of Naples Federico II, Italy

Flavio Spagnuolo
https://orcid.org/0009-0000-0251-0299
University of Naples Federico II, Italy

Rosanna Spanò
https://orcid.org/0000-0003-0557-3011
University of Naples Federico II, Italy

ABSTRACT

The chapter aims to understand how ESG dynamics can be shaped through a dialogical process between organizations and stakeholders, overcoming the mainstream view that considers ESG as a static disclosure element. For this purpose, the authors rely on a case study based on an Italian company operating in the utilities sector, which is particularly exposed to ESG matters and engages ESG reporting on a voluntary basis since 2021. Specifically, they exploit the theoretical model proposed by Merkl Davies and Brennan to investigate the evolution of ESG within the firm, focusing on information as a transactional process rather than as a mere transmission of informative flows. The case study shows how the materiality level—which operatizes and surrounds ESG issues—depends on a two-way conversation in which stakeholders are not simply referred to as primary users but become real "co-producers" of information. The work offers valuable insights to companies and policymakers, nudging towards effective ESG information, beyond the attempts for

DOI: 10.4018/979-8-3693-5663-0.ch010

formal compliance.

INTRODUCTION

In today's era of growing environmental, social, and economic concerns, companies face complex and ever-changing challenges. Specifically, sustainability matters are becoming of increasing importance, particularly pushing companies to take into account the responsibility for adopting high ethical practices in their decision-making processes. While nowadays the sustainable orientation provides for new and concrete opportunities for business development, it also entails new risks that can no longer be overlooked. Hence, Companies are required to adapt their business models in light of the climate and environmental emergency the world is experiencing (Orazalin et al., 2024). This assumption entails that sustainability is currently intended as a "process", which imposes the need to go beyond the common view to integrate such practices by a strict ethical approach but including strategic and operational concerns in business behaviors day after day.

From this perspective, the present chapter starts with the awareness that Environmental, Social, Governance (ESG) factors are continuing to evolve over time, and that a potential lack in the literature could emerge whereas extant research mainly treated ESG from a "static" point of view. The ESG paradigm is a result of the reinterpretation of various constructs that have already been addressed during the last years. Specifically, ESG dynamics started to become pivotal for firms in 2000, with the United Nations 15 Millennium Development Goals, which include topic as environmental sustainability, poverty eradication, ensuring primary education, reducing infant mortality, improving maternal health, and combating HIV and malaria. Subsequently, the plan was extended with the introduction of the UN 2030 Agenda for Sustainable Development in 2015. This program consists of 17 goals agreed by all UN Member States to be achieved within 15 years to reduce poverty, improve people's well-being, promote a better quality of life, and ensure the protection of our planet.

For instance, several studies only document how ESG is relevant for the economic outcomes of companies that face with such issues. Friede et al. (2015) analyzed the link between ESG standards and the financial success of companies since the 1970s, concluding that in 90% of cases, there is a positive correlation between ESG and the firm's financial performance. The same analysis was repeated in 2021 by Rockefeller Asset Management and the NYU Stern Center for Sustainable Business and it emerged that between 2015 and 2020 the correlation tends to be positive, but that the results (for 21%) are still divergent on the issue.

Interestingly, the hype around ESG has led to a proliferation of reporting attempts by companies and the setting of standards by *Global Reporting Initiative* (GRI), *International Sustainability Standards Board* (ISSB), *European Financial Reporting Advisory Group* (EFRAG), which nevertheless overlap and influence each other because they are variously employed by companies.

Accounting scholars have explored these themes, and they generally agree on the importance of deepening this area of attention (Arvidsson and Dumay, 2022; Bebbington and Larrinaga, 2014; Bebbington et al., 2021; Bolt and Tregidga, 2022; Du Rietz, 2014; Khan, 2022; Laine et al., 2021; Lehman and Kuruppu, 2017; Michelon et al., 2022).

Many studies on ESG reporting have shown a common focus on what is disclosed, paying attention to aspects such as the quantity, quality, and materiality of ESG information. In greater detail, a first strand of research examined the issues that can or should be addressed in the documents (Agostini et al., 2022; Arif et al., 2021; Romolini et al., 2014; Yoo and Managi, 2022; Zeisel, 2020), highlighting how much information is quantitatively dedicated to each topic, also to assess its quality. Other studies have sought to identify the determinants that improve the quality of ESG disclosures (D'Apice et al., 2021; Ellili, 2022; Minutiello and Tettamanzi, 2022; Lokuwaduge and Heenetigala 2017). In these papers, quality is understood as the ability of companies to faithfully adopt the guidelines suggested by the standards, to disclose more ESG information, as well as the degree of consistency and comparability of ESG information (from one period to another, from one company to another, across sectors and within sectors). Yet other works, on the other hand, deal with the conceptualization of materiality for the disclosure of ESG information, i.e. what information disclosed (or not) by a company would be relevant (Busco et.al, 2020; Gerwanski et al., 2019; Sepúlveda-Alzate et al. 2021; Schiehll and Kolahgar, 2021; Torelli et al., 2020).

A common feature of this literature is the focus on reporting, i.e. the final output of the disclosure process, while issues related to the process itself, as far as ESG issues are concerned, have not yet been fully addressed and remain rather confusing and unexplored.

Therefore, in the paper at hand, we examine the issue of ESG reporting as a process aimed at pursuing effective sustainability approaches, deepening how – in the perspective of the materiality analysis – the chance of this happening derives from an open dialogue and collaboration with stakeholders. From this perspective, the concept of materiality plays a key role, representing the filter through which the sustainable issues – that are most relevant to the company and its stakeholders – are selected. Through an accurate materiality assessment, an organization can identify key issues that have the potential to significantly affect its financial value and reputation. This targeted selection process allows company resources to be focused on those areas where risk is greatest and positive impact can be maximized.

On the basis of all the above, our chapter examines how ESG disclosure can be shaped through a two-way conversation process between organization and stakeholders, using a case-study approach based on the Italian company Optima Italia S.p.A. (hereafter mentioned as *Optima* or *Optima Italia*), which operates in the crucial utilities' sector that is particularly exposed to ESG dynamics and issues.

The case study takes advantage of the theoretical model proposed by Merkl Davies and Brennan (2017) to explore the process of ESG dynamics, focusing on information as a transactional process rather than a mere transmission. More specifically, we try to understand how materiality can be achieved by approaching it as a conversation – better "communication" – in which stakeholders are not simply referred to as primary users but become real "co-producers" of information.

The rest of the chapter is organized as follows. The second section presents the complex regulatory background for ESG reporting. The third section summarizes relevant literature and introduces the model by Merkl Davies and Brennan (2017). The fourth section describes the methodological approach, while the fifth section presents and discusses the results of our analysis. Finally, conclusions and directions for future research are reported in the sixth section.

THE REGULATORY BACKGROUND FOR ESG

Over the last years a hype in the regulatory efforts surrounding ESG has progressively challenged companies, with multiple efforts by both governmental and non-governmental bodies. This has progressively fostered attention for ESG issues but has also increased complexity in reporting (Laine et al., 2021). Thus, a heterogeneous landscape emerges as for ESG reporting, due to possible overlaps deriving from co-existence of various regulations, standards, and guidelines, either at national or international levels (Lokuwaduge and Heenetigala 2017; Romolini et al., 2014).

To better grasp this complex picture, we provide below a brief explanation of the possible elements deriving from the regulations issued by European and national institutions and from the standards/guidelines issued by standard setters and task forces.

More specifically, the European Union started to engage in a regulatory effort for ESG back in 2014 with Directive 2014/95/EU, towards a harmonization process aimed at favoring adequate disclosures to meet the ESG information needs of stakeholders. More recently, the *Corporate Sustainability Reporting Directive* (CSRD) attempted to overcome some limitations of the previous cited regulation, offering a deeper identification of elements relating to the content of ESG reporting. Nevertheless, a closer inspection of the two directives allows us to indicate that some shortcomings may affect companies' reporting process, and specially: 1) the lack of detailed *disclosure* requirements for each subject area possibly leading to heterogeneity, also in the absence of shared meanings on relevant issues such as the concept of materiality; 2) the lack of substantive *comparability* even though more recent updates suggest the mandatory adoption of ESRSs (European Sustainability Reporting Standards) standards as reporting guidelines. On this latter point, in fact, it is worth noting that there is a spread in the guidelines already available (GRI, ISSB, EFRAG), some already employed by companies, which can arguably generate confusion due to the mobilization and mixing of standards or frameworks with substantially different approaches, while ESRS are still a work in progress and lag behind in terms of coverage. Yet, the various standards recall different primary users, and founding conceptions, not to say categories of information and material themes to be disclosed, that may impinge the chances for actual harmonization in the foreseeable future.

There are fundamental differences between the standards promulgated. The main differences are explained below. The ISSB's proposal aims to meet the information needs of investors, while the EFRAG and GRI proposals aim to meet the information needs of stakeholders. The ISSB standards require the reporting of general principles, with a focus on industry-specific climate-related risks and opportunities, the EFRAG standards require general principles but also specific environmental, social and governance metrics (ESG approach), the GRI requires general information but also specific information on economic, social and environmental impacts. The material themes of the ISSB are based on financial materiality, those of EFRAG on double materiality, and those of the GRI on the materiality of impact. This situation reveals that, to facilitate a more effective harmonization process, there would be a need for greater cooperation between standard-setters on standard-setting drivers and achieving uniformity and comparability of disclosure.

In addition, the European Union (EU) has issued additional regulations such as the Taxonomy Regulation (Regulation 2020/852/EU). This regulation requires companies to report additional information on sustainable investments in addition to that already required by Directive 2014/95/EU, requiring large public-interest entities information how their business activities align with the climate objectives set out in the EU Taxonomy Regulation from 2022. Again, a regulation which entails different objectives, primary users, and minimum disclosure requirements than those of the *Non Financial Reporting Directive* (NFRD) and the more recent CSRD. On this regard, even though the CSRD has included detailed information on environmental taxonomy, it remains fairly theoretical (Correa-Mejía et al., 2024).

Moreover, the multiplicity of frameworks for ESG reporting, has also been reinforced by the *Task Force on Climate-Related Financial Disclosures*' (TFCD) guidelines which requires non-financial disclosures to be included in financial documents. This encourages – *de facto* – large companies to produce more than one report at the end of the year, attempting to meet more requirements, which again is something unlikely to improve the comparability and transparency of the information reported (Pizzi et al., 2023).

LITERATURE REVIEW AND THEORETICAL FRAMEWORK

The topic of ESG dynamics as a process is of fundamental importance, especially in industries for which the pressures deriving from a complex regulatory framework such as the one described above, and the concerns of multiple stakeholders determine the need for dynamic balancing and the need to ensure effective changes and increasing efforts by the parties involved. (Manes-Rossi et al. 2020; Manes-Rossi et al. 2022).

Previous literature focused on ESG reporting (Bebbington and Unerman 2018; Al-Htaybat et al. 2019; Di Vaio and Varriale 2020; Guthrie et al. 2017) examines the role of *disclosure* in the pursuit of the United Nations (UN) Sustainable Development Goals (SDGs) (Bebbington and Unerman 2018); the intersection between accounting practices and new technologies to support both value creation and SDGs (Al-Htaybat et al. 2019; Di Vaio and Varriale 2020); and the links between integrated reporting (IR) and the internal processes of organizations (Guthrie et al. 2017).

Further ESG-related studies focus on the amount of information (Arif et al., 2021; Arvidsson and Dumay, 2022; Chen and Xie, 2022; Guthrie et al., 2017; Karpoff et al., 2022; Nicolò et al., 2021; Yoo and Managi, 2022), the main topics to be disseminated (Agostini et al., 2022; Bebbington and Larrinaga, 2014; Bebbington et al., 2021; Busco et al, 2020; Cordazzo et al., 2020; Du Rietz, 2014, 2018; Farneti et al., 2011; Laine et al., 2021; Lokuwaduge and Heenetigala 2017; Merkl-Davies and Brennan, 2017; Michelon et al., 2022; Romolini et al, 2014), and more recently to issues related to materiality (in its many aspects) (Bolt and Tregidga, 2022; Busco et.al, 2020; Gerwanski et al., 2019; Sepúlveda-Alzate et al. 2021; Schiehll and Kolahgar, 2021; Torelli et al., 2020).

A common feature of this literature is the focus on the analysis of the reports disclosed by companies, i.e. the output of the *disclosure* process, while the questions related to the process itself, as far as ESG issues are concerned, have not yet found an unequivocal answer, and remain rather confused and unexplored.

A relevant starting point for considering how ESG reporting is placed in the pursuit of sustainability objectives is the effective incorporation of the latter into companies' business models, due to their "material" nature (Tulder and Lucht, 2019). A sustainable issue is material if it is "capable of substantially influencing the organization's ability to create value in the short, medium or long term" (IIRC 2013, p. 33). Given the importance of the topic, numerous authors have begun to study the concept of materiality in the context of non-financial disclosure (Pizzi et al., 2023; Correa-Mejía et al., 2024; Setia et al., 2024).

In general, ESG materiality helps to determine what information should be presented in sustainability reports to provide a comprehensive representation of the company's effort in sustainability-related activities (Baumüller and Sopp, 2022). Specifically, a certain ESG information is considered as *material* if its omission (or misstatement) could reasonably affect stakeholders' needs. It is worth noting that the materiality assessment for non-financial information seems to be different from that for financial information, as the latter is more sector-specific and difficult to quantify (Abhayawansa, 2022).

Indeed, when measuring financial materiality items, the preparers of financial statements consider just that information the omission or misstatement of which may influence primary users' decisions (i.e., investors) (Edgley, 2014). On the contrary, for measuring the materiality of non-financial information, there has been introduced the concept of "double materiality" (EFRAG, 2022), which considers both the impact of the environment and society on companies' business ("outside-in" financial materiality) and the influence of their business on the environment and society ("inside-out" impact materiality).

In other words, companies need to assess their materiality based on the needs of society and the planet, and not just their vision of their interests. This approach allows for a more comprehensive view of the organization, activities, and their impact on the social and environmental context, and as investors have begun to comply with investment policies containing sustainability rules, the demand for more detailed information on environmental impact has increased, fueling the need for stricter reporting guidelines.

Despite the efforts made by standard setters (e.g., GRI, ISSB, EFRAG) to clarify a definition of materiality applicable to sustainability reporting, it suffers several limitations in its application (Adams et al. 2021; Baumüller and Sopp, 2022; Cooper and Michelon, 2022; Gerwanski et al., 2019; De Villiers et al., 2022; Khan et al., 2016). For instance, Pizzi et al. (2023) reveal that materiality applies differently basing on GRI and SASB's frameworks. This can lead to ineffective applications of such a concept and, consequentially, a likely mismatch may arise between what companies do and what they actually say (Correa-Mejía et al., 2024).

In this regard, many companies around the world have gradually implemented social and sustainability reporting to establish a communication with stakeholders. Non-financial reporting has become one of the best ways to communicate CSR initiatives, making stakeholders aware of the efforts made. In this regard, the main dilemma for companies is figuring out how to recognize the relevant issues to be disclosed in sustainability reporting and prioritize those material issues by stakeholder demands. Hence, the accountability process requires the company to understand the need for information from management, investors, and all stakeholders that can influence the company's performance in the long run.

For this reason, a materiality analysis and the definition of a materiality matrix are necessary to clarify which topics are relevant and, among these, which are most relevant. This is where the importance of the stakeholder engagement process comes into play: their direct or indirect involvement allows companies to properly understand their expectations and needs, which in turn facilitates an effective reporting system.

Thus, the focus on materiality requires internal exchange within companies and external validation to assist an open dialogue with stakeholders, that would also shape strategic decision-making process and, in turn, would encourage a real business model change.

The dialogue and process aspects mentioned above have been examined to a limited extent (Bolt and Tregidga, 2022; Cooper and Michelon, 2022). The research by Merkl-Davies and Brennan (2017) is one of the few that provides a theoretical framework of external communication based on two broad research perspectives: a functionalist-behavioral transmission perspective and a symbolic-interpretative narrative perspective.

Merkl-Davies and Brennan (2017) propose a rethinking starting from Barnlund (1970) and Littlejohn and Foss (2011), who developed an early conception of transactional communication. The transactional communication model moves away from the transmissive model, which is the traditional accounting communication model, theorized by Shannon and Weaver (1949), in which communication is a one-way linear process focused on transmitting messages from a sender to a receiver. These two accounting communication models have many different features. In the transmission model, only the sender, the receiver, and the message are incorporated into the communication process, while in the transactional model, eight other aspects of communication come into play, proposed and elaborated by Littlejohn and Foss (2011): (1) the communicator, (2) the message, (3) the conversation, (4) the relationship, (5) the group, (6) the external organizations, (7) the media and (8) society. It is worth noting that the "receiver" is not included in the Littlejohn and Foss (2011) model as he becomes a "communicator". The logic of the framework is to emphasize the fact that those who actually receives the information also communicates such information in a dialogical way, differently from the transmission (one-way) model. In addition, contextual factors such as psychological, relational, social, and cultural dimensions are ignored in the transmission model, which are instead included in the transactional model.

Merkl-Davies and Brennan (2017), in their rethinking, compare the two models, including the enrichments of Littlejohn and Foss (2011) and Berglund (1970) in the transactional one (see Figure 1). The focus is on changing accounting communication. A drastic change emerges in accounting communication from a "disclosure vehicle" in the transmission model to a "conversation" in the transactional model. In the transactional model, therefore, accounting communication becomes a "message" or rather a "corporate narrative", which arises from a conversation between organizations and shareholders/stakeholders in a two-way direction.

We adopt this theoretical framework to explore the ESG disclosure process, focusing on information as a transactional process rather than a mere transmission. More specifically, we seek to understand how the long-desired materiality of ESG disclosure can be achieved by approaching it as a conversation – better 'narrative communication' – in which stakeholders are not simply referred to as 'primary users' but become true 'co-producers' of ESG disclosure. Therefore, ESG disclosures include stakeholder interests with the aim of being accountable to a variety of stakeholders for the impacts of organizations' environmental, social, and governance activities.

Figure 1. Merkl Davies and Brennan (2017) Model

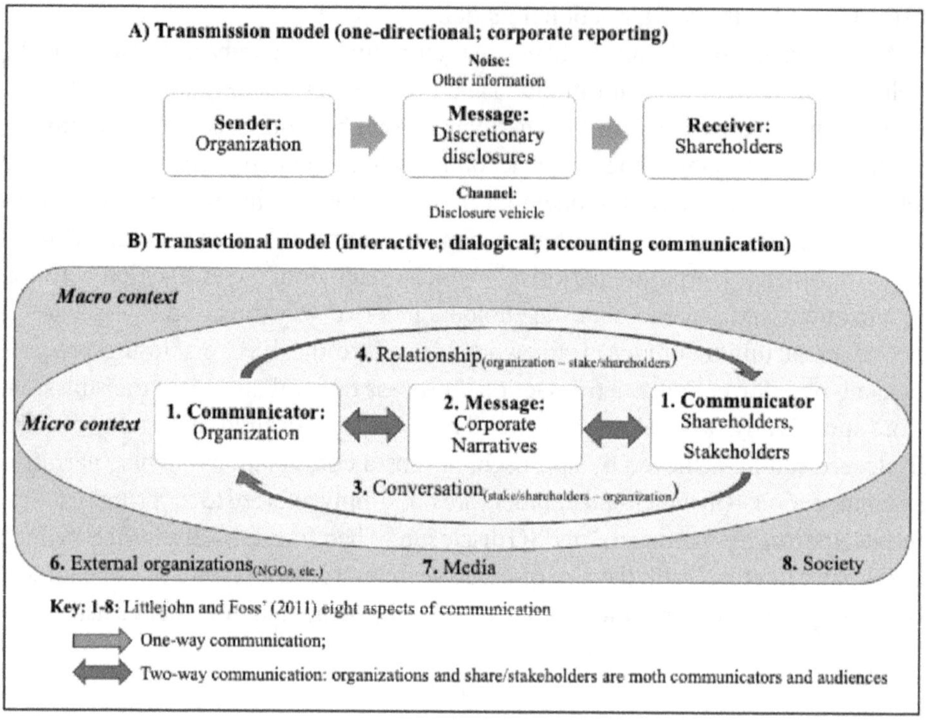

Source: personal elaboration from Merkl Davies and Brennan, 2017, p.9.

RESEARCH DESIGN

In this section, we address the research design employed in this study, which is centered around a case study approach (Yin, 2011). Specifically, Section 4.1 provide a comprehensive background on Optima Italia (the subject of our case study), delving into the history and strategic initiatives of the company, providing a thorough understanding of its business environment and the factors which should have affected its sustainability disclosures practices. Then, in Section 4.2 provides adequate information for data sources and the analysis conducted based on the gathered information.

Setting the Context of the Case Study: The Story of Optima Italia

Optima Italia is a multi-utility company specializing in the integrated management of electricity, gas, telephony, internet, mobile, and VAS. The company was founded in 1999 from an innovative project by two young entrepreneurs from Campania: Danilo Caruso and Alessio Matrone to create a service company that could simplify everyone's day, families, and businesses, offering integrated solutions for individuals and businesses for utilities and services in a single solution and with a single interlocutor.

Starting from 2003, due to the continuous investments in Human Resources and Training, the company has been able to compete on the national territory with a solid network in 18 Italian regions (out of 20). In 2009, Optima became a joint-stock company under the name Optima Italia S.p.A. and continues to work on its brand identity based on a simple and direct approach to the customers and broader stakeholders in general. In a short time, 2010 saw the entry of Optima into the gas market, always with a view to progressive integration for customers.

Since 2011, growth has been a constant figure in terms of turnover, human resources, and sales network, making Optima one of the main multi-utilities in the energy and telecommunications sector in Italy with over 80,000 client companies and over 150 consultants distributed throughout the country. At the same time, dialogues and contacts with several stakeholders continue to growth also thanks to the *Optima digital magazine* born in 2012 as a simple experiment but which quickly exceeds one million monthly visits.

These are the focal years for a conscious transition to B2C that integrates and completes the initial focus on B2B customers, through the offer to private customers of the new integrated offer with Electricity, Gas, Telephone, and Internet at a single monthly fee and a single bill.

In 2021, also downstream of the effects of the pandemic, a new Optima business unit was born: *YouHealthy*, the platform that allows users to have a doctor always available, 7 days a week, 24 hours a day and to receive assistance and services in the field of Telemedicine, Psychological Wellness, Nutrition, and DNA analysis. The following year saw further integrations of 24-hour assistance services, with qualified technicians always ready to intervene in the event of damage at home or in the company and Medical Teleconsultation with a general practitioner always available for every need, while the focus of the 2023 strategy is to expand the offer with products related to the energy transition.

The current ownership structure includes Optima Holding Spa, which refers to the founders, and Optiworld S.a.r.l., which refers to Alpha Private Equity Funds Management Company S.a.r.l., which became part of the Optima corporate structure in 2015, acquiring 20% of the share capital.

Data Collection and Analysis

The work use a case study approach (Yin, 2011) based on a data collection carried out between April and May 2024. The analysis includes various sources such as sustainability reports for the years 2021 and 2022, documents published on the company's communication channels, internal documents that the top management rendered available, as well as 5 interviews (each lasting about two hours) with the company subjects involved in the process of analysis and definition of ESG reporting and materiality.

In particular, interviews have been conducted with the following members of the group:

- Vincenzo Pisano, CEO of Optima Albania and COO of Optima Italia;
- Stefano Russo, Head of Customer Management at Optima Italia;
- Gabriella Pirozzi Head of Customer Experience at Optima Italia;
- Sabatino Castellone, Head of Customer Value Management, Optima Italia;
- Bledar Pojani, General Manager of Optima Albania.

The analysis of the documentary sources, together with that of the internal documents, made it possible to identify relevant issues for the preparation of the interviews, which were also prepared using the interpretative coordinates provided by the theoretical model presented in the previous section.

Specifically, the interviews focused on the following questions.

1. How does the company conceptualize the topic of materiality? What are the main challenges related to this?
2. What processes have been put in place to implement a materiality analysis in Optima and for what reasons?
3. What are the competitive advantages you see in sustainability reporting and materiality analysis?
4. How do you involve internal and external stakeholders in the materiality assessment and management process?
5. What are the main obstacles you have faced?

6. What are the prospects of Optima's materiality analysis, also concerning the incorporation of double materiality in decision-making processes and corporate reporting, also considering the evolutionary context in which we find ourselves?

Before concluding the data collection, respondents were asked to review the transcripts and make any corrections. The above themes have also been used to analyze transcripts and identify relevant areas to shape the findings.

RESULTS AND DISCUSSION

This section presents the results of the analysis conducted on Optima Italia, based on the information collected as per the above section, and especially taking into consideration the company's disclosure and the insights from the interviews.

Overall, both from reading the documents published on the company's website and from the interviews with managers, it seems clear that attention to sustainability and its reporting represents a priority for Optima, which in the current period is preparing to publish a Sustainability Report for the third consecutive year, by GRI standards.

It is worth noting that, as a starting point, the analysis of the Sustainability Report prepared by Optima has played a key role in mapping the ESG dynamics of the company under scrutiny, since nowadays is undoubtedly an essential reporting tool for any company that wants to keep up with the times.

It seems clear from the recognition of the company's history how the goal of simplifying the lives of customers, aiming at an offer of multiple services provided in innovative ways and with the advantage of having a single interlocutor for every need, has been since the very beginning a cornerstone of the company's strategy and a factor of competitive advantage. Optima's sustainability reporting starts from the explication of such a company's mission, aimed at improving the lives of customers with ever-changing and innovative solutions.

As the management explains, Optima *has rooted its competitive positioning on three essential pillars: customer centricity, sustainability, and speed of response due to the needs of a wide range of stakeholders.*

Specifically, as far as sustainability is concerned, it should be emphasized that Optima *preserves and increases the strong bond with the local community and is managed in the firm opinion, which permeates the corporate culture at every level, that it must do its part to ensure sustainable and responsible development.* This logic does not only concern, by way of example, the most recent choices to offer services that can play an important role in the energy transition, dialoguing with customers and stakeholders to develop solutions aimed at energy efficiency and raising awareness among customers and employees on the relevance of environmental issues. The desire to effectively implement extensive sustainability actions involves the social dimension of doing business at Optima well beyond the mere commitment to people. It involves actions aimed at strengthening the firm's community in spite of any cultural distance, and also initiatives to intervening with concrete aid as in the case of social projects involving local communities and customers.

For clarity, the following Table (1), based on the analysis of Optima reports, shows in detail the several activities carried out by the company, which entailed the huge participation of several categories of stakeholders.

Table 1. Engagement activities

Stakeholders	Activity	Description
Dependents	*Company intranet*	The Group leverages the company intranet to share key initiatives and enhance career opportunities by posting job openings for employees.
	Performance review	Optima implements a comprehensive performance review system that engages all employees, offering numerous opportunities for dialogue and multiple annual feedback exchanges between staff and managers.
	Optima Campus	The group annual training program engaged employees through in-person and webinar courses to develop both soft and hard skills. It also included seminars, workshops, and conferences to enhance the organization's human capital.
Local Communities	*Innovation Village*	In 2022, Optima actively participated in organizing the Innovation Village Award, presenting an annual award that highlights sustainable innovation efforts within communities, contributing to the achievement of the 17 Sustainable Development Goals outlined by the UN 2030 Agenda.
	Optimagazine	Founded in 2012 as a company blog, Optimagazine has evolved into a vibrant webzine offering top-notch content on cinema, technology, trending news, and more. In 2022, the addition of the "Life" section brought tips to promote responsible consumption among readers.
Customers	*Caring campaigns*	Optima keeps engagement soaring by regularly reaching out to customers, proactively addressing needs, and ensuring satisfaction levels remain top-notch.
	Energetic training	In 2021, Optima introduced Super Ecò, its energy trainer seamlessly integrated into the apps, offering personalized guidance to all Consumer Customers. It empowers users to trim energy usage, cut waste, and unlock both economic and environmental advantages.

continued on following page

Table 1. Continued

Stakeholders	Activity	Description
Suppliers	*Optivendo and Optiman*	Optivendo and Optiman are the two training programs dedicated to sales agents, which aim to grow technical and soft skills in the sales network.
	Code of Ethics in Supply Contracts	The Group requires suppliers to review and sign the Optima Code of Ethics. This document outlines the core values and principles guiding all activities within the company.
Shareholders and lenders	*Periodic Communications*	The Group periodically communicates with the reference shareholder about the economic, financial, and sustainability performance.
Public Administration and Regulatory Authorities	*Regulatory Updates*	Operating in regulated sectors, Optima maintains a vigilant eye on legal updates and provisions. With a dedicated team, it ensures internal processes seamlessly align with Regulatory Authorities' requirements, fostering compliance and staying ahead of the curve.

Source: Our elaboration based upon Optima Italia disclosure.

Overall, the general objective to be more aware and closer to stakeholders has prompted the company to make a further effort to interpret ESG dynamics in light of the *materiality analysis*, which exploits (and it is based on) the commitment of several stakeholders.

Specifically, the definition of the ESG issues explored in the Sustainability Strategy is accurately based on such an analysis, carried out through an evaluation process allowed by the involvement of Companies' directors, top managers, and external stakeholders.

The start-up phase of materiality assessment required Optima's use of benchmarking analyses and mapping of the context, essentially aimed at identifying current and potential ESG impacts, which were then discussed with management in one-to-one meetings and assessed, both by the heads of the corporate functions and by the external stakeholders identified, through questionnaires.

Firstly, it seems worth noting that Optima Italia realized a list of *material* items, defined – in line with the requirements of the GRI Standards – as *those issues that may have a significant environmental, social, and economic impact on the Company's strategic objectives and activities or, conversely, that are significantly impacted by Optima's activities, or that can significantly influence the decisions of internal and external stakeholders* (Optima Italia, 2022).

On this basis, we noticed that the company has been able to build its Sustainability Framework (on which the production of ESG disclosure is based) particularly focusing on stakeholders' engagement and co-participation. In this regards, we recognized three phases which operatize the continuous dialogue between the company and the stakeholders.

First, the Reporting team carries out a benchmark analysis on the issues that peers or comparable companies deem relevant, together with an analysis of industry standards and guidelines completed with an open discussion with the first line of management. This comparison was carried out to better select potentially relevant issues based on corporate strategies and the main ESG risks and impacts to which the company is exposed, as well as to map the categories of stakeholders relevant to the company according to the criteria of the AA1000 standard.

Second, the team involves 50 stakeholders, including external parties and internal managers, as respondents to a questionnaire aimed at prioritizing the ESG impacts that emerged in the first phase of work and were potentially relevant. Specifically, this phase was based on the assessment of the impacts (in terms of scope, diffusion, irreparability, and probability) using an evaluation scale by the GRI 3 *Material Topics*.

The third phase saw the consolidation of the results of the analyses conducted internally and externally, thus identifying the 12 most relevant issues, which were then subjected to a process of validation by top management. In this regard, see Figure 2 below from the Optima Sustainability Report (2022).

Figure 2. Material Themes

#	MATERIAL ISSUES	SCOPE
1	Quality of Service and Customer Centrity	Social
2	Climate Change	Environmantal
3	Diversity, Equality, Inclusion	Social
4	Local Community	Social
5	Energy efficiency and renewable energy	Environmantal
6	R&D and innovation	Governance
7	Enhancement of human capital	Social
8	Ethics & Compliance	Governance
9	Supply Chain Management	Governance
10	Privacy e Cybersecurity	Governance
11	Reduction of paper usage	Environmantal
12	Circular economy and waste management	Environmantal

Source: Optima Sustainability report, 2022.

As the company ranked the topic in order of importance, it can be noticed that the most important material issues refer – for the company and its stakeholders – to "Quality of Service and Customer Centricity" and "Climate Change". As for the former, this is a proof of the high and constant attention that the company dedicates to the customers, while for the latter it seems that climate change sensitiveness is particularly important. Hence, it is reasonable to believe that a two-way communication between the company and primary stakeholders (i.e., customers and community at large) affects the importance of ESG issues considered as highly material.

Topics such as "Diversity, Equality, Inclusion", "Energy Efficiency and Renewable Energy", "R&D and Innovation" and "Enhancement of Human Capital" are also highly relevant by both internal and external stakeholders, consistently with 1) Optima's positioning choices in the market as a digital leader; and 2) with the consolidated approaches to human capital management oriented towards the satisfaction and enhancement of people, differences and, more generally, a corporate culture based on innovation and inclusion.

The topic of "Privacy and Cybersecurity" is relevant, as expected also considering the context, in line with the growing investments aimed at increasing IT security and the protection of sensitive data.

Awareness of the "Local Community" and "Supply Chain Management" issues is increasing, revealing, albeit from different angles, an orientation of the company to pursue sustainability goals also as an agent of change for the subjects and contexts with which it is in relationship.

Further topics, those related to "Reduction of paper use" and "Circular economy and waste management" are mainly related to the context effect and Optima's goal of increasing digital invoicing, digitizing internal processes, and raising customer awareness about the disposal of IoT devices.

Moreover, with regard to materiality analyses and the gradual consolidation of reporting practices, it should be noted that certain aspects of primary importance emerged during the interviews that deserve deeper attention.

Firstly, the interviewees highlighted the burden of the processes related to the integration of sustainability practices was significant in terms of increased responsibilities and new operational tasks (especially for the top managers). In any case, it is worth noting that the actors involved showed a broad appreciation for the benefits identified in the face of this new way of working, engaging dialogical discussions and generally re-considering the company as an entity which impacts stakeholders' thinking. By way of example, the actions implemented to mentor customers in order to achieve real energy efficiency were found to be conducive to a better brand identity for the company, greater customer satisfaction in terms of spending less and more consciously, and a positive impact of the company from an environmental perspective.

This positive feedback prompted the company to provide, for the 2023 reporting, additional sections of educational tips useful to its stakeholders, building a dialogue around issues also related to their protection, (e.g., actions against aggressive telemarketing).

Last but not least, the company has also initiated a reflection, albeit a medium-term one, given the onerousness and risks associated with possible errors, on the correct application of the so-called double materiality.

In this regards, the interviewees have indeed reiterated that although they are not currently implementing a tangible process that considers double materiality, for the future this concept will represents a driving force to which they will devote greater attention, mainly to 1) comply with the progressive pressures that directly or indirectly emanate from the regulatory evolution taking place in Europe; 2) satisfy the constantly evolving characteristics of the context in which the company operates; 3) formalize an approach characterizing decision-making processes.

It is reasonable advance that through these three phases, the needs of stakeholders are a source of value for production of the company's disclosure information. Such an inference find a concrete feedback from both Optima's reports and interviews, in which it clearly emerges that sustainability issues (as operatized by ESG materiality analysis) are based *on transparent, proactive, and continuous communication with its stakeholders, to stimulate growth and promote stakeholder satisfaction with the company* (Optima Italia, 2022). This is, on closer inspection, a very important Optima's feature, which implies an (indirect) active role of stakeholders in both the ESG materiality analysis and the production of ESG disclosure.

CONCLUSIONS AND FUTURE RESEARCH AVENUES

The case study of Optima Italia has made it possible to empirically deepen the issue of materiality and its analysis for sustainability reporting, thanks to the consultation of documentary sources of different types and interviews conducted with 5 managers actively involved in these processes.

These results offer several contributions. Particularly, the study provides insights about how the company conceptualizes the topic of materiality, the main challenges related to this aspect, the processes put in place to implement a materiality analysis, and the underlying motivations. In addition, it has been possible to explore what competitive advantages the company sees concerning sustainability reporting and materiality analysis, how stakeholders are involved, and, above all, what obstacles have arisen and what objectives the company reserves to pursue in the future, also concerning the integration of double materiality into decision-making processes and corporate reporting, also considering the current evolutionary context.

Specifically, the chapter prompt the idea that, by treating materiality analysis as a communication process, companies can go beyond a mere "checklist approach" to identify and prioritize ESG issues, deeply weaving them into a cohesive narrative that reflects the company's values, purpose, and long-term vision.

Based on the results discussed in the previous paragraphs, it was also possible, in light of the theoretical model adopted, to understand how Optima is approaching the transition from a type of communication of a purely informative nature and based on the transmission of the news to third parties and recipients, to a transactional model that intends to build a conversation with stakeholders, based on a corporate narrative that stems from an active and conscious exchange between the actors involved. Materiality and its analysis, in Optima, are understood precisely as a "narrative communication" - in which stakeholders are not simply "primary users" but act as "co-producers" of ESG reporting. In practical terms, this shift towards a dialogical approach to ESG dynamics within Optima carries a deep engagement in a two-way conversation with stakeholders rather than simply disseminating information, that allows Optima to better understand perspectives, concerns, and expectations of its stakeholders. This not only fosters a sense of partnership among stakeholders, but also ensures that companies' sustainability efforts are aligned with needs and ethical values of a wider range of its counterparts.

These results constitute an important basis for the current debate as they corroborate the idea that ESG reporting is a process to be built over time and should not be understood and interpreted as a simplistic output, but rather observed as a valuable input for the integration of the company's strategic resources.

In this sense, reporting constitutes a virtuous circle that leads to the creation of value by beneficiaries, thanks to a dynamic and interactive process that includes all stakeholders. This perspective can overcome the attention so far limited to the quantity, quality, and materiality of information, providing a more integrated understanding of the latter as part of a holistic process of construction of narrative discourses by companies.

This perspective is also useful for other companies, operators, and policymakers.

First, companies can gain a better understanding of how to deliver truly effective and relevant ESG disclosure, beyond attempts at formal compliance and towards greater satisfaction of stakeholder disclosure needs. This could lay the groundwork for improving two-way communication processes, overcoming the highly confusing open questions of quantity, quality, and materiality of information, and possibly leading to more substantive mutual reflections and dialogic responsibilities across ESG objectives and not just for ESG itself.

Secondly, this case study may sow the seeds for more informed approaches by ESG reporting professionals, who can draw suggestions on the appropriateness of promoting the adoption of participatory reporting models, in other words, the implementation of a public consultation process, which allows for the inclusion of the pluralistic interests of stakeholders and integrates them into the strategy at a higher level.

Finally, on a policy level, it is necessary to reiterate that a paradigm shift is necessary at several levels concerning a broader acceptance of the role of shareholders/stakeholders not only as primary users but as co-producers of information.

Overall, the chapter suggest that by embracing a dialogical approach to ESG dynamics, companies can enhance both accountability and stakeholder engagement, while they can also pursuit a concrete sustainable development. This shift from a stationary to a relational model of communication not only benefits companies and their stakeholders (i.e., at a micro-level context) but also contributes to the broader societal transition (i.e., at a macro-level context) towards a more sustainable future.

Despite contributions and implications, our study is not without limitations. First, although the use of a single case study appears as the most suitable approach to deeply analyze dialogical dynamics, it does not allow to generalize our results. Thus, we encourage here future studies to replicate our analysis basing on different settings (industry or country) in order to augment research comparability and evidence around the topic.

Secondly, our analysis cover years after COVID-19 pandemic, as company public disclosure was not available before 2021. We suggest an avenue for future studies to capture the switch in the context (before and after a macroeconomic crisis), which might easily justify progress and engagement in companies-stakeholders dialogue. Specifically, further research may attempt to analyze how the recent social (rather than mere economic) crisis due to COVID-19 might have catalyzed a dynamic dialogical approach to ethical issues and disclosure production.

REFERENCES

Abhayawansa, S. (2022). Swimming against the tide: back to single materiality for sustainability reporting. Sustainability Accounting, Management and Policy Journal, (ahead-of-print).

Adams, C. A., Alhamood, A., He, X., Tian, J., Wang, L., & Wang, Y. (2021). *The Double-Materiality Concept: Application and Issues*. Global Reporting Initiative.

Agostini, M., Costa, E., & Korca, B. (2022). Non-financial disclosure and corporate financial performance under directive 2014/95/EU: Evidence from Italian listed companies. *Accounting in Europe*, 19(1), 78–109. DOI:10.1080/17449480.2021.1979610

Al-Htaybat, K., Hutaibat, K., & von Alberti-Alhtaybat, L. (2019). Global brain-reflective accounting practices: Forms of intellectual capital contributing to value creation and sustainable development. *Journal of Intellectual Capital*, 20(6), 733–762. DOI:10.1108/JIC-01-2019-0016

Arif, M., Gan, C., & Nadeem, M. (2022). Regulating non-financial reporting: Evidence from European firms' environmental, social and governance disclosures and earnings risk. *Meditari Accountancy Research*, 30(3), 495–523. DOI:10.1108/MEDAR-11-2020-1086

Arvidsson, S., & Dumay, J. (2022). Corporate ESG reporting quantity, quality and performance: Where to now for environmental policy and practice? *Business Strategy and the Environment*, 31(3), 1091–1110. DOI:10.1002/bse.2937

Barker, R., & Mayer, C. (2023). Seeing double corporate reporting through the materiality lenses of both investors and nature. [Routledge.]. *Accounting Forum*, •••, 1–31.

Barnlund, D. C. (1970). "A transactional model of communication", in Language Behaviour: A Book of Readings in Communications. In Akin, J., Goldberg, A., Myers, G., & Stewart, J. (Eds.), *Mouton Publishers* (pp. 43–61).

Baumüller, J., & Sopp, K. (2022). Double materiality and the shift from non-financial to European sustainability reporting: Review, outlook and implications. *Journal of Applied AccountingResearch*, 23(1), 8–28. DOI:10.1108/JAAR-04-2021-0114

Bebbington, J., & Larrinaga, C. (2014). Accounting and sustainable development: An exploration. *Accounting, Organizations and Society*, 39(6), 395–413. DOI:10.1016/j.aos.2014.01.003

Bebbington, J., Larrinaga, C., O'Dwyer, B., & Thomson, I. (Eds.). (2021). *Routledge handbook of environmental accounting*. Routledge. DOI:10.4324/9780367152369

Bebbington, J., & Unerman, J. (2018). Achieving the United Nations Sustainable Development Goals: An enabling role for accounting research. *Accounting, Auditing & Accountability Journal*, 31(1), 2–24. DOI:10.1108/AAAJ-05-2017-2929

Bolt, R., & Tregidga, H. (2023). Methodological Insights "Materiality is…": Sense-making and sensegiving through storytelling. *Accounting, Auditing & Accountability Journal*, 36(1), 403–427. DOI:10.1108/AAAJ-06-2021-5314

Busco, C., Consolandi, C., Eccles, R. G., & Sofra, E. (2020). A preliminary analysis of SASB reporting: Disclosure topics, financial relevance, and the financial intensity of ESG materiality. *The Bank of America Journal of Applied Corporate Finance*, 32(2), 117–125. DOI:10.1111/jacf.12411

Chen, Z., & Xie, G. (2022). ESG disclosure and financial performance: Moderating role of ESG investors. *International Review of Financial Analysis*, 83, 102291. DOI:10.1016/j.irfa.2022.102291

Cooper, S., & Michelon, G. (2022). Conceptions of materiality in sustainability reporting frameworks: commonalities, differences and possibilities. In Adams, C. A. (Ed.), *Handbook of Accounting and Sustainability* (pp. 44–66). Edward Elgar Publishing. DOI:10.4337/9781800373518.00010

Cooper, S., & Michelon, G. (2022). Conceptions of materiality in sustainability reporting frameworks: Commonalities, differences and possibilities. In *Handbook of accounting and sustainability* (pp. 44–66). Edward Elgar Publishing. DOI:10.4337/9781800373518.00010

Cordazzo, M., Bini, L., & Marzo, G. (2020). Does the EU Directive on non-financial information influence the value relevance of ESG disclosure? Italian evidence. *Business Strategy and the Environment*, 29(8), 3470–3483. DOI:10.1002/bse.2589

Correa-Mejía, D. A., Correa-García, J. A., & García-Benau, M. A. (2024). Analysis of double materiality in early adopters. Are companies walking the talk? *Sustainability Accounting. Management and Policy Journal*, 15(2), 299–329.

D'Apice, V., Ferri, G., & Intonti, M. (2021). Sustainable disclosure versus ESG intensity: Is there a cross effect between holding and SRI funds? *Corporate Social Responsibility and Environmental Management*, 28(5), 1496–1510. DOI:10.1002/csr.2178

De Villiers, C., La Torre, M., & Molinari, M. (2022). The global reporting initiative's (GRI) past, present and future: Critical reflections and a research agenda on sustainability reporting (standard-setting). *Pacific Accounting Review*, 34(5), 728–747. Advance online publication. DOI:10.1108/PAR-02-2022-0034

Di Vaio, A., & Varriale, L. (2020). SDGs and airport sustainable performance: Evidence from Italy on organisational, accounting and reporting practices through financial and non-financial disclosure. *Journal of Cleaner Production*, 249, 119431. DOI:10.1016/j.jclepro.2019.119431

Du Rietz, S. (2014). When accounts become information: A study of investors' ESG analysis practice. *Scandinavian Journal of Management*, 30(4), 395–408. DOI:10.1016/j.scaman.2014.09.002

Edgley, C. (2014). A genealogy of accounting materiality. Critical Perspectives on Accounting, 25(3), 255-271.

EFRAG (2022). ESRS S1 General principles, Exposure Draft, April 2022.

Ellili, N. O. D. (2022). Impact of ESG disclosure and financial reporting quality on investment efficiency. Corporate Governance: The International Journal of Business in Society.

European Commission. (2020). Regolamento (UE) 2020/852 del Parlamento europeo e del Consiglio del 27 novembre 2019 relativo all'istituzione di un quadro per la promozione di investimenti sostenibili. Available at https://eur-lex.europa.eu/legal-content/IT/TXT/PDF/?uri=CELEX:32020R0852

European Commission. (2022). Corporate Social Responsibility Directive n. 2464. Available at https://finance.ec.europa.eu/capital-markets-union-and-financial-markets/company-reporting-and-auditing/company-reporting/corporate-sustainability-reporting_en

Farneti, F., Guthrie, J., & Siboni, B. (2011). Social and sustainability reporting in Italian local governments: What is not reported? In Ball, A., & Osborne, S. P. (Eds.), *Social Accounting and Public Management. Accountability for the Common Good*. Routledge.

Friede, G., Busch, T., & Bassen, A. (2015). ESG and financial performance: Aggregated evidence from more than 2000 empirical studies. *Journal of Sustainable Finance & Investment*, 5(4), 210–233. DOI:10.1080/20430795.2015.1118917

Gerwanski, J., Kordsachia, O., & Velte, P. (2019). Determinants of materiality disclosure quality in integrated reporting: Empirical evidence from an international setting. *Business Strategy and the Environment*, 28(5), 750–770. DOI:10.1002/bse.2278

Guthrie, J., Manes-Rossi, F., & Orelli, R. L. (2017). Integrated reporting and integrated thinking in Italian public sector organisations. *Meditari Accountancy Research*, 25(4), 553–573. DOI:10.1108/MEDAR-06-2017-0155

IIRC. (2013). The international IR framework. Available at https://integratedreporting.ifrs.org/wp-content/uploads/2013/12/13-12-08-THE-INTERNATIONAL-IR-FRAMEWORK-2-1.pdf

Karpoff, J. M., Litan, R., Schrand, C., & Weil, R. L. (2022). What ESG-Related Disclosures Should the SEC Mandate? *Financial Analysts Journal*, 78(2), 9–18. DOI:10.1080/0015198X.2022.2044718

Khan, M., Serafeim, G., & Yoon, A. (2016). Corporate sustainability: First evidence on materiality. *The Accounting Review*, 91(6), 1697–1724. www.aaajournals.org/doi/abs/10.2308/accr-51383. DOI:10.2308/accr-51383

Khan, M. A. (2022). ESG disclosure and Firm performance: A bibliometric and Meta Analysis. *Research in International Business and Finance*, 61, 101668. DOI:10.1016/j.ribaf.2022.101668

Laine, M., Tregidga, H., & Unerman, J. (2021). *Sustainability accounting and accountability*. Routledge. DOI:10.4324/9781003185611

Lehman, G., & Kuruppu, S. C. (2017, September). A framework for social and environmental accounting research. *Accounting Forum*, 41(3), 139–146. DOI:10.1016/j.accfor.2017.07.001

Littlejohn, S. W., & Foss, K. A. (2011). *Theories of Human Communication* (10th ed.). Waveland Press.

Lokuwaduge, C. S. D. S., & Heenetigala, K. (2017). Integrating environmental, social and governance (ESG) disclosure for a sustainable development: An Australian study. *Business Strategy and the Environment*, 26(4), 438–450. DOI:10.1002/bse.1927

Manes-Rossi, F., Nicolò, G., & Argento, D. (2020). Non-financial reporting formats in public sector organizations: A structured literature review. *Journal of Public Budgeting, Accounting & Financial Management*, 32(4), 639–669. DOI:10.1108/JPBAFM-03-2020-0037

Manes-Rossi, F., Spanò, R., Martin-Sardesai, A., & Guthrie, J. (2022). Performance management change: Discourses at play in an Italian university. *Journal of Public Budgeting, Accounting & Financial Management*, 34(4), 534–556. DOI:10.1108/JPBAFM-11-2021-0156

Merkl-Davies, D. M., & Brennan, N. M. (2017). A theoretical framework of external accounting communication: Research perspectives, traditions, and theories. *Accounting, Auditing & Accountability Journal*, 30(2), 433–469. DOI:10.1108/AAAJ-04-2015-2039

Michelon, G., Trojanowski, G., & Sealy, R. (2022). Narrative reporting: State of the art and future challenges. *Accounting in Europe*, 19(1), 7–47. DOI:10.1080/17449480.2021.1900582

Minutiello, V., & Tettamanzi, P. (2022). The quality of nonfinancial voluntary disclosure: A systematic literature network analysis on sustainability reporting and integrated reporting. *Corporate Social Responsibility and Environmental Management*, 29(1), 1–18. DOI:10.1002/csr.2195

Nicolò, G., Zanellato, G., Manes-Rossi, F., & Tiron-Tudor, A. (2021). Corporate reporting metamorphosis: Empirical findings from state-owned enterprises. *Public Money & Management*, 41(2), 138–147. DOI:10.1080/09540962.2020.1719633

Optima Italia. (2022). Bilancio di Sostenibilità. Available on https://www.optimaitalia.com/public/files/pdf/Bilancio_Sostenibilita%CC%80_2022.pdf

Orazalin, N. S., Ntim, C. G., & Malagila, J. K. (2024). Board sustainability committees, climate change initiatives, carbon performance, and market value. *British Journal of Management*, 35(1), 295–320. DOI:10.1111/1467-8551.12715

Pizzi, S., Principale, S., & De Nuccio, E. (2023). Material sustainability information and reporting standards. Exploring the differences between GRI and SASB. *Meditari Accountancy Research*, 31(6), 1654–1674. DOI:10.1108/MEDAR-11-2021-1486

Romolini, A., Fissi, S., & Gori, E. (2014). Scoring CSR reporting in listed companies–Evidence from Italian best practices. *Corporate Social Responsibility and Environmental Management*, 21(2), 65–81. DOI:10.1002/csr.1299

Schiehll, E., & Kolahgar, S. (2021). Financial materiality in the informativeness of sustainability reporting. *Business Strategy and the Environment*, 30(2), 840–855. DOI:10.1002/bse.2657

Sepúlveda-Alzate, Y. M., García-Benau, M. A., & Gómez-Villegas, M. (2022). Materiality assessment: The case of Latin American listed companies. *Sustainability Accounting. Management and Policy Journal*, 13(1), 88–113.

Setia, N., Abhayawansa, S., Joshi, M., & Wasantha Pathiranage, N. (2024). *Shifting perspectives: unveiling the dual nature of sustainability materiality in integrated reports*. Meditari Accountancy Research.

Shannon, C. E., & Weaver, W. (1949). *The Mathematical Theory of Communication*. University of Illinois Press.

Torelli, R., Balluchi, F., & Furlotti, K. (2020). The materiality assessment and stakeholder engagement: A content analysis of sustainability reports. *Corporate Social Responsibility and Environmental Management*, 27(2), 470–484. DOI:10.1002/csr.1813

United Nations (UN). (2015). *Transforming Our World: The 2030 Agenda for Sustainable Development*. United Nations.

van Tulder, R., & Lucht, L. (2019). Reversing materiality: from a reactive matrix to a proactive SDG agenda. *Innovation for sustainability: Business transformations towards a better world*, 271-289.

Yin, R. K. (2011). *Applications of case study research*. sage.

Yoo, S., & Managi, S. (2022). Disclosure or action: Evaluating ESG behavior towards financial performance. *Finance Research Letters*, 44, 102108. DOI:10.1016/j.frl.2021.102108

Zeisel, S. (2020). Is sustainability a moving target? A methodology for measuring CSR dynamics. *Corporate Social Responsibility and Environmental Management*, 27(1), 283–296. DOI:10.1002/csr.1805

KEY TERMS AND DEFINITIONS

Case Study: A case study is a research method that involves the detailed examination of a single instance or event (a case). This method is used to explore complex issues in real-life contexts. It involves an in-depth, longitudinal examination of a single case or a small number of cases, providing a comprehensive understanding of the phenomenon under study.

Dialogic Process: A process that arises from continuous and bidirectional communication between an entity and a variety of actors. Dialogic process leads to a reporting that meets a wider range of stakeholders' information needs. It is seen as a vehicle with the potential to foster democratic interaction rather than a set of techniques to maximize shareholder wealth or privilege only certain stakeholders.

Double Materiality: The principle according to which companies must report not only on how ESG factors influence their operations and financial performance but also on how their activities impact the environment and society.

ESG: The paradigm that evaluates a company's performance based on three key criteria: Environmental, Social, and Governance.

GRI: An international independent standards organization that helps businesses, governments, and other organizations understand and communicate their impacts on sustainability issues.

Merkl Davies and Brennan Model: Theoretical model which proposes a change in accounting communication from a transmission model to transactional model. In the latter, the communication becomes a "message" which arises from a conversation between organizations and shareholders/stakeholders in a two-way direction rather than in a one-way.

Stakeholders: Any individual, group, or organization that has an interest in or is affected by the activities, decisions, and outcomes of a business or project.

Chapter 11
CSR Practices in Brazilian Construction Firms

Adamilton Ferreira Pimenta Júnior
Federal University of Rondônia, Brazil

Talissa Nunes Lima
Federal University of Rondônia, Brazil

Lívia Maria da Silva Santos
https://orcid.org/0000-0001-9839-9424
Federal University of Rondônia, Brazil

Risolene Alves de Macena Araújo
https://orcid.org/0000-0001-6423-6299
Federal University of Pará, Brazil

Adriana Rodrigues Silva
https://orcid.org/0000-0003-1538-6877
Polytechnic Institute of Santarem, Portugal

ABSTRACT

Corporate social responsibility (CSR) is vital for business success, particularly in the competitive and evolving landscape of the construction industry. Companies increasingly adopt CSR to incorporate environmental and social practices into their operations, meeting stakeholder needs and promoting a sustainable balance between business performance and social well-being. This approach enhances corporate image, stakeholder satisfaction, and engagement. The construction sector, a key contributor to Brazil's GDP, has immense potential to drive urban development and improve public health, urban mobility, and housing. This study identifies and analyzes CSR practices of construction companies listed on the Brazilian Stock

DOI: 10.4018/979-8-3693-5663-0.ch011

Exchange, offering practical insights for managers and enriching the literature with a contextualized analysis of CSR's impact on corporate performance, thereby supporting future research and public policy development.

INTRODUCTION

Corporate Social Responsibility (CSR) is essential for business success. With increased competition and the emergence of new challenges, many companies are adopting CSR to integrate environmental and social practices into their operations. This approach aims to meet the needs of stakeholders, promoting a sustainable balance between business performance and social well-being. In addition to strengthening the corporate image, CSR contributes to stakeholder satisfaction and engagement (Bhatti et al., 2017).

According to Mazzer (2015), there has been a significant increase in the attraction of companies and investors towards CSR actions in recent years. A survey conducted by Union + Webster and published by the Federation of Industries of the State of Paraná (2019) reveals that 87% of the Brazilian population is interested in sustainable services and products. Additionally, 70% of respondents stated they do not mind paying more for these products, demonstrating an apparent concern for sustainability. Thus, it becomes increasingly evident that companies should adopt CSR practices to stand out and differentiate themselves in the competitive market.

When organizations engage in CSR activities, they overcome agency problems, generating relational assets and moral capital, thus boosting organizational performance. In addition, reduced employee turnover rates, more outstanding employee commitment, higher levels of customer satisfaction and, consequently, greater customer loyalty are benefits that improve the company's reputation (Rehman et al., 2015; Shahzad et al., 2022).

Besides providing advantages and competitive differentials, CSR adds value to a company's image. Therefore, it becomes an excellent strategic opportunity to improve service quality, meet consumer needs, reduce costs, increase productivity, and elevate product value with customer consent. This results in companies' satisfactory corporate social performance (CSP) (Leite, 2011). While CSR focuses on social practices and activities, CSP aims to achieve economic, environmental, and social results (Salazar et al., 2012).

According to the Brazilian Association of Real Estate Developers (2021), the construction sector plays an important role in the Brazilian economy, as a large part of the investment in the industry returns as Gross Domestic Product (GDP), taxes, jobs, and income for the population. The construction sector has the potential to boost various essential urban areas for society, such as the expansion of basic sanitation, which improves public health; the amplification of urban mobility; and the increase in the number of housing units, thus reducing the housing deficit and bringing improvements in quality of life. According to a survey by the Brazilian Institute of Geography and Statistics (IBGE), published by the Brazilian Chamber of the Construction Industry Agency (2022), the GDP of the construction sector grew by 9.7% in 2021 compared to 2020 after recording a 6.3% drop due to the COVID-19 pandemic.

The construction sector is increasingly inclined to adopt sustainable practices, incorporating social responsibility in project operation, implementation, and maintenance. The increase in competition in the construction market has led companies in this sector to show more interest in CSR, as this practice helps improve the brand image (Hoang; Huyen, 2020). Given this scenario, the following question arises: what are the Corporate Social Responsibility practices adopted by the construction companies listed on the Brazilian Stock Exchange?

This study aims to contribute, from a practical point of view, by identifying and analyzing the CSR practices adopted by companies listed on the Brazilian Stock Exchange, providing valuable insights for managers and professionals in the sector, allowing them to implement more effective strategies aligned with stakeholder expectations, improving corporate image and market competitiveness. Theoretically, the research aims to expand the existing literature by providing a detailed and contextualized analysis of CSR practices specific to the construction sector, a vital segment of the Brazilian economy. Furthermore, by exploring the relationship between CSR investments and corporate performance, the study seeks to contribute to understanding the dynamics between sustainable practices and business outcomes, offering a solid foundation for future research and the development of public policies that encourage adopting sustainable practices in the sector.

THEORETICAL FRAMEWORK

Stakeholder Theory

According to Freeman (1984), an organization's survival depends on the support of its stakeholders, emphasizing the partnership between stakeholders and the company. Stakeholder theory aims to boost the company's profit by taking actions that align with the stakeholders' interests. This approach is grounded in social responsibility and is geared towards improving the company's performance, with a primary focus on the stakeholders' well-being. In today's competitive market, organizations are continually seeking opportunities to enhance their performance indicators (Singhy & Misra, 2021).

Stakeholders can be categorized into two groups: primary and secondary. Primary stakeholders directly impact business operations and are indispensable for the company's survival. This group comprises investors, shareholders, customers, suppliers, and employees. On the other hand, secondary stakeholders exert an indirect influence and are not crucial for the company's survival. They include entities such as the media, government, and the community (Clarkson, 1995). According to Reis (2018), shareholders in publicly traded companies are mainly concerned with economic issues due to their role as investors. In contrast, stakeholders may include individuals who do not necessarily make financial investments but are interested in both economic aspects and social responsibility, highlighting their significant differences. The investments but are concerned with both economic aspects and social responsibility, highlighting their fundamental differences.

According to Santos (2016), stakeholder theory contributes to understanding the company's social, economic, and political landscape, emphasizing responsibility towards all those affected by organizational decisions, both internally and externally. Stakeholders need managers who monitor the company's activities efficiently and effectively, tracking each individual or group and identifying and analyzing their profiles based on their interests related to the enterprise.

Traditional strategies are needed to help managers create new paths and opportunities to keep up with changes in the landscape. Therefore, to reverse this situation and seek effective strategic management, it is necessary to identify and implement all the requirements for stakeholder satisfaction. The main focus is to meet the interests of shareholders, suppliers, employees, and other groups to ensure the company's long-term success (Freeman & McVea, 2001).

The involvement of stakeholders in the company's decision-making serves two primary objectives. Firstly, it enhances the organization's understanding, enabling the tracking of their demands and ensuring a robust base of participants during decision-making moments. Secondly, it facilitates the evaluation of the company's actions in relation to stakeholder demands and interests, with the aim of securing a competitive advantage. The active participation of stakeholders in decision-making processes is pivotal, as their influence and power directly correlate with their engagement in the company's decision-making (Stocker & Mascena, 2019).

According to Freeman et al. (2010), stakeholder theory integrates social and financial dimensions, promoting the wealth growth of shareholders and community members. The social and financial dimensions must be in harmony to benefit all stakeholders and avoid conflicts. Another fundamental aspect of the theory is value creation, where managers seek different perspectives on how to share information about the generated value (Harrison et al., 2015).

Stakeholder theory is a cornerstone of business ethics, integrating ethical considerations into the core operations of a company, alongside the pursuit of economic gains. This theory strives to align moral conduct with value creation. While business ethics professionals provide valuable insights for stakeholders, it is crucial for them to fully comprehend the key managerial issues addressed by experts (Freeman et al., 2010).

Barchiesi and Colladon (2021) suggest that managers should periodically assess the involvement of each stakeholder category in the organization's core values to enhance the effectiveness of their corporate social responsibility (CSR) strategies. This recommendation stems from an integrated approach combining Stakeholder Theory and CSR, which posits that companies engage in socially responsible behaviour due to stakeholder pressure (Shnayder et al., 2016; Tolmie et al., 2020).

Therefore, integrating CSR into Stakeholder Management Theory allows for a deeper understanding of the roles and relationships of organizations within society. The rationale is that CSR initiatives may prove ineffective if they fail to address the diverse attitudes and interests of key stakeholders (Barchiesi & Colladon, 2021).

Corporate Social Responsibility

Corporate Social Responsibility (CSR) has increasingly become a critical issue in the organizational sphere, evolving into a central concept in discussions about business and social relations (Han & Lee, 2021; Islam et al., 2021). This heightened importance is due to large corporations being subject to greater public scrutiny, as major corporate incidents—such as significant spills, occupational fatalities, and ethical scandals—can severely damage a company's image and threaten its legitimacy (Lin, 2021). The literature offers a myriad of definitions of CSR, reflecting its complex and constantly evolving nature, which is driven by the increasing pressure on businesses to enhance their social responsibility. The growing awareness of market participants regarding environmental and social issues, coupled with intense product market competition, has created moral and strategic pressures (Valiente et al., 2012). Stakeholders such as green movements generally utilize public shaming to hold companies accountable for socially irresponsible behaviour. Strategically, it is argued that CSR initiatives should be designed and implemented to promote differentiation at both the product and company levels, enhancing the company's competitiveness (Chkir et al., 2021).

CSR encompasses a company's responsibilities towards its consumers, communities, and the environment while producing profits and fulfilling obligations to its shareholders and employees. According to Kong et al. (2021), effective CSR generates long-term benefits for the organization, mitigates negative impacts on the business environment, and promotes sustainable outcomes for both the company and society. Emphasizing stakeholders is crucial for developing a robust CSR strategy (Almeida, 2002).

The result of CSR actions is Corporate Social Performance (CSP). CSP offers a framework for evaluating and managing an organization's societal relationships and activities, with a focus on actions related to the environment, social aspects, and governance, as perceived by its stakeholders (Ye et al., 2021). In essence, CSP emphasizes the outcomes of CSR efforts, serving as an extension and natural consequence of the CSR concept (Sage, 2012).

According to Carroll (1979), in his model on CSP, different perspectives of social responsibility highlight the complexity of attributing this responsibility to an organization in three main topics: (i) economic, legal, and voluntary topics; (ii) social topics; and (iii) philosophical topics. Carroll argues that it is not enough to detail only the economic, legal, ethical, and discretionary parts of social responsibility; it is also essential to analyze the origins of these social issues, which vary according to the type of organization. Regarding Young & Marais (2012) high-risk industries demonstrate more robust CSR practices than low-risk industries.

Wood's (1991) study on corporate social responsibility (CSR) is a comprehensive exploration. It defines CSP as a descriptive class of activities that focus on the consequences for the organization, its stakeholders, and society. The model is designed to integrate the conceptions of corporate responsibility at various levels-institutional, organizational, and personal. It takes into account environmental studies, interactions with stakeholders, and social challenges, providing a holistic view of CSR.

Organizations that implement corporate social actions, such as social programs aiming to achieve specific objectives, and integrate these actions into their social policies to authenticate their socially conscious causes need to respond to or meet precise demands through the application of valuable resources. The social repercussions of Corporate Social Performance (CSP) can impact organizations and stakeholders on environmental and social issues (Wood, 1991).

In the context of corporate social performance, it serves as a tool to achieve results that align with the interests of an entity's stakeholders. In this light, conducting a stakeholder analysis is of utmost importance. This analysis can significantly contribute to the formation of CSP, thereby aligning the organization's actions with the expectations and needs of its stakeholders (Boaventura et al., 2012).

Wood (1991) suggests that to assess the extent to which organizations embrace social responsibility, they must implement socially responsible actions, such as social policies and programs, to foster positive connections and impacts. This emphasizes the influence of actions on the organization's programs and policies, positioning Corporate Social Performance (CSP) as a guide for a management model oriented towards the business environment. Complementing this, Santos (2022) underscores the significant role of CEO characteristics in shaping CSP. Her research on Brazilian companies listed on B3 found that the personal attributes of CEOs, including the duality of roles, gender, education, age, and experience, have notable impacts on CSP. These findings highlight the necessity of considering organizational actions and leadership attributes in effectively implementing socially responsible practices.

By adopting a socially responsible stance, organizations address the diverse demands of their stakeholders, enhance their legitimacy, and bolster their reputation and corporate image. CSR also aids organizations in gaining and maintaining a competitive edge in the market, which, in turn, contributes to improved financial performance (Saeidi et al. 2015; Ye et al., 2021).

METHODOLOGY

Research Design

This research is descriptive regarding its objective, as it seeks to verify and describe the Corporate Social Responsibility (CSR) practices adopted by construction companies listed on B3. Regarding procedures, this research is classified as a documentary since it analyzed Standardized Financial Statements (DFPs), Explanatory Notes, Management Reports, Reference Forms, and Sustainability and/or Annual Reports of the companies. Regarding the problem approach, the research employs a mixed methods that combining qualitative and quantitative methodology. This approach allows for a comprehensive study of the characteristics of construction companies concerning their CSR actions. According to Creswell (2014), mixed methods enable researchers to draw on the strengths of both qualitative and quantitative data, providing a fuller understanding of the research problem. Bryman (2016) and Tashakkori & Teddlie (2002) further support the use of mixed methods in social research, emphasizing its effectiveness in capturing complex phenomena.

Research Sample

The research sample consists of 28 construction companies listed in Brasil, Bolsa, and Balcão (B3), according to the B3 Sector Classification of November 12, 2021. The study covers the period from 2010 to 2020 and considers the availability of Reference Forms on the B3 website from 2010 onwards. These forms contain a specific section on the social and environmental actions undertaken by the companies, thus serving as an indispensable source for the analysis, especially for those companies that do not publish Sustainability Reports. Six categories were broken down into 20 items to evaluate corporate social responsibility practices, as presented in Table 1.

Table 1. Categories for Analysis of Corporate Social Responsibility Practices

Category	Items
Labor	Equal opportunities; staff recruitment
	Occupational safety and health, risk prevention plans
	Employee education/human development, training/careers
Ethics	Establishment of a corporate code of conduct
	Whistleblowing function
Community	Health programs
	Education programs
	Local employment development
Environment	Efficient use and reuse of water
	Waste treatment/recycling initiatives
	Risk management
	Partnerships in environmental projects
Business Behavior	Channels for processing customer complaints and suggestions
	Consumer rights advocacy
	Fair competition (avoiding anti-competitive behavior)
	Anti-corruption policy
Corporate Governance	Investor relations
	Respect for governance principles
	Definition of CSR objectives
	Training program for corporate employees in CSR
	Training programs for corporate stakeholders in CSR

Source: Adapted from the works of Valiente et al. (2012), Young and Marais (2012), and Santos (2022)

Data Analysis

Based on the content analysis conducted on the Standardized Financial Statements (Explanatory Notes and Management Reports), Reference Forms, Sustainability and Annual Reports available on the B3 website, except for the Sustainability Reports, which are available on the companies' websites under the "investor relations" menu, it was possible to identify the CSR practices adopted by the construction companies. We organized the data using Excel spreadsheets, and descriptive statistics were performed to analyze the frequency of CSR practices developed by the companies studied from 2010 to 2020.

ANALYSIS OF RESULTS

This section aims to present the research results, to demonstrate which CSR practices are used by construction companies based on their reports.

Table 2. Practices Related to the Labor Category

Category	Items	2010	2011	2012	2013	2014	2015	2016	2017	2018	2019	2020
Labor	Equal opportunities; staff recruitment	12	12	12	12	12	12	12	13	13	14	15
		42.86 %	42.86 %	42.86 %	42.86 %	42.86 %	42.86 %	42.86 %	46.43 %	46.43 %	50.00 %	53.57 %
	Occupational safety and health, risk prevention plans	17	17	17	17	17	17	17	19	19	21	25
		60.71 %	60.71 %	60.71 %	60.71 %	60.71 %	60.71 %	60.71 %	67.89 %	67.89 %	75.00 %	89.29 %
	Employee education/human development, training/careers	13	12	13	13	13	13	13	16	17	19	24
		46.43 %	42.86 %	46.43 %	46.43 %	46.43 %	46.43 %	46.43 %	57.14 %	60.71 %	67.86 %	85.71 %
Total Companies		28	28	28	28	28	28	28	28	28	28	28
		100 %	100 %	100 %	100 %	100 %	100 %	100 %	100 %	100 %	100 %	100 %

Source: Research Data (2022).

According to the results in Table 2, the items "Occupational safety and health, risk prevention plans" and "Employee education/human development, training/ careers" were the most utilized by construction companies, especially in 2020, when they were adopted by 89.29% and 58.71% of the companies, respectively. These results reflect the emphasis that companies place on their employees' quality of work life, implementing practices that promote a healthier and more productive work environment. A well-structured career management can bring various benefits, such as experienced and skilled employees and competitive advantages (Harrison et al., 2015; Stocker & Mascena, 2019).

On the other hand, according to Table 2, the least practiced item was "Equal opportunities; staff recruitment." Despite this, the adoption of this practice has increased since 2017, although it is still not widely utilized. Shnayder et al. (2016) e Tolmie et al. (2020) explain that dealing with and coordinating diversity is still a significant challenge for modern companies due to the difficulties that organizations face, even though promoting diversity is a priority in their corporate social responsibilities.

Table 3. Practices related to the Ethics Category

Category	Items	2010	2011	2012	2013	2014	2015	2016	2017	2018	2019	2020
Ethics	Establishment of a corporate code of conduct	17	17	17	17	17	17	17	19	19	20	26
		60,71%	60,71%	60,71%	60,71%	60,71%	60,71%	60,71%	67,86%	67,86%	71,43%	92,86%
	Whistleblowing function	13	13	13	13	13	13	13	15	17	19	24
		46,43%	46,43%	46,43%	46,43%	46,43%	46,43%	46,43%	53,57%	60,71%	67,86%	85,71%
Total Companies		**28**	**28**	**28**	**28**	**28**	**28**	**28**	**28**	**28**	**28**	**28**
		100%	**100%**	**100%**	**100%**	**100%**	**100%**	**100%**	**100%**	**100%**	**100%**	**100%**

Source: Research Data (2022).

Table 3 shows that most organizations have a code of conduct for establishing a corporate code of conduct. From 2011 to 2020, there was a 32.15% increase in the number of companies that now have this document to conduct business activities. The Code of Ethics/Conduct is a resource for implementing the company's philosophy, mission, and values. It is used to designate the conduct of its employees and to substantiate the organization's stance towards the public with which it interacts, bringing value to the company, such as increasing the association between employees, a qualifying work environment, and adding value to the company's image, among others (Freeman et al., 2010; Shahzad et al., 2022).

With the proliferation of companies in Brazil and the media's exposure of questionable behavior and fraud, organizations have been compelled to place ethics and good conduct at the forefront of their operations. This shift has led to the adoption of management practices that foster an ethical, transparent corporate environment, thereby upholding the company's principles and values. In this context, the establishment of a code of conduct and a whistleblowing channel becomes not just a choice but a necessity, to ensure the formation of an ethical organization (Valiente et al., 2012).

It was also found that the 'Whistleblowing function' is used by most of the companies analyzed, with the highest percentage of applications in 2020 (85.71%). Implementing whistleblowing channels in organizations is of paramount importance since it is part of the Compliance program. The practice of this item generates excellent privileges for the organization, such as greater trust and credibility for its stakeholders and other organizations, providing an image of transparency for the company about society (Young & Marais, 2012; Santos, 2022).

Table 4. Practices related to the Community Category

Category	Items		2010	2011	2012	2013	2014	2015	2016	2017	2018	2019	2020
Community	Health Programs		11	11	11	11	11	11	11	11	12	13	17
			39,29%	39,29%	39,29%	39,29%	39,29%	39,29%	39,29%	39,29%	42,86%	46,43%	60,71%
	Education Programs		9	9	10	10	10	10	10	10	11	12	14
			32,14%	32,14%	35,71%	35,71%	35,71%	35,71%	35,71%	35,71%	39,29%	42,86%	50,00%
	Development of local employment		5	5	5	6	6	6	6	6	7	7	8
			17,86%	17,86%	17,86%	21,43%	21,43%	21,43%	21,43%	21,43%	25,00%	25,00%	28,57%
Total Companies			28	28	28	28	28	28	28	28	28	28	28
			100%	100%	100%	100%	100%	100%	100%	100%	100%	100%	100%

Source: Research Data (2022).

Table 4 shows that the items "Health programs" and "Education programs" had the highest percentages over the 11 years analyzed and are therefore the practices most adopted by construction companies in the Community category. This highlights the organizations' commitment to community-oriented actions.

On the other hand, the item "Development of local employment" had the lowest percentage of use by companies. In 2010, only 17.88% of organizations implemented this practice, and in 2020, the rate increased to 28.57%. Local development requires a deep and multifaceted process, which involves a combination of initial factors, such as quality governance, strategic policies, and responsive actions, to promote local and regional growth (Dreher et al., 2009; Stocker & Mascena 2019).

Table 5. Practices related to the Environment Category

Category	Items	2010	2011	2012	2013	2014	2015	2016	2017	2018	2019	2020
Environment	Efficient use and reuse of water	8	8	8	9	11	11	11	11	11	12	15
		28,57%	28,57%	28,57%	32,14%	39,29%	39,29%	39,29%	39,29%	39,29%	42,86%	53,57%
	Waste treatment/ recycling initiatives	10	10	10	11	12	12	12	12	12	14	20
		35,71%	35,71%	35,71%	39,29%	42,86%	42,86%	42,86%	42,86%	42,86%	50,00%	71,43%
	Risk management	18	18	18	18	18	18	18	18	18	20	25
		64,29%	64,29%	64,29%	64,29%	64,29%	64,29%	64,29%	64,29%	64,29%	71,43%	89,29%
	Partnerships in environmental projects	8	8	8	8	8	8	8	8	8	8	10
		28,57%	28,57%	28,57%	28,57%	28,57%	28,57%	28,57%	28,57%	28,57%	28,57%	35,71%
Total Companies		28	28	28	28	28	28	28	28	28	28	28
		100%	100%	100%	100%	100%	100%	100%	100%	100%	100%	100%

Source: Research Data (2022).

In Table 5, in the Environment category, we can see that the items "Efficient use and reuse of water", "Waste treatment/recycling initiatives", and "Risk management" showed a gradual evolution in 2018, 2019 and 2020, with an increasing number of companies adhering to these sustainable practices. According to Almeida

(2002), this trend is justified by the need for companies to effectively measure their sustainability, not just by declaring themselves socially responsible but by proving their practices.

An organization's commitment to effectively using resources on construction sites is essential since good energy and water consumption management allows for efficient use. In addition, it is crucial to monitor this use to assess performance and identify possible flaws in the systems, enabling them to be optimized. Thus, improvement actions are fundamental, along with investments, maintenance of the work, and the use of technologies and development with employees (Valiente et al., 2012 and Young & Marais, 2012)

Before starting a building project, it is important to identify the possible environmental impacts that construction may cause and seek practical and effective solutions to mitigate them. There are various solutions for managing waste, transforming the environment into a more sustainable place and reducing future environmental impacts and damage. As a result, the construction industry has improved its techniques, technologies and equipment, obtaining satisfactory results and creating a greener and more viable environment (Valiente et al., 2012)

Table 6. Practices related to the Corporate Behavior Category

Category	Items	2010	2011	2012	2013	2014	2015	2016	2017	2018	2019	2020
Business Behavior	Channels for processing customer complaints and suggestions	15	16	16	16	15	16	16	17	17	19	23
		53,57%	57,14%	57,14%	57,14%	53,57%	57,14%	57,14%	60,71%	60,71%	67,86%	82,14%
	Defense of consumer rights	12	12	12	12	12	12	12	14	16	18	23
		42,86%	42,86%	42,86%	42,86%	42,86%	42,86%	42,86%	50,00%	57,14%	64,29%	82,14%
	Normal competition (avoiding anti-competitive behavior)	16	16	16	16	16	16	16	18	19	21	25
		57,14%	57,14%	57,14%	57,14%	57,14%	57,14%	57,14%	64,29%	67,86%	75,00%	89,29%
	Anti-corruption policy	8	8	8	10	11	12	12	14	16	19	25
		28,57%	28,57%	28,57%	35,71%	39,29%	42,86%	42,86%	50,00%	57,14%	67,86%	89,29%
Total Companies		28	28	28	28	28	28	28	28	28	28	28
		100%	100%	100%	100%	100%	100%	100%	100%	100%	100%	100%

Source: Research Data (2022).

In the corporate behaviour category, the items "Defense of consumer rights", "Normal competition (avoiding anti-competitive behaviour)", and "Anti-corruption policy" have seen a significant and expressive increase in the last four years. The item "Anti-Corruption Policy" showed the greatest growth: in 2010, only 28.57% of companies had such a policy, while in 2020 this figure rose to 89.29%, showing the growing interest of organizations in this issue.

This result is justified because the effective implementation of anti-corruption policies increases the company's credibility in the market. Internally, it promotes greater satisfaction among employees, increasing loyalty and productivity. Externally, it generates more stable relationships, improves the organization's reputation, facilitates negotiations and makes the company safer, positively impacting its results (Saeidi et al., 2015; Ye et al., 2021)

Regarding the item "Defense of consumer rights," 42.86% of companies adopted this practice in 2012; in 2020, this percentage rose to 82.14%. Suppliers must support consumers regarding complaints, clarifications, and defects. Mutual trust is essential; a satisfied and respected customer tends to return and recommend the company to others (Freeman et al., 2010):

Table 7. Practices related to the Corporate Governance Category

Category	Items	2010	2011	2012	2013	2014	2015	2016	2017	2018	2019	2020
Corporate governance	Investor relations	19	19	19	19	19	19	19	20	20	22	28
		67,86%	67,86%	67,86%	67,86%	67,86%	67,86%	67,86%	71,43%	71,43%	78,57%	100%
	Respect for governance principles	12	12	12	12	12	12	13	16	16	18	25
		42,86%	42,86%	42,86%	42,86%	42,86%	42,86%	46,43%	57,14%	57,14%	64,29%	89,29%
	Definition of CSR objectives	2	2	2	2	2	1	1	1	2	3	4
		7,14%	7,14%	7,14%	7,14%	7,14%	3,57%	3,57%	3,57%	7,14%	10,71%	14,29%
	Training program for corporate employees on CSR	2 7,14%	2 7,14%	2 7,14%	2 7,14%	2 7,14%	1 3,57%	1 3,57%	1 3,57%	1 3,57%	2 7,14%	3 10,71%
	Training programs for corporate stakeholders on CSR	2 7,14%	2 7,14%	2 7,14%	2 7,14%	2 7,14%	1 3,57%	1 3,57%	1 3,57%	1 3,57%	2 7,14%	3 10,71%
Total Companies		**28**	**28**	**28**	**28**	**28**	**28**	**28**	**28**	**28**	**28**	**28**
		100%	**100%**	**100%**	**100%**	**100%**	**100%**	**100%**	**100%**	**100%**	**100%**	**100%**

Source: Research Data (2022).

In Table 7, about the corporate governance category, the items "Investor relations" and "Respect for governance principles" were the most prominent, especially in 2019 and 2020. The item that stood out the most was "Investor relations": in 2010, 67.86% of companies adopted this practice, and in 2020, all 28 companies in the sector (100%) became concerned with investor relations.

Communication between the organization and its investors is essential, as is the search for continuous improvement. It is a competitive differentiator in the capital markets. A good relationship with investors guarantees a secure source of funds for the company (Barchiesi & Colladon, 2021)

Corporate governance consists of a set of mechanisms that increase the likelihood of raising funds and guarantee a return on investment. Among the various governance mechanisms are the capital structure, the board of directors, competition in the product market, the publication of regular reports, and the remuneration policy (Freeman & McVea, 2001; Freeman et al., 2010; Harrison et al., 2015; Santos, 2016).

FINAL CONSIDERATIONS

This research aimed to verify the Corporate Social Responsibility (CSR) practices adopted by companies in the construction sector listed on B3 between 2010 and 2020.

In the "Work" category, the "Occupational health and safety, occupational risk prevention plans" and "Employee education/human development, training/careers" practices stood out. In the "Ethics" category, the items "Establishment of a corporate code of conduct" and "Whistleblowing function" were the most adopted. About "Community", the highlight was "Health programs".

In the "Environment" category, "Risk management" was the most prominent item. In the "Business Behavior" category, in 2020, the items "Normal Competition (avoiding anti-competitive behaviour)" and "Anti-Corruption Policy" were adopted by 89.29% of companies. Finally, in the "Corporate Governance" category, the items "Investor relations" and "Respect for governance principles" showed the highest percentages of adoption, being used by 100% and 89.29% of companies, respectively, in 2020.

The results indicate an evolution in the adoption of CSR practices over the 11 years of the study. This concern on the part of organizations to maintain a positive relationship with their stakeholders is motivated by the pressure they are under to present solutions and immediate commitments to social problems, such as racial prejudice, pollution, inclusion of people with disabilities, unemployment, social exclusion, environmental degradation, among other issues that directly or indirectly impact companies and their stakeholders (Dreher, Ullrich & Moro, 2009).

The research offers significant practical contributions by providing an overview of the CSR practices adopted by companies in the construction sector over a decade, highlighting key areas such as occupational safety, employee education, and environmental management, which can guide other companies in the industry in implementing sustainable and ethical strategies. Theoretically, this research provides empirical data on the evolution of CSR practices, identifying trends and patterns that may be useful for future academic study and developing theories on corporate governance, business behaviour and sustainability in the construction sector.

Also contributes to Brazil's literature on Corporate Social Responsibility (CSR). According to Shu and Chiang (2020) and Ye et al. (2021), the adoption of CSR practices in emerging countries is relatively slow compared to developed countries. In this context, the research findings indicate a positive evolution in the social stance of organizations within the construction sector despite these practices being not mandatory.

The research's limitations include the subjectivity inherent in the content analysis carried out to collect data on corporate social responsibility in construction companies' reports. For future studies, we suggest investigating the measurement of construction companies' corporate social performance, considering that this reflects the results of the organization's corporate social responsibility actions.

REFERENCES

Abrainc. (2021). ABRAINC Explica: A importância da Construção Civil para impulsionar a economia brasileira. Associação Brasileira de Incorporadoras Imobiliárias. Disponível em: https://www.abrainc.org.br/abrainc-explica/2021/06/28/abrainc-explica-a-importancia-da-construcao-civil-para-impulsionar-a-economia-brasileira/

Agência, C. B. I. C. (2022). PIB da construção fecha o ano com crescimento de 9,7%, a maior alta em 11 anos. Câmara Brasileira da Indústria da Construção. Disponível em: https://cbic.org.br/pib-da-construcao-fecha-o-ano-com-crescimento-de-97-a-maior-alta-em-11-anos

Agência Sistema Fiep. (2019). 87% dos consumidores brasileiros preferem comprar de empresas sustentáveis. Disponível em: https://www.agenciafiep.com.br/2019/02/28/consumidores-preferem-empresas-sustentaveis/

Almeida, F. (2002). *O Bom Negócio da Sustentabilidade*. Nova Fronteira.

Barchiesi, M. A., & Colladon, A. F. (2021). Corporate core values and social responsibility: What really matters to whom. *Technological Forecasting and Social Change*, 170, 1–9. DOI:10.1016/j.techfore.2021.120907

Bhatti, A., Arif, S., Marium, M., & Younas, S. (2017). The Impact of Corporate Social Responsibility (CSR) and Relationship Marketing on Relationship Maintenance and Customer Loyalty through the Mediating Role of Customer Satisfaction. *Management Information Journal*, 4(4), 19–24.

Boaventura, J. M. G., da Silva, R. S., & Bandeira-de-Mello, R. (2012). Performance Financeira Corporativa e Performance Social Corporativa: Desenvolvimento metodológico e contribuição teórica dos estudos empíricos. *Revista Contabilidade & Finanças*, 23(60), 232–245. DOI:10.1590/S1519-70772012000300008

Bryman, A. (2016). *Social research methods*. Oxford University Press.

Carroll, A. B. (1979). A Three Dimensional conceptual model of corporate performance. *Academy of Management Review*, 4(4), 497–505. DOI:10.2307/257850

Carroll, A. B. (1991). The pyramid of corporate social responsibility: Toward the moral management of organizational stakeholders. *Business Horizons*, 34(4), 39–46. DOI:10.1016/0007-6813(91)90005-G

Chkir, I., Hassan, B. E. H., Rjiba, H., & Saadi, S. (2021). Does corporate social responsibility influence corporate innovation? International evidence. *Emerging Markets Review*, 46, 1–19. DOI:10.1016/j.ememar.2020.100746

Clarkson, M. E. A. (1995). A stakeholder framework for analyzing and evaluating corporate social performance. *Academy of Management Review*, 20(1), 92–117. DOI:10.2307/258888

Creswell, J. (2016). *Research Design.: Qualitative, Quantitative, Mixed Methods Approaches*. University Of Nebraska-Lincoln.

Dreher, M., Ullrich, D., & Moro, R. (2009). *Stakeholder e Responsabilidade Social: As experiências das organizações de Blumenau*. ABEPRO - Associação Brasileira de Engenharia de Produção.

Freeman, R., Parmar, B., Harrison, J., Wicks, A., De Colle, S., & Purnell, L. (2010). Stakeholder Theory: The State of the Art. *The Academy of Management Annals*, 4(1), 403–445. DOI:10.5465/19416520.2010.495581

Freeman, R. E. (1984). *Strategic Management: A Stakeholders Approach*. Pitman.

Freeman, R. E., & McVea, J. (2005). A stakeholder approach to strategic management. *The Blackwell Handbook of strategic management*, 183-201.

Han, S., & Lee, J. W. (2021). Does corporate social responsibility matter even in the B2B market?: Effect of B2B CSR on customer trust. *Industrial Marketing Management*, 93, 115–123. DOI:10.1016/j.indmarman.2020.12.008

Harrison, J., Freeman, R., & Abreu, M. (2015). Stakeholder Theory as an Ethical Approach to Effective Management: Applying the theory to multiple contexts. *Revista Brasileira de Gestão de Negócios*, 17(55), 858–869. DOI:10.7819/rbgn.v17i55.2647

Hoang, A., & Huyen, T. (2020). A corporate social responsibility indicator system for construction enterprises in Vietnam. *International Journal of Civil Engineering*, 7(6), 12–20. DOI:10.14445/23488352/IJCE-V7I6P102

Islam, T., Islam, R., Pitafi, A. H., Xiaobei, L., Rehmani, M., Irfan, M., & Mubarak, M. S. (2021). The impact of corporate social responsibility on customer loyalty: The mediating role of corporate reputation, customer satisfaction, and trust. *Sustainable Production and Consumption*, 25, 123–135. DOI:10.1016/j.spc.2020.07.019

Kawa, L. (2016). Responsabilidade social na construção civil. Disponível em: http://professoralucianekawa.blogspot.com

Kong, D., Shu, Y., & Wang, Y. (2021). Corruption and corporate social responsibility: Evidence from a quasi-natural experiment in China. *Journal of Asian Economics*, 75, 1–16. DOI:10.1016/j.asieco.2021.101317

Leite, L. (2011). Responsabilidade Social Corporativa como Estratégia de Negócio: Modelos Conceituais e Exemplos Ilustrativos (Tese de Mestrado, Escola de Administração de Empresas de São Paulo).

Lin, Y. (2021). Legitimation strategies in corporate discourse: A comparison of UK and Chinese corporate social responsibility reports. *Journal of Pragmatics*, 177, 157–169. DOI:10.1016/j.pragma.2021.02.009

Mazzer, L. (2015). Responsabilidade Social Corporativa e Desempenho Econômico Financeiro: Um Estudo em Empresas Brasileiras (Tese de Doutorado, Universidade de Brasília).

Oliva, A., & De Oliveira, R. (2008). Social Responsibility in Civil Construction in Brazil: A Path that Can Support Housing Access. *Revista INVI*, 23, 121–134.

Rehman, A., Baloch, Q., & Sethi, S. (2015). Understanding the relationship between firm's corporate social responsibility and financial performance: Empirical analysis. *Abasyn Journal of Social Sciences*, 8(1), 98–107.

Reis, T. (2018). Stakeholder: O que é e qual sua importância em uma empresa? Suno. Disponível em: https://www.suno.com.br/artigos/stakeholder/. Acesso em: 12 de junho de 2022.

Saeidi, S. P., Sofian, S., Saeidi, P., Saeidi, S. P., & Saaeidi, S. A. (2015). How does corporate social responsibility contribute to firm financial performance? The mediating role of competitive advantage, reputation, and customer satisfaction. *Journal of Business Research*, 68(2), 341–350. DOI:10.1016/j.jbusres.2014.06.024

Salazar, J., Husted, B. W., & Biehl, M. (2012). Thoughts on the evaluation of corporate social performance through projects. *Journal of Business Ethics*, 105(2), 175–186. DOI:10.1007/s10551-011-0957-z

Santos, D. (2016). Stakeholders e o Desempenho Social Corporativo De Entidades Desportivas Do Terceiro Setor: Proposta De Mensuração (Dissertação de Mestrado, Universidade Nove de Julho).

Santos, L. M. S. (2022). Influência da Discrição Gerencial dos CEOs no Desempenho Social Corporativo: Uma Análise nas Empresas Listadas na B3 (Tese de Doutorado, Universidade Federal da Paraíba).

Shahzad, F., Baig, M. H., Rehman, I. U., Saeed, A., & Asim, G. A. (2022). Does intellectual capital efficiency explain corporate social responsibility engagement-firm performance relationship? Evidence from environmental, social and governance performance of US listed firms. *Borsa Istanbul Review*, 22(2), 295–305. DOI:10.1016/j.bir.2021.05.003

Shnayder, L., van Rijnsoever, F. J., & Hekkert, M. P. (2016). Motivations for Corporate Social Responsibility in the packaged food industry: An institutional and stakeholder management perspective. *Journal of Cleaner Production*, 122, 212–227. DOI:10.1016/j.jclepro.2016.02.030

Shu, P., & Chiang, S. (2020). The impact of corporate governance on corporate social performance: Cases from listed firms in Taiwan. *Pacific-Basin Finance Journal*, 61, 1–20. DOI:10.1016/j.pacfin.2020.101332

Singh, K., & Misra, M. (2021). Linking Corporate Social Responsibility (CSR) and Organizational Performance: The Moderating Effect of Corporate Reputation. *Research in Management and Business Economics*, 27.

Stocker, F., & Mascena, K. M. C. (2019). Orientação e gestão para stakeholders no processo de decisão organizacional. *R.G.Secr.GESEC*, 10(1), 167–191. DOI:10.7769/gesec.v10i1.864

Tashakkori, A., & Teddlie, C. (2002). Handbook of mixed methods in social & behavioural research. Sage Publications.

Tolmie, C. R., Lehnert, K., & Zhao, H. (2020). Formal and informal institutional pressures on corporate social responsibility: A cross-country analysis. *Corporate Social Responsibility and Environmental Management*, 27(2), 786–802. DOI:10.1002/csr.1844

Valiente, J. M. A., Ayerbe, C. G., & Figueras, M. S. (2012). Social responsibility practices and evaluation of corporate social performance. *Journal of Cleaner Production*, 35, 25–38. DOI:10.1016/j.jclepro.2012.05.002

Wartick, S., & Cochran, P. (1985). The evolution of the corporate social performance model. *Academy of Management Review*, 10(4), 758–769. DOI:10.2307/258044

Wood, D. J. (1991). Corporate social performance revisited. *Academy of Management Review*, 16(4), 691–718. DOI:10.2307/258977

Ye, M., Wang, H., & Lu, W. (2021). Opening the "black box" between corporate social responsibility and financial performance: From a critical review on moderators and mediators to an integrated framework. *Journal of Cleaner Production*, 313, 1–10. DOI:10.1016/j.jclepro.2021.127919

Young, S., & Marais, M. (2012). A Multi Level Perspective of CSR Reporting: The Implications of National Institutions and Industry Risk Characteristics. *Corporate Governance*, 20(5), 432–450. DOI:10.1111/j.1467-8683.2012.00926.x [illegible], J., van [illegible], E., & Hekkert, M. P. (2020). [illegible] social Responsibility in the [illegible] and [illegible] in [illegible] and [illegible] behaviour [illegible]. *Journal of Cleaner Production*, [illegible]. Doi:10.1016/j.jclepro.2020.[illegible]

Shi, P., & [illegible], S. (2020). The [illegible] of [illegible] [illegible] social [illegible] [illegible]. [illegible]

Singh, A., [illegible], M. (2021). [illegible]. [illegible] International [illegible]. [illegible]

[illegible] (2001). [illegible]

[illegible] (2011). Handbook of [illegible]. [illegible] Sage Publications.

[illegible] (2020). [illegible] corporate social responsibility: A [illegible] analysis [illegible]. [illegible]

[illegible] (2018). [illegible]

[illegible], S., & [illegible] (1988). The [illegible]. [illegible]

[illegible]

[illegible] (2020). [illegible]. Doi:10.1016/j.jclepro.[illegible]

[illegible] (2017). [illegible] and [illegible]. Doi:10.1007/[illegible]

Chapter 12
Organisational and Individual Accountability for Sustainability Through Control

Leanne Johnstone
https://orcid.org/0000-0003-0916-7889
Örebro University, Sweden

ABSTRACT

This chapter elaborates on the connections between organisational and individual-level accountabilities for sustainability control purposes. This aim is achieved through a conceptual study that draws on accountability as the theoretical lens and some recent sustainability control works in different contexts to highlight potential research avenues for scholars conducting research into sustainability management, accounting, and/or control. The chapter finds that building on the individual level of accountability and socialising accountability form is important to incorporate into sustainability control studies given that such research is often conceptualised at the organisational level of external accounts. For practitioners, the chapter suggests that formalised control system design is not enough to ensure that sustainable performance outcomes are achieved in practice, and that managers in different types of organisational forms should integrate the views, perspectives, and beliefs systems of other (non-managerial) employees into their daily sustainability work.

DOI: 10.4018/979-8-3693-5663-0.ch012

INTRODUCTION

Although stemming from the socio-environmental movements of the 1960s and 1970s, scholarly works dealing with sustainability control have grown exponentially since the turn of the 21st century as organisations attempt to meet various institutional demands relating to sustainability. Much like the more traditional definitions of management control (e.g. Anthony et al., 2014; Chenhall, 2003), sustainability controls are put in place to support decision-making and monitor, motivate and guide employee behaviour related to a specific sustainability control problem (Johnstone, 2019). While such problems have typically dealt with the environmental facets of sustainability such as those related to climate, waste, water and biodiversity (e.g. Gomez-Conde et al., 2019; Henri and Journeault, 2010), issues related to social sustainability issues, such as modern slavery, diversity and employee health are emerging (e.g. Gunarathne et al., 2016), and increasingly the subject of current special issue calls.

Sustainability controls have been conceptualised under various thematic categories, which often stem from extant management control system frameworks such as Simons' (1995) levers of control (e.g. Arjaliès & Mundy 2013; Beusch et al., 2022) or Malmi and Brown's (2008) conceptual package (e.g. Bouten & Hoozée, 2016; Crutzen et al., 2017). Drawing on these works, there are several types of controls that can be discerned from the literature for sustainability purposes that, combined, form the sustainability control system. These are now briefly overviewed.

Planning control sets out the strategic and tactical goals for the organisation based on its wider context. *Performance-related control* regards implementing targets to meet such plans. Some common examples include budgets and non-financial performance measures related to carbon and biodiversity. Meanwhile, *administrative control* regards the official policies and procedures of an organisation, as well as its (reporting) structures to ensure strategic plans are met. *Socio-ideological or cultural control* regards the symbols, values and belief systems of the organisation that are used to influence employee behaviours to align with organisational strategy as a function of control. Finally, *compensation controls* are those put in place to incentivise or reward individual employee behaviour and, for example, achievement of specific key performance indicators. Sustainability controls therefore include a wide variety of tools (e.g. sustainability performance indicators, governance structures and incentive systems etc.) that can be used by managers to ensure that organisational aims are met. These control tools can be both formal and informal in nature, as part of the official control system design. This means that while the formal tools regard the more tangible policies or targets of the organisation, the informal control tools regard the communication and reporting pathways between managers and other employees (see Pondeville et al. [2013] for more examples of this distinction).

In the European context, the increasing use of sustainability controls to support corporate strategic is clear. This is arguably because of the recent wave of directives and international guidelines within Europe that support sustainability. As examples, the Non-Financial Reporting Directive (Directive 2014/95/EU) and the Corporate Sustainability Reporting Directive (Directive 2022/2464/EU) illustrate a move that supports the European Green Deal and Task Force on Climate-related Financial Disclosures (2015), as well as other social sustainability issues (e.g. employee welfare, human rights, anti-corruption and bribery, and diversity on company boards). These mandates, therefore, have sought to impose certain *accountability* demands on organisations to account and control their sustainability operations.

Accountability is a theoretical perspective that is often used to help explain why organisations conduct certain actions in response to their accountability demands; that is, the mandates, expectations or requirements placed upon them within a particular context. In this sense, accountability has clear links to organisational control in that strategic sustainability controls are designed in response to particular contextual demands (see Pondeville et al., 2013; Wijethilake & Ekanayake, 2018). Notwithstanding the strategic focus of 'external' accountability demands in prior sustainability control works, the seminal accountability works (e.g. Roberts, 1991, 2001; Roberts & Scapens, 1985) emphasise that accountability demands are placed on both institutional (i.e. organisational) *and* individual levels; thus, signalling that accountability relationships exist between organisations and employees as accountors, *and* external accountees (e.g. government, industry, society) as the demanders of such accounts (see also Johnstone et al., 2023). As will be argued in this chapter, sustainability control tools thereby become important for organisations to meet their accountability demands; although rarely conceptualised as the means of accountability in prior literature. This is where the current chapter aims to fill such a gap.

Recent sustainability control research calls for the theoretical perspective of accountability to be integrated with conceptualisations of control to help more fully explain and understand, particularly, employee action in practice (e.g. Frostenson & Johnstone, 2023; Johnstone et al., 2023). Building on these emerging studies, the aim of this chapter is *to elaborate on the connections between accountability for sustainability control purposes, putting forward proposals for future sustainability control research to be framed by accountability as the theoretical lens*. This aim is achieved through a conceptual study that draws on accountability theorisations and some recent sustainability control works to highlight potential research avenues for scholars conducting research into sustainability management, accounting and/or control. In this sense, the inclusion of different case studies (e.g. Frostenson & Johnstone, 2023; Johnstone et al., 2023; Johnstone, 2021, 2022) in different contexts (i.e. multinational companies, public sector organisations and small businesses) that link accountability theorisations (more or less explicitly) to control serves an illustrative purpose to support the analytical generalisability of the chapter's key propositions.

The paper begins by overviewing the theoretical perspective of accountability and its relationship to control, drawing on important accountability works. Following from this, the method approach is briefly given before more explicit examples regarding how accountability for sustainability is being achieved in practice from empirical cases in different organisational contexts (i.e. multinational companies, public sector organisations and small businesses) are presented. The chapter concludes by putting forward some propositions regarding the relationship between sustainability control and accountability that can be tested and built upon in future works, as well as the research and practical implications stemming from such findings.

ACCOUNTABILITY FOR SUSTAINABILITY CONTROL

Accountability is defined as providing *"an account (by no means necessarily a financial account) or reckoning of those actions for which one is held responsible"* (Gray et al., 1996, p. 38). Through this definition, a twofold responsibility position is inferred of: *1)* (not) enacting certain actions and *2)* providing accounts of those (non) actions (ibid.). When relating this to the function of control, accountability therefore relates to the decision-making function in terms of deciding what/how to act, considering the wider accountability demands on both organisational and individual levels. Here, 'providing accounts' additionally relates to the second function of control for behavioural alignment, i.e. to monitor, motivate and guide employee behaviour in light of such accountability demands.

Most social and environmental accounting research that uses accountability as a theoretical perspective, however, concentrates on the organisational level of accounts to external demands; rather than how accountability relationships for sustainability are achieved through the internal functions of sustainability control. This is illustrated in the manifold studies that focus on sustainability reporting and disclosure at the organisation-environment interface (see Brown & Dillard, 2013; Dillard & Vinnari 2019). In contrast, the seminal accountability works in accounting scholarship often frame accountability as intra-organisational; the result of two complementary forms (i.e. hierarchical and socialising) that work together as a dynamic (Roberts, 1991, 2001).

In short, hierarchical accountability regards how *"individuals or unit groups are controlled and held accountable by those with the power to do so, granted by superior status in the respective organisational hierarchy"* (Yates et al., 2019, p. 169). This type of accountability is often conceptualised as being individualising in that it implies that individual agency is reduced by formalised tools in the organisation that hold employees accountable (see Roberts, 1991). Stemming from Foulcault's (1977, 1979) disciplinary control and the panopticon metaphor, the seminal accountability works of Roberts (1991, 2001) posit the account-givers as subject to those to which the accounts are made. In an intra-organisational context and related to control, this means that managers or superiors are the account-givers and the general employees or subordinates are the accountees. Such conceptualisations of hierarchical accountability have the clearest links to controls in that through the formalised design of controls, managers can impose certain conditions for behavioural alignment as one function of control.

Meanwhile, socialising accountability (Roberts, 1991) stems from Habermas' (1971, 1984) works and emphasises the 'other' accountability relationships (see also Levinas, 1991) that may call (some) employees to account; that is, those relationships beyond the formal organisational hierarchy that are nevertheless important for guiding employee action:

> *Those who one happens to work with or alongside, become those with whom one shares and builds a common interpretation of one's world of work. Journeys to and from work, lunches and after work drinks, toilets, corridors, all the unsurveilled 'back regions' of organizational life serve as locations for such sense-making talk. Through such talk not only is the official version of organizational reality penetrated and reinterpreted, but also it is the basis for a diffuse set of loyalties and ties, of enmity as well as friendship, that humanize and socialize the experience of work (Roberts, 1991, p. 362).*

Socialising accountability is therefore distinct from informal control in that it also incorporates relationships and 'meetings' that are not embedded into the formalised control system design and/or the organisational hierarchy. Nevertheless, the socialising accountability form may not be any freer than the 'individualising' hierarchical accountability form (Jacobs & Walker 2004). This is because responsibility to 'others' also has controlling effects in terms of how one acts.

While much has been written on the two types of accountability, and conceptualised in different ways in the literature (e.g. Boomsma & O'Dwyer, 2014; Sinclair, 1995), Roberts (1991) emphasises that the accountability forms work together as a dynamic (see also Yates et al., 2019). In this sense, the hierarchical and socialising accountability forms should not be viewed as a dichotomy but rather as complementary ways for accounts to be expressed. Notwithstanding, extant control research tends to put focus on the hierarchical or structural form as *the* means for achieving particular performance outcomes. In doing so, the formalised design of controls is seen as *the* main way to connect the organisational level accountability demands to individual employee behaviours. Nevertheless, some subtle nuances remain in terms of this hierarchical accountability form when related to what is known about control.

For some time, there has been a debate over the role of control for behavioural alignment in terms of reducing employee agency in that some controls, even though part of the formalised control system design, are designed to stimulate employee autonomy and empowerment. This has key implications for the individualising role of hierarchical accountability when related to control.

One such discussion that nuances the effects of 'hierarchical' control on employees is those wider control studies that build upon Adler and Borys' (1996) enabling and coercive bureaucracy/control (e.g. Ahrens & Chapman 2004; Jordan & Messner, 2012). In brief, coercive features of control system design regard hierarchy, compliance, constraint and low trust, while enabling features regard flat organisational structures, autonomy, flexibility and high trust. Meanwhile, both are part of the formalised control system design and thus, hierarchical in conceptualisation. What can be ascertained from such studies is that while characteristically coercive controls can be seen as reducing individual agency through compliance, enabling controls may allow for more agency through the flexibility and autonomy built into their design. This essentially means that both coercive and enabling controls can be viewed as the formalised means for managers to achieve particular performance outcomes, embedded into organisational hierarchy (whether hierarchical or flat) but where the degree of individual agency ranges from low (coercive) to high (enabling).

However, as the more recent sustainability control research - whether implicitly or explicitly – suggests, the formalised design of controls by (top) managers is not the only factor to consider for explaining sustainable employee behaviour as one important function of control (see Johnstone, 2019). This is where drawing on the two accountability forms (i.e. hierarchical and socialising) becomes useful to add to what is already known about control and the primarily organisational level of accountability to external demands through the strategic design of controls. In the cases that follow, different examples will help shed light on how accountability theorisations can be applied to sustainability control studies to more fully explain or capture employee behaviour as one function of control, and particularly through the socialising accountabilities that can provide more reason behind individual workplace actions. First, the method is briefly described.

METHOD

Already explained in the introduction section, the use of different cases in this chapter is to serve an illustrative purpose for analytical generalisations in terms of the propositions put forward. The four studies reviewed come from three different contexts. They are important for providing a brief review of the limited - yet emerging - sustainability control works that draw on both forms of accountability (i.e. the hierarchical and the socialising) for sustainability performance. Importantly, these studies elaborate on accountability *within* the organisational context in alignment with the intentions of the seminal accountability works (e.g. Roberts, 1991, 2001; Roberts & Scapens, 1985). The papers used in the case examples are overviewed in Table 1.

Table 1. Papers used in the case analysis

Context	Author(s) & year	Title & Journal	Accountability focus
Multinational company	Frostenson, M. & Johnstone, L. (2023)	Moving beyond the external face of accountability: constructing accountability for sustainability from within. *Sustainability Accounting, Management and Policy Journal*, 14(7), 124-151.	Explicit, Roberts' (1991) hierarchical and socialising accountability forms
Public sector organisation	Johnstone, L. Yates, D., & Nylander, S. (2023)	Taking shape within the structural and the personal: sustainability accountability within a Swedish public sector organisation. *Sustainability Accounting, Management and Policy Journal*, 14(7), 287-312.	Explicit Roberts' (1991) hierarchical and socialising accountability forms, as well as Sinclair's (1995) structural and personal accountability.
Small businesses	Johnstone, L. (2021)	Facilitating sustainability control in SMEs through the implementation of an environmental management system. *Journal of Management Control*, 32(4), 559-605.	Accountability theorisations less explicit but offers examples of 'other' types of accountability relationships beyond the formal hierarchy for inciting employee action.
	Johnstone, L. (2022)	The means to substantive performance improvements–environmental management control systems in ISO 14001–certified SMEs. Sustainability Accounting, Management and Policy Journal, 13(5), 1082-1108.	Elaborates on connections between control system design and external accountability demands.

All papers used in this study used in-depth qualitative research in the forms of interviews with employees (managers and non-managers on different levels), site visits and secondary data analysis, among others. The method description in each paper overviews these in more detail. Nevertheless, drawing on such qualitative studies was considered beneficial to elaborate on the connections between accountability for sustainability control purposes, thereby establishing analytical generalisations from these contexts that could be developed into future research proposals. Particularly, a qualitative research design is considered useful to *"examine how accounting influences particular members of society and how they influence accounting"* (de

Villiers et al. 2019, 1477); which relates to the accountability demands on organisations and individuals as members of the societies to which they are accountable to.

In the case examples that follow, each context is taken in turn and described in more detail, before being summarised together in the form of a table which connects the findings to accountability theorisations. It is this analytical summary that forms the basis for the propositions that follow.

Method Limitations

Given that this study is based on a limited review of recent sustainability control papers that link to the internal and/or individual elements of accountability to the external and/or organisational-level, other case contexts should be added to increase the analytical and thus, the theoretical generalisability of the initial propositions put forward in this chapter. This should be achieved in future empirical research that continues along this vein, which is especially important considering that studies which explicitly relate sustainability control to 'internal' and 'individual' accountability are few. Related to this point, there may be the critiqued that qualitative studies cannot be generalised. However, the term generalisability here does not refer to statistical generalisability but rather in terms of general patterns regarding the (potential) connections between accountability and control. Further limitations are suggested in the future research opportunities put forward at the end of this paper.

CASE EXAMPLES

Case 1. The Multinational Company

Frostenson and Johnstone (2023) explore how accountability for sustainability is constructed whilst establishing a control system for sustainability. In doing so, they provide empirical evidence of the connections between the accountability dynamic and sustainability control system design. The case context is that of decentralised industrial group, following a qualitative approach from 2017 to 2020, with data such as semi-structured interviews, informal conversations, site visits and document analyses. The case company has its headquarters in Sweden but operates in nine (mainly Northern European) countries. The main product categories relate to heavy industrial products and services, including steel and recycling.

Since 2014, sustainability has become a key corporate ambition of the company and - at the time of data collection - was centrally coordinated at the group level. The external demands of customers had then triggered the development of a new sustainability strategy. This strategy required the development of internal control and reporting structures within the group to make people accountable for sustainability within the different business areas. This meant that while the sustainability strategy, as a form of planning control, was formulated at the group level, the respective subsidiary companies were permitted relative autonomy in terms of designing and implementing particular sustainability controls at the tactical level to meet this strategy.

During the beginning of the research period, a sustainability network structure had been established with the aim of appointing one key responsibility from each of the subsidiary companies to guide and drive the internal sustainability work. There were also clearer hierarchical accountability mechanisms illustrated through the Code of Conduct and traditional key performance indicators (KPIs) to guide employees towards sustainable targets. Nevertheless, there was little follow-up or discipline for not following guidelines or meeting targets. This suggested a lack of 'discipline' for bad performance when related to sustainability issues. Rather, much of the accountability illustrated in the case was characterised as beyond the formalised design of controls, through relationships between people who were motivated to work with sustainability issues; that is, mainly those tactical level managers who were part of the formal sustainability coordination network. These individuals were driven to establish further controls in their respective subsidiary companies but were rarely held accountable for sustainability (non) results. In this sense, their role was one of facilitating sustainability integration further down the organisational hierarchy through the formalised design of controls that imply other hierarchical accountability relationships between middle-managers and subordinates.

The findings of the case illustrate the need for socialising accountability relationships at the tactical level (between employees or relatively equal status) to mobilise the design of further hierarchical accountability forms in the lower tiers of the company (i.e. to construct more effective sustainability control systems in each subsidiary company). This means that middle managers (rather than the strategic level) are important for the construction of sustainable accounts in terms of what to account for, in what ways and by whom. Yet, it was those very individuals that negotiated what to account for, rather than having those conditions imposed on them from the group level. In doing so, this implies that hierarchical accountability may well be decentralised in large multinational companies like the one describe as the control systems are decentralised. In such multinational companies, it may well be the tactical managers who are striving to make sense of the (non) official accountability demands placed upon them and their respective subsidiary companies.

Overall, the findings of this paper reason that socialising accountability relationships may be behind the attempts to construct hierarchical accountability forms. This contributes to the wider literature on the accountability dynamic by elaborating on the dynamic processes behind the establishment of formalised sustainability control systems. These processes regard a consideration of how individuals within organisations work to reconcile strategic objectives with their perceived accountability demands; a theme that continues into the next empirical context.

Case 2. The Public Sector Organisation

Johnstone et al. (2023) conducted a study on a Swedish local authority with the aim of understanding "how accountability for sustainability takes shape" and particularly, what makes these public sector employees act. In doing so, the study again went further into the internal, intra-organisational aspects of accountability wherein organisational level accountability demands were discussed considering those individual-level factors. It also went deeper into the individual level of accountability for public sector employees who exist in a complex accountability position as both the accountors (i.e. those giving the accounts) and accountees (i.e. as part of the wider society demanding such accounts). The case is discussed in more detail in the following paragraphs.

The case local authority is in central Sweden and provides health care, research and education services, among others. Given that it is a local authority, it is mandated by Swedish legislation to report on certain sustainability issues such as anti-discrimination and the environment. The local authority is a key employer, with around 10,000 employees in the region ranging from the regional board at the top, to a wide range of employees such as doctors, nurses and cleaners. While the board is responsible for the long-term strategic planning and the external accountability demands of constituents and the prevailing political party, there are six administrative departments related to its services. These departments entail a degree of decentralisation in that they contain further organisational hierarchies and sub-divisions.

Through drawing on interviews and document analyses, the findings reveal that although formal governance documents existed (e.g. the master budget, development strategy and sustainability programme), these were ineffective in ensuring employee action and thus limited for inciting individual accountability for sustainability. The general perception of individual employees was that such documents serve to 'obscure' responsibility in that they feel that it is not them alone who were responsibility for meeting the sustainability accountability demands of the public sector organisation. Rather, individual employees appeared (more) motivated to act because of certain socialising accountability relationships both within and outside the organisation. As examples, employees incorporated the felt accountability demands from their friends and family (e.g. in terms of gender equality issues) and took them into the workplace. Additionally, informal discussions in the coffee room seemed particularly important for both promoting sustainable workplace behaviours and/or shaming unsustainable ones. Combined, such accountability forms changed individual employee behaviours into more sustainable ones on a more localised level of the individual employee's daily working tasks.

Overall, the findings of this paper suggest that hierarchical accountability does not (in all instances) individualise as Roberts' (1991, 2001) suggests, but rather can obscure individual responsibility. Further, socialising accountability relationships appear especially important for guiding employee behaviour in this example of a public sector organisation. Here, the employees made sense and reconciled the personal ethical expectations placed upon them in the less formal spaces of the organisation - and even at home - regarding various sustainability issues, and then acted based on these. This suggests a more limited role of control for the behavioural alignment of organisational aims and individual actions as previously assumed in much extant sustainability control research. Rather, it appears a more haphazard or incremental nature of change from the bottom-up is also important for explaining changes in workplace behaviours that cannot be captured through traditional conceptualisations of management control systems from the wider accounting field.

Case 3. Small Businesses

The final case context overviews two studies conducted on environmental management systems in SMEs (i.e. Johnstone, 2021, 2022). SMEs are defined as companies with less than 250 employees and/or a turnover of ≤ €50m (European Union Commission. 2003/361/EC, 2003). Notwithstanding, the 18 SMEs used in these studies tended to be on the smaller side, incorporating various sectors such as transport and construction, yet all with the key characteristic in that they were certified to the environmental management system, ISO 14001. The SMEs were in various countries in Northern Europe such as Sweden, the United Kingdom and the Republic of Ireland.

The first paper (Johnstone, 2021) explored the characteristic type and use of sustainability control through the implementation of an environmental management system. It found that the SMEs perceive the types of controls needed for certification purposes as primarily formal and procedure based (i.e. relying on documentation and policies as forms of administrative controls). Notwithstanding, it also found that the sustainable action of SMEs also comes down to the individual belief systems of owners, managers and employees, whereby such actors perceive it as their duty to act sustainably. One example noted includes the community litter project whereby a SME owner-manager engages his employees to go around the local community to pick up litter. This is not part of the business' activities and this example extends beyond the business purpose to the wider community effects of environmental management. Therefore, the findings of this paper make (more) explicit the different accountability relationships at both organisational and individual levels as important for guiding action; action that is imperative to wider accountability demands, not always business performance.

The second paper (Johnstone, 2022) elaborated on the relationship between external accountability demands and the implementation of controls for environmental performance improvements. Even though external demands such as customer and legislative pressures conditioned the implementation of controls related to environmental management systems, indicative of a traditional strategic understanding of control system design, this study also found that the design and monitoring of controls are sometimes beyond the role of (top) management in SMEs. Some examples included landfill allowances and the prescription of antibiotics that come from the state or controlling health bodies. This moves beyond the intra-organisational focus of controls in prior research to imply an extra-organisational characteristic of not only their design, but also their monitoring and measurement.

Another finding stemming from this study regarded the role of gamification tools through performance measurement for individualising accountability effects. These included the use of computer programs by SMEs to analyse and benchmark employee performance, which are often related to rewards (e.g. team nights or higher salaries).

Finally, the socialising aspects within the studied SMEs seem especially important for accountability. Dialogue and informal discussions between term members were important for fostering an internal culture that supported environmental management.

Summary

Together, the findings from the different empirical contexts illustrate the role of external accountability relationships for employee action at the individual level; a point that has often been missing in prior sustainability control works that assert their focus on the strategic level of formalised control system design (e.g. Arjaliès & Mundy 2013; Pondeville et al., 2013; Wijethilake & Ekanayake, 2018) and thus focus on organisational-level accountability, similar to the wider social and environmental accounting literature and its focus on reporting and disclosure (e.g. Perego & Kolk, 2012; Perkiss et al., 2021). They also offer some examples of both hierarchical and socialising accountability forms that work together as a dynamic (see also Yates et al., 2019). These are overviewed in the following table that summarises the findings.

Table 2. Summary of empirical connections between accountability and control

	Accountability form & links to extant control typologies
Strategic level	**Hierarchical forms** • External accountees instrumental for the design monitoring of internal performance in some instances (i.e. planning and performance controls) • Gamification as a control tool to individualise employees and teams (i.e. performance and compensation controls) • Hierarchical accountability means (e.g. documents, policies) sometimes serve to obscure responsibility; not individualise employees to perform (i.e. administrative controls)
Tactical & operational levels	**Socialising forms** • Wider and personal ethical calls to act (i.e. accountability demands) on the individual level are also important for organisational performance (not currently captured through extant conceptualisations of control) • Socialising accountability sometimes necessary for the hierarchical form (not currently captured through extant conceptualisations of control) • Socialising accountability not necessarily freer as it can individualise or isolate employees with different beliefs systems than the group (i.e. links to socio-ideological or cultural controls)

While many of the hierarchical accountability forms can be clearly related to extant concetualisations of control, this is not the case for the socialising accountability form; thus, signalling some limitations in extant control system frameworks in explaining employee behaviour as one main function of control. Additionally, while some of these findings are already presented in accountability theorisations or prior works (e.g. the socialising form not necessarily any freer [Jacobs & Walker, 2004]), others are novel. Particularly, the findings suggest an element of individual agency through the socialising accountability form that can help explain why some employees act sustainably in practice. Additionally, the interaction of both accountability forms as a dynamic imply that employee behaviour is not only the result of formalised sustainability controls but also because of some personal or ethical calls to account. This signals that beyond what is already known about control and its focus on organisational (managerial) beliefs systems is the need to incorporate the more personal, individual belief systems of employees to help more fully explain and understand action. It is with these thoughts that the following sub-section offers some propositions stemming from this chapter.

PROPOSITIONS

Although sustainability control signals a legitimate approach by organisations to account for their various sustainability demands in different contexts, the findings imply that its focus on the organisational level of accountability, whereby individuals are passive recipients of formalised control system design, needs redressing. The case examples suggest incorporating the socialising accountability into conceptualisations of control to be able to capture what guides and motivates employees to act (sustainably) in practice more fully. This is also important for elaborating on both the institutional (organisational) *and* individual level accountabilities (i.e. those of various employees not only top managers) proposed back in the 1980s by the seminal accountability scholars (e.g. Roberts & Scapens, 1985). This brings us to a series of propositions that should stimulate scholarly thought and debate on future theorisations and conceptualisations of sustainability control work.

The first proposition asserts the importance of employees throughout the hierarchy for sustainability control purposes whereby the monitoring, motivating and guiding function can also come from socialising accountability relationships:

Proposition 1. Individual employee belief systems combined with organisational ones (represented by managerial belief systems) reinforce the monitoring, motivating and guiding function of sustainability control.

As implied by other sustainability control scholars (e.g. Bouten & Hoozée, 2022; Crutzen et al., 2017) and suggested in this chapter, individual values and beliefs about sustainability are often as important as organisational ones for guiding workplace action. However, these are not captured through informal and/or socio-ideological/cultural controls. Particularly, the distinction between socialising accountability and informal control is important in that the former can regard other relationships that are not part of the organisational hierarchy or formalised control system design. These are illustrated in the papers above in terms of collegial interactions in the coffee room, conversations at home, expectations as part of a wider local community etc.

When related to the wider accountability literature, various scholars have already addressed these multiple accountability demands on employees as felt, emotive, personal and intelligent forms (cf. Boomsma & O'Dwyer, 2015; O'Regan et al., 2021; Yates, 2019). Surprisingly, though, the control literature in general embeds these forms, almost exclusively, into intra-organisational relationships or expectations; for example, conceptualised through informal, horizontal or self-control, among others (see De Jong et al., 2014; Gerdin & Englund, 2022).

Building on this individual level of accountability as important to incorporate into conceptualisations of control, the findings also suggest that individual accountability for sustainability is achieved through the two accountability forms, working together as a dynamic. This leads to the second proposition:

Proposition 2. The interaction of hierarchical and socialising accountability forms, working together as a dynamic, are needed to achieve individual level accountability for sustainability in daily working tasks.

This individual accountability stance can be related to each of the accountability forms as follows, through:

1. Compliance (hierarchical means)

2. Activism (socialising forms in response to perceived inefficiencies in hierarchical means)
3. Incrementalism (socialising forms)

These lead to the following three sub-propositions being put forward, which are taken in turn:

Proposition 2a. Accountability for sustainability at the individual employee level is partly mediated through 'compliance' controls that are embedded into the organisational hierarchy.

This proposition asserts that accountability for sustainability can be partly explained through the formalised design of controls, which can broadly be grouped as the hierarchical accountability means in that the design of such controls is tied to the organisational 'hierarchy', even if coercive or enabling in form. Often, key individuals are assigned roles as sustainability specialists or coordinators to achieve performance ends and it is rarely the accountants doing the sustainability management accounting and control work (see Egan & Tweedie, 2018; Rodrigue & Picard, 2022). Moreover, there are various formalised policies and codes of conducts put in place to guide, motivate and monitor sustainable behaviours. These findings are not new as they relate to the traditional notion and conceptualisation of control for guiding employee behaviour (cf. Chenhall, 2003). What is new, however, is the explicit connection of such controls to internal accountability theorisations. Having sustainability roles, policies and procedures inside the organisation also serve a legitimising function to external accountability demands. They signal the clear attempts being made to meet these demands. This is exemplified in the case of the multinational corporation through the establishment of its sustainability coordination network as sustainability demands became higher on the customer and legislative agenda. This is also illustrated in the public sector context through the emphasis on three overarching governance documents that served as administrative controls to guide behaviour; even if they had limited success in actually doing so.

Notwithstanding, accountability for sustainability can also be explained by the actions of other employees from the 'bottom-up', or through the middle to incite different rates of change. On the one hand, the pace of change is explained due to the perceived inadequacies of existing control system design by personnel who function as activists, and on the other hand, it is explained due to more personal explanatory factors. This leads to the following sub-propositions being put forward:

Proposition 2b. *Accountability for sustainability at the individual employee level is partly mediated through tactical and operational employee activism to change existing sustainability control systems from below.*

Proposition 2c. *Accountability for sustainability at the individual employee level is partly mediated through the more personal socialising accountability relationships (from both within and beyond the organisation) that incite changes to daily workplace behaviours as a function of control.*

Notably, accountability for sustainability in most case contexts normally resides within key individuals who are either assigned or self-assign themselves sustainability roles. The network coordination structure in the multinational company provides an example of the former and those more passionately engaged individuals in the public sector organisation (e.g. the coffee room accountability peer pressure) the latter. This means that individuals who are not necessarily part of the formal organisational sustainability structure can also be important for developing or implementing sustainability controls due to their passionate interests about sustainability causes. Both types of individuals are motivated (for some reason) to drive sustainability forward in their respective companies from tactical or operational levels; thus, driving change from below. This finding in itself contrasts the prior control research focus on functionalist frameworks such as Simons' (1995) levers of control which emphasise managerially-designed, vertical controls from the top-down (e.g. Simons, 1995).

Meanwhile, on the receiving end of, for example, 'coffee-room accountability, peer or collegial pressures, and the other types of socialising accountability relationships that come into the workplace, are other individual employees who change their workplace behaviours regarding sustainability, but on a more localised or incremental level. Such individuals do not seek to make drastic changes to existing structures but make small changes to their daily working practices as a result of various socialising accountability demands. Therefore, Proposition 2c extends what we already know from the institutional entrepreneurship literature (see Greenwood & Suddaby 2006) and, in this case, control systems from below but elaborating the pace of change as less radical. Nevertheless, both paces of change through activism and incrementalism can complement the more common, compliance driven hierarchical accountability form that manifests itself though formalised control system design; working together as an accountability dynamic that helps more fully explain what motivates, monitors and guides sustainable employee behaviour as one function of sustainability control.

CONCLUSION

In putting forward the propositions in the previous section, this chapter has achieved its first aim by elaborating on the connections between accountability for sustainability control purposes. In this concluding chapter, these are now summarised through proposals for future research directions as the second research aim by using accountability as a theoretical lens to explain more fully what motivates, guides and monitors sustainable workplace behaviours as one function of control.

Research Implications

This chapter yields contributions to sustainability control research and accountability theorisations. It also signals some recommendations for future research development in the field of sustainability control.

First, the chapter contributes by suggesting that extant conceptualisations of control for sustainability issues require something more than the formalised design of controls by top managers in response to external accountability demands. Rather, motivating, monitoring and guiding employee action also regards the incorporating of socialising accountability forms at the individual level. This implies that future sustainability control research either draw on accountability as a theoretical perspective to more fully capture this function of control or reconceptualise sustainability control systems. While some attempts towards and calls for have been made for the latter (e.g. Guenther et al., 2016; Johnstone, 2019), there is still some way to go.

Particularly, future research could build upon the above propositions to illustrate how sustainability control is both designed and used at different organisational levels (e.g. strategic, tactical and operational), through different accountability forms (e.g. hierarchical and socialising) and because of different accountability relationships (e.g. between superior-subordinate, peer-peer, individual-family, individual-society). This would benefit from qualitative studies in different contexts whereby an elaboration of the different types of controls (e.g. Malmi & Brown, 2008) could be made at different levels and relationships. Embedding control within different intra-organisational accountability relationships could pose a promising avenue of research as it places emphasis on individual accountabilities for sustainability, rather than the extant research focus on organisational ones. As Proposition 1 suggests, this individual focus on belief systems, ethics and values has not been adequately incorporated into extant conceptualisations of control that often treats employees as a homogenous group to be 'managed'. This requires, particularly, an elaboration of the types of controls that can be considered under the socialising accountability form.

Second, this chapter contributes to accountability scholarship in social and environmental accounting research more generally, and sustainability control research specifically by providing empirical examples of the 'internal' face of accountability; moving away from the prevalent external accountability focus of sustainability reporting and disclosure studies (Brown & Dillard, 2013). Additionally, this returns to the fundamentals of accountability theorisations (e.g. Roberts & Scapens, 1985; Roberts, 1991, 2001). It also supports the necessity of an accountability dynamic being at play for inciting individual employee action through compliance, activism and incrementalism as elaborated in the second proposition.

Future studies could build on these concepts of compliance, activism and incrementalism, elaborating more specifically what controls could be categorised under or designed within each category, as well as their type (formal or informal) and nature (tight or flexible) in relation to the accountability relationships that they stem from in different case organisations. Conducting further qualitative studies to understand what drives employee behaviour as one function of control could prove a useful starting point. From this, more inductive conceptualisations of control for guiding, monitoring and motivating purposes would arise; that is, rather than using extant functionalistic or managerialist frameworks such as Simons' (1995) levers of control which have been applied (often partially) in extant sustainability control studies. More inductive and explorative studies could prove useful for conceptualising sustainability control from within the field (see also Guenther et al., 2016; Johnstone, 2019; Leug & Radlach, 2016). Additionally, the propositions put forward could also be tested quantitatively in other empirical contexts to increase their theorising potential.

Third, the chapter's findings imply the need to incorporate external accountability demands not only at the strategic level, conceptualised through the beliefs systems of top managers designing the strategic controls, but also the external accountability demands on individual employees. Together the organisational and individual level accountabilities work together to monitor, motivate and guide action. Yet, prior sustainability control research focuses on the former. Future research could open the boundaries of 'intra' organisational control for sustainability issues by explicitly recognising the role of external accountabilities in shaping internal workplace behaviours at the individual level. Further studies are also needed to elaborate on the internal and individual elements of constructing accountability for sustainability (in what ways and by whom) in different empirical contexts to increase the analytical generalisability of the findings of this chapter.

Practical Implications

While the contributions from this chapter are mainly research-related, they nevertheless have some important practical implications that should be considered by managers and other sustainability strategists in different types of organisations. Notably, introducing formalised performance, administrative and/or planning-related controls is not enough to ensure sustainable employee behaviours that align with organisational strategic goals. This means that the formalised control tools in themselves are not an ends in themselves for organisations to achieved their desired sustainability performance goals. Rather, they should be considered one (of the) means to achieve this. Additionally, the individual views, beliefs and ethics of employees throughout the hierarchy may also be important – but not only that. The relationship employees have with one another as well as friends and family in the private sphere may also impact how they work with sustainability on a day-to-day basis.

Although such socialising accountability relationships are more difficult to 'control', owner-managers in various organisational forms should make themselves (more) aware of the attitudes and beliefs of employees, meeting them on frequent bases (e.g. through informal controls) or spending the time getting to know employees and what motivates them to work 'sustainably' in practice (i.e. through other socialising accountability forms not part of the official control system design). In doing so, owner-managers can place their own sustainability expectations on employees through the socialising accountability form, which is seen to be preferred in all cases. It will also help managers better understand any potential moral and ethical conflicts that they may face through the construction of formalised control systems on certain (groups of) employees when it comes to certain sustainability issues.

REFERENCES

Adler, P. S., & Borys, B. (1996). Two types of bureaucracy: Enabling and coercive. *Administrative Science Quarterly*, 41(1), 61–89. DOI:10.2307/2393986

Ahrens, T., & Chapman, C. S. (2007). Management accounting as practice. *Accounting, Organizations and Society*, 32(1-2), 1–27. DOI:10.1016/j.aos.2006.09.013

Anthony, R. N., Govindarajan, V., Hartmann, F. G. H., Karus, Kl., & Nilsson, G. (2014). *Management Control Systems* (13th European Edition). McGraw-Hill Education.

Arjaliès, D. L., & Mundy, J. (2013). The use of management control systems to manage CSR strategy: A levers of control perspective. *Management Accounting Research*, 24(4), 284–300. DOI:10.1016/j.mar.2013.06.003

Beusch, P., Frisk, J. E., Rosén, M., & Dilla, W. (2022). Management control for sustainability: Towards integrated systems. *Management Accounting Research*, 54, 100777. DOI:10.1016/j.mar.2021.100777

Boomsma, R., & O'Dwyer, B. (2014). The nature of NGO accountability: conceptions, motives, forms and mechanisms. In Bebbington, J., Unerman, J., & O'Dwyer, B. (Eds.), *Sustainability Accounting and Accountability* (pp. 157–175). Routledge.

Bouten, L., & Hoozée, S. (2016). Let's do it safely: How Altrad Balliauw configured a package of control systems. *Journal of Cleaner Production*, 136, 172–180. DOI:10.1016/j.jclepro.2016.01.105

Bouten, L., & Hoozée, S. (2022). Hybridity in a hotel chain: Designing a package of controls to sustain a hybrid mission. *Accounting, Auditing & Accountability Journal*, 35(8), 1862–1891. DOI:10.1108/AAAJ-06-2020-4622

Brown, J., & Dillard, J. (2013). Agonizing over engagement: SEA and the "death of environmentalism" debates. *Critical Perspectives on Accounting*, 24(1), 1–18. DOI:10.1016/j.cpa.2012.09.001

Chenhall, R. H. (2003). Management control systems design within its organizational context: Findings from contingency-based research and directions for the future. *Accounting, Organizations and Society*, 28(2-3), 127–168. DOI:10.1016/S0361-3682(01)00027-7

Crutzen, N., Zvezdov, D., & Schaltegger, S. (2017). Sustainability and management control: Exploring and theorizing control patterns in large European firms. *Journal of Cleaner Production*, 143, 1291–1301. DOI:10.1016/j.jclepro.2016.11.135

De Jong, B. A., Bijlsma-Frankema, K. M., & Cardinal, L. B. (2014). Stronger than the sum of its parts? The performance implications of peer control combinations in teams. *Organization Science*, 25(6), 1703–1721. DOI:10.1287/orsc.2014.0926

de Villiers, C., Dumay, J., & Maroun, W. (2019). Qualitative accounting research: Dispelling myths and developing a new research agenda. *Accounting and Finance*, 59(3), 1459–1487. DOI:10.1111/acfi.12487

Dillard, J., & Vinnari, E. (2019). Critical dialogical accountability: From accounting-based accountability to accountability-based accounting. *Critical Perspectives on Accounting*, 62, 16–38. DOI:10.1016/j.cpa.2018.10.003

Egan, M., & Tweedie, D. (2018). A "green" accountant is difficult to find: Can accountants contribute to sustainability management initiatives? *Accounting, Auditing & Accountability Journal*, 31(6), 1749–1773. DOI:10.1108/AAAJ-03-2017-2891

European Union Commission. 2003/361/EC (2003). Commission recommendation of 6 May 2003 concerning the definition of micro, small and medium-sized enterprises. *Official Journal of the European Union*, 46, 36-41.

Foucault, M. (1977). *Discipline and Punish: The Birth of the Prison* (Sheridan, A., Trans.). Allen Lane.

Foucault, M. (1979). Omnes et singulatim: towards a criticism of political reason, paper presented at Stanford University, in McMurrin, S. (Ed). (1981), *The Tanner Lectures on Human Values*, 2, Cambridge University Press: Cambridge.

Frostenson, M., & Johnstone, L. (2023). Moving beyond the external face of accountability: Constructing accountability for sustainability from within. *Sustainability Accounting. Management and Policy Journal*, 14(7), 124–151.

Gerdin, J., & Englund, H. (2022). Vertical, horizontal, and self control in academia: Survey evidence on their diverging effects on perceived researcher autonomy and identity. *The British Accounting Review*, 54(5), 101055. DOI:10.1016/j.bar.2021.101055

Gomez-Conde, J., Lunkes, R. J., & Rosa, F. S. (2019). Environmental innovation practices and operational performance: The joint effects of management accounting and control systems and environmental training. *Accounting, Auditing & Accountability Journal*, 32(5), 1325–1357. DOI:10.1108/AAAJ-01-2018-3327

Gray, R., Owen, D., & Adams, C. (1996). *Accounting & Accountability: Changes and Challenges in Corporate Social and Environmental Reporting*. Prentice Hall.

Greenwood, R., & Suddaby, R. (2006). Institutional entrepreneurship in mature fields: The big five accounting firms. *Academy of Management Journal*, 49(1), 27–48. DOI:10.5465/amj.2006.20785498

Guenther, E., Endrikat, J., & Guenther, T. W. (2016). Environmental management control systems: A conceptualization and a review of the empirical evidence. *Journal of Cleaner Production*, 136, 147–171. DOI:10.1016/j.jclepro.2016.02.043

Gunarathne, N., Samudrage, D., Wijesinghe, D. N., & Lee, K. H. (2016). Fostering social sustainability management through safety controls and accounting: A stakeholder approach in the mining sector. *Accounting Research Journal*, 29(2), 179–197. DOI:10.1108/ARJ-04-2015-0062

Habermas, J. (1971). *Towards a Rational Society*. Heineman.

Habermas, J. (1984). Reason and the Rationalization of Society, Volume 1 of The Theory of Communicative Action, English translation by Thomas McCarthy. Boston: Beacon Press (originally published in German in 1981).

Henri, J. F., & Journeault, M. (2010). Eco-control: The influence of management control systems on environmental and economic performance. *Accounting, Organizations and Society*, 35(1), 63–80. DOI:10.1016/j.aos.2009.02.001

Jacobs, K., & Walker, S. P. (2004). Accounting and accountability in the Iona Community. *Accounting, Auditing & Accountability Journal*, 17(3), 361–381. DOI:10.1108/09513570410545786

Johnstone, L. (2019). Theorising and conceptualising the sustainability control system for effective sustainability management. *Journal of Management Control*, 30(1), 25–64. DOI:10.1007/s00187-019-00277-w

Johnstone, L. (2021). Facilitating sustainability control in SMEs through the implementation of an environmental management system. *Journal of Management Control*, 32(4), 559–605. DOI:10.1007/s00187-021-00329-0

Johnstone, L. (2022). The means to substantive performance improvements–environmental management control systems in ISO 14001–certified SMEs. *Sustainability Accounting. Management and Policy Journal*, 13(5), 1082–1108.

Johnstone, L., Yates, D., & Nylander, S. (2023). Taking shape within the structural and the personal: Sustainability accountability within a Swedish public sector organisation. *Sustainability Accounting. Management and Policy Journal*, 14(7), 287–312. DOI:10.1108/SAMPJ-08-2022-0450

Jordan, S., & Messner, M. (2012). Enabling control and the problem of incomplete performance indicators. *Accounting, Organizations and Society*, 37(8), 544–564. DOI:10.1016/j.aos.2012.08.002

Levinas, E. (1991). *Otherwise than Being or Beyond Essence*. Kluwer Academic Publishers. DOI:10.1007/978-94-015-7906-3

Lueg, R., & Radlach, R. (2016). Managing sustainable development with management control systems: A literature review. *European Management Journal*, 34(2), 158–171. DOI:10.1016/j.emj.2015.11.005

O'Regan, B., King, R., & Smith, D. (2021). Combining accountability forms: Transparency and "intelligent" accountability in a public service organization. *Accounting, Auditing & Accountability Journal*.

Perego, P., & Kolk, A. (2012). Multinationals' accountability on sustainability: The evolution of third-party assurance of sustainability reports. *Journal of Business Ethics*, 110(2), 173–190. DOI:10.1007/s10551-012-1420-5

Perkiss, S., Bayerlein, L., & Dean, B. A. (2021). Facilitating accountability in corporate sustainability reporting through Spotlight Accounting. *Accounting, Auditing & Accountability Journal*, 34(2), 397–420. DOI:10.1108/AAAJ-08-2019-4142

Pondeville, S., Swaen, V., & De Rongé, Y. (2013). Environmental management control systems: The role of contextual and strategic factors. *Management Accounting Research*, 24(4), 317–332. DOI:10.1016/j.mar.2013.06.007

Roberts, J. (1991). The possibilities of accountability. *Accounting, Organizations and Society*, 16(4), 355–368. DOI:10.1016/0361-3682(91)90027-C

Roberts, J. (2001). Trust and control in Anglo-American systems of corporate governance: The individualizing and socializing effects of processes of accountability. *Human Relations*, 54(12), 1547–1572. DOI:10.1177/00187267015412001

Roberts, J., & Scapens, R. (1985). Accounting systems and systems of accountability—Understanding accounting practices in their organisational contexts. *Accounting, Organizations and Society*, 10(4), 443–456. DOI:10.1016/0361-3682(85)90005-4

Rodrigue, M., & Picard, C. F. (2022). Non-accountants and Accounting: On the Emancipatory Mobilization of Accounting by Sustainability Managers. *European Accounting Review*, 32(5), 1217–1245. DOI:10.1080/09638180.2022.2052921

Simons, R. (1995). Control in an age of empowerment. *Harvard Business Review*, 73(2), 80–88.

Sinclair, A. (1995). The chameleon of accountability: Forms and discourses. *Accounting, Organizations and Society*, 20(2-3), 219–237. DOI:10.1016/0361-3682(93)E0003-Y

Wijethilake, C., & Ekanayake, A. (2018). Proactive strategic responses to corporate sustainability pressures: a sustainability control system framework. In *Advances in Management Accounting* (pp. 129–173). Emerald Publishing Limited. DOI:10.1108/S1474-787120180000030006

Yates, D., Gebreiter, F., & Lowe, A. (2019). The internal accountability dynamic of UK service clubs: Towards (more) intelligent accountability? *Accounting Forum*, 42(1), 161–192. DOI:10.1080/01559982.2019.1589907

ADDITIONAL READING

Baker, M., & Schaltegger, S. (2015). Pragmatism and new directions in social and environmental accountability research. *Accounting, Auditing & Accountability Journal*, 28(2), 263–294. DOI:10.1108/AAAJ-08-2012-01079

Ditillo, A., & Lisi, I. E. (2016). Exploring sustainability control systems' integration: The relevance of sustainability orientation. *Journal of Management Accounting Research*, 28(2), 125–148. DOI:10.2308/jmar-51469

Ghosh, B., Herzig, C., & Mangena, M. (2019). Controlling for sustainability strategies: Findings from research and directions for the future. *Journal of Management Control*, 30(1), 5–24. DOI:10.1007/s00187-019-00279-8

Laine, M., Laine, M., Tregidga, H., Tregidga, H., & Unerman, J. (2021). *Sustainability Accounting and Accountability* (3rd ed.). Routledge. DOI:10.4324/9781003185611

Merchant, K. A., & Otley, D. T. (2006). A review of the literature on control and accountability. *Handbooks of Management Accounting Research*, 2, 785–802. DOI:10.1016/S1751-3243(06)02013-X

KEY TERMS AND DEFINITIONS

Accountability: The means that can help explain why organisations and individuals conduct such actions and report on such actions in response to certain demands.

Administrative Control: A type of control that regards the official policies, procedures, organisational and reporting structure of the organisation put in place to ensure strategic plans are met.

Compensation Controls: A type of control put in place to incentivise or reward individual employee behaviour and, for example, achievement of specific key performance indicators.

Performance-Related Control: A type of control that regards implementing targets to meet the strategic plans of organisations.

Planning Control: A type of control that sets out the strategic and tactical goals for the organisation based on its wider context.

Socio-Ideological Control: A broad collection of controls that regard the symbols, values and belief systems of the organisation that are used to influence employee behaviours that align with organisational strategy.

Sustainability Controls: The tools put in place within organisations to meet strategic goals by motivating, monitoring and guiding employee sustainable workplace behaviours.

Compilation of References

Abdelfattah, T., Elmahgoub, M., & Elamer, A. A. (2021). Female audit partners and extended audit reporting: UK evidence. *Journal of Business Ethics*, 174(1), 177–197. DOI:10.1007/s10551-020-04607-0

Abdullatif, M., & Al-Rahahleh, A. S. (2020). Applying a New Audit Regulation: Reporting Key Audit Matters in Jordan. *International Journal of Auditing*, 24(2), 268–291. DOI:10.1111/ijau.12192

Abhayawansa, S. (2022). Swimming against the tide: back to single materiality for sustainability reporting. Sustainability Accounting, Management and Policy Journal, (ahead-of-print).

Abrainc. (2021). ABRAINC Explica: A importância da Construção Civil para impulsionar a economia brasileira. Associação Brasileira de Incorporadoras Imobiliárias. Disponível em: https://www.abrainc.org.br/abrainc-explica/2021/06/28/abrainc-explica-a-importancia-da-construcao-civil-para-impulsionar-a-economia-brasileira/

Adams, C. A., Alhamood, A., He, X., Tian, J., Wang, L., & Wang, Y. (2021). *The Double-Materiality Concept: Application and Issues*. Global Reporting Initiative.

Adams, R. B., & Ferreira, D. (2009). Women in the boardroom and their impact on governance and performance. *Journal of Financial Economics*, 94(2), 291–309. DOI:10.1016/j.jfineco.2008.10.007

Adler, P. S., & Borys, B. (1996). Two types of bureaucracy: Enabling and coercive. *Administrative Science Quarterly*, 41(1), 61–89. DOI:10.2307/2393986

Agência Sistema Fiep. (2019). 87% dos consumidores brasileiros preferem comprar de empresas sustentáveis. Disponível em: https://www.agenciafiep.com.br/2019/02/28/consumidores-preferem-empresas-sustentaveis/

Agência, C. B. I. C. (2022). PIB da construção fecha o ano com crescimento de 9,7%, a maior alta em 11 anos. Câmara Brasileira da Indústria da Construção. Disponível em: https://cbic.org.br/pib-da-construcao-fecha-o-ano-com-crescimento-de-97-a-maior-alta-em-11-anos

Agostini, M., Costa, E., & Korca, B. (2022). Non-financial disclosure and corporate financial performance under directive 2014/95/EU: Evidence from Italian listed companies. *Accounting in Europe*, 19(1), 78–109. DOI:10.1080/17449480.2021.1979610

Águas de Portugal. (2024). *Relatório de Sustentabilidade 2021*. https://www.adp.pt/pt/sustentabilidade/relatorios-de-sustentabilidade/downloads/file507_pt.pdf

Ahrens, T., & Chapman, C. S. (2007). Management accounting as practice. *Accounting, Organizations and Society*, 32(1-2), 1–27. DOI:10.1016/j.aos.2006.09.013

Al Fadli, A., Sands, J., Jones, G., Beattie, C., & Pensiero, D. (2019). Board gender diversity and CSR reporting: Evidence from Jordan. *Australasian Accounting. Business and Finance Journal*, 13(3), 29–52.

Albuquerque, R., Koskinen, Y., & Zhang, C. (2019). Corporate social responsibility and firm risk: Theory and empirical evidence. *Management Science*, 65(10), 4451–4949. DOI:10.1287/mnsc.2018.3043

Al-Hiyari, A., Ismail, A. I., Kolsi, M. C., & Kehinde, O. H. (2023). Environmental, social and governance performance (ESG) and firm investment efficiency in emerging markets: The interaction effect of board cultural diversity. Corporate Governance. *Corporate Governance (Bradford)*, 23(3), 650–673. DOI:10.1108/CG-03-2022-0133

Al-Htaybat, K., Hutaibat, K., & von Alberti-Alhtaybat, L. (2019). Global brain-reflective accounting practices: Forms of intellectual capital contributing to value creation and sustainable development. *Journal of Intellectual Capital*, 20(6), 733–762. DOI:10.1108/JIC-01-2019-0016

Ali, I., Sami, S., Senan, N. A. M., Baig, A., & Khan, I. A. (2022). A study on corporate sustainability performance evaluation and management: The sustainability balanced scorecard. *Corporate Governance and Organizational Behavior Review*, 6(2), 150–162. DOI:10.22495/cgobrv6i2p15

Allemand, I., Brullebaut, B., & Raimbault, S. (2014). Recommendations for boards of directors of investor owned firms from the co-operative model. In *Research Handbook on Sustainable Co-operative Enterprise* (pp. 206–220). Edward Elgar Publishing. DOI:10.4337/9781783472024.00019

Almeida, F. (2002). *O Bom Negócio da Sustentabilidade*. Nova Fronteira.

Al-Shaer, H., & Zaman, M. (2016). Board gender diversity and sustainability reporting quality. *Journal of Contemporary Accounting & Economics*, 12(3), 210–222. DOI:10.1016/j.jcae.2016.09.001

Aluchna, M., Roszkowska-Menkes, M., & Kamiński, B. (2022). From talk to action: The effects of the non-financial reporting directive on ESG performance. *Meditari Accountancy Research*, 31(7), 1–25. DOI:10.1108/MEDAR-12-2021-1530

Alvares, K. P., & de Souza, I. M. (2016). Sustentabilidade na gestão de pessoas: Práticas e contribuições às organizações. *Revista Gestão Organizacional*, 9(2), 24–38. DOI:10.22277/rgo.v9i2.3285

Anthony, R. N., Govindarajan, V., Hartmann, F. G. H., Karus, Kl., & Nilsson, G. (2014). *Management Control Systems* (13th European Edition). McGraw-Hill Education.

Araújo, L., Oliveira, H. C., & Gomes, L. (2020). Sustainability Balanced Scorecard for a Brazilian agricultural and livestock company. E3S Web of Conferences, 159, 04005. DOI:10.1051/e3sconf/202015904005

Arayakarnkul, , Chatjuthamard, P., & Treepongkaruna, S. (2022). Arayakarnkul, P., Chatjuthamard, P., and Treepongkaruna, S. (2022). Board gender diversity, corporate social commitment and sustainability. *Corporate Social Responsibility and Environmental Management*, 29(5), 1706–1721. DOI:10.1002/csr.2320

Arayssi, M., Jizi, M., & Tabaja, H. H. (2020). The impact of board composition on the level of ESG disclosures in GCC countries. Sustainability Accounting. *Management and Policy Journal*, 11(1), 137–161.

Arena, M., Azzone, G., Ratti, S., Urbano, V. M., & Vecchio, G. (2023). Sustainable development goals and corporate reporting: An empirical investigation of the oil and gas industry. *Sustainable Development (Bradford)*, 31(1), 12–25. DOI:10.1002/sd.2369

Arif, M., Gan, C., & Nadeem, M. (2022). Regulating non-financial reporting: Evidence from European firms' environmental, social and governance disclosures and earnings risk. *Meditari Accountancy Research*, 30(3), 495–523. DOI:10.1108/MEDAR-11-2020-1086

Arjaliès, D. L., & Mundy, J. (2013). The use of management control systems to manage CSR strategy: A levers of control perspective. *Management Accounting Research*, 24(4), 284–300. DOI:10.1016/j.mar.2013.06.003

Armstrong, A. (2020). Ethics and ESG. Australasian Accounting. *Business and Finance Journal*, 14(3), 6–17.

Arslan, H. M., Chengang, Y., Bilal, , Siddique, M., & Yahya, Y. (2022). Influence of senior executives' characteristics on corporate environmental disclosures: A bibliometric analysis. *Journal of Risk and Financial Management*, 15(3), 136. DOI:10.3390/jrfm15030136

Arvidsson, S., & Dumay, J. (2022). Corporate ESG reporting quantity, quality and performance: Where to now for environmental policy and practice? *Business Strategy and the Environment*, 31(3), 1091–1110. DOI:10.1002/bse.2937

Ashraf, A., Qi, B., Meile, Z., & Marie, M. (2024). CEO career horizons, foreign experience, and state ownership impact on the adoption of the Global Reporting Initiative standards for corporate social responsibility reporting. Business Ethics, the Environment & Responsibility. DOI:10.1111/beer.12673

Ashraf, M. Z., Wei, W., Usman, M., & Mushtaq, S. (2024). How can natural resource dependence, environmental-related technologies and digital trade protect the environment: Redesigning SDGs policies for sustainable environment? *Resources Policy*, 88, 104456. DOI:10.1016/j.resourpol.2023.104456

Avrampou, A., Skouloudis, A., Iliopoulos, G., & Khan, N. (2019). Advancing the sustainable develpment goals: Evidence from leading European banks. *Sustainable Development (Bradford)*, 27(4), 743–757. DOI:10.1002/sd.1938

Aydoğmuş, M., Gülay, G., & Ergun, K. (2022). Impact of ESG performance on firm value and profitability. *Borsa Istanbul. RE:view*, 22, S119–S127.

Azzam, M., AlQudah, A., Abu Haija, A., & Shakhatreh, M. (2020). The association between sustainability disclosures and the financial performance of Jordanian firms. *Cogent Business & Management*, 7(1), 1859437. DOI:10.1080/23311975.2020.1859437

Bachoo, K., Tan, R., & Wilson, M. (2013). Firm Value and the Quality of Sustainability Reporting in Australia: Firm Value and the Quality of Sustainability Reporting. *Australian Accounting Review*, 23(1), 67–87. DOI:10.1111/j.1835-2561.2012.00187.x

Baden, D., & Harwood, I. (2013). Terminology matters: A critical exploration of corporate social responsibility terms. *Journal of Business Ethics*, 116(3), 615–627. DOI:10.1007/s10551-012-1498-9

Bae, K.-H., El Ghoul, S., Guedhami, O., Kwok, C. C. Y., & Zheng, Y. (2019). Does corporate social responsibility reduce the costs of high leverage? Evidence from capital structure and product market Interactions. *Journal of Banking & Finance*, 100, 135–150. DOI:10.1016/j.jbankfin.2018.11.007

Bae, K., Kang, J., & Wang, J. (2011). Employee treatment and firm leverage: A test of the stakeholder theory of capital structure. *Journal of Financial Economics*, 100(1), 130–153. DOI:10.1016/j.jfineco.2010.10.019

Baker, N., & Nazer, K. (2000). Empirical evidence on corporate social disclosure (CSD) practices in Jordan. *International Journal of Commerce and Management*, 10(3&4), 18–34. DOI:10.1108/eb047406

Balluchi, F., Lazzini, A., & Torelli, R. (2020). Credibility of environmental issues in non-financial mandatory disclosure: Measurement and determinants. *Journal of Cleaner Production*, 288, 25744.

Baraibar-Diez, E., & Odriozola, , M. (2019). CSR committees and their effect on ESG performance in UK, France, Germany, and Spain. *Sustainability*, 11(18), 5077. DOI:10.3390/su11185077

Barauskaite, G., & Streimikiene, D. (2021). Corporate social responsibility and financial performance of companies: The puzzle of concepts, definitions and assessment methods. *Corporate Social Responsibility and Environmental Management*, 28(1), 278–287. DOI:10.1002/csr.2048

Barchiesi, M. A., & Colladon, A. F. (2021). Corporate core values and social responsibility: What really matters to whom. *Technological Forecasting and Social Change*, 170, 1–9. DOI:10.1016/j.techfore.2021.120907

Barker, R., & Mayer, C. (2023). Seeing double corporate reporting through the materiality lenses of both investors and nature. [Routledge.]. *Accounting Forum*, •••, 1–31.

Barnea, A., & Rubin, A. (2010). Corporate Social Responsibility as a Conflict Between Shareholders. *Journal of Business Ethics*, 97(1), 71–86. DOI:10.1007/s10551-010-0496-z

Barnlund, D. C. (1970). "A transactional model of communication", in Language Behaviour: A Book of Readings in Communications. In Akin, J., Goldberg, A., Myers, G., & Stewart, J. (Eds.), *Mouton Publishers* (pp. 43–61).

Barros, C., Boubakar, S., & Hamrouni, A. (2013). Corporate governance and voluntary disclosure in France. *Journal of Applied Business Research*, 29(2), 561–578. DOI:10.19030/jabr.v29i2.7657

Bartolacci, F., Bellucci, M., Corsi, K., & Soverchia, M. (2022). A Systematic Literature Review of Theories Underpinning Sustainability Reporting in Non-financial Disclosure. In Cinquini, L., & De Luca, F. (Eds.), *Non-financial Disclosure and Integrated Reporting* (pp. 87–113). Springer International Publishing. DOI:10.1007/978-3-030-90355-8_4

Baumüller, J., & Sopp, K. (2022). Double materiality and the shift from non-financial to European sustainability reporting: Review, outlook and implications. *Journal of Applied AccountingResearch*, 23(1), 8–28. DOI:10.1108/JAAR-04-2021-0114

Bear, S., Rahman, N., & Post, C. (2010). The impact of board diversity and gender composition on corporate social responsibility and firm reputation. *Journal of Business Ethics*, 97(2), 207–221. DOI:10.1007/s10551-010-0505-2

Bebbington, J., & Larrinaga, C. (2014). Accounting and sustainable development: An exploration. *Accounting, Organizations and Society*, 39(6), 395–413. DOI:10.1016/j.aos.2014.01.003

Bebbington, J., Larrinaga, C., O'Dwyer, B., & Thomson, I. (Eds.). (2021). *Routledge handbook of environmental accounting*. Routledge. DOI:10.4324/9780367152369

Bebbington, J., & Unerman, J. (2018). Achieving the United Nations Sustainable Development Goals. *Accounting, Auditing & Accountability Journal*, 31(1), 2–24. DOI:10.1108/AAAJ-05-2017-2929

Bedard, J., Coram, P., Esphbodi, R., & Mock, T. J. (2016). Does recent academic research support changes to audit reporting standards? *Accounting Horizons*, 30(2), 255–275. DOI:10.2308/acch-51397

Beji, R., Yousfi, O., Loukil, N., & Omri, A. (2021). Board diversity and corporate social responsibility: Empirical evidence from France. *Journal of Business Ethics*, 173(1), 133–155. DOI:10.1007/s10551-020-04522-4

Bell, S., & Morse, S. (2008). *Sustainability indicators: Measuring the immeasurable*. Earthscan.

Benlemlih, M. (2017). Corporate Social Responsibility and Firm Debt Maturity. *Journal of Business Ethics*, 144(3), 491–517. DOI:10.1007/s10551-015-2856-1

Benlemlih, M., Shaukat, A., Qiu, Y., & Trojanowski, G. (2018). Environmental and social disclosures and firm risk. *Journal of Business Ethics*, 152(3), 613–626. DOI:10.1007/s10551-016-3285-5

Benvenuto, M., Aufiero, C., & Viola, C. (2023). A systematic literature review on the determinants of sustainability reporting systems. *Heliyon*, 9(4), e14893. DOI:10.1016/j.heliyon.2023.e14893 PMID:37064487

Berg, F., Fabisik, K., & Sautner, Z. (2021). Is History Repeating Itself? The(un) predictable Past of ESG Ratings. *European Corporate Governance Institute–Finance Working Paper*: 708. DOI:10.2139/ssrn.3722087

Beusch, P., Frisk, J. E., Rosén, M., & Dilla, W. (2022). Management control for sustainability: Towards integrated systems. *Management Accounting Research*, 54, 100777. DOI:10.1016/j.mar.2021.100777

Bhatti, A., Arif, S., Marium, M., & Younas, S. (2017). The Impact of Corporate Social Responsibility (CSR) and Relationship Marketing on Relationship Maintenance and Customer Loyalty through the Mediating Role of Customer Satisfaction. *Management Information Journal*, 4(4), 19–24.

Bianchi, R. J., Drew, M. E., & Walk, A. N. (2010). On the responsible investment disclosure practices of the world's largest pension funds. *Accounting Research Journal*, 23(3), 302–318. DOI:10.1108/10309611011092619

Bieker, . (2001). *Sustainability management with the Balanced Scorecard*. The Institute for Economy and the Environment at the University of St. Gallen.

Bifulco, G. M., Savio, R., Paolone, F., & Tiscini, R. (2023). The CSR committee as moderator for the ESG score and market value. *Corporate Social Responsibility and Environmental Management*, 30(6), 3231–3241. DOI:10.1002/csr.2549

Boaventura, J. M. G., da Silva, R. S., & Bandeira-de-Mello, R. (2012). Performance Financeira Corporativa e Performance Social Corporativa: Desenvolvimento metodológico e contribuição teórica dos estudos empíricos. *Revista Contabilidade & Finanças*, 23(60), 232–245. DOI:10.1590/S1519-70772012000300008

Bo, H., Li, T., & Toolsema, L. (2009). Corporate social responsibility investment and social objectives: An examination on social welfare investment of Chinese state owned enterprises. *Scottish Journal of Political Economy*, 56(3), 267–295. DOI:10.1111/j.1467-9485.2009.00484.x

Bolt, R., & Tregidga, H. (2023). Methodological Insights "Materiality is…": Sensemaking and sensegiving through storytelling. *Accounting, Auditing & Accountability Journal*, 36(1), 403–427. DOI:10.1108/AAAJ-06-2021-5314

Boomsma, R., & O'Dwyer, B. (2014). The nature of NGO accountability: conceptions, motives, forms and mechanisms. In Bebbington, J., Unerman, J., & O'Dwyer, B. (Eds.), *Sustainability Accounting and Accountability* (pp. 157–175). Routledge.

Bose, S., Khan, H. Z., & Bakshi, S. (2024). Determinants and consequences of sustainable development goals disclosure: International evidence. *Journal of Cleaner Production*, 434, 140021. DOI:10.1016/j.jclepro.2023.140021

Boulouta, I. (2013). Hidden connections: The link between board gender diversity and corporate social performance. *Journal of Business Ethics*, 113(2), 185–197. DOI:10.1007/s10551-012-1293-7

Bouten, L., & Hoozée, S. (2016). Let's do it safely: How Altrad Balliauw configured a package of control systems. *Journal of Cleaner Production*, 136, 172–180. DOI:10.1016/j.jclepro.2016.01.105

Bouten, L., & Hoozée, S. (2022). Hybridity in a hotel chain: Designing a package of controls to sustain a hybrid mission. *Accounting, Auditing & Accountability Journal*, 35(8), 1862–1891. DOI:10.1108/AAAJ-06-2020-4622

Boutin-Dufresne, F., & Savaria, P. (2004). Corporate social responsibility and financial risk. *Journal of Investing Spring, 13*(1), 57-66.

Boyle, F., & Sherman, D. (2006). Scopus: The product and its development. *The Serials Librarian*, 49(3), 147–153. DOI:10.1300/J123v49n03_12

Braam, G., & Peeters, R. (2018). Corporate sustainability performance and assurance on sustainability reports: Diffusion of accounting practices in the realm of sustainable development. *Corporate Social Responsibility and Environmental Management*, 25(2), 164–181. DOI:10.1002/csr.1447

Brammer, S., Millington, A., & Pavelin, S. (2009). Corporate reputation and women on the board. *British Journal of Management*, 20(1), 17–29. DOI:10.1111/j.1467-8551.2008.00600.x

Branco, A. P. C., Bianchi, M. T., & Castelo Branco, M. (2022). Board demographic diversity and human rights reporting in Western Europe. *PSU Research Review*, 6(3), 158–174. DOI:10.1108/PRR-06-2020-0018

Branco, M. C., Delgado, C. J., Sá, M., & Sousa, C. (2014). Comparing CSR communication on corporate websites in Sweden and Spain. *Baltic Journal of Management*, 9(2), 231–250. DOI:10.1108/BJM-10-2013-0151

Branco, M. C., & Rodrigues, L. L. (2008). Factors influencing social responsibility disclosure by Portuguese companies. *Journal of Business Ethics*, 83(4), 685–701. DOI:10.1007/s10551-007-9658-z

Bravo, F., & Reguera-Alvarado, N. (2019). Sustainable development disclosure: Environmental, social, and governance reporting and gender diversity in the audit committee. *Business Strategy and the Environment*, 28(2), 418–429. DOI:10.1002/bse.2258

Brickley, J. A., Coles, J. L., & Jarrell, G. (1997). Leadership structure: Separating the CEO and chairman of the board. *Journal of Corporate Finance*, 3(3), 189–220. DOI:10.1016/S0929-1199(96)00013-2

Bromley, P., & Powell, W. W. (2012). From smoke and mirrors to walking the talk: Decoupling in the contemporary world. *The Academy of Management Annals*, 6(1), 483–530. DOI:10.5465/19416520.2012.684462

Brown, B. J., Hanson, M. E., Liverman, D. M., & Merideth, R. W.Jr. (1987). Global sustainability: Toward definition. *Environmental Management*, 11(6), 713–719. DOI:10.1007/BF01867238

Brown, J., & Dillard, J. (2013). Agonizing over engagement: SEA and the "death of environmentalism" debates. *Critical Perspectives on Accounting*, 24(1), 1–18. DOI:10.1016/j.cpa.2012.09.001

Bryman, A. (2016). *Social research methods*. Oxford University Press.

Buniamin, S., Jaffar, R., Ahmad, N., & Johari, N. H. (2022). The role of corporate governance in achieving SDGs among Malaysian companies. *European Journal of Sustainable Development*, 11(3), 326–326. DOI:10.14207/ejsd.2022.v11n3p326

Burgwal, D., & Vieira, R. (2014). Environmental disclosure determinants in dutch listed companies. *Revista de Contabilidade e Finanças de São Paulo*, 25(64), 60–78. DOI:10.1590/S1519-70772014000100006

Burhan, A. H. N., & Rahmanti, W. (2012). The impact of sustainability reporting on company performance. *Journal of Economics, Business, &Accountancy Ventura*, 15(2), 257–272. DOI:10.14414/jebav.v15i2.79

Busco, C., Consolandi, C., Eccles, R. G., & Sofra, E. (2020). A preliminary analysis of SASB reporting: Disclosure topics, financial relevance, and the financial intensity of ESG materiality. *The Bank of America Journal of Applied Corporate Finance*, 32(2), 117–125. DOI:10.1111/jacf.12411

Business Council for Sustainable Development (BCSD) Portugal. (2024). *Objetivos de Desenvolvimento Sustentável - Objetivo 6: Água Potável e Saneamento*. https://ods.pt/objectivos/6-agua-e-saneamento/

Butler, J. B., Henderson, S. C., & Raiborn, C. (2011). Sustainability and the balanced scorecard: Integrating green measures into business reporting. *Management Accounting Quarterly*, 12(2), 1.

Cabeza-García, L., Fernández-Gago, R., & Nieto, M. (2018). Do board gender diversity and director typology impact CSR reporting? *European Management Review*, 15(4), 559–575. DOI:10.1111/emre.12143

Caetano, D., & Eugénio, T. (2014). Relato de Sustentabilidade de Empresas da Construção Civil em Portugal e Espanha. *Revista Ambiente Contábil, 10(1)*, 273-290.

Callado, A. L. C., & Fensterseifer, J. E. (2010). Indicadores de sustentabilidade: uma abordagem empírica a partir de uma perspectiva de especialistas. *Simpósio de administração da produção, logística e operações internacionais*, 13, 2010.

Campbell, K., & Mínguez-Vera, A. (2008). Gender diversity in the boardroom and firm financial performance. *Journal of Business Ethics*, 83(3), 435–451. DOI:10.1007/s10551-007-9630-y

Campra, M., Esposito, P., & Lombardi, R. (2020). The engagement of stakeholders in nonfinancial reporting: New information-pressure, stimuli, inertia, under short-termism in the banking industry. *Corporate Social Responsibility and Environmental Management*, 27(3), 1436–1444. DOI:10.1002/csr.1896

Cancela, B. L., Neves, M. E. D., Rodrigues, L. L., & Dias, A. C. (2020). The influence of corporate governance on corporate sustainability: New evidence using panel data in the Iberian macroeconomic environment. *International Journal of Accounting and Information Management*, 28(4), 785–806. DOI:10.1108/IJAIM-05-2020-0068

Caputo, F., Leopizzi, R., Pizzi, S., & Milone, V. (2020). The non-financial reporting harmonization in Europe: Evolutionary pathways related to the transposition of the directive 95/2014/EU within the italian context. *Sustainability (Basel)*, 12(1), 92. DOI:10.3390/su12010092

Carmo, C., & Ribeiro, C. (2022). Mandatory Non-Financial Information Disclosure under European Directive 95/2014/EU: Evidence from Portuguese Listed Companies. *Sustainability (Basel)*, 14(8), 4860. DOI:10.3390/su14084860

Carroll, A. B. (1979). A Three Dimensional conceptual model of corporate performance. *Academy of Management Review*, 4(4), 497–505. DOI:10.2307/257850

Carroll, A. B. (1991). The pyramid of corporate social responsibility: Toward the moral management of organizational stakeholders. *Business Horizons*, 34(4), 39–46. DOI:10.1016/0007-6813(91)90005-G

Carter, D. A., D'Souza, F., Simkins, B. J., & Simpson, W. G. (2010). The gender and ethnic diversity of US boards and board committees and firm financial performance. *Corporate Governance*, 18(5), 396–414. DOI:10.1111/j.1467-8683.2010.00809.x

Carvajal, M., & Nadeem, M. (2022). Financially material sustainability reporting and firm performance in New Zealand. *Meditari Accountancy Research*, 31(4), 938–969. DOI:10.1108/MEDAR-06-2021-1346

Carvalho, A., Schmidt, L., Santos, F. D., & Delicado, A. (2014). Climate change research and policy in Portugal. *Wiley Interdisciplinary Reviews: Climate Change*, 5(2), 199–217. DOI:10.1002/wcc.258

Carvalho, F., Santos, G., & Gonçalves, J. (2018). The disclosure of information on sustainable development on the corporate website of the certified Portuguese organisations. *International Journal of Qualitative Research*, 12(1), 253–276. DOI:10.18421/IJQR12.01-14

Catalyst. (2004). The bottom line: Connecting corporate performance and gender diversity. Catalyst.

Cepeda, C. (2024). Can Crisis Periods Affect the ESG Reporting Scope? The Portuguese Euronext Entities Case. *Journal of Risk and Financial Management*, 17(5), 191. DOI:10.3390/jrfm17050191

Chadegani, A., Salehi, H., Yunus, M., Farhadi, H., Fooladi, M., Farhadi, M., & Ebrahim, N. (2013). A comparison between two Main academic literature collections: Web of science and Scopus databases. *Asian Social Science*, 9(5), 18–26. DOI:10.5539/ass.v9n5p18

Chang, Y.-T., Chi, W., & Stone, D. N. (2024). Is Client-Specific Information Useful to Investors? Evidence From Key Audit Matter Reports. *Journal of Accounting, Auditing & Finance*, 39(3), 786–806. DOI:10.1177/0148558X221091804

Chen, G., Wang, B., & Wang, X. (2020). Corporate social responsibility and information flow. *Accounting and Finance*, 61(2), 2759–2807. DOI:10.1111/acfi.12683

Cheng, B., Ioannou, I., & Serafeim, G. (2014). Corporate social responsibility and access to finance. *Strategic Management Journal*, 35(1), 1–23. DOI:10.1002/smj.2131

Chenhall, R. H. (2003). Management control systems design within its organizational context: Findings from contingency-based research and directions for the future. *Accounting, Organizations and Society*, 28(2-3), 127–168. DOI:10.1016/S0361-3682(01)00027-7

Chen, K., Chen, Z., & Wei, K. (2009). Legal protection of investors, corporate governance, and the cost of equity capital. *Journal of Corporate Finance*, 15(3), 273–289. DOI:10.1016/j.jcorpfin.2009.01.001

Chen, Z., & Xie, G. (2022). ESG disclosure and financial performance: Moderating role of ESG investors. *International Review of Financial Analysis*, 83, 102291. DOI:10.1016/j.irfa.2022.102291

Chkir, I., Hassan, B. E. H., Rjiba, H., & Saadi, S. (2021). Does corporate social responsibility influence corporate innovation? International evidence. *Emerging Markets Review*, 46, 1–19. DOI:10.1016/j.ememar.2020.100746

Cho, C. H., & Patten, D. M. (2007). The role of environmental disclosures as tools of legitimacy: A research note. *Accounting, Organizations and Society*, 32(7-8), 639–647. DOI:10.1016/j.aos.2006.09.009

Cho, Y., Kim, S., You, J., Moon, H., & Sung, H. (2021). Application of ESG measures for gender diversity and equality at the organizational level in a Korean context. *European Journal of Training and Development*, 45(4/5), 346–365. DOI:10.1108/EJTD-05-2020-0090

Christensen, H. B., Hail, L., & Leuz, C. (2019). Adoption of CSR and sustainability reporting standards: economic analysis and review. *NBER Working Paper*.

Christmann, P. (2000). Effects of 'Best Practices' of Environmental Management on Cost Advantage. *Academy of Management Journal*, 43(4), 663–680. DOI:10.2307/1556360

Church, B., Davis, S., & McCracken, S. (2008). The auditor's reporting model: A literature overview and research synthesis. *Accounting Horizons*, 22(1), 69–90. DOI:10.2308/acch.2008.22.1.69

Clarkson, M. E. A. (1995). A stakeholder framework for analyzing and evaluating corporate social performance. *Academy of Management Review*, 20(1), 92–117. DOI:10.2307/258888

Clarkson, P. M., Li, Y., Richardson, G. D., & Vasvari, F. P. (2008). Revisiting the relation between environmental performance and environmental disclosure: An empirical analysis. *Accounting, Organizations and Society*, 33(4-5), 303–327. DOI:10.1016/j.aos.2007.05.003

Cobbold, I., & Lawrie, G. (2001). Strategic Alignment: Cascading the Balanced Scorecard in a Multi-national Company, Balanced Scorecard Case Study - Crosshouse.2GC Working Paper, Active Management, December

Cobo, M., Matínez, M., Gutiérrez-Salcedo, M., Fujita, H., & Herrera-Viedma, E. (2015). 25 years at knowledge-based systems: A bibliometric analysis. *Knowledge-Based Systems*, 80, 3–13. DOI:10.1016/j.knosys.2014.12.035

Colglazier, W. (2015). Sustainable development agenda: 2030. *Science*, 349(6252), 1048–1050. DOI:10.1126/science.aad2333 PMID:26339011

Commission of the European Communities. (2001). Green Paper: Promoting a European framework for Corporate Social Responsibility. Retrieved from https://ec.europa.eu/commission/presscorner/detail/en/DOC_01_9

Conselho das Finanças Públicas. (2024). *Relatório nº 2 de 2023 Setor Empresarial do Estado 2020-2021*. https://www.cfp.pt/uploads/publicacoes_ficheiros/cfp_rel-02-2023.pdf

Consolandi, C., Phadke, H., Hawley, J., & Eccles, R. G. (2020). Material ESG outcomes and SDG externalities: Evaluating the health care sector's contribution to the SDGs. *Organization & Environment*, 33(4), 511–533. DOI:10.1177/1086026619899795

Conte, F., Sardanelli, D., Vollero, A., & Siano, A. (2023). CSR signaling in controversial and noncontroversial industries: CSR policies, governance structures, and transparency tools. *European Management Journal*, 41(2), 274–281. DOI:10.1016/j.emj.2021.12.003

Cooper, E. W., & Uzun, H. (2015). Corporate social responsibility and the cost of debt. *Journal of Accounting & Finance*, 15(8), 11–29.

Cooper, S., & Michelon, G. (2022). Conceptions of materiality in sustainability reporting frameworks: commonalities, differences and possibilities. In Adams, C. A. (Ed.), *Handbook of Accounting and Sustainability* (pp. 44–66). Edward Elgar Publishing. DOI:10.4337/9781800373518.00010

Cordazzo, M., Bini, L., & Marzo, G. (2020). Does the EU Directive on non-financial information influence the value relevance of ESG disclosure? Italian evidence. *Business Strategy and the Environment*, 29(8), 3470–3483. DOI:10.1002/bse.2589

Cormier, D., & Gomez-Gutierrez, L. (2018). On the search for mimetic patterns in environmental disclosure: An international perspective. *International Journal of Sustainable Development and World Ecology*, 25(7), 655–671. DOI:10.1080/13504509.2018.1439849

Correa-Mejía, D. A., Correa-García, J. A., & García-Benau, M. A. (2024). Analysis of double materiality in early adopters. Are companies walking the talk? *Sustainability Accounting. Management and Policy Journal*, 15(2), 299–329.

Corvino, A., Doni, F., & Bianchi Martini, S. (2020). Corporate governance, integrated reporting and environmental disclosure: Evidence from the South African context. *Sustainability (Basel)*, 12(12), 4820. DOI:10.3390/su12124820

Costa, R., Menichini, T., & Salierno, G. (2022). Do SDGs really matter for business? Using GRI sustainability reporting to answer the question. *European Journal of Sustainable Development*, 11(1), 113. DOI:10.14207/ejsd.2022.v11n1p113

Crane, A., Matten, D., & Spence, L. (2014). *Corporate Social Responsibility: Readings and Cases in a Global Context*. Routledge.

Creswell, J. (2016). *Research Design.: Qualitative, Quantitative, Mixed Methods Approaches*. University Of Nebraska-Lincoln.

Crutzen, N., Zvezdov, D., & Schaltegger, S. (2017). Sustainability and management control: Exploring and theorizing control patterns in large European firms. *Journal of Cleaner Production*, 143, 1291–1301. DOI:10.1016/j.jclepro.2016.11.135

Cui, J., Dai, J., Wang, Z., & Zhao, X. (2022). Does environmental regulation induce green innovation? A panel study of Chinese listed firms. *Technological Forecasting and Social Change*, 176, 121492. DOI:10.1016/j.techfore.2022.121492

D'Apice, V., Ferri, G., & Intonti, M. (2021). Sustainable disclosure versus ESG intensity: Is there a cross effect between holding and SRI funds? *Corporate Social Responsibility and Environmental Management*, 28(5), 1496–1510. DOI:10.1002/csr.2178

Dai, J., Lu, C., & Qi, J. (2019). Corporate social responsibility disclosure and stock price crash risk: Evidence from China. *Sustainability (Basel)*, 11(2), 448. DOI:10.3390/su11020448

Dainelli, F., Manetti, G., & Sibilio, B. (2013). Web-Based Accountability Practices in Non-profit Organisations: The Case of National Museums. *Voluntas*, 24(3), 649–665. DOI:10.1007/s11266-012-9278-9

Dani, A. C., Picolo, J. D., & Klann, R. C. (2019). Gender influence, social responsibility and governance in performance. *RAUSP Management Journal*, 54(2), 154–177. DOI:10.1108/RAUSP-07-2018-0041

Datta, S., & Goyal, S. (2022). Determinants of SDG Reporting by Businesses: A Literature Analysis and Conceptual Model. *Vision (Basel)*. DOI:10.1177/09722629221096047

Davie, S. (2008). An autoethnography of accounting knowledge production: Serendipitous and fortuitous choices for understanding our social world. *Critical Perspectives on Accounting*, 19(7), 1054–1079. DOI:10.1016/j.cpa.2007.03.011

Davis, J. H., Schoorman, F. D., & Donaldson, L. (1997). Towards a stewardship theory of management. *Academy of Management Review*, 22(1), 20–47. DOI:10.2307/259223

De Andrade Guerra, J. B. S. O., Garcia, J., De Andrade Lima, M., Barbosa, S. B., Heerdt, M. L., & Berchin, I. I. (2018). A proposal of a Balanced Scorecard for an environmental education program at universities. *Journal of Cleaner Production*, 172, 1674–1690. DOI:10.1016/j.jclepro.2016.11.179

De Jong, B. A., Bijlsma-Frankema, K. M., & Cardinal, L. B. (2014). Stronger than the sum of its parts? The performance implications of peer control combinations in teams. *Organization Science*, 25(6), 1703–1721. DOI:10.1287/orsc.2014.0926

De Lucia, C. D., Pazienza, P., & Bartlett, M. (2020). Does good ESG lead to better financial performances by firms? Machine learning and logistic regression models of public enterprises in Europe. *Sustainability (Basel)*, 12(13), 5317. DOI:10.3390/su12135317

de Villiers, C., Dumay, J., & Maroun, W. (2019). Qualitative accounting research: Dispelling myths and developing a new research agenda. *Accounting and Finance*, 59(3), 1459–1487. DOI:10.1111/acfi.12487

De Villiers, C., La Torre, M., & Molinari, M. (2022). The global reporting initiative's (GRI) past, present and future: Critical reflections and a research agenda on sustainability reporting (standard-setting). *Pacific Accounting Review*, 34(5), 728–747. Advance online publication. DOI:10.1108/PAR-02-2022-0034

Decree-Law n.º 89/2017, from 28 de july. Retrived from Diário da República Eletrónico: https://dre.pt/dre/detalhe/decreto-lei/89-2017-107773645

Decree-Law no. 119/83. *Official Journal of the Portuguese Republic*, no. 46 - Series I, of 25 February.

Decree-Law no. 172-A/2014. *Official Journal of the Portuguese Republic*, no. 221 - Series I, of 14 November.

Decree-Law no. 89/2017. *Official Journal of the Portuguese Republic*, no. 145 - Series I, of 28 July.

Decree-Law no. 98/2015. *Official Journal of the Portuguese Republic*, no. 106 - Series I, of 2 June.

Deegan, C. (2002). Introduction: The legitimising effect of social and environmental disclosures: A theoretical foundation. *Accounting, Auditing & Accountability Journal*, 15(3), 282–311. DOI:10.1108/09513570210435852

del Mar Alonso-Almeida, M., Llach, J., & Marimon, F. (2014). A closer look at the 'Global Reporting Initiative'sustainability reporting as a tool to implement environmental and social policies: A worldwide sector analysis. *Corporate Social Responsibility and Environmental Management*, 21(6), 318–335. DOI:10.1002/csr.1318

Dhanani, A., & Connolly, C. (2014). Non-governmental organisational accountability: Talking the talk and walking the walk? *Journal of Business Ethics*, 129(3), 613–637. DOI:10.1007/s10551-014-2172-1

Di Vaio, A., & Varriale, L. (2020). SDGs and airport sustainable performance: Evidence from Italy on organisational, accounting and reporting practices through financial and non-financial disclosure. *Journal of Cleaner Production*, 249, 119431. DOI:10.1016/j.jclepro.2019.119431

Diamond, D. (1991). Monitoring and reputation: The choice between bank loans and directly placed debt. *Journal of Political Economy*, 99(4), 689–721. DOI:10.1086/261775

Díaz-Sarachaga, J. M. (2021). Shortcomings in reporting contributions towards the Sustainable Development Goals. *Corporate Social Responsibility and Environmental Management*, 28(4), 1–14. DOI:10.1002/csr.2129

Dienes, D., Sassen, R., & Fisher, J. (2016). What are the drivers of sustainability reporting? A systematic review. *Sustainability Accounting. Management and Policy Journal*, 7(2), 154–189.

Dillard, J., & Vinnari, E. (2019). Critical dialogical accountability: From accounting-based accountability to accountability-based accounting. *Critical Perspectives on Accounting*, 62, 16–38. DOI:10.1016/j.cpa.2018.10.003

DiMaggio, P. J., & Powell, W. W. (1983). The Iron Cage Revisited: Institutional Isomorphism and Collective Rationality in Organizational Fields. *American Sociological Review* 48:147–60. Crossref. ISI. Directive 2014/95/UE from European Parliament and the Council, from 22 October. Retrived from Official Journal of the European Union: https://eur-lex.europa.eu/legal-content/PT/TXT/?uri=CELEX:32014L0095

DiMaggio, P. J., & Powell, W. W. (1983). The Iron Cage Revisited: Institutional Isomorphism and Collective Rationality in Organizational Fields. *American Sociological Review*, 48(2), 147. DOI:10.2307/2095101

Dincer, C., & Dincer, B. (2010). An investigation of Turkish small and medium-sized enterprises online CSR communication. *Social Responsibility Journal*, 6(2), 197–207. DOI:10.1108/17471111011051711

Ding, W., Levine, R., Lin, C., & Xie, W. (2021). Corporate immunity to the COVID-19 pandemic. *Journal of Financial Economics*, 141(2), 802–830. DOI:10.1016/j.jfineco.2021.03.005 PMID:34580557

Directive 2022/2464/EU of the European Parliament and of the Council of 14 December 2022 amending Regulation (EU) No 537/2014, Directive 2004/109/EC, Directive 2006/43/EC and Directive 2013/34/EU as regards corporate sustainability reporting. https://eur-lex.europa.eu/legal-content/PT/TXT/PDF/?uri=CELEX:32022L2464

DiSegni, D. M., Huly, M., & Akron, S. (2015). Corporate social responsibility, environmental leadership and financial performance. *Social Responsibility Journal*, 11(1), 131–148. DOI:10.1108/SRJ-02-2013-0024

Dong, S., Xu, L., & McIver, R. P. (2023). Sustainability reporting quality and the financial sector: Evidence from China. *Meditari Accountancy Research*, 31(5), 1190–1214. DOI:10.1108/MEDAR-05-2020-0899

Doni, F., Gasperini, A., & Soares, J. T. (2020). Monitoring, evaluation and reporting on SDG 13 implementation. In *SDG13–climate action: combating climate change and its impacts* (pp. 73–84). Emerald Publishing Limited. DOI:10.1108/978-1-78756-915-720201009

Donner, E. K., Meißner, A., & Bort, S. (2024). Moving from voluntary to mandatory sustainability reporting—Transparency in sustainable development goals (SDG) reporting: An analysis of Germany's largest MNCs. *Business Ethics, the Environment & Responsibility*, 00, 1–12. DOI:10.1111/beer.12687

Donthu, N., Kumar, S., & Pattnaik, D. (2020). Forty-five years of Journal of Business Research: A bibliometric analysis. *Journal of Business Research*, 109, 1–14. DOI:10.1016/j.jbusres.2019.10.039

Dragomir, V. D., & Dragomir, V. D. (2020). Ethical aspects of environmental strategy. *Corporate Environmental Strategy: Theoretical, Practical, and Ethical Aspects*, 75-113.

Dreher, M., Ullrich, D., & Moro, R. (2009). *Stakeholder e Responsabilidade Social: As experiências das organizações de Blumenau*. ABEPRO - Associação Brasileira de Engenharia de Produção.

Du Rietz, S. (2014). When accounts become information: A study of investors' ESG analysis practice. *Scandinavian Journal of Management*, 30(4), 395–408. DOI:10.1016/j.scaman.2014.09.002

Duboisée de Ricquebourg, A., & Maroun, W. (2023). How do auditor rotations affect key audit matters? Archival evidence from South African audits. *The British Accounting Review*, 55(2), 101099. DOI:10.1016/j.bar.2022.101099

Dunphy, D., Benveniste, J., Griffiths, A., & Sutton, P. (Eds.). (2000). *Sustainability: The corporate challenge of the 21st century*. Allen & Unwin.

Dyllick, T., & Muff, K. (2016). Clarifying the meaning of sustainable business: Introducing a typology from business-as-usual to true business sustainability. *Organization & Environment*, 29(2), 156–174. DOI:10.1177/1086026615575176

Ebrahim, A. (2005). Accountability myopia: Losing sight of organisational learning. *Nonprofit and Voluntary Sector Quarterly*, 34(1), 56–87. DOI:10.1177/0899764004269430

Ebrhahim, A. (2003). Accountability in practice: Mechanisms for NGOs. *World Development*, 31(5), 813–829. DOI:10.1016/S0305-750X(03)00014-7

Eccles, R. G., & Spiesshofer, B. (2015). Integrated reporting for a re-imagined capitalism. *Harvard Business School General Management Unit Working Paper*, (16-032).

Ece, O., & Sari, S. S. (2020). Relationship between corporate sustainability reporting and firm efficiency, productivity, and profitability and firm value: Evidence from Turkey. *Academic studies in economics and administrative sciences*. 83-113

Edgley, C. (2014). A genealogy of accounting materiality. Critical Perspectives on Accounting, 25(3), 255-271.

EFRAG (2022). ESRS S1 General principles, Exposure Draft, April 2022.

Egan, M., & Tweedie, D. (2018). A "green" accountant is difficult to find: Can accountants contribute to sustainability management initiatives? *Accounting, Auditing & Accountability Journal*, 31(6), 1749–1773. DOI:10.1108/AAAJ-03-2017-2891

El Ghoul, S., Guedhami, O., Kwok, C. C., & Mishra, D. R. (2011). Does corporate social responsibility affect the cost of capital? *Journal of Banking & Finance*, 35(9), 2388–2406. DOI:10.1016/j.jbankfin.2011.02.007

Elbanna, S., Eid, R., & Kamel, H. (2015). Measuring hotel performance using the balanced scorecard: A theoretical construct development and its empirical validation. *International Journal of Hospitality Management*, 51, 105–114. DOI:10.1016/j.ijhm.2015.09.004

Ellili, N. O. D. (2022). Impact of ESG disclosure and financial reporting quality on investment efficiency. Corporate Governance: The International Journal of Business in Society.

Ellili, N. O. (2020). Environmental, social, and governance disclosure, ownership structure and cost of capital: Evidence from the UAE. *Sustainability (Basel)*, 12(18), 7706. DOI:10.3390/su12187706

Elsevier (2020). Scopus: Content Coverage Guide. Retrieved from https://www.elsevier.com/__data/assets/pdf_file/0007/69451/Scopus_ContentCoverage_Guide_WEB.pdf

Engelmann, W., & Nascimento, H. C. P. (2021). O desenvolvimento dos direitos humanos nas empresas por meio do ESG como forma de qualificar as relações de trabalho. *Revista da Escola Judicial do TRT4,3*(6).

Epstein, M., Flamholtz, E., & McDonough, J. J. (1976). Corporate social accounting in the United States of America: State of the art and future prospects. *Accounting, Organizations and Society*, 1(1), 23–42. DOI:10.1016/0361-3682(76)90005-2

Erin, O. A., Bamigboye, O. A., & Oyewo, B. (2022). Sustainable development goals (SDG) reporting: An analysis of disclosure. *Journal of Accounting in Emerging Economies*, 12(5), 761–789. DOI:10.1108/JAEE-02-2020-0037

Erin, O. A., & Olojede, P. (2024). *Do nonfinancial reporting practices matter in SDG disclosure? An exploratory study*. Meditari Accountancy Research. DOI:10.1108/MEDAR-06-2023-2054

Esken, B., Franco-García, M. L., & Fisscher, O. A. (2018). CSR perception as a signpost for circular economy. *Management Research Review*, 41(5), 586–604. DOI:10.1108/MRR-02-2018-0054

European Commission. (2012). Communication from the commission to the european parliament, the council, the european economic and social committee and the committee of the regions a Roadmap for moving to a competitive low carbon economy in 2050. https://eur-lex.europa.eu/legal-content/EN/TXT/?uri=celex:52011DC0112

European Commission. (2020). Regolamento (UE) 2020/852 del Parlamento europeo e del Consiglio del 27 novembre 2019 relativo all'istituzione di un quadro per la promozione di investimenti sostenibili. Available at https://eur-lex.europa.eu/legal-content/IT/TXT/PDF/?uri=CELEX:32020R0852

European Commission. (2022). Corporate Social Responsibility Directive n. 2464. Available at https://finance.ec.europa.eu/capital-markets-union-and-financial-markets/company-reporting-and-auditing/company-reporting/corporate-sustainability-reporting_en

European Parliament. (2022). Directive (EU) 2022/2464 of the European Parliament and of the Council of 14 December 2022 amending Regulation (EU) No 537/2014, Directive 2004/109/EC, Directive 2006/43/EC and Directive 2013/34/EU, as regards corporate sustainability reporting. https://eur-lex.europa.eu/legal-content/EN/TXT/PDF/?uri=CELEX:32022L2464

European Union (2014). Directive 2014/95/EU of the european parliament and of the council of 22 october 2014 amending Directive 2013/34/EU as regards disclosure of non-financial and diversity information by certain large undertakings and groups. *Official Journal of the European Union, 2014,* L 330, 1–9. https://eur-lex.europa.eu/legal-content/EN/TXT/HTML/?uri=CELEX:32014L0095

European Union (2022). Directive 2022/2464/EU of the european parliament and of the council of 14 December 2022 amending Regulation (EU) No 537/2014, Directive 2004/109/EC, Directive 2006/43/EC and Directive 2013/34/EU, as regards corporate sustainability reporting. *Official Journal of the European Union, 2022,* L 322, 15–80. https://eur-lex.europa.eu/legal-content/EN/TXT/HTML/?uri=CELEX:32022L2464

European Union Commission. 2003/361/EC (2003). Commission recommendation of 6 May 2003 concerning the definition of micro, small and medium-sized enterprises. *Official Journal of the European Union*, 46, 36-41.

Evangelinos, K., Fotiadis, S., Skouloudis, A., Khan, N., Konstandakopoulou, F., Nikolaou, I., & Lundy, S. (2018). Occupational health and safety disclosures in sustainability reports: An overview of trends among corporate leaders. *Corporate Social Responsibility and Environmental Management*, 25(5), 961–970. DOI:10.1002/csr.1512

Ezzi, F., Jarboui, A., & Zouari-Hadiji, R. (2020). CSR categories and R&D investment: The moderating role of managerial emotional intelligence. *Management & Marketing*, 15(1), 17–37. DOI:10.2478/mmcks-2020-0002

Fama, E. F., & Jensen, M. C. (1983). Separation of ownership and control. *The Journal of Law & Economics*, 26(2), 301–325. DOI:10.1086/467037

Farisyi, S., Musadieq, M., Utami, H., & Damayanti, C. (2022). A Systematic Literature Review: Determinants of Sustainability Reporting in Developing Countries. *Sustainability (Basel)*, 14(16), 10222. DOI:10.3390/su141610222

Farneti, F., Guthrie, J., & Siboni, B. (2011). Social and sustainability reporting in Italian local governments: What is not reported? In Ball, A., & Osborne, S. P. (Eds.), *Social Accounting and Public Management. Accountability for the Common Good*. Routledge.

Fearnside, P. M. (2005). Deforestation in Brazilian Amazonia: History, rates, and consequences. *Conservation Biology*, 19(3), 680–688. DOI:10.1111/j.1523-1739.2005.00697.x

Federal Law 13.303, from 30 june 2016. https://legislacao.presidencia.gov.br/atos/?tipo=LEI&numero=13303&ano=2016&ato=264ETT650dZpWT936. (accessed on 05 May 2024).

Felo, A. J., & Transparency, C. R.Board Independence and Expertise, and CEO Duality. (2010). DOI:10.2139/ssrn.1373942

Fernandez-Feijoo, B., Romero, S., & Ruiz-Blanco, S. (2014). Women on Boards: Do They Affect Sustainability Reporting? *Corporate Social Responsibility and Environmental Management*, 21(6), 351–364. DOI:10.1002/csr.1329

Fernandez-Feijoo, B., Romero, S., & Ruiz, S. (2014). Commitment to corporate social responsibility measured through global reporting initiative reporting: Factors affecting the behavior of companies. *Journal of Cleaner Production*, 81, 244–254. DOI:10.1016/j.jclepro.2014.06.034

Fernandez-Feijoo, B., Romero, S., & Ruiz, S. (2014). Effect of Stakeholders' Pressure on Transparency of Sustainability Reports within the GRI Framework. *Journal of Business Ethics*, 122(1), 53–63. DOI:10.1007/s10551-013-1748-5

Ferrero-Ferrero, I., Muñoz-Torres, M. J., Rivera-Lirio, J. M., Escrig-Olmedo, E., & Fernández-Izquierdo, M. Á. (2023). SDG reporting: An analysis of corporate sustainability leaders. *Marketing Intelligence & Planning*, 41(4), 457–472. DOI:10.1108/MIP-07-2022-0332

Figge, F., Hahn, T., Schaltegger, S., & Wagner, M. (2002). The Sustainability Balanced Scorecard-Linking sustainability management to business strategy. *Business Strategy and the Environment*, 11(5), 269–284. DOI:10.1002/bse.339

Filatotchev, I., Jackson, G., & Nakajima, C. (2013). Corporate governance and national institutions: A review and emerging research agenda. *Asia Pacific Journal of Management*, 30(4), 965–986. DOI:10.1007/s10490-012-9293-9

Financial Reporting Council. (2015). *Extended auditors' reports: A review of experience in the first year*. https://frc.org.uk/Extended-auditors-reports.pdf

Florêncio, M., Oliveira, L., & Oliveira, H. C. (2023). Management Control Systems and the Integration of the Sustainable Development Goals into Business Models. *Sustainability (Basel)*, 15(3), 2246. DOI:10.3390/su15032246

Fonseca, A., McAllister, M. L., & Fitzpatrick, P. (2014). Sustainability reporting among mining corporations: A constructive critique of the GRI approach. *Journal of Cleaner Production*, 4, 70–83. DOI:10.1016/j.jclepro.2012.11.050

Foucault, M. (1979). Omnes et singulatim: towards a criticism of political reason, paper presented at Stanford University, in McMurrin, S. (Ed). (1981), *The Tanner Lectures on Human Values*, 2, Cambridge University Press: Cambridge.

Foucault, M. (1977). *Discipline and Punish: The Birth of the Prison* (Sheridan, A., Trans.). Allen Lane.

Freeman, R. E., & McVea, J. (2005). A stakeholder approach to strategic management. *The Blackwell Handbook of strategic management*, 183-201.

Freeman, R., & Mcvea, J. (2001). A Stakeholder Approach to Strategic Management. SSRN *Electronic Journal*. https://doi.org/DOI:10.2139/ssrn.263511

Freeman, R. E. (1984). *Strategic management: A stakeholder approach*. Pitman.

Freeman, R. E. (1984). *Strategic Management: A Stakeholders Approach*. Pitman.

Freeman, R. E. (1994). The politics of stakeholder theory: Some future directions. *Business Ethics Quarterly*, 4(4), 409–421. DOI:10.2307/3857340

Freeman, R. E., & Reed, D. L. (1983). Stockholders and stakeholders: A new perspective on corporate governance. *California Management Review*, 25(3), 93–94. DOI:10.2307/41165018

Freeman, R., Parmar, B., Harrison, J., Wicks, A., De Colle, S., & Purnell, L. (2010). Stakeholder Theory: The State of the Art. *The Academy of Management Annals*, 4(1), 403–445. DOI:10.5465/19416520.2010.495581

Frias-Aceituno, J. V., Rodriguez-Ariza, L., & Garcia-Sanchez, I. M. (2013). The role of the board in the dissemination of integrated corporate social reporting. *Corporate Social Responsibility and Environmental Management*, 13(20), 219–233. DOI:10.1002/csr.1294

Friede, G., Busch, T., & Bassen, A. (2015). ESG and financial performance: Aggregated evidence from more than 2000 empirical studies. *Journal of Sustainable Finance & Investment*, 5(4), 210–233. DOI:10.1080/20430795.2015.1118917

Frooman, J. (1999). Stakeholder influence strategies. *Academy of Management Review*, 24(2), 191–205. DOI:10.2307/259074

Frostenson, M., & Johnstone, L. (2023). Moving beyond the external face of accountability: Constructing accountability for sustainability from within. *Sustainability Accounting. Management and Policy Journal*, 14(7), 124–151.

Fu, W., & Deshpande, S. (2012). Factors impacting ethical behaviour in a Chinese state-owned steel company. *Journal of Business Ethics*, 105(2), 231–237. DOI:10.1007/s10551-011-0962-2

Gainet, C. (2010). Exploring the Impact of Legal Systems and Financial Structure on Corporate Responsibility. *Journal of Business Ethics*, 95(S2, SUPPL. 2), 195–222. DOI:10.1007/s10551-011-0854-5

Galani, D., Gravas, E., & Stavropoulos, A. (2012). Company characteristics and environmental policy. *Business Strategy and the Environment*, 21(4), 236–247. DOI:10.1002/bse.731

Galeazzo, A., Miandar, T., & Carraro, M. (2024). SDGs in corporate responsibility reporting: A longitudinal investigation of institutional determinants and financial performance. *The Journal of Management and Governance*, 28(1), 113–136. DOI:10.1007/s10997-023-09671-y

Gallego-Álvarez, I., Lozano, M. B., & Rodríguez-Rosa, M. (2018). An analysis of the environmental information in international companies according to the new GRI standards. *Journal of Cleaner Production*, 182, 57–66. DOI:10.1016/j.jclepro.2018.01.240

Gambetta, N., Sierra-García, L., García-Benau, M. A., & Novejarque-Civera, J. (2023). The Informative Value of Key Audit Matters in the Audit Report: Understanding the Impact of the Audit Firm and KAM Type. *Australian Accounting Review*, 104(33), 114–134. DOI:10.1111/auar.12396

Gandía, L. J. (2009). Internet disclosure by nonprofit organisations: Empirical evidence of nongovernmental organisations for development in Spain. *Nonprofit and Voluntary Sector Quarterly*, 40(1), 57–78. DOI:10.1177/0899764009343782

García-Meca, E., & Martínez-Ferrero, J. (2021). Is SDG reporting substantial or symbolic? An examination of controversial and environmentally sensitive industries. *Journal of Cleaner Production*, 298, 126781. DOI:10.1016/j.jclepro.2021.126781

García-Sánchez, I. M., Aibar-Guzmán, B., Aibar-Guzmán, C., & Rodríguez-Ariza, L. (2020). "Sell" recommendations by analysts in response to business communication strategies concerning the Sustainable Development Goals and the SDG compass. *Journal of Cleaner Production*, 255, 1–12. DOI:10.1016/j.jclepro.2020.120194

García-Sánchez, I. M., Hussain, N., Khan, S. A., & Martínez-Ferrero, J. (2020). Managerial entrenchment, corporate social responsibility, and earnings management. *Corporate Social Responsibility and Environmental Management*, 27(4), 1818–1833. DOI:10.1002/csr.1928

García-Sánchez, I. M., Rodríguez-Ariza, L., Aibar-Guzmán, B., & Aibar-Guzmán, C. (2020). Do institutional investors drive corporate transparency regarding business contribution to the sustainable development goals? *Business Strategy and the Environment*, 29(5), 2019–2036. DOI:10.1002/bse.2485

Garde-Sanchez, R., López-Pérez, M. V., & López-Hernández, A. M. (2018). Current trends in research on social responsibility in state-owned enterprises: A review of the literature from 2000 to 2017. *Sustainability (Basel)*, 10(2403), 2403. Advance online publication. DOI:10.3390/su10072403

Gazi, F., Atan, T., & Kiliç, M. (2022). The Assessment of Internal Indicators on The Balanced Scorecard Measures of Sustainability. *Sustainability (Basel)*, 14(14), 8595. DOI:10.3390/su14148595

Gerdin, J., & Englund, H. (2022). Vertical, horizontal, and self control in academia: Survey evidence on their diverging effects on perceived researcher autonomy and identity. *The British Accounting Review*, 54(5), 101055. DOI:10.1016/j.bar.2021.101055

Gerged, A. M. (2021). Factors affecting corporate environmental disclosure in emerging markets: The role of corporate governance structures. *Business Strategy and the Environment*, 30(1), 609–629. DOI:10.1002/bse.2642

Gerwanski, J., Kordsachia, O., & Velte, P. (2019). Determinants of materiality disclosure quality in integrated reporting: Empirical evidence from an international setting. *Business Strategy and the Environment*, 28(5), 750–770. DOI:10.1002/bse.2278

Gh Popescu, C. R. (2019). Corporate social responsibility, corporate governance and business performance: Limits and challenges imposed by the implementation of directive 2013/34/EU in Romania. *Sustainability (Basel)*, 11(19), 5146. DOI:10.3390/su11195146

Giannarakis, G., Konteos, G., & Sariannidis, N. (2014). Financial, governance and environmental determinants of corporate social responsible disclosure. *Management Decision*, 52(10), 1928–1951. DOI:10.1108/MD-05-2014-0296

Gladwin, T. N., Kennelly, J. J., & Krause, T. (1995). Shifting paradigms for sustainable development: Implications for management theory and research. *Academy of Management Review*, 20(4), 874–907. DOI:10.2307/258959

Glass, C., & Cook, A. (2018). Do women leaders promote positive change? Analyzing the effect of gender on business practices and diversity initiatives. *Human Resource Management*, 57(4), 823–837. DOI:10.1002/hrm.21838

Global Sustainability Standards Board. (2023). GRI: Foundation 2021. https://globalreporting.org/

Gomez-Conde, J., Lunkes, R. J., & Rosa, F. S. (2019). Environmental innovation practices and operational performance: The joint effects of management accounting and control systems and environmental training. *Accounting, Auditing & Accountability Journal*, 32(5), 1325–1357. DOI:10.1108/AAAJ-01-2018-3327

Goss, A., & Roberts, G. S. (2011). The impact of corporate social responsibility on the cost of bank loans. *Journal of Banking & Finance*, 35(7), 1794–1810. DOI:10.1016/j.jbankfin.2010.12.002

Grabinska, B., Kedzior, D., Kedzior, M., & Grabinski, K. (2021). The Impact of CSR on the Capital Structure of High-Tech Companies in Poland. *Sustainability (Basel)*, 13(10), 5467. DOI:10.3390/su13105467

Gray, R. (2010). A Re-Evaluation of Social, Environmental and Sustainability Accouning: An Exploration of an Emerging Trans-Disciplinary Field? *Sustainability Accounting. Management and Policy Journal*, 1(1), 11–32.

Gray, R. (2010). A re-evaluation of social, environmental and sustainability accounting: An exploration of an emerging trans-disciplinary field? *Sustainability Accounting. Management and Policy Journal*, 1(1), 11–32. DOI:10.1108/20408021011059205

Gray, R., Kouhy, R., & Lavers, S. (1995). Corporate social and environmental reporting: A review of the literature and a longitudinal study of UK disclosure. *Accounting, Auditing & Accountability Journal*, 8(2), 44–47. DOI:10.1108/09513579510146996

Gray, R., Owen, D., & Adams, C. (1996). *Accounting & Accountability: Changes and Challenges in Corporate Social and Environmental Reporting*. Prentice Hall.

Greenwood, R., & Suddaby, R. (2006). Institutional entrepreneurship in mature fields: The big five accounting firms. *Academy of Management Journal*, 49(1), 27–48. DOI:10.5465/amj.2006.20785498

GRI. (2024). *About GRI*. GRI. https://www.globalreporting.org/about-gri/

Guenther, E., Endrikat, J., & Guenther, T. W. (2016). Environmental management control systems: A conceptualization and a review of the empirical evidence. *Journal of Cleaner Production*, 136, 147–171. DOI:10.1016/j.jclepro.2016.02.043

Guenther, E., Guenther, T., Schiemann, F., & Weber, G. (2016). Stakeholder relevance for reporting: Explanatory factors of carbon disclosure. *Business & Society*, 55(3), 361–397. DOI:10.1177/0007650315575119

Guesser, T., Hein, N., Pfitscher, E. D., & Lunkes, R. J. (2015). Environmental impact management of Brazilian companies: Analyzing factors that influence disclosure of waste, emissions, effluents, and other impacts. *Journal of Cleaner Production*, 96, 148–160. DOI:10.1016/j.jclepro.2013.10.035

Gunarathne, N., Samudrage, D., Wijesinghe, D. N., & Lee, K. H. (2016). Fostering social sustainability management through safety controls and accounting: A stakeholder approach in the mining sector. *Accounting Research Journal*, 29(2), 179–197. DOI:10.1108/ARJ-04-2015-0062

Gunningham, K. N., & Thornton, D. (2003). *Shades of green*. Stanford University.

Guthrie, J., Manes-Rossi, F., & Orelli, R. L. (2017). Integrated reporting and integrated thinking in Italian public sector organisations. *Meditari Accountancy Research*, 25(4), 553–573. DOI:10.1108/MEDAR-06-2017-0155

Gutiérrez-Ponce, H., & Wibowo, S. A. (2023). Do sustainability activities affect the financial performance of banks? The case of Indonesian Banks. *Sustainability (Basel)*, 15(8), 6892. DOI:10.3390/su15086892

Guziana, B., & Dobers, P. (2013). How sustainability leaders communicate corporate activities of sustainable development. *Corporate Social Responsibility and Environmental Management*, 20(4), 193–204. DOI:10.1002/csr.1292

Habermas, J. (1984). Reason and the Rationalization of Society, Volume 1 of The Theory of Communicative Action, English translation by Thomas McCarthy. Boston: Beacon Press (originally published in German in 1981).

Habermas, J. (1971). *Towards a Rational Society*. Heineman.

Habermas, J. (1987). *The theory of communicative action: Lifeworld and systems, a critique of functionalist reason*. Polity Press.

Hahn, R., & Kühnen, M. (2013). Determinants of sustainability reporting: A review of results, trends, theory, and opportunities in an expanding field of research. *Journal of Cleaner Production*, 59, 5–21. DOI:10.1016/j.jclepro.2013.07.005

Hahn, R., Reimsbach, D., & Wickert, C. (2023). Nonfinancial Reporting and Real Sustainable Change: Relationship Status-It's Complicated. *Organization & Environment*, 36(1), 3–16. DOI:10.1177/10860266231151653

Hail, L., & Leuz, C. (2006). International differences in cost of equity capital: Do legal institutions and securities regulations matter? *Journal of Accounting Research*, 44(3), 485–531. DOI:10.1111/j.1475-679X.2006.00209.x

Hair, J. F., Sarstedt, M., Ringle, C. M., & Gudergan, S. P. (2018). *Advanced Issues in Partial Least Squares Structural Equation Modeling (PLS-SEM)*. Sage., DOI:10.3926/oss.37

Hair, J., Hult, G., Ringle, C., & Sarstedt, M. (2017). *A Primer on Partial Least Squares Structural Equation Modeling (PLS-SEM)* (2nd ed.). Sage.

Hair, J., Risher, J., Sarstedt, M., & Ringle, C. (2019). When to use and how to report the results of PLS-SEM. *European Business Review*, 31(1), 2–24. DOI:10.1108/EBR-11-2018-0203

Håkanson, L., Ambos, B., Schuster, A., & Leicht-Deobald, U. (2016). The psychology of psychic distance: Antecedents of asymmetric perceptions. *Journal of World Business*, 51(2), 308–318. DOI:10.1016/j.jwb.2015.11.005

Hakimdavar, R., Hubbard, A., Policelli, F., Pickens, A., Hansen, M., Fatoyinbo, T., & Schollaert Uz, S. (2020). Monitoring water-related ecosystems with earth observation data in support of Sustainable Development Goal (SDG) 6 reporting. *Remote Sensing (Basel)*, 12(10), 1634. DOI:10.3390/rs12101634

Halkos, G., & Nomikos, S. (2021). Corporate social responsibility: Trends in global reporting initiative standards. *Economic Analysis and Policy*, 69, 106–117. DOI:10.1016/j.eap.2020.11.008

Hamad, S., Draz, M. U., & Lai, F.-W. (2020). The Impact of Corporate Governance and Sustainability Reporting on Integrated Reporting: A Conceptual Framework. *SAGE Open*, 10(2), 215824402092743. DOI:10.1177/2158244020927431

Hamad, S., Lai, F. W., Shad, M. K., Khatib, S. F. A., & Ali, S. E. A. (2023). Assessing the implementation of sustainable development goals: Does integrated reporting matter? *Sustainability Accounting. Management and Policy Journal*, 14(1), 49–74. DOI:10.1108/SAMPJ-01-2022-0029

Haniffa, R., & Cooke, T. (2002). Culture, corporate governance and disclosure in Malaysian corporations. *Abacus*, 38(3), 317–349. DOI:10.1111/1467-6281.00112

Haniffa, R., & Hudaib, M. (2007). Locating audit expectations gap within a cultural context: The case of Saudi Arabia. *Journal of International Accounting, Auditing & Taxation*, 16(2), 179–206. DOI:10.1016/j.intaccaudtax.2007.06.003

Han, S., & Lee, J. W. (2021). Does corporate social responsibility matter even in the B2B market?: Effect of B2B CSR on customer trust. *Industrial Marketing Management*, 93, 115–123. DOI:10.1016/j.indmarman.2020.12.008

Hansen, E. G., & Schaltegger, S. (2016). The Sustainability Balanced Scorecard: A Systematic Review of Architectures. *Journal of Business Ethics*, 133(2), 193–221. DOI:10.1007/s10551-014-2340-3

Hansmann, H. B. (1980). The role of nonprofit enterprise. *The Yale Law Journal*, 89(5), 835–902. http://hdl.handle.net/20.500.13051/4588. DOI:10.2307/796089

Harjoto, M. A. (2017). Corporate social responsibility and degrees of operating and financial leverage. *Review of Quantitative Finance and Accounting*, 49(2), 487–513. DOI:10.1007/s11156-016-0598-5

Harjoto, M., Laksmana, I., & Lee, R. (2015). Board diversity and corporate social responsibility. *Journal of Business Ethics*, 132(4), 641–660. DOI:10.1007/s10551-014-2343-0

Harrison, J., Freeman, R., & Abreu, M. (2015). Stakeholder Theory as an Ethical Approach to Effective Management: Applying the theory to multiple contexts. *Revista Brasileira de Gestão de Negócios*, 17(55), 858–869. DOI:10.7819/rbgn.v17i55.2647

Harzing, A. W. (2019). Two new kids on the block: How do Crossref and Dimensions compare with Google Scholar, Microsoft Academic, Scopus and the Web of Science? *Scientometrics*, 120(1), 341–349. DOI:10.1007/s11192-019-03114-y

Hebb, T. (2006). The Economic Inefficiency of Secrecy: Pension Fund Investors' Corporate Transparency Concerns. *Journal of Business Ethics*, 63(4), 385–405. DOI:10.1007/s10551-005-3968-9

Hegazy, M. A. A., & Kamareldawla, N. M. (2021). Key audit matters: Did IAASB unravel the knots of confusion in audit reports decisions? *Managerial Auditing Journal*, 36(8), 1025–1052. DOI:10.1108/MAJ-11-2019-2464

Helm, S. (2013). A matter of reputation and pride: Associations between perceived external reputation, pride in membership, job satisfaction and turnover intentions. *British Journal of Management*, 24(4), 542–556. DOI:10.1111/j.1467-8551.2012.00827.x

Henri, J. F., & Journeault, M. (2010). Eco-control: The influence of management control systems on environmental and economic performance. *Accounting, Organizations and Society*, 35(1), 63–80. DOI:10.1016/j.aos.2009.02.001

Henseler, J., Dijkstra, T. K., Sarstedt, M., Ringle, C. M., Diamantopoulos, A., Straub, D. W., Ketchen, D. J.Jr, Hair, J. F., Hult, G. T. M., & Calantone, R. J. (2014). Common Beliefs and Reality About PLS: Comments on Ronkko and Evermann (2013). *Organizational Research Methods*, 17(2), 182–209. DOI:10.1177/1094428114526928

Hepburn, C. (2006). Regulation by prices, quantities, or both: A review of instrument choice. *Oxford Review of Economic Policy*, 22(2), 226–247. DOI:10.1093/oxrep/grj014

Hera-Saizarbitoria, I. (2022). Organizations' engagement with sustainable development goals: From cherry-picking to SDG-washing? *Corporate Social Responsibility and Environmental Management*, 29(2), 316–328. DOI:10.1002/csr.2202

Herremans, I. M., Nazari, J. A., & Mahmoudian, F. (2016). Stakeholder relationships, engagement, and sustainability reporting. *Journal of Business Ethics*, 138(3), 417–435. DOI:10.1007/s10551-015-2634-0

Hirsch, J. (2005). An index to quantify an individual's scientific research output. *Proceedings of the National Academy of Sciences of the United States of America*, 102(46), 16569–16572. DOI:10.1073/pnas.0507655102 PMID:16275915

Hoang, A., & Huyen, T. (2020). A corporate social responsibility indicator system for construction enterprises in Vietnam. *International Journal of Civil Engineering*, 7(6), 12–20. DOI:10.14445/23488352/IJCE-V7I6P102

Hoffmann, E., Dietsche, C., & Hobelsberger, C. (2018). Between mandatory and voluntary: Non-financial reporting by German companies. *Sustainability Management Forum*, 26(1–4), 47–63.

Holy House of Mercy of Passos. (2016). *The history of the Holy Houses*. Imprensa. Retrieved June 3, 2021, from http://www.scmp.org.br/materia/61/a-historia-das-santas-casas

Hsu, S. C., Wu, K. T., Wang, Q., & Chang, Y. (2023). Is capital structure associated with corporate social responsibility? *International Journal of Corporate Social Responsibility*, 8(1), 6. DOI:10.1186/s40991-023-00081-9

Hsu, Y.-L., & Liu, C.-C. (2010). Environmental performance evaluation and strategy management using balanced scorecard. *Environmental Monitoring and Assessment*, 170(1-4), 599–607. DOI:10.1007/s10661-009-1260-7 PMID:20020324

Huang, H., & Ye, Y. (2021). Rethinking capital structure decision and corporate social responsibility in response to COVID-19. *Accounting and Finance*, 61(3), 4757–4788. DOI:10.1111/acfi.12740

Hummel, K., & Schlick, C. (2016). The relationship between sustainability performance and sustainability disclosure reconciling voluntary disclosure theory and legitimacy theory. *Journal of Accounting and Public Policy*, 35(5), 455–476. DOI:10.1016/j.jaccpubpol.2016.06.001

Hummel, K., & Szekely, M. (2022). Disclosure on the sustainable development goals–Evidence from Europe. *Accounting in Europe*, 19(1), 152–189. DOI:10.1080/17449480.2021.1894347

Hussain, M. J., Tian, G., Ashraf, A., Khan, M. K., & Ying, L. (2023). Chief executive officer ability and corporate environmental sustainability information disclosure. *Business Ethics, the Environment & Responsibility*, 32(1), 24–39. DOI:10.1111/beer.12485

IBGC Instituto brasileiro de Governança Corporativa (IBGC) (2011). Relatório de mulheres na administração das empresas brasileiras listadas – 2010 e 2011. *Available at:*http://hotsite.mma.gov.br/redemulheres/wpcontent/uploads/Pesquisa_Mulheres_no_Conselho.pdf

IFRS Foundation. (2021). IFRS Advisory Council Update International Sustainability Standards Board. https://www.ifrs.org/content/dam/ifrs/meetings/2021/november/advisory-council/ap4-update-on-international-sustainability-standards-board.pdf

IIRC. (2013). The International Integrated Reporting Framework. Available at https://integratedreporting.org/wpcontent/uploads/2013/12/13-12-08-the-international-ir-framework-2-1.pdf

IIRC. (2013). The international IR framework. Available at https://integratedreporting.ifrs.org/wp-content/uploads/2013/12/13-12-08-THE-INTERNATIONAL-IR-FRAMEWORK-2-1.pdf

Ikram, M., Sroufe, R., Mohsin, M., Solangi, Y. A., Shah, S. Z., & Shahzad, F. (2019). Does CSR influence firm performance? A longitudinal study of SME sectors of Pakistan. *Journal of Global Responsibility*, 11(1), 27–53. DOI:10.1108/JGR-12-2018-0088

International Auditing and Assurance Standards Board. (2018a). *ISA 315 (Revised) - Identifying and Assessing the Risks of Material Misstatement through Understanding the Entity and Its Environment*. https://www.ifac.org/_flysystem/azure-private/publications/files/A017%202013%20IAASB%20Handbook%20ISA%20315%20Revised.pdf

International Auditing and Assurance Standards Board. (2018b). *ISA 500 - Audit Evidence*. https://www.ifac.org/_flysystem/azure-private/publications/files/A023%202012%20IAASB%20Handbook%20ISA%20500.pdf

International Auditing and Assurance Standards Board. (2018c). *ISA 700 (Revised) - Forming an Opinion and Reporting on Financial Statements*. https://www.iaasb.org/publications/international-standard-auditing-isa-700-revised-forming-opinion-and-reporting-financial-statements

International Auditing and Assurance Standards Board. (2018d). *ISA 701 - Communicating Key Audit Matters in the Independent Auditor's Report*. https://www.iaasb.org/publications/international-standard-auditing-isa-701-new-communicating-key-audit-matters-independent-auditors

Ioannou, I., & Serafeim, G. (2017). The consequences of mandatory corporate sustainability reporting. *Harvard Business School research working paper*, (11-100).

Islam, T., Islam, R., Pitafi, A. H., Xiaobei, L., Rehmani, M., Irfan, M., & Mubarak, M. S. (2021). The impact of corporate social responsibility on customer loyalty: The mediating role of corporate reputation, customer satisfaction, and trust. *Sustainable Production and Consumption*, 25, 123–135. DOI:10.1016/j.spc.2020.07.019

Iwanowicz, T., & Iwanowicz, B. (2019). ISA 701 and Materiality Disclosure as Methods to Minimize the Audit Expectation Gap. *Journal of Risk and Financial Management*, 12(4), 1–20. DOI:10.3390/jrfm12040161

Izzo, M. F., Ciaburri, M., & Tiscini, R. (2020). The challenge of Sustainable Development Goal reporting: The first evidence from Italian listed companies. *Sustainability (Basel)*, 12(8), 3494. DOI:10.3390/su12083494

Jacobs, K., & Walker, S. P. (2004). Accounting and accountability in the Iona Community. *Accounting, Auditing & Accountability Journal*, 17(3), 361–381. DOI:10.1108/09513570410545786

Jain, A., Ripa, D., & Torres, L. (2024). Have companies arisen to the challenge of promoting sustainable work? The role of responsible business practices in the context of evolving employment and working conditions. *Safety Science*, 170, 106364. DOI:10.1016/j.ssci.2023.106364

Jensen, M. C. (1986). Agency costs of free cash flow, corporate finance, and takeovers. *The American Economic Review*, 76, 323–329.

Jensen, M. C., & Meckling, W. H. (1976). Theory of the firm: Managerial behavior, agency costs and ownership structure. *Journal of Financial Economics*, 3(4), 305–360. DOI:10.1016/0304-405X(76)90026-X

Jo, H., & Harjoto, M. (2011). Corporate governance and firm value: The impact of corporate social responsibility. *Journal of Business Ethics*, 103(3), 351–383. DOI:10.1007/s10551-011-0869-y

Jo, H., & Na, H. (2012). Does CSR reduce firm risk? Evidence from controversial industry sectors? *Journal of Business Ethics*, 110(4), 441–456. DOI:10.1007/s10551-012-1492-2

Johnston, A., & Samanta, N. (2024). ESG and workforce engagement: Experiences in the UK. In Research Handbook on Environmental, Social and Corporate Governance (pp. 158-178). Edward Elgar Publishing.

Johnstone, L. (2019). Theorising and conceptualising the sustainability control system for effective sustainability management. *Journal of Management Control*, 30(1), 25–64. DOI:10.1007/s00187-019-00277-w

Johnstone, L. (2021). Facilitating sustainability control in SMEs through the implementation of an environmental management system. *Journal of Management Control*, 32(4), 559–605. DOI:10.1007/s00187-021-00329-0

Johnstone, L. (2022). The means to substantive performance improvements–environmental management control systems in ISO 14001–certified SMEs. *Sustainability Accounting. Management and Policy Journal*, 13(5), 1082–1108.

Johnstone, L., Yates, D., & Nylander, S. (2023). Taking shape within the structural and the personal: Sustainability accountability within a Swedish public sector organisation. *Sustainability Accounting. Management and Policy Journal*, 14(7), 287–312. DOI:10.1108/SAMPJ-08-2022-0450

Jordan, S., & Messner, M. (2012). Enabling control and the problem of incomplete performance indicators. *Accounting, Organizations and Society*, 37(8), 544–564. DOI:10.1016/j.aos.2012.08.002

Kalender, Z. T., & Vayvay, Ö. (2016). The Fifth Pillar of the Balanced Scorecard: Sustainability. *Procedia: Social and Behavioral Sciences*, 235, 76–83. DOI:10.1016/j.sbspro.2016.11.027

Kang, S., & Norton, H. E. (2004). Nonprofit organisations' use of the world wide web: Are they sufficiently fulfilling organisational goals? *Public Relations Review*, 30(3), 279–284. DOI:10.1016/j.pubrev.2004.04.002

Kaplan, R. S., & Norton, D. P. (1996). *The balanced scorecard: Translating strategy into action*. Harvard Business School Press.

Kapri, S. S. (2023). The role of corporate governance in mitigating financial risk: An Indian experiences. *Journal of Cardiovascular Research*, 12(6), 2114–2121.

Karpoff, J. M., Litan, R., Schrand, C., & Weil, R. L. (2022). What ESG-Related Disclosures Should the SEC Mandate? *Financial Analysts Journal*, 78(2), 9–18. DOI:10.1080/0015198X.2022.2044718

Kawa, L. (2016). Responsabilidade social na construção civil. Disponível em: http://professoralucianekawa.blogspot.com

Keay, A. (2017). Stewardship theory: Is board accountability necessary? *International Journal of Law and Management*, 59(6), 1292–1314. DOI:10.1108/IJLMA-11-2016-0118

Khakimovna, N. F., & Oktyamovna, S. A. (2022). Sustainability Reporting Towards Common Standards. *European Journal of Innovation In Nonformal Education*, 2(4), 236–239.

Khan, M. A. (2022). ESG disclosure and Firm performance: A bibliometric and Meta Analysis. *Research in International Business and Finance*, 61, 101668. DOI:10.1016/j.ribaf.2022.101668

Khan, M., & Lockhart, J. (2022). Corporate social responsibility decoupling in developing countries: Current research and a future agenda. *Business and Society Review*, 127(1), 127–143. DOI:10.1111/basr.12254

Khan, M., Serafeim, G., & Yoon, A. (2016). Corporate sustainability: First evidence on materiality. *The Accounting Review*, 91(6), 1697–1724. www.aaajournals.org/doi/abs/10.2308/accr-51383. DOI:10.2308/accr-51383

Khatib, S. F. A., Abdullah, D. F., Elamer, A. A., & Abueid, R. (2021). Nudging toward diversity in the boardroom: A systematic literature review of board diversity of financial institutions. *Business Strategy and the Environment*, 30(2), 985–1002. DOI:10.1002/bse.2665

Kiel, G. C., & Nicholson, G. J. (2003). Board composition and corporate performance: How the Australian experience informs contrasting theories of corporate governance. *Corporate Governance*, 11(3), 189–205. DOI:10.1111/1467-8683.00318

Kim, S., Lee, G., & Kang, H. G. (2021). Risk management and corporate social responsibility. *Strategic Management Journal*, 42(1), 202–230. DOI:10.1002/smj.3224

Kiroyan, N. (2015). NCSR Sustainability Reporting. *SKK Migas Indonesian Petroleum Association 39th Convention, 11.*

Knott, S., & Wilson, J. P. (2024). Core charitable purpose and voluntary CSR activities in charity organisations: Do they conflict? *Social Responsibility Journal*, 20(6), 1056–1071. DOI:10.1108/SRJ-09-2023-0498

Knut, B., & Heß, P. (2023). Stakeholder perceptions of the role of standards for addressing the sustainable development goals. *Sustainable Production and Consumption*, 37, 180–190. DOI:10.1016/j.spc.2023.02.016

Kolk, A. (2008). Sustainability, accountability and governance: Exploring multinational reporting practice. *Business Strategy and the Environment*, 17(1), 1–15. DOI:10.1002/bse.511

Kong, D., Shu, Y., & Wang, Y. (2021). Corruption and corporate social responsibility: Evidence from a quasi-natural experiment in China. *Journal of Asian Economics*, 75, 1–16. DOI:10.1016/j.asieco.2021.101317

Kornieieva, Y. (2020). Non-financial reporting challenges in monitoring SDGs achievement: Investment aspects for transition economy. *International Journal of Economics and Business Administration*, VIII(1), 62–71. DOI:10.35808/ijeba/409

Kouloukoui, D., Sant'Anna, Â. M. O., da Silva Gomes, S. M., de Oliveira Marinho, M. M., de Jong, P., Kiperstok, A., & Torres, E. A. (2019). Factors influencing the level of environmental disclosures in sustainability reports: Case of climate risk disclosure by Brazilian companies. *Corporate Social Responsibility and Environmental Management*, 26(4), 791–804. DOI:10.1002/csr.1721

KPMG. (2020). *The time has come. The KPMG survey of sustainability reporting 2020.* KPMG. https://assets.kpmg.com/content/dam/kpmg/be/pdf/2020/12/The_Time_Has_Come_KPMG_Survey_of_Sustainability_Reporting_2020.pdf

Kramer, M. R., & Porter, M. E. (2006). Strategy and society: The link between competitive advantage and corporate social responsibility. *Harvard Business Review*, 84(12), 78–92. PMID:17183795

Krasodomska, J., Zarzycka, E., & Zieniuk, P. (2023). Voluntary sustainability reporting assurance in the European Union before the advent of the corporate sustainability reporting directive: The country and firm-level impact of Sustainable Development Goals. *Sustainable Development*.

Krasodomska, J., Zieniuk, P., & Kostrzewska, J. (2022). Reporting on Sustainable Development Goals in the European Union: What drives companies' decisions? *Competitiveness Review*, 33(1), 120–146. DOI:10.1108/CR-12-2021-0179

Krivačić, D. (2017). Sustainability Reporting Quality: The Analysis of Companies in Croatia. *Journal of Accounting and Management*, 07(01).

Księżak, P., & Fischbach, B. (2017). Triple bottom line: The pillars of CSR. *Journal of corporate responsibility and leadership, 4*(3), 95-110.

Kücükgül, E., Cerin, P., & Liu, Y. (2022). Enhancing the value of corporate sustainability: An approach for aligning multiple SDGs guides on reporting. *Journal of Cleaner Production*, 333, 130005. DOI:10.1016/j.jclepro.2021.130005

Lagasio, V., & Cucari, N. (2019). Corporate governance and environmental social governance disclosure: A meta-analytical review. *Corporate Social Responsibility and Environmental Management*, 26(4), 701–711. DOI:10.1002/csr.1716

Lai, A., Melloni, G., & Stacchezzini, R. (2018). Integrated reporting and narrative accountability: The role of preparers. *Accounting, Auditing & Accountability Journal*, 31(5), 1381–1405. DOI:10.1108/AAAJ-08-2016-2674

Laine, M., Tregidga, H., & Unerman, J. (2021). *Sustainability accounting and accountability*. Routledge. DOI:10.4324/9781003185611

Landrum, N. E., & Ohsowski, B. (2018). Identifying Worldviews on Corporate Sustainability: A Content Analysis of Corporate Sustainability Reports. *Business Strategy and the Environment*, 27(1), 128–151. DOI:10.1002/bse.1989

Langevoort, D. C. (2000). The human nature of corporate boards: Law, norms, and the unintended consequences of independence and accountability. *Geological Journal*, 89, 797.

Lanka, S., Khadaroo, I., & Bohm, S. (2017). Agroecology accounting: Biodiversity and sustainable livelihoods from the margin. *Accounting, Auditing & Accountability Journal*, 30(7), 1592–1613. DOI:10.1108/AAAJ-12-2015-2363

Latapí Agudelo, M. A., Jóhannsdóttir, L., & Davídsdóttir, B. (2019). A literature review of the history and evolution of corporate social responsibility. *International Journal of Corporate Social Responsibility*, 4(1), 1–23. DOI:10.1186/s40991-018-0039-y

Law 12/2008 of Assembly of the Republic (2008). Republic Diary No. 40/2008, Series I of 2008-02-26. https://diariodarepublica.pt/dr/detalhe/lei/12-2008-247453

Law 148/2015 of Assembly of the Republic (2015). Republic Diary No. 176/2015, Series I of 2015-09-09. https://diariodarepublica.pt/dr/legislacao-consolidada/lei/2015-74094268

Law 23/96 of Assembly of the Republic (1996). Republic Diary No. 172/1996, Series I-A of 1996-07-26. https://diariodarepublica.pt/dr/detalhe/lei/23-1996-408366

Law 58/2005 of Assembly of the Republic (2005). Republic Diary No. 249/2005, Series I-A of 2005-12-29. https://diariodarepublica.pt/dr/detalhe/lei/58-2005-469068

Law no. 30/2013. *Official Journal of the Portuguese Republic*, no. 88 - Series I, of 8 May.

Lazzaretti, K., Godoi, C. K., Camilo, S. P. O., & Marcon, R. (2013). Gender diversity in the boards of directors of Brazilian businesses. *Gender in Management*, 28(2), 94–110. DOI:10.1108/17542411311303239

Leardini, C., Rossi, G., & Landi, S. (2020). Organisational factors affecting charitable giving in the environmental nonprofit context. *Sustainability (Basel)*, 12(21), 8947. DOI:10.3390/su12218947

Lee, D., & Faff, R. (2009). Corporate sustainability performance and idiosyncratic risk: A global perspective. *Financial Review*, 44(2), 213–237. DOI:10.1111/j.1540-6288.2009.00216.x

Lee, E., Walker, M., & Zeng, C. (2017). Do Chinese state subsidies affect voluntary corporate social responsibility disclosure? *Journal of Accounting and Public Policy*, 36(3), 179–200. DOI:10.1016/j.jaccpubpol.2017.03.004

Lee, J., Lee, J., Lee, C., & Kim, Y. (2023). Identifying ESG trends of International container shipping companies using semantic network analysis and multiple case theory. *Sustainability (Basel)*, 15(12), 9441. DOI:10.3390/su15129441

Legaspi, J. L. R. (2023). The current state of sustainability reporting: Evidence from publicly listed financial institutions. *Corporate Governance and Sustainability Review*, 7(2), 18–28. DOI:10.22495/cgsrv7i2p2

Lehman, G., & Kuruppu, S. C. (2017, September). A framework for social and environmental accounting research. *Accounting Forum*, 41(3), 139–146. DOI:10.1016/j.accfor.2017.07.001

Leite, L. (2011). Responsabilidade Social Corporativa como Estratégia de Negócio: Modelos Conceituais e Exemplos Ilustrativos (Tese de Mestrado, Escola de Administração de Empresas de São Paulo).

Lennox, C. S., Schmidt, J. J., & Thompson, A. M. (2023). Why are expanded audit reports not informative to investors? Evidence from the United Kingdom. *Review of Accounting Studies*, 28(2), 497–532. DOI:10.1007/s11142-021-09650-4

Lettieri, C. (2003). Quem realmente interessa às empresas? Contribuições analíticas da teoria dos stakeholders ao estudo da responsabilidade corporativa.

Levinas, E. (1991). *Otherwise than Being or Beyond Essence*. Kluwer Academic Publishers. DOI:10.1007/978-94-015-7906-3

Liang, C., Lourie, B., Nekrasov, A., & Yoo, I. S. (2023). Voluntary disclosure of workforce gender diversity. *Available atSSRN* 3971818.

Li, D., Huang, M., Ren, S., Chen, X., & Ning, L. (2018). Environmental legitimacy, green innovation, and corporate carbon disclosure: Evidence from CDP China 100. *Journal of Business Ethics*, 150(4), 1089–1104. DOI:10.1007/s10551-016-3187-6

Lii, Y., Wu, K., & Ding, M. (2013). Doing good does good? sustainable marketing of CSR and consumer evaluations. *Corporate Social Responsibility and Environmental Management*, 20(1), 15–28. DOI:10.1002/csr.294

Lindblom, C. K. (1993). The implications of organizational legitimacy for corporate social performance and disclosure. *Paper presented at the Critical Perspectives on Accounting Conference*, New York, NY.

Lin, J. (2023). Does the disclosure of key audit matters improve the audit quality for sustainable development: Empirical evidence from China. *PLoS One*, 18(5), e0285340. DOI:10.1371/journal.pone.0285340 PMID:37141326

Lins, K. V., Servaes, H., & Tamayo, A. (2017). Social capital, trust, and firm performance: The value of corporate social responsibility during the financial crisis. *The Journal of Finance*, 72(4), 1785–1824. DOI:10.1111/jofi.12505

Lin, Y. (2021). Legitimation strategies in corporate discourse: A comparison of UK and Chinese corporate social responsibility reports. *Journal of Pragmatics*, 177, 157–169. DOI:10.1016/j.pragma.2021.02.009

Li, R., & Henderson, G. V.Jr. (1991). Combined leverage and stock risk. *Quarterly Journal of Business Economics*, 30(1), 18–39. https://www.jstor.org/stable/40473011

Littlejohn, S. W., & Foss, K. A. (2011). *Theories of Human Communication* (10th ed.). Waveland Press.

Liu, L., & Nemoto, N. (2021). Environmental, social and governance (ESG) evaluation and organizational attractiveness to prospective employees: Evidence from Japan. *Journal of Accounting and Finance*, 21(4), 14–29. DOI:10.33423/jaf.v21i4.4522

Liu, L., & Tian, G. G. (2019). Mandatory CSR disclosure, monitoring and investment efficiency: Evidence from China. *Accounting and Finance*, 61(1), 595–644. DOI:10.1111/acfi.12588

Liu, Y., Heinberg, M., Huang, X., & Eisingerich, A. B. (2023). Building a competitive advantage based on transparency: When and why does transparency matter for corporate social responsibility? *Business Horizons*, 66(4), 517–527. DOI:10.1016/j.bushor.2022.10.004

Li, X., Zheng, C., Liu, G., & Sial, M. S. (2018). The effectiveness of internal control and corporate social responsibility: Evidence from Chinese capital market. *Sustainability (Basel)*, 10(11), 4006. DOI:10.3390/su10114006

Lock, I., & Seele, P. (2016). The credibility of CSR (corporate social responsibility) reports in Europe. Evidence from a quantitative content analysis in 11 countries. *Journal of Cleaner Production*, 122, 186–200. DOI:10.1016/j.jclepro.2016.02.060

Lokuwaduge, C. S. D. S., & Heenetigala, K. (2017). Integrating environmental, social and governance (ESG) disclosure for a sustainable development: An Australian study. *Business Strategy and the Environment*, 26(4), 438–450. DOI:10.1002/bse.1927

López-Gamero, M. D., Molina-Azorín, J. F., & Claver-Cortés, E. (2009). The whole relationship between environmental variables and firm performance: Competitive advantage and firm resources as mediator variables. *Journal of Environmental Management*, 90(10), 3110–3121. DOI:10.1016/j.jenvman.2009.05.007 PMID:19482410

López, M. V., Garcia, A., & Rodriguez, L. (2007). Sustainable development and corporate performance: A study based on the Dow Jones sustainability index. *Journal of Business Ethics*, 75(3), 285–300. DOI:10.1007/s10551-006-9253-8

Lueg, R., & Radlach, R. (2016). Managing Sustainable development with management control systems: A literature review. *European Management Journal*, 34(2), 158–171. DOI:10.1016/j.emj.2015.11.005

Lu, F., Kozak, R., Toppinen, A., D'Amato, D., & Wen, Z. (2017). Factors influencing levels of CSR disclosure by forestry companies in China. *Sustainability (Basel)*, 9(10), 1800. DOI:10.3390/su9101800

Lu, J., & Wang, J. (2021). Corporate governance, law, culture, environmental performance and CSR disclosure: A global perspective. *Journal of International Financial Markets, Institutions and Money*, 70, 101264. DOI:10.1016/j.intfin.2020.101264

Luo, L., & Tang, Q. (2023). The real effects of ESG reporting and GRI standards on carbon mitigation: International evidence. *Business Strategy and the Environment*, 32(6), 2985–3000. DOI:10.1002/bse.3281

Lu, S., & Cheng, B. (2023). Does environmental regulation affect firms' ESG performance? Evidence from China. *MDE. Managerial and Decision Economics*, 44(4), 2004–2009. DOI:10.1002/mde.3796

Mahmood, A. N., Arslan, H. M., Younas, Z. I., Komal, B., Ali, K., & Mubeen, M. (2023). Understanding the dynamics of capital structure, corporate governance, and corporate social responsibility in high and low-leveraged US and Chinese firms. *Environmental Science and Pollution Research International*, 30(16), 1–18. DOI:10.1007/s11356-022-24843-3 PMID:36710308

Majeed, S., Aziz, T., & Saleem, S. (2015). The Effect of Corporate Governance Elements on Corporate Social Responsibility (CSR) Disclosure: An Empirical Evidence from Listed Companies at KSE Pakistan. *International Journal of Financial Studies*, 3(4), 530–556. DOI:10.3390/ijfs3040530

Makeen Energy (2022) Responsible energy solutions on a sustainability journey Available online: global-compact-2022_responsible-energy-solutions-on-a-sustainability-journey.pdf

Makeen Energy. (2023a) About us Available online: https://www.makeenenergy.com/about-us/who-we-are

Makeen Energy. (2023b) Our work with the UN SDGs Available online: https://www.makeenenergy.com/commitments/sustainable-development-goals

Manes-Rossi, F., Nicolò, G., & Argento, D. (2020). Non-financial reporting formats in public sector organizations: A structured literature review. *Journal of Public Budgeting, Accounting & Financial Management*, 32(4), 639–669. DOI:10.1108/JPBAFM-03-2020-0037

Manes-Rossi, F., Spanò, R., Martin-Sardesai, A., & Guthrie, J. (2022). Performance management change: Discourses at play in an Italian university. *Journal of Public Budgeting, Accounting & Financial Management*, 34(4), 534–556. DOI:10.1108/JPBAFM-11-2021-0156

Manita, R., Bruna, M. G., Dang, R., & Houanti, L. H. (2018). Board gender diversity and ESG disclosure: Evidence from the USA. *Journal of Applied Accounting Research*, 19(2), 206–224. DOI:10.1108/JAAR-01-2017-0024

Manoel, J., & Quel, L. F. (2017). Innovation in the International Standards for the New Independent Audit Report. *Journal on Innovation and Sustainability*, 8(1), 130–143. DOI:10.24212/2179-3565.2017v8i1p130-143

Manyaga, C. B., Muturi, W., & Oluoch, O. (2020). Board gender diversity and financial performance of commercial banks in Kenya. *Journal of Finance and Accounting*, 8(1), 1–10.

Margolis, J., Elfenbein, H., & Walsh, J. (2009). Does it pay to be good? A meta-analysis and redirection of research on the relationship between corporate social and financial performance (March 1, 2009). Retrieved from https://ssrn.com/abstract=1866371

Marlowe, J., & Clarke, A. (2022). Carbon accounting: A systematic literature review and directions for future research. *Green Finance*, 4(1), 71–87. DOI:10.3934/GF.2022004

Martin Curran, M., & Moran, D. (2007). Impact of the FTSE4 Good Index on firm price: An event study. *Journal of Environmental Management*, 82(4), 529–537. DOI:10.1016/j.jenvman.2006.02.010 PMID:16678334

Martín-Martín, A., Thelwall, M., Orduna-Malea, E., & Delgado López-Cózar, E. (2020). Google Scholar, Microsoft Academic, Scopus, Dimensions, Web of Science, and OpenCitations' COCI: A multidisciplinary comparison of coverage via citations. *Scientometrics*, 126(1), 871–906. DOI:10.1007/s11192-020-03690-4 PMID:32981987

Mazzer, L. (2015). Responsabilidade Social Corporativa e Desempenho Econômico Financeiro: Um Estudo em Empresas Brasileiras (Tese de Doutorado, Universidade de Brasília).

Mebratu, D. (1998). Sustainability and sustainable development: Historical and conceptual review. *Environmental Impact Assessment Review*, 18(6), 493–520. DOI:10.1016/S0195-9255(98)00019-5

Mendes, P., Santos, A. C., Perna, F., & Ribau Teixeira, M. (2012). The balanced scorecard as an integrated model applied to the Portuguese public service: A case study in the waste sector. *Journal of Cleaner Production*, 24, 20–29. DOI:10.1016/j.jclepro.2011.11.007

Menz, K. M. (2010). Corporate social responsibility: Is it rewarded by the corporate bond market? A critical note. *Journal of Business Ethics*, 96(1), 117–134. DOI:10.1007/s10551-010-0452-y

Merkl-Davies, D. M., & Brennan, N. M. (2017). A theoretical framework of external accounting communication: Research perspectives, traditions, and theories. *Accounting, Auditing & Accountability Journal*, 30(2), 433–469. DOI:10.1108/AAAJ-04-2015-2039

Meyer, H. D., & Rowan, B. (2006). Institutional analysis and the study of education. *The new institutionalism in education*, 113.

Michelon, G. (2011). Sustainability disclosure and reputation: A comparative study. *Corporate Reputation Review*, 14(2), 79–96. DOI:10.1057/crr.2011.10

Michelon, G., Boesso, G., & Kumar, K. (2013). Examining the link between strategic corporate social responsibility and company performance: An analysis of the best corporate citizens. *Corporate Social Responsibility and Environmental Management*, 20(2), 81–94. DOI:10.1002/csr.1278

Michelon, G., Trojanowski, G., & Sealy, R. (2022). Narrative reporting: State of the art and future challenges. *Accounting in Europe*, 19(1), 7–47. DOI:10.1080/17449480.2021.1900582

Minutiello, V., & Tettamanzi, P. (2022). The quality of nonfinancial voluntary disclosure: A systematic literature network analysis on sustainability reporting and integrated reporting. *Corporate Social Responsibility and Environmental Management*, 29(1), 1–18. DOI:10.1002/csr.2195

Mio, C., Costantini, A., & Panfilo, S. (2022). Performance measurement tools for sustainable business: A systematic literature review on the sustainability balanced scorecard use. *Corporate Social Responsibility and Environmental Management*, 29(2), 367–384. DOI:10.1002/csr.2206

Mion, G., & Adaui, C. R. (2019). Mandatory Nonfinancial Disclosure and Its Consequences on the Sustainability Reporting Quality of Italian and German Companies. *Sustainability (Basel)*, 11(17), 4612. DOI:10.3390/su11174612

Mitchell, R. K., Agle, B. R., & Wood, D. J. (1997). Toward a theory of stakeholder identification and salience: Defining the principle of who and what really counts. *Academy of Management Review*, 22(4), 853–886. DOI:10.2307/259247

Mobus, J., & Tacoma, T. (2005). Mandatory environmental disclosures in a legitimacy theory context. *Accounting, Auditing & Accountability Journal*, 18(4), 492–517. DOI:10.1108/09513570510609333

Mock, T. J., Bedard, J., Coram, J. P., Davis, S. M., Esphabodi, R., & Wrane, R. C. (2013). The audit reporting model: Current research synthesis and implications. *Auditing*, 32(1, Supplement 1), 323–351. DOI:10.2308/ajpt-50294

Moneva, J. M., & Llena, F. (2000). Environmental disclosures in the annual reports of large companies in Spain. *European Accounting Review*, 9(1), 7–29. DOI:10.1080/096381800407923

Monteiro, A. P. (2022). *Social Accounting: analysis of the disclosure on labor practices and human rights and its determinants* [Doctoral dissertation]. University of Santiago de Compostela, Spain.

Monteiro, A. P., Cepêda, C., Borges, A. P., & Vieira, E. (2024). Does CSR committee presence, stakeholder engagement, gender equality (SDG 5) and firm value influence ESG performance reporting? An EU pre and during Covid-19 analysis. *Measuring Business Excellence*. DOI:10.1108/MBE-03-2024-0034

Monteiro, A. P., Pereira, C., & Barbosa, F. M. (2023). Environmental disclosure on mandatory and voluntary reporting of Portuguese listed firms: the role of environmental certification, lucratively and corporate governance. *Meditari accountancy research, 31*(3), 524-553.

Monteiro, S., Marques, R., & Lemos, K. (2023). Fatores determinantes do relato não financeiro obrigatório vs voluntário em grandes empresas portuguesas. International Workshop on Accounting and Taxation - IWAT2023, Oporto, 17 february

Monteiro, A. P. (2022). *Social Accounting: Analysis of the disclosure on labor practices and human rights and its determinants*. Phd in Economics and Business. Universidade de Santiago de Compostela.

Monteiro, A. P., Cepêda, C., & da Silva, A. F. (2024a). Does the Workforce and Sustainability Reports Strengthen the Relationship between Gender Diversity and Sustainability Performance Reporting? *Administrative Sciences*, 14(6), 105. DOI:10.3390/admsci14060105

Monteiro, A. P., Cepêda, C., Pereira, C., & Silva, A. (2023). Social Performance Disclosed by European Companies: The Role of the Board Attributes and the Country's Legal System. *Journal of Risk and Financial Management*, 16(6), 284. DOI:10.3390/jrfm16060284

Monteiro, A. P., García-Sánchez, I. M., & Aibar-Guzmán, B. (2022). Labour practice, decent work and human rights performance and reporting: The impact of women managers. *Journal of Business Ethics*, 180(2), 523–542. DOI:10.1007/s10551-021-04913-1

Monteiro, A. P., Pereira, C., & Silva, A. (2021). *Corporate Social Responsailty Reporting*. Ponte Editora.

Monteiro, S. M., & Guzmán, B. A. (2010). The influence of the Portuguese environmental accounting standard on the environmental disclosures in the annual reports of large companies operating in Portugal - A first view (2002-2004). *Management of Environmental Quality*, 21(4), 414–435. DOI:10.1108/14777831011049070

Monteiro, S., & Aibar-Guzmán, B. (2009). Determinants of environmental disclosure in the annual reports of large companies operating in Portugal. *Corporate Social Responsibility and Environmental Management*, 17(4), 185–204. DOI:10.1002/csr.197

Monteiro, S., & Aibar-Guzmán, B. (2010). Organizational and accounting change within the context of the environmental agenda: Evidence from Portugal. *Journal of Accounting & Organizational Change*, 6(4), 404–435. DOI:10.1108/18325911011091800

Monteiro, S., Ribeiro, V., Vilhena, E., Lemos, K., & Molho, C. (2024). Determinants of online-reporting on sustainable development goals: The case of Portuguese Higher Education Institutions. *Social Responsibility Journal*, 20(3), 462–484. DOI:10.1108/SRJ-01-2023-0044

Naciti, V. (2019). Corporate governance and board of directors: The effect of a board composition on firm sustainability performance. *Journal of Cleaner Production*, 237, 117727. DOI:10.1016/j.jclepro.2019.117727

Navarro-Galera, A., Ruiz-Lozano, M., Tirado-Valencia, P., & de los Ríos-Berjillos, A. (2017). Promoting sustainability transparency in European local governments: An empirical analysis based on administrative cultures. *Sustainability (Basel)*, 9(3), 432. DOI:10.3390/su9030432

Nelling, E., & Webb, E. (2009). Corporate social responsibility and financial performance: The "virtuous circle" revisited. *Review of Quantitative Finance and Accounting*, 32(2), 197–209. DOI:10.1007/s11156-008-0090-y

Nicolò, G., Zanellato, G., Manes-Rossi, F., & Tiron-Tudor, A. (2021). Corporate reporting metamorphosis: Empirical findings from state-owned enterprises. *Public Money & Management*, 41(2), 138–147. DOI:10.1080/09540962.2020.1719633

O'Regan, B., King, R., & Smith, D. (2021). Combining accountability forms: Transparency and "intelligent" accountability in a public service organization. *Accounting, Auditing & Accountability Journal.*

Oboreh, M., Justina, D. E., & Agbarha, K., Egberi, M., & Onyeyime, E. (2022). Workforce gender diversity and performance of multinational companies in Nigeria. *Journal of Positive School Psychology*, 1582–1590.

Oliva, A., & De Oliveira, R. (2008). Social Responsibility in Civil Construction in Brazil: A Path that Can Support Housing Access. *Revista INVI*, 23, 121–134.

Optima Italia. (2022). Bilancio di Sostenibilità. Available on https://www.optimaitalia.com/public/files/pdf/Bilancio_Sostenibilita%CC%80_2022.pdf

Orazalin, N. S., Ntim, C. G., & Malagila, J. K. (2024). Board sustainability committees, climate change initiatives, carbon performance, and market value. *British Journal of Management*, 35(1), 295–320. DOI:10.1111/1467-8551.12715

Orazalin, N., & Baydauletov, M. (2020). Corporate social responsibility strategy and corporate environmental and social performance: The moderating role of board gender diversity. *Corporate Social Responsibility and Environmental Management*, 27(4), 1664–1676. DOI:10.1002/csr.1915

Ortega-Rodríguez, C., Licerán-Gutiérrez, A., & Moreno-Albarracín, A. L. (2020). Transparency as a key element in accountability in non-profit organisations: A systematic literature review. *Sustainability (Basel)*, 12(14), 5834. DOI:10.3390/su12145834

Ottenstein, P., Erben, S., Jost, S., Weuster, C., & Zulch, H. (2022). From voluntarism to regulation: Effects of directive 2014/95/EU on sustainability reporting in the EU. *Journal of Applied Accounting Research*, 23(1), 55–98. DOI:10.1108/JAAR-03-2021-0075

Ouni, Z., Ben Mansour, J., & Arfaoui, S. (2020). Board/Executive gender diversity and firm financial performance in Canada: The mediating role of environmental, social, and governance (ESG) orientation. *Sustainability (Basel)*, 12(20), 8386. DOI:10.3390/su12208386

Ouyang, Y., Zhang, Y., & Xue, X. (2022, April). The impact of board cultural diversity on company ESG performance under different risk backgrounds. In Proceedings of the 5th International *Conference on Financial Management*, Education and Social Science, Hohhot, China (pp. 9-10).

Oware, K. M., & Mallikarjunappa, T. (2021). Corporate social responsibility and debt financing of listed firms: A quantile regression approach. *Journal of Financial Reporting and Accounting*, 19(4), 615–639. DOI:10.1108/JFRA-07-2020-0202

Page, M. J., McKenzie, J. E., Bossuyt, P. M., Boutron, I., Hoffmann, T. C., Mulrow, C. D., & Moher, D. (2021). Updating guidance for reporting systematic reviews: Development of the PRISMA 2020 statement. *Journal of Clinical Epidemiology*, 134, 103–112. DOI:10.1016/j.jclinepi.2021.02.003 PMID:33577987

Paolone, F., Pozzoli, M., Chhabra, M., & Di Vaio, A. (2024). Cultural and gender diversity for ESG performance towards knowledge sharing: Empirical evidence from European banks. *Journal of Knowledge Management*, 28(11), 106–131. DOI:10.1108/JKM-05-2023-0445

Papaj, E. (2017). *Non-financial information regarding the amended accounting act bill*. https://api.semanticscholar.org/CorpusID:169622468

Papoutsi, A., & Sodhi, M. S. (2020). Does disclosure in sustainability reports indicate actual sustainability performance? *Journal of Cleaner Production*, 260, 121049. DOI:10.1016/j.jclepro.2020.121049

Parris, D. L., Dapko, J. L., Arnold, R. W., & Arnold, D. (2016). Exploring transparency: A new framework for responsible business management. *Management Decision*, 54(1), 222–247. DOI:10.1108/MD-07-2015-0279

Pastoriza, D., & Ariño, M. A. (2008, June). When agents become stewards: Introducing learning in the stewardship theory. In *1st IESE Conference, Humanizing the Firm & Management Profession*, Barcelona, IESE Business School. DOI:10.2139/ssrn.1295320

Pastor, L., Sinha, M., & Swaminathan, B. (2008). Estimating the intertemporal risk-return trade off using the implied cost of capital. *The Journal of Finance*, 63(6), 2859–2897. DOI:10.1111/j.1540-6261.2008.01415.x

Paun, D. (2018). Corporate sustainability reporting: An innovative tool for the greater good of all. *Business Horizons*, 61(6), 925–935. DOI:10.1016/j.bushor.2018.07.012

Perego, P., & Kolk, A. (2012). Multinationals' accountability on sustainability: The evolution of third-party assurance of sustainability reports. *Journal of Business Ethics*, 110(2), 173–190. DOI:10.1007/s10551-012-1420-5

Pereira, I., & Oliveira, H. C. (2020). Public Sector Sustainability in the Balanced Scorecard – A Portuguese City Council Case. In W. Strielkowski, E. Animitsa, & E. Dvoryadkina (Eds.) *1st Conference on Sustainable Development: Industrial Future of Territories (IFT 2020). E3S Web Conferences, 208*(06017). DOI:10.1051/e3sconf/202020806017

Pereira, L., Lemos, K., Monteiro, S., & Ribeiro, V. (2020), The Determinants of Non-Financial Reporting in Portuguese Listed Companies, Proceedings 35th International Business Information Management Association Conference (IBIMA)-Education Excellence and Innovation Management, 1-2 April 2020 Seville, Spain.

Perkiss, S., Bayerlein, L., & Dean, B. A. (2021). Facilitating accountability in corporate sustainability reporting through Spotlight Accounting. *Accounting, Auditing & Accountability Journal*, 34(2), 397–420. DOI:10.1108/AAAJ-08-2019-4142

Permatasari, P., & Gunawan, J. (2023). Sustainability policies for small medium enterprises: Who are the actors? *Cleaner and Responsible Consumption*, 9, 100122. DOI:10.1016/j.clrc.2023.100122

Pessarossia, P., & Weill, L. (2013). Choice of corporate debt in China: The role of state ownership. *China Economic Review*, 26, 1–16. DOI:10.1016/j.chieco.2013.03.005

Pham, C. V., Liu, S. F., & Chen, S. H. (2024). *Corporate ESG performance and intellectual capital: International evidence*. Asia Pacific Management Review. DOI:10.1016/j.apmrv.2023.12.003

Pinelli, M., & Maiolini, R. (2017). Strategies for sustainable development: Organizational motivations, stakeholders' expectations and sustainability agendas. *Sustainable Development (Bradford)*, 25(4), 288–298. DOI:10.1002/sd.1653

Pinto, I., Morais, A. I., & Quick, R. (2020). The impact of the precision of accounting standards on the expanded auditor's report in the European Union. *Journal of International Accounting, Auditing & Taxation*, 40, 100333. DOI:10.1016/j.intaccaudtax.2020.100333

Pizzi, S., Principale, S., & De Nuccio, E. (2023). Material sustainability information and reporting standards. Exploring the differences between GRI and SASB. *Meditari Accountancy Research*, 31(6), 1654–1674. DOI:10.1108/MEDAR-11-2021-1486

Pondeville, S., Swaen, V., & De Rongé, Y. (2013). Environmental management control systems: The role of contextual and strategic factors. *Management Accounting Research*, 24(4), 317–332. DOI:10.1016/j.mar.2013.06.007

Popescu, C.R.G. (2020). Sustainability assessment: Does the oecd/g20 inclusive framework for beps (base erosion and profit shifting project) put an end to disputes over the recognition and measurement of intellectual capital? *Sustainability, 12*(23), 1-22.

Porter, M., & Kramer, M. (2006). *Strategy & Society: The link between Competitive Advantage and Corporate Social Responsibility, Harvard Business Review (HBR), Estados Unidos da América*. Harvard Business Publishing.

Posadas, S., Ruiz-Blanco, S., Fernandez-Feijoo, B., & Tarquinio, L. (2022). Institutional isomorphism under the test of Non-financial Reporting Directive. Evidence from Italy and Spain. *Meditari Accountancy Research*, 31(7), 26–48. DOI:10.1108/MEDAR-02-2022-1606

Pradhan, A. K., & Nibedita, B. (2021). The determinants of corporate social responsibility: Evidence from Indian firms. *Global Business Review*, 22(3), 753–766. DOI:10.1177/0972150918814318

Pucheta-Martínez, M. C., Bel-Oms, I., & Gallego-Alvarez, I. (2022). Corporate social responsibility reporting and capital structure: Does board gender diversity mind in such association? *Corporate Social Responsibility and Environmental Management*, 1–13. DOI:10.1002/csr.2437

Pucheta-Martínez, M. C., Olcina-Sempere, G., & Lopez-Zamora, B. (2020). Female directorship on boards and corporate sustainability policies: Their effect on sustainable development. *Sustainable Development (Bradford)*, 28(1), 56–72. DOI:10.1002/sd.1965

Radu, O. M., Dragomir, V. D., & Ionescu-Feleagă, L. (2023). The Conceptual Link between Country Competitiveness and Corporate ESG Performance. *InProceedings of the International Conference on Business Excellence, 17*(1),763-775. DOI:10.2478/picbe-2023-0071

Rainey, D. (2006). *Sustainable Business Development: Inventing the Future Through Strategy, Innovation, and Leadership*. Cambridge University Press. DOI:10.1017/CBO9780511617607

Rajesh, R., & Rajendran, C. (2020). Relating environmental, social, and governance scores and sustainability performances of firms: An empirical analysis. *Business Strategy and the Environment*, 29(3), 1247–1267. DOI:10.1002/bse.2429

Ramos, D. L., Chen, S., Rabeeu, A., & Abdul Rahim, A. B. (2022). Does SDG coverage influence firm performance? *Sustainability (Basel)*, 14(9), 4870. DOI:10.3390/su14094870

Ramos, T. B., Montano, M., De Melo, J. J., Souza, M. P., de Lemos, C. C., Domingues, A. R., & Polido, A. (2015). Strategic Environmental Assessment in higher education: Portuguese and Brazilian cases. *Journal of Cleaner Production*, 106, 222–228. DOI:10.1016/j.jclepro.2014.12.088

Ramus, C. A., & Montiel, I. (2005). When are corporate environmental policies a form of green-washing? *Business & Society*, 44(4), 377–414. DOI:10.1177/0007650305278120

Refinitiv. (2020). Environmental, Social and Governance (ESG) Scores from Refinitiv. Refinitiv.

Rehman, A., Baloch, Q., & Sethi, S. (2015). Understanding the relationship between firm's corporate social responsibility and financial performance: Empirical analysis. *Abasyn Journal of Social Sciences*, 8(1), 98–107.

Reis, T. (2018). Stakeholder: O que é e qual sua importância em uma empresa? Suno. Disponível em: https://www.suno.com.br/artigos/stakeholder/. Acesso em: 12 de junho de 2022.

Ren, S., Hu, Y., Zheng, J., & Wang, Y. (2020). Emissions trading and firm innovation: Evidence from a natural experiment in China. *Technological Forecasting and Social Change*, 155, 119989. DOI:10.1016/j.techfore.2020.119989

Resolution nº 2014/4.327, from 25 April, https://www.bcb.gov.br/pre/normativos/res/2014/pdf/res_4327_v1_O.pdf

Reverte, C. (2012). The impact of better corporate social responsibility disclosure on the cost of equity capital. *Corporate Social Responsibility and Environmental Management*, 19(5), 253–272. DOI:10.1002/csr.273

Reverte, C. (2016). Corporate social responsibility disclosure and market valuation: Evidence from Spanish listed firms. *Review of Managerial Science*, 10(2), 411–435. DOI:10.1007/s11846-014-0151-7

Ribeiro, V. P., Aibar-Guzman, B., Aibar-Guzmán, C., & Monteiro, S. (2016). Determinants of environmental accounting and reporting practices in Portuguese local entities. *Corporate Communications*, 21(3), 352–370. DOI:10.1108/CCIJ-11-2015-0071

Rizzato, F., Tonelli, A., Fiandrino, S., & Devalle, A. (2024). Analysing SDG disclosure and its impact on integrated thinking and reporting. *Meditari Accountancy Research*, 32(3), 803–831. DOI:10.1108/MEDAR-07-2022-1751

Robalo, R., & Patrocínio, W. (2019). Disclosure of corporate social responsibility on the websites of Portuguese foundations. In A. Ferreira, R. Marques, G. Azevedo, H. Inácio, & C. Santos (Eds.), *Modernisation and accountability in the social economy sector* (pp. 176-195). DOI:10.4018/978-1-5225-8482-7.ch010

Roberts, J. (1991). The possibilities of accountability. *Accounting, Organizations and Society*, 16(4), 355–368. DOI:10.1016/0361-3682(91)90027-C

Roberts, J. (2001). Trust and control in Anglo-American systems of corporate governance: The individualizing and socializing effects of processes of accountability. *Human Relations*, 54(12), 1547–1572. DOI:10.1177/00187267015412001

Roberts, J., & Scapens, R. (1985). Accounting systems and systems of accountability—Understanding accounting practices in their organisational contexts. *Accounting, Organizations and Society*, 10(4), 443–456. DOI:10.1016/0361-3682(85)90005-4

Rodrigue, M., & Picard, C. F. (2022). Non-accountants and Accounting: On the Emancipatory Mobilization of Accounting by Sustainability Managers. *European Accounting Review*, 32(5), 1217–1245. DOI:10.1080/09638180.2022.2052921

Rodríguez, M. D., Pérez, M. D., & Godoy, M. L. (2011). Determining factors in online transparency of NGOs: A Spanish case study. *Voluntas*, 23(3), 661–683. DOI:10.1007/s11266-011-9229-x

Romero, S., Ruiz, S., & Fernandez-Feijoo, B. (2019). Sustainability Reporting and stakeholder engagement in Spain: Different instruments, different quality. *Business Strategy and the Environment*, 28(1), 221–232. DOI:10.1002/bse.2251

Romolini, A., Fissi, S., & Gori, E. (2014). Scoring CSR reporting in listed companies–Evidence from Italian best practices. *Corporate Social Responsibility and Environmental Management*, 21(2), 65–81. DOI:10.1002/csr.1299

Rosati, F., & Faria, L. G. (2019). Addressing the SDGs in sustainability reports: The relationship with institutional factors. *Journal of Cleaner Production*, 215, 1312–1326. DOI:10.1016/j.jclepro.2018.12.107

Rösner, T., & Bredebach, C. (2022). Integrating the United Nations sustainable development goals into organizational strategy: A sustainability balanced scorecard approach using ANP and TOPSIS. *Journal of Sustainability Outreach*, 3(1), 1–18. DOI:10.37357/1068/jso/3.1.01

Rossi, G., Leardini, C., & Landi, S. (2020). The more you know, the more you give: Influence of online disclosure on European community foundations' donations. *Nonprofit Management & Leadership*, 31(1), 81–101. DOI:10.1002/nml.21412

Rousseau, L. M., & Zehms, K. M. (2020). Audit partner style in key audit matter reporting decisions. SSRN *Electronic Journal*. http://dx.doi.org/DOI:10.2139/ssrn.3625651

Saeidi, S. P., Sofian, S., Saeidi, P., Saeidi, S. P., & Saaeidi, S. A. (2015). How does corporate social responsibility contribute to firm financial performance? The mediating role of competitive advantage, reputation, and customer satisfaction. *Journal of Business Research*, 68(2), 341–350. DOI:10.1016/j.jbusres.2014.06.024

Salazar, J., Husted, B. W., & Biehl, M. (2012). Thoughts on the evaluation of corporate social performance through projects. *Journal of Business Ethics*, 105(2), 175–186. DOI:10.1007/s10551-011-0957-z

Salinas-Ríos, K., & García López, A. J. (2022). Bibliometrics, a useful tool within the field of research. *Journal of Basic and Applied Psychology Research*, 3(6), 9–16. DOI:10.29057/jbapr.v3i6.6829

Santos, D. (2016). Stakeholders e o Desempenho Social Corporativo De Entidades Desportivas Do Terceiro Setor: Proposta De Mensuração (Dissertação de Mestrado, Universidade Nove de Julho).

Santos, L. M. S. (2022). Influência da Discrição Gerencial dos CEOs no Desempenho Social Corporativo: Uma Análise nas Empresas Listadas na B3 (Tese de Doutorado, Universidade Federal da Paraíba).

Savitz, A. W., & Weber, K. (2007). The sustainability sweet spot. *Environmental Quality Management*, 17(2), 17–28. DOI:10.1002/tqem.20161

Saxton, G. D., & Guo, C. (2009). Accountability online: Understanding the web-based accountability practices of nonprofit organisations. *Nonprofit and Voluntary Sector Quarterly*, 40(2), 270–295. DOI:10.1177/0899764009341086

Schiehll, E., & Kolahgar, S. (2021). Financial materiality in the informativeness of sustainability reporting. *Business Strategy and the Environment*, 30(2), 840–855. DOI:10.1002/bse.2657

Schleich, M. V. (2022). What are the human resources policies and practices most used by companies with the best ESG ratios in Brazil? *RAE*, 62(5), e2021–e0370. DOI:10.1590/s0034-759020220511x

Schwartz, M. S. (2013). Developing and sustaining an ethical corporate culture: The core elements. *Business Horizons*, 56(1), 39–50. DOI:10.1016/j.bushor.2012.09.002

Sepúlveda-Alzate, Y. M., García-Benau, M. A., & Gómez-Villegas, M. (2022). Materiality assessment: The case of Latin American listed companies. *Sustainability Accounting. Management and Policy Journal*, 13(1), 88–113.

Setia, N., Abhayawansa, S., Joshi, M., & Wasantha Pathiranage, N. (2024). *Shifting perspectives: unveiling the dual nature of sustainability materiality in integrated reports*. Meditari Accountancy Research. DOI:10.1108/MEDAR-08-2023-2128

Shahab, Y., Ntim, C. G., Chen, Y., Ullah, F., Li, H. X., & Ye, Z. (2020). Chief executive officer attributes, sustainable performance, environmental performance, and environmental reporting: New insights from upper echelons perspective. *Business Strategy and the Environment*, 29(1), 1–16. DOI:10.1002/bse.2345

Shahbaz, M., Karaman, A. S., Kilic, M., & Uyar, A. (2020). Board attributes, CSR engagement, and corporate performance: What is the nexus in the energy sector? *Energy Policy*, 143, 111582. DOI:10.1016/j.enpol.2020.111582

Shahzad, F., Baig, M. H., Rehman, I. U., Saeed, A., & Asim, G. A. (2022). Does intellectual capital efficiency explain corporate social responsibility engagement-firm performance relationship? Evidence from environmental, social and governance performance of US listed firms. *Borsa Istanbul Review*, 22(2), 295–305. DOI:10.1016/j.bir.2021.05.003

Shahzad, M., Qu, Y., Javed, S. A., Zafar, A. U., & Rehman, S. U. (2020). Relation of environment sustainability to CSR and green innovation: A case of Pakistani manufacturing industry. *Journal of Cleaner Production*, 253, 119938. DOI:10.1016/j.jclepro.2019.119938

Shannon, C. E., & Weaver, W. (1949). *The Mathematical Theory of Communication*. University of Illinois Press.

Sharfman, M., & Fernando, C. (2008). Environmental risk management and the cost of capital. *Strategic Management Journal*, 29(6), 569–592. DOI:10.1002/smj.678

Shen, H., Lin, H., Han, W., & Wu, H. (2023). ESG in China: A review of practice and research, and future research avenues. *China Journal of Accounting Research*, 100325(4). Advance online publication. DOI:10.1016/j.cjar.2023.100325

Shields, D. J., Šolar, S. V., & Martin, W. E. (2002). The role of values and objectives in communicating indicators of sustainability. *Ecological Indicators*, 2(1-2), 149–160. DOI:10.1016/S1470-160X(02)00042-0

Shmueli, G., Ray, S., Estrada, J. M. V., & Chatla, S. B. (2016). The elephant in the room: Predictive performance of PLS models. *Journal of Business Research*, 69(10), 4552–4564. DOI:10.1016/j.jbusres.2016.03.049

Shnayder, L., van Rijnsoever, F. J., & Hekkert, M. P. (2016). Motivations for Corporate Social Responsibility in the packaged food industry: An institutional and stakeholder management perspective. *Journal of Cleaner Production*, 122, 212–227. DOI:10.1016/j.jclepro.2016.02.030

Shu, P., & Chiang, S. (2020). The impact of corporate governance on corporate social performance: Cases from listed firms in Taiwan. *Pacific-Basin Finance Journal*, 61, 1–20. DOI:10.1016/j.pacfin.2020.101332

Sierra-García, L., Gambetta, N., García-Benau, M. A., & Orta-Pérez, M. (2019). Understanding the determinants of the magnitude of entity-level risk and account-level risk key audit matters: The case of the United Kingdom. *The British Accounting Review*, 51(3), 227–240. DOI:10.1016/j.bar.2019.02.004

Silva, G. M., Styles, C., & Lages, L. F. (2017). Breakthrough innovation in international business: The impact of tech-innovation and market-innovation on performance. *International Business Review*, 26(2), 391–404. DOI:10.1016/j.ibusrev.2016.10.001

Simons, R. (1995). Control in an age of empowerment. *Harvard Business Review*, 73(2), 80–88.

Sinclair, A. (1995). The chameleon of accountability: Forms and discourses. *Accounting, Organizations and Society*, 20(2-3), 219–237. DOI:10.1016/0361-3682(93)E0003-Y

Singh, K., & Misra, M. (2021). Linking Corporate Social Responsibility (CSR) and Organizational Performance: The Moderating Effect of Corporate Reputation. *Research in Management and Business Economics*, 27.

Sirois, L. P., Bédard, J., & Bera, P. (2018). The informational value of key audit matters in the auditor's report: Evidence from an eye-tracking study. *Accounting Horizons*, 32(2), 141–162. DOI:10.2308/acch-52047

Skouloudis, A., Evangelinos, K., & Kourmousis, F. (2010). Assessing non-financial reports according to the Global Reporting Initiative guidelines: Evidence from Greece. *Journal of Cleaner Production*, 18(5), 426–438. DOI:10.1016/j.jclepro.2009.11.015

Slack, R., & Shrives, P. (2008). Social disclosure and legitimacy in Premier League football clubs: The first ten years. *Journal of Applied Accounting Research*, 9(1), 17–28. DOI:10.1108/09675420810886105

Stahlschmidt, S., & Stephen, D. (2022). From indexation policies through citation networks to normalized citation impacts: Web of Science, Scopus, and Dimensions as varying resonance chambers. *Scientometrics*, 127(5), 2413–2431. DOI:10.1007/s11192-022-04309-6

Steurer, R., Martinuzzi, A., & Margula, S. (2018). Public policies on CSR in Europe: Themes, instruments, and regional differences. *Corporate Social Responsibility and Environmental Management*, 19(4), 206–227. DOI:10.1002/csr.264

Stiles, P. (2001). The impact of the board on strategy: An empirical examination. *Journal of Management Studies*, 38(5), 627–650. DOI:10.1111/1467-6486.00252

Stocker, F., & Mascena, K. M. C. (2019). Orientação e gestão para stakeholders no processo de decisão organizacional. *R.G.Secr.GESEC*, 10(1), 167–191. DOI:10.7769/gesec.v10i1.864

Stoyanova, T. (2019). CSR strategies applied in terms of circular economy. *Economic Alternatives*, 2, 263–274.

Street, D. L., & Gordon, E. A. (2023). An interview with IASB Chair Dr. Andreas Barckow. *Journal of International Financial Management & Accounting*, 34(2), 358–377. DOI:10.1111/jifm.12171

Stuart, S. (2017), Brasil Board Index 2017, available at: https://www.spencerstuart.com/-/media/pdf%20files/research%20and%20insight%20pdfs/bi-brazil-2017.pdf

Tang, P., Wang, C., Jiang, Q., Liu, X., & Wang, J. (2023). Symbol or substance? Environmental regulations and corporate environmental actions decoupling. *Journal of Environmental Management*, 346, 118950. DOI:10.1016/j.jenvman.2023.118950 PMID:37696070

Tashakkori, A., & Teddlie, C. (2002). Handbook of mixed methods in social & behavioural research. Sage Publications.

Tilling, M. (2004). *Refinements to legitimacy theory in social and environmental accounting*. Flinders University.

Tiron-Tudor, A., Hurghis, R., Lacurezeanu, R., & Podoaba, L. (2020). The Level of European Companies' Integrated Reports Alignment to the< IR> Framework: The Role of Boards' Characteristics. *Sustainability (Basel)*, 12(21), 8777. DOI:10.3390/su12218777

Tolmie, C. R., Lehnert, K., & Zhao, H. (2020). Formal and informal institutional pressures on corporate social responsibility: A cross-country analysis. *Corporate Social Responsibility and Environmental Management*, 27(2), 786–802. DOI:10.1002/csr.1844

Torelli, R., Balluchi, F., & Furlotti, K. (2020). The materiality assessment and stakeholder engagement: A content analysis of sustainability reports. *Corporate Social Responsibility and Environmental Management*, 27(2), 470–484. DOI:10.1002/csr.1813

Tremblay-Boire, J., & Prakash, A. (2014). Accountability.org: Online disclosures by U.S. nonprofits. *Voluntas*, 26(2), 693–719. DOI:10.1007/s11266-014-9452-3

Trezevant, R. (1992). Debt financing and tax status: Tests of the substitution effect and the tax exhaustion hypothesis using firms' responses to the economic recovery tax act of 1981. *The Journal of Finance*, 47(4), 1557–1568. DOI:10.1111/j.1540-6261.1992.tb04670.x

Tudor, A., Silvia, N., Ştefănescu, C., & Zanellato, G. (2019). Encompassing Non-Financial Reporting in a Coercive Framework for Enhancing Social Responsibility: Romanian Listed Companies Case. *Amfiteatru Economic*, 21(52), 590. DOI:10.24818/EA/2019/52/590

Ugoani, J. (2019). Business ethics and its effect on organizational sustainability. *Global Journal of Social Sciences Studies*, 5(2), 119–131. DOI:10.20448/807.5.2.119.131

UNDP. (n.d.). *The SDGS in Action*. Sustainable Development Goals. https://www.undp.org/es/sustainable-development-goals

Unerman, J. (2000). Methodological issues – reflections on quantification in corporate social reporting content analysis. *Accounting, Auditing & Accountability Journal*, 13(5), 667–681. DOI:10.1108/09513570010353756

Union of Portuguese Mercies. (2015). *Statutes of the Union of Portuguese Mercies*. Union of Portuguese Mercies. https://cdn.ump.pt/files/files/Estatutos.pdf

Union of Portuguese Mercies. (2018). *Presentation of the UPM*. Retrieved March 1, 2021, from Union of Portuguese Mercies. https://www.ump.pt/Home/uniao/apresentacao/

United Nations (UN). (2015). *Transforming Our World: The 2030 Agenda for Sustainable Development*. United Nations.

United Nations. (2015). *SDG Compass. The guide for business action on the SDGs*. https://sdgcompass.org/wp-content/uploads/2015/12/019104_SDG_Compass_Guide_2015.pdf

United Nations. (2015). Transforming Our World: The 2030 Agenda for Sustainable Development. Available online: https://www.undp.org/ukraine/publications/transforming-our-world-2030-agenda-sustainable-development?utm _ source=EN&utm_medium=GSR&utm_content=US_UNDP_PaidSearch_Brand_English&utm_campaign=CENTRAL&c_ src=CENTRAL&c_src2=GS-R&gclid=EAIaIQobChMIvuLS5s_a_AIVBKuWCh2dgg8tEAAYASAAEgLW-g_D_BwE

United Nations. (2024). *Tier Classification for Global SDG Indicators*. Sustainable Development Goals. https://unstats.un.org/sdgs/iaeg-sdgs/tier-classification/

Uyar, A., Kuzey, C., Kilic, M., & Karaman, A. S. (2021). Board structure, financial performance, corporate social responsibility performance, CSR committee, and CEO duality: Disentangling the connection in healthcare. *Corporate Social Responsibility and Environmental Management*, 28(6), 1730–1748. DOI:10.1002/csr.2141

Valiente, J. M. A., Ayerbe, C. G., & Figueras, M. S. (2012). Social responsibility practices and evaluation of corporate social performance. *Journal of Cleaner Production*, 35, 25–38. DOI:10.1016/j.jclepro.2012.05.002

Vallet-Bellmunt, T., Fuertes-Fuertes, I., & Flor, M. L. (2023). Reporting Sustainable Development Goal 12 in the Spanish food retail industry. An analysis based on Global Reporting Initiative performance indicators. *Corporate Social Responsibility and Environmental Management*, 30(2), 695–707. DOI:10.1002/csr.2382

Van Hoang, T. H., Przychodzen, W., Przychodzen, J., & Segbotangni, E. A. (2021). Environmental transparency and performance: Does the corporate governance matter? *Environmental and Sustainability Indicators*, 10, 100123. DOI:10.1016/j.indic.2021.100123

Van Puyvelde, S., Caers, R., Du Bois, C., & Jegers, M. (2013). Agency problems between managers and employees in nonprofit organizations: A discrete choice experiment. *Nonprofit Management & Leadership*, 24(1), 63–85. DOI:10.1002/nml.21081

van Tulder, R., & Lucht, L. (2019). Reversing materiality: from a reactive matrix to a proactive SDG agenda. *Innovation for sustainability: Business transformations towards a better world*, 271-289.

Vanstraelen, A., Schelleman, C., Meuwissen, R., & Hofmann, I. (2012). The audit reporting debate: Seemingly intractable problems and feasible solutions. *European Accounting Review*, 21(2), 193–215. DOI:10.1080/09638180.2012.687506

Vaz, N., Fernandez-Feijoo, B., & Ruiz, S. (2016). Integrated reporting: An international overview. *Business Ethics (Oxford, England)*, 25(4), 577–591. DOI:10.1111/beer.12125

Velte, P. (2019). Associations between the Financial and Industry Expertise of Audit Committee Members and Key Audit Matters within Related Audit Reports. *Journal of Applied Accounting Research*, 21(1), 185–200. DOI:10.1108/JAAR-10-2018-0163

Velte, P. (2020). Does CEO power moderate the link between ESG performance and financial performance? A focus on the German two-tier system. *Management Research Review*, 43(5), 497–520. DOI:10.1108/MRR-04-2019-0182

Verwijmeren, P., & Derwall, J. (2010). Employee well-being, firm leverage, and bankruptcy risk. *Journal of Banking & Finance*, 34(5), 956–964. DOI:10.1016/j.jbankfin.2009.10.006

Vieira, E. S., & Gomes, J. A. N. F. (2009). A comparison of Scopus and Web of Science for a typical university. *Scientometrics*, 81(2), 587–600. DOI:10.1007/s11192-009-2178-0

Vildåsen, S. S. (2018). Corporate sustainability in practice: An exploratory study of the sustainable development goals (SDGs). *Business Strategy & Development*, 1(4), 256–264. DOI:10.1002/bsd2.35

Villarón-Peramato, Ó., Martínez-Ferrero, J., & García-Sánchez, I.-M. (2018). CSR as entrenchment strategy and capital structure: Corporate governance and investor protection as complementary and substitutive factors. *Review of Managerial Science*, 12(1), 27–64. DOI:10.1007/s11846-016-0212-1

Villiers, C., & Sharma, U. (2020). A critical reflection on the future of financial, intellectual capital, sustainability and integrated reporting. *Critical Perspectives on Accounting*, 70, 101999. DOI:10.1016/j.cpa.2017.05.003

Wang, L., Liu, B., Zhu, Y., Yang, M., Du, C., Han, Z., & Cao, C. (2022). General metal–organic framework-derived strategy to synthesize yolk-shell carbon-encapsulated nickelic spheres for sodium-ion batteries. *Journal of Colloid and Interface Science*, 613, 23–34. DOI:10.1016/j.jcis.2021.12.157 PMID:35032774

Wartick, S., & Cochran, P. (1985). The evolution of the corporate social performance model. *Academy of Management Review*, 10(4), 758–769. DOI:10.2307/258044

Wasiuzzaman, S., & Subramaniam, V. (2023). Board gender diversity and environmental, social and governance (ESG) disclosure: Is it different for developed and developing nations? *Corporate Social Responsibility and Environmental Management*, 30(5), 2145–2165. Advance online publication. DOI:10.1002/csr.2475

Waters, R. D. (2007). Nonprofit organisations' use of the internet: A content analysis of communication trends on the internet sites of the Philanthropy 400. *Nonprofit Management & Leadership*, 18(1), 59–76. DOI:10.1002/nml.171

Weiss, J. W. (2021). *Business ethics: A stakeholder and issues management approach*. Berrett-Koehler Publishers.

Wijethilake, C., & Ekanayake, A. (2018). Proactive strategic responses to corporate sustainability pressures: a sustainability control system framework. In *Advances in Management Accounting* (pp. 129–173). Emerald Publishing Limited. DOI:10.1108/S1474-787120180000030006

Williams, B. (2015). Reporting on sustainability by Australian Councils - A Communication Perspective. *Asian Review of Accounting*, 23(2), 186–203. DOI:10.1108/ARA-12-2013-0079

Wood, D. J. (1991). Corporate social performance revisited. *Academy of Management Review*, 16(4), 691–718. DOI:10.2307/258977

Wu, M., Shen, C., & Chen, T. (2016). Application of multi-level matching between financial performance and corporate social responsibility in the banking industry. *Review of Quantitative Finance and Accounting*, 49(1), 29–63. DOI:10.1007/s11156-016-0582-0

Wu, Q., Furuoka, F., & Lau, S. C. (2022). Corporate social responsibility and board gender diversity: A meta-analysis. *Management Research Review*, 45(7), 956–983. DOI:10.1108/MRR-03-2021-0236

Xu, H., Xu, X., & Yu, J. (2021). The impact of mandatory CSR disclosure on the cost of debt financing: Evidence from China. *Emerging Markets Finance & Trade*, 57(8), 2191–2205. DOI:10.1080/1540496X.2019.1657401

Xu, L. D., Xu, E. L., & Li, L. (2018). Industry 4.0: State of the art and future trends. *International Journal of Production Research*, 56(8), 2941–2962. DOI:10.1080/00207543.2018.1444806

Xu, S., Liu, D., & Huang, J. (2015). Corporate social responsibility, the cost of equity capital and ownership structure: An analysis of Chinese listed firms. *Australian Journal of Management*, 40(2), 245–276. DOI:10.1177/0312896213517894

Yalcin, N. (2022). Content analysis of audit reports in stock indices EURONEXT 100 vs BIST 100. *Istanbul Business Research*, 51(2), 433–458. DOI:10.26650/ibr.2022.51.938151

Yang, S., He, F., Zhu, Q., & Li, S. (2018). How does corporate social responsibility change capital structure? *Asia-Pacific Journal of Accounting & Economics*, 25(3-4), 352–387. DOI:10.1080/16081625.2017.1354710

Yasser, Q. R., Al Mamun, A., & Ahmed, I. (2017). Corporate social responsibility and gender diversity: Insights from Asia Pacific. *Corporate Social Responsibility and Environmental Management*, 24(3), 210–221. DOI:10.1002/csr.1400

Yates, D., Gebreiter, F., & Lowe, A. (2019). The internal accountability dynamic of UK service clubs: Towards (more) intelligent accountability? *Accounting Forum*, 42(1), 161–192. DOI:10.1080/01559982.2019.1589907

Yeh, C.-C., Lin, F., Wang, T.-S., & Wu, C.-M. (2020). Does corporate social responsibility affect cost of capital in China? *Asia Pacific Management Review*, 25(1), 1–12. DOI:10.1016/j.apmrv.2019.04.001

Ye, K., & Zhang, R. (2011). Do lenders value corporate social responsibility? Evidence from China. *Journal of Business Ethics*, 104(2), 197–206. DOI:10.1007/s10551-011-0898-6

Ye, M., Wang, H., & Lu, W. (2021). Opening the "black box" between corporate social responsibility and financial performance: From a critical review on moderators and mediators to an integrated framework. *Journal of Cleaner Production*, 313, 1–10. DOI:10.1016/j.jclepro.2021.127919

Yin, R. K. (2011). *Applications of case study research*. sage.

Yoo, S., & Managi, S. (2022). Disclosure or action: Evaluating ESG behavior towards financial performance. *Finance Research Letters*, 44, 102108. DOI:10.1016/j.frl.2021.102108

Young, S., & Marais, M. (2012). A Multi Level Perspective of CSR Reporting: The Implications of National Institutions and Industry Risk Characteristics. *Corporate Governance*, 20(5), 432–450. DOI:10.1111/j.1467-8683.2012.00926.x

Zampone, G., Nicolò, G., Sannino, G., & De Iorio, S. (2024). Gender diversity and SDG disclosure: The mediating role of the sustainability committee. *Journal of Applied Accounting Research*, 25(1), 171–193. DOI:10.1108/JAAR-06-2022-0151

Zeisel, S. (2020). Is sustainability a moving target? A methodology for measuring CSR dynamics. *Corporate Social Responsibility and Environmental Management*, 27(1), 283–296. DOI:10.1002/csr.1805

Zeng, S. X., Xu, X. D., Dong, Z. Y., & Tam, V. W. (2010). Towards corporate environmental information disclosure: An empirical study in China. *Journal of Cleaner Production*, 18(12), 1142–1148. DOI:10.1016/j.jclepro.2010.04.005

Zerbini, F. (2017). CSR initiatives as market signals: A review and research agenda. *Journal of Business Ethics*, 146(1), 1–23. DOI:10.1007/s10551-015-2922-8

Zhang, P. F., & Shailer, G. (2021). Changes in audit effort and changes in auditors' disclosures of risks of material misstatement. *The British Accounting Review*, 53(3), 100970. DOI:10.1016/j.bar.2020.100970

Zheng, Z., Li, J., Ren, X., & Guo, J. M. (2023). Does corporate ESG create value? New evidence from M&As in China. *Pacific-Basin Finance Journal*, 77, 101916. DOI:10.1016/j.pacfin.2022.101916

Zhou, D., Saeed, U. F., & Agyemang, A. O. (2024). Assessing the Role of Sustainability Disclosure on Firms' Financial Performance: Evidence from the Energy Sector of Belt and Road Initiative Countries. *Sustainability (Basel)*, 16(2), 930. DOI:10.3390/su16020930

Zhou, G., Liu, L., & Luo, S. (2022). Sustainable development, ESG performance and company market value: Mediating effect of financial performance. *Business Strategy and the Environment*, 31(7), 3371–3387. DOI:10.1002/bse.3089

Zhou, H., Li, G., & Lin, W. (2016). Corporate social responsibility and credit spreads: An empirical study in Chinese context. *Annals of Economics and Finance*, 17(1), 79–103.

Zwetsloot, G. I. (2003). From management systems to corporate social responsibility. *Journal of Business Ethics*, 44(2), 201–208. DOI:10.1023/A:1023303917699

About the Contributors

Albertina Paula Moreira Monteiro holds a PhD in Economics and Business, specialising in accounting (University of Santiago de Compostela) and a PhD in Marketing and Strategy (University of Minho). Coordinating Professor at Porto Accounting and Business School of the Polytechnic Institute of Porto (ISCAP.IPP) in the scientific area of Accounting. Researcher at Centre for Organisational and Social Studies of the Polytechnic Institute of Porto (CEOS.PP) and CICF (Polytechnic Institute of Cávado and Ave) and OSEAN (University of Madeira). Author of several publications (papers and book chapters) indexed to the main bibliographic databases.

Ana Pinto Borges holds a PhD in Economics, Faculty of Economics, University of Porto from 2009. Since 2010 She is Coordinating Professor at ISAG - European Business School specializing on the areas of Economics, Management, and Finance, and since 2015 Coordinator of the Master's Degree in Business Management and President of the Pedagogical Council of ISAG. She is Scientific Coordinator of Research Centre in Business Sciences and Tourism (CICET – FCVC) since 2021 and coordinated the ISAG Research Centre (NIDISAG) between 2015 and 2021. Since 2018, she is researcher of the Centre for Research in Organizations, Markets and Industrial Management (COMEGI). She supervised various PhD theses and master's theses. She published more than 200 publications (indexed in Scopus/ WoS databases) in journals/book chapters/proceedings and various books (indexed in Scopus). She is associate editor at the Eurasian Business Review and editor and one of the founding members of the European Journal of Applied Business and Management (EJABM). She founded, integrated the organizer and scientific committees and did the co-editor of the proceedings of International Conference in Applied Business and Management (ICABM), International Workshop in Tourism and Hospitality Management (IWTHM), and in Accounting and Taxation (IWAT). All these academic events have been indexed or are in evaluation by WoS and by EBSCO, among others. Furthermore, she is the coordinator and co-author of several applied projects financed by external entities (companies, municipalities, among others). She is Economist at the Portuguese Health Regulatory Authority since 2010 with the main function of carrying out sectoral studies and issuing opinions in the scope of access, quality and competition. Member of the Associação Portuguesa de Economia da Saúde (since 2005).

Elvira Vieira holds a PhD in Applied Economics, University of Santiago de Compostela. Professor, member of the Scientific Council at Institute of Marketing Management between 2007-2009 and Invited Professor at Minho University between 2009-2012. Professor at Polytechnic Institute of Viana do Castelo and Coordinating Professor at ISAG - European Business School since 2009. General Director at ISAG - European Business School since 2012, researcher in UNIAG, scientific coordinator of NIDISAG Research Center (between 2014 - 2021) and of Center in Business Sciences and Tourism (CICET - FCVC) since 2021. Author of several publications (papers and book chapters) indexed to the main bibliographic databases. Editor and one of the founding members of the European Journal of Applied Business and Management (EJABM). 2009 1st prize winner for research of the "Catedra da Euroregión Galicia – Norte of Portugal" and President of the European Grouping of Territorial Cooperation Galicia – North of Portugal, from 2010-2012.

* * *

Catarina Cepeda: Professor at ISCAP-IPP and UTAD, PhD student at University of Minho, researcher at CEOS-PP and COMEGI and certified accountant. Her research interests are Financial Accounting, Corporate Social Responsibility, Accounting Information System, Digital Accounting and Decision-Making. She has published at international conferences and in international scientific journals such as RBGN, Accounting, Systems, Journal of Entrepreneurship and Sustainability Issues and Universal Journal of Accounting and Finance. Email: catarinac@utad.pt

Amélia Ferreira da Silva is a Coordinating Professor at Porto Accounting and Business School, Polytechnic University of Porto. She has taught Management Accounting since 2000. She holds a PhD in Accounting from the University of Vigo, Spain. Her research interests are in accounting and management control in healthcare, accountability in public organizations, business failure prediction, and digital transformation in accounting. She supervised several Master´s dissertations and PhD's thesis. She has participated in several projects, namely STAMP (2020-1-UK01-KA203-0 KA203-080299), DIPCAT (2018-1-UK01-KA203-048027), ASSET (2023-1-IT02-KA220-HED-000156791) and GAMSTRA - Gamification Strategies for Management Skills. She has also several scientific publications and collaborations as a peer reviewer in index journals. She was head of CEOS. PP – Centre for Organizational and Social Studies of Porto Polytechnic, by FCT – Fundação para Ciência e Tecnologia. Since 2022, she has been the coordinator of the accounting department at Porto Accounting and Business School. Details about her research profile can be found in Scopus Author ID: 57191034656; Researcher ID: A-9163-2017; or Google Scholar.

Leanne Johnstone is a senior lecturer in Business Administration at Örebro University, Sweden. She completed her PhD at the same institution in 2022 on sustainability control, within the Centre for Empirical Research on Organisational Control. Her research interests span both accounting and marketing fields, including a variety of topics with a sustainability focus such as sustainable control and integration in organisations, ISO 14001 standardisation and certification, influencer marketing for sustainability, circular economy and product-service systems, and strategic networks for sustainability initiatives, among others. Her current research project is focused on biodiversity accounting and control. She currently serves as a reviewer for various business journals and teaches graduate level courses on environmental management and sustainability supply networks.

Kátia Lemos is an associate professor at the Management School of the Polytechnic University of Cávado and Ave (Portugal). PhD in Business sciences from Santiago de Compostela University. Member of Research Center on Accounting and Taxation. Her main research areas are financial accounting and financial and non-financial reporting, Accounting for financial instruments.

Natália Lemos holds a Master's degree in Management from the Polytechnic University of Cávado and Ave (IPCA), Portugal; she was a research fellow in the area of management at the Applied Artificial Intelligence Laboratoty (2Ai), and nowadays she is a research fellow in the area of management at the Research Center for Accounting and Taxation (CICF), both of the Polytechnic University of Cávado and Ave (IPCA).

Mara Madaleno is Associate Professor, DEGEIT, University of Aveiro. She is researcher at the GOVCOPP and vice-coordinator of a research group. She has a PhD in Economics from the University Nova, Lisbon. Her research topics are economics, corporate finance, capital markets, energy, sustainable finance.

Ilaria Martino is a ph.D student in Management at the Department of Economics, Management, Institutions of the University of Naples "Federico II". Her main area of interest and research are international accounting standard, materiality judgments and financial reporting decisions.

Patrícia Quesado is a coordinator professor at the Management School of the Polytechnic University of Cávado and Ave (Portugal). PhD in Business Sciences from Santiago de Compostela University. Member of Research Center on Accounting and Taxation. Her main research areas are management accounting, management control and cost accounting.

Rui Costa Robalo holds a PhD in Business Sciences by Faculty of Economics at University of Porto (Portugal). He is associate professor at the School of Management and Technology of the Polytechnic Institute of Santarém (Portugal) and integrated member of the Center for Research in Accounting and Taxation at IPCA, located in Barcelos (Portugal). His teaching has covered various accounting subjects, namely management accounting, management control, financial accounting, nonfinancial reporting, and research methods in accounting and finance. He has supervised several internships of graduate and master students. He has also supervised research from master students, which has covered several topics. He has published research in national and international accounting journals and books. His current research focus on trends and developments in the accounting profession, mainly related with the roles of accountants in digitalization processes of accounting tasks and in nonfiancial reporting practices.

Vanda Roque is an associate professor in the School of Management of the Polytechnic University of Cavado and Ave, in Barcelos, Portugal. She has been teaching at this school for more than 20 years, lecturing Financial Mathematics, Corporate Finance and Derivatives and Risk Management. She has a PhD in Business Sciences from the University of Minho (2013) and her main areas of interest are international portfolio investment and sustainable investment. She is a contributing member of UNIAG – Applied Management Research Unit.

Lívia Santos is a PhD in Accounting Sciences from the Postgraduate Program in Accounting Sciences at the Federal University of Paraíba. Professor of Accounting Sciences.

Sara Serra completed her PhD in Accounting on 02/10/2014 from the University of Minho, a Master's in Accounting and Auditing on 03/17/2008, and a Degree in Management in 2003. She has been an Adjunct Professor at the Higher School of Management of the Polytechnic University of Cávado and Ave (IPCA) since 2003. She is the director of the Masters in Auditing and is responsible for the auditing disciplinary area. He belongs to the Scientific Technical Council of the Higher School of Management of the IPCA, the Advisory Council of the IPCA and several committees of the Higher School of Management of the IPCA. She has published several papers in specialized journals and book chapters. She supervised 31 master's dissertations and over 40 bachelor's internship reports. She received seven awards. She participated as a researcher in 2 projects at the Center for Research in Accounting and Taxation, where she is an integrated member. She participated in the scientific committee of several international conferences and is also a reviewer for many international journals in her area of research and auditing.

Adriana Silva is an Adjunct Professor in Management Accounting at the Polytechnic Institute of Santarém. Integrated member researcher of the CICF, School of Management, IPCA, Barcelos, Portugal. Member researcher of the Laboratory of Critical and Interpretive Studies in Accounting (LECIC) at the Federal University of Pará (UFPA). Associated Editor of journal "Revista Contemporânea de Economia e Gestão". PhD in Accounting from the University of Minho. Research interest focuses on critical and interpretative accounting and accounting history, specifically on themes that give prominence to subordinated voices.

Lurdes Silva is an associate professor at the Management School of the Polytechnic University of Cávado and Ave (Portugal). PhD in Business Sciences from Vigo University. Member of Research Center on Accounting and Taxation. Her main research areas are financial accounting and financial and non-financial reporting, Intellectual Capital, Intangible Assets.

Flavio Spagnuolo is Postdoctoral fellow in Accounting at the Department of Economics, Management, Institutions of the University of Naples "Federico II". He took a PhD in Management, and his main area of interest and research are International accounting standards, ESG dynamics, financial analysis and financial reporting in the context of mergers and acquisitions.

Elisabete S. Vieira is Principal Coordinator Professor, ISCA-UA, University of Aveiro. She is researcher at the Research Unit on Governance, Competitiveness and Public Policies (GOVCOPP). She has a PhD. in Finance from the ISCTE, Lisbon. Her research topics include corporate finance, corporate behavior finance, corporate governance and sustainable finance.

Corneliu Zabolotnic holds a master's degree in accounting and finance from the School of Management and Technology of the Polytechnic Institute of Santarém in Portugal. He has research interests in the issue of disclosure of social responsibility information by profit and non-profit organizations.

Index

A

B

C

D

E

F

G

H

I

K

M

N

O

P

Q

R

S

T

W

www.ingramcontent.com/pod-product-compliance
Lightning Source LLC
LaVergne TN
LVHW081349300926
849161LV00008B/2112